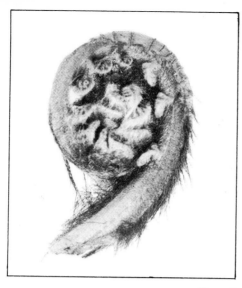

FIG. 9

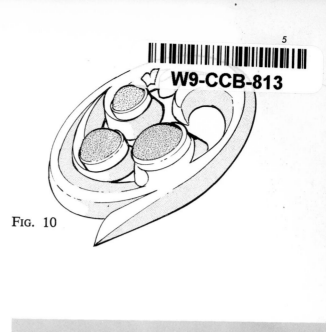

FIG. 10

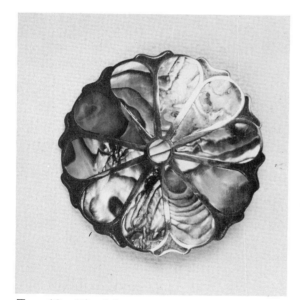

FIG. 12 Pin inlay, sterling silver with abalone shell.
Mexican design.

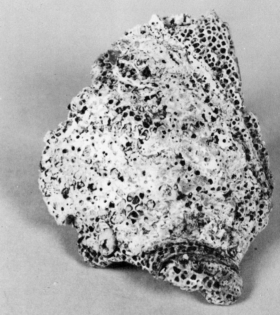

FIG. 11

FIG. 13

Fig. 11). It does not remotely resemble the outer shell surface that has been used for many years by Mexican artisans for inlay jewelry (see Fig. 12).

FIG. 14

Small ceramic figures purchased for nominal sums from museums, archaeological buffs, and gem and mineral dealers are particularly attractive when used as the focal point or points for a metal design (see Fig. 13). Often these are centuries old which, of course, adds to the value of the article. In the same category are small Venetian glass beads of contemporary manufacture which, when strung on a rod or attached to a stud or a pin with a ball end, bring a diffusion of color to the surrounding metal (see Fig. 14).

Designs can be either simple or complicated, but there must always be a sense of order and coherence. Fine proportion, the relationship of depth and space, exciting and interesting textures, and the feeling of movement—rhythmic, static, radial, and curved—all contribute to good design.

CREATIVE
GOLD- AND SILVERSMITHING

List of Color Plates

(between pages 154 and 155)

All black-and-white photographs and drawings are by the author, except Fig. 25A, which is courtesy of the Tescom Corporation. All color photographs are by the author, except JEWEL BOX by Henrietta Norton (photograph by Lou White), and the works of Ellen Broker, which are by herself.

CREATIVE GOLD- AND SILVERSMITHING

Jewelry · Decorative Metalcraft

BY SHARR CHOATE

WITH BONNIE CECIL DE MAY

CROWN PUBLISHERS, INC., NEW YORK

Also by SHARR CHOATE
with BONNIE CECIL DE MAY
CREATIVE CASTING: Jewelry • Silverware • Sculpture

Acknowledgments

THE AUTHOR WISHES TO EXPRESS GRATITUDE to the following craftsmen who contributed examples of their fine work for use as illustrations:

Miss Ellen Brøker, Master Goldsmith, Copenhagen, Denmark

Mr. Hakon Jonnson, Master Goldsmith, Designer-Jeweler, Mountain View, Calif. (Formerly of Iceland)

Miss Alberta Best, Richmond, Calif.

Mrs. Henrietta Norton, Santa Rosa, Calif.

Wayne Smith, Stanford, Calif.

Pamela Healey, Mountain View, Calif.

and to Marilyn Larke, who patiently acted as a model for the action photos; to Glennys Taylor, who did an excellent job of typing the manuscript, and to the W. H. Haney, and Gems Galore Companies of Mountain View, Calif., for materials and tools.

Special thanks go to my good friend Hugh Leiper, editor of the *Lapidary Journal,* who called the attention of the publisher to her articles on casting and metalsmithing that appeared monthly over a period of five years in his magazine, and which led to the publishing of this book.

Crown Publishers, Inc., One Park Avenue, New York, N.Y. 10016
Library of Congress Catalog Card Number: 74–108087
ISBN: 0-517-L00036
ISBN: 0-517-524139 pbk
Printed in the United States of America
Published simultaneously in Canada by
General Publishing Company Limited

Thirteenth Printing, January, 1979

Contents

Foreword

THE PURPOSE OF THIS BOOK IS TO PRESENT the techniques necessary for making customized pieces of metalcraft. Because there is such a wide range of techniques possible for the craftsman, and as some of them are either used infrequently or require expensive tools and equipment, the techniques presented are those that are most useful, practical, and at the same time versatile.

Skill in the basic processes, such as sawing, filing, texturing, hammering, forming, soldering, and surface finishing will lead to the creating of more intricate designs that require additional techniques.

The aspiring craftsman should never cease the search for new materials, new forms for old materials, new combinations and ways of working the old and the new in techniques or methods not yet suggested by manufacturers or other craftsmen.

After all is said and done, nothing can take the place of experience. Each one must have his own trial-and-error experiences in order to become proficient in any skill. It is the author's desire in these pages to share her own experiences and discoveries of what to do and what not to do, so that satisfactory achievement will far outweigh any failures for those taking up the fascinating and richly rewarding craft of goldsmithing and silversmithing.

The ready access to cut stones, rough material, polishing equipment, the availability of all the necessary tools, to say nothing of the opportunities for good instruction, open the metalsmithing crafts to everyone.

CHAPTER 1

Design

DESIGN IDEAS ARE TO BE FOUND EVERYWHERE. Nature alone, from the smallest seed to a star, offers an endless variety of form and texture, and reflections, light and shadow, geometrical figures, free forms, and man-made objects of all kinds and dimensions add endless possibilities. All is in the eye of the beholder, for even one small flower has an amazing potential for suggesting design motifs (see Figs. 1 and 2). Indispensable is an awareness of even the most insignificant details, and that indefinable quality called good taste that enables the artist to select from such an abundance that which will best express his ideas.

The work of the best artists of past and present must be studied analytically and continuously in order to develop the ability to create original articles of good design. A focal point of interest, contrast, and a unifying balance of proportions will always be evident in the best work, for these are the necessary elements in all art forms.

The material to be used, the tools available, the technical skill of the craftsman, and the ultimate purpose of the finished article provide a framework of limitation within which appropriate design ideas develop. It is wise for the neophyte to limit himself to the more uncomplicated variations of conventional designs until he gains some proficiency in handling the necessary techniques for goldsmithing and silversmithing. However, in spite of such restrictions, there is room for originality in the bending, twisting, pounding, stretching, and finishing of the metal. Such requirements as intricate curves may be found difficult at first, but subtle variations and combinations of simple lines can be made to conceal limitations that will gradually disappear as knowledge and skill increase with practice.

A handy sketch pad will enable one to capture fleeting impressions for designs that can be modified and combined in countless unexpected ways, even to the modification of a sketch until it only faintly resembles the original. After a design idea has been sketched, a tracing paper placed over it will permit additional sketches and variations of the original idea. Several consecutive tracings may be made in this manner, altering and modifying each successive sketch until it evolves into something new and original. Thickening lines in some areas, thinning or tapering others, adding new ones, turning the paper to a different position, making cutouts, and inserting or overlaying other sections of paper are useful means of revealing new aspects of a basic design.

Symmetrical designs can be developed from any linear sketch, whether geometric, abstract, or nonobjective, simply by standing a mirror on edge and observing what develops as the mirror is moved fanwise across the design. Whenever a pleasing design appears, a line should be drawn across the paper along the edge of the mirror to mark the center. The complete design can then be traced on a piece of tracing paper (see Fig. 3).

Abstract designs, such as unusual and humorous interpretations of animals, birds, insects, etc., can be developed into interesting contemporary pieces. However, such objects should never be complicated or overworked in detail.

"Doodling" is an excellent way to break into working in more abstract forms. Here the line and shape will be suggested, but the craftsman is left free to choose and to combine until he discovers a design that pleases him. Shading various areas with different values of gray combined with black and white brings out a nonobjective design that can be clearly defined by outlining (see Fig. 4). Inkblots made either on a flat sheet or in the fold of a paper will also suggest ideas for unusual nonobjective designs.

All design ideas should be filed for future reference. At the time they have been noted there may be no application in mind for them, but later they can prove to be an invaluable resource.

Sketched designs are often difficult for the beginner to envision as a three-dimensional form, but by experimenting with soft materials, such as clay, dental carving wax (used for casting), and a plastic typewriter cleaner, he can mold various designs that will enable him to envision and evaluate an idea before attempting to make it in precious metal. In this way exact patterns can be made for contored shapes after all modifications and improvements are worked out, and an additional advantage is that gemstones can be embedded in the soft material

FIG. 1

FIG. 2

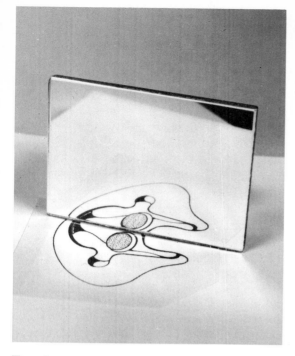

FIG. 3

permitting study of how best to position them in the design.

Soft metal and discarded toothpaste and shaving cream tubes slit, spread open, and cleaned can also be used for experimentation (see Fig. 5). However, as they can be easily shaped, there is sometimes a tendency to form and bend them into forms far too intricate to fashion in less malleable and ductile metal.

Random pieces of paper cut with small scissors and then intertwined and overlaid will suggest many different design ideas. Jigsaw puzzle pieces stacked in random layers will also suggest interesting designs for appliqué.

A dark-colored length of string dropped carelessly on a sheet of light-colored paper will form itself into an interesting nonobjective pattern that can be traced. Soft lead, annealed copper, or brass wire, bent or twisted into pleasing shapes, will also give no end of ideas for original designs (see Figs. 6 and 7). An advantage in using wire is that bending and twisting to alter the design can be done without losing the original idea. Also the wire may be ham-

FIG. 4

FIG. 5

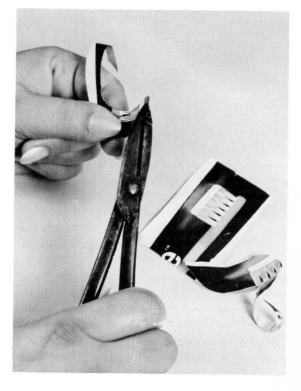

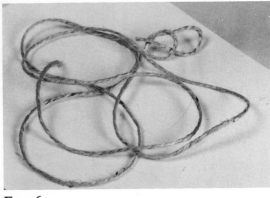

FIG. 6

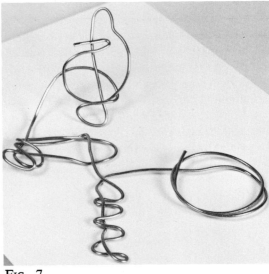

FIG. 7

FIG. 8

mered to give added dimension and character to the design. Square and triangular wire bent and curved will give even more variety.

A magnifying lens or microscope used to study and sketch cross sections of flowers, seed pods, or any organic material will reveal fascinating and unsuspected suitable patterns for designs (see Figs. 8, 9, and 10).

Those who feel deficient in the ability to sketch can make good use of closeup photos of objects in nature. The photos can be blown up to reveal details from which an area that suggests ideas for design motifs can be selected.

One of the easiest ways to accomplish a focal point of interest is by means of accent material, the most common, of course, being gemstones (see Figs. 113 and 115). Areas of texture, form, and color should be treated so as to direct attention to the gem material. Faceted stones, because of their brilliance, need very little surrounding area to emphasize their beauty (see Fig. 117). They require prongs or belcher settings because light is necessary to set them off. The effect of beautiful gems can be lost by being improperly mounted. Cabochons appear to best advantage in handwrought pieces. Gemstone material should be of good quality, and its appropriateness to the metal that surrounds it must be carefully considered. Naturally, agate should not be used with platinum, or diamonds mounted with copper or brass.

By using informal or free-form shapes and the most unusual shapes of natural crystals (see Fig. 116), single crystals, and clusters of natural gem or mineral materials, the stone can be made the nucleus of the design, but each should be placed in a setting compatible with its inherent nature. Drusy coating on mineral, or common rock matrices, slices of patterned material, irregularly shaped pieces of opal that permit the play of color fire should never be used in a standard or formal design.

Often it is impossible to find a particular color in a gemstone that is desired for a particular design. Instead of making a long search for it in a natural material, sections of clay or bisque fired and glazed to the specific color can be substituted.

The porous side of the abalone shell with its crusty, pockmarked surface sanded smooth or sandblasted gives a pearlescent tone that brings a new dimension to a common material (see

CHAPTER 2

Metals

ACCORDING TO THE DICTIONARY, METAL IS ANY class of elementary substance characterized by opacity, ductility, conductivity, and malleability such as is found in gold, silver, platinum, copper, tin, zinc, nickel, etc. All these metals, referred to as elements, are peculiar in that they are basically pure. When an elemental metal is combined with any other metal, the combination is defined as an alloy. The platinum family includes five other elements, namely, rhodium, palladium, osmium, iridium, and ruthenium. These elements are constituents of a natural alloy found only in platinum.

Metal categories

Element metals in their pure state except silver, are seldom used for jewelry and other decorative metalcrafts. Blended in various combinations, they form important alloys. Such metals and alloys are classified as ferrous and nonferrous. Ferrous metal refers mainly to iron, the primary alloy being steel, and nonferrous metals indicate a complete absence of iron and are classified as precious metals: gold, silver, platinum; base metals—copper, nickel, zinc, aluminum, lead; alloy metals—karat gold, sterling silver,

gold solder and silver solder, brass, bronze, pewter, nickel silver, and duraluminum.

Each pure metal and alloy has individual characteristics of color, hardness, ductility, malleability, and melting point and requries different heat treatment methods. Alloys are generally more desirable than their individual constituents. They are often either harder, heavier, more dense, or all of these when combined.

Pure gold and fine silver are too soft for some kinds of jewelry and must be alloyed to produce a harder metal so that they will be longer wearing, hold their shape better, and take a higher polish.

The addition of alloying metals to pure gold produces a different weight for each karat (k) alloy. Gold alloyed with copper will result in a lighter alloy, and when alloyed with platinum, a heavier alloy. Karat gold alloys vary because of the different percentages of combining metals. Manufacturers order alloys from refiners to meet particular requirements such as a hard alloy to produce a smooth, hard surface when cast; an extremely ductile alloy that can be drawn extensively without breaking, or an alloy that will need to be age-hardened after shaping. All these characteristics are possible with various alloys of the same karat content. Generally, the metal offered by suppliers is the best all-around alloy for use by the craftsman.

Alloys

Alloys consisting of two metals in combination, such as sterling silver (silver and copper), are called binary alloys. A combination of three metals—gold, silver, and copper—that forms 14-karat gold, is a ternary alloy. A four-metal combination is called a quarternary alloy, and a five-metal combination is a quinary alloy.

It is not practical for the craftsman to attempt to alloy metals, as one cannot be assured of a completely homogeneous mass, and the price of rolling mills is financially unfeasible for home workshops.

Metal characteristics and qualities

The metalsmith must be familiar with the basic properties, characteristics, and inherent qualities of the various metals he uses, which consist of malleability, ductility, tensile strength, fusibility, brittleness, and elasticity.

Malleability is the quality that allows the metal to be worked easily by hammering or pressure without crumbling. Gold is the most malleable metal; silver is second, and copper third.

Ductility is the quality of a metal such as is inherent in gold, wherein one ounce of pure gold can be drawn into a fine wire fifty miles long. Ductility and malleability are similar qualities, but some malleable metals, such as lead, cannot be drawn into wire by any means.

Tensile strength is the degree of tenacity that enables a metal when worked to withstand longitudinal stress without cracking. The tensile strength is measured by the minimum amount of longitudinal stress required to rupture the metal.

Fusibility refers to the capability of a metal to be combined with other metals to produce alloys. All elements and alloys become liquid when heated at different degrees of temperature, and return to a solid stage as they cool, or "freeze." Mercury, the one exception to this, remains liquid at room temperature, becoming an absolute solid only when it reaches a temperature of minus 40° F.

Brittleness, the opposite of ductility, indicates sudden breaking without warning. With some exceptions, very hard metals are usually brittle.

Elasticity is the ability of a metal to return to its original form when the force applied to change it has been removed.

Fig. 15

Gauging metals

Metals can be measured or gauged with a Brown and Sharpe circular wire gauge, a sliding gauge graduated in millimeters; and for the weight with a gold scale, which is mounted on a platform, held in a case, or in the hand, or a triple beam scale (see Figs. 15, 16 and 17). Of these, the Brown and Sharpe circular wire gauge with slots around the perimeter is preferred. On one side of the tool the gauges are indicated, and on the reverse side the decimal equivalent of each gauge is noted. Drill and hole gauges for measuring wire instead of sheet are manufactured in the same manner.

When ordering metals to a desired gauge or thickness, not only the gauge should be mentioned, but its decimal equivalent as well, in the event that the metal stock is improperly marked as to gauge size. (See the Appendix for a comparative table of weights of different sizes of metal.)

Choosing a metal

The first step after creating a design suitable for a certain metal is to determine the thickness of the metal. Heavier metals, although malleable and ductile, are more difficult to work. In addition, heavy metals used for jewelry will tend to sag, and bracelets, rings, and pendants will be uncomfortable to wear. The thinnest metal that will hold its shape without bending when handled or worn is always preferable. Most jewelry is constructed of 14-24-gauge metals. Only precious metals should be used in objects that will be worn next to the skin, though other metals can be used if a protective precious metal backing is used.

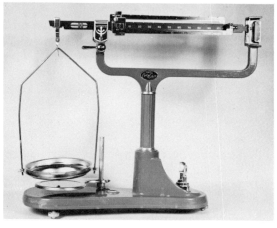

FIG. 16

FIG. 17

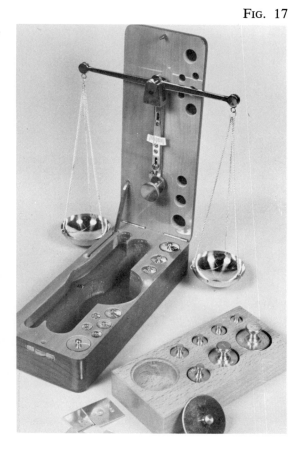

Gold

Gold is the king of metals. Its bright yellow glitter has made it, since the dawn of history, the metal par excellence. The earliest craftsmen used gold to fashion decorative pieces of all kinds. In the Middle Ages most craftsmen were trained as goldsmiths to create jewelry and ornaments of the highest order, some surpassing that done by the craftsmen of today.

Gold found in its native state is rarely pure 24k, but is usually associated with silver and often with mercury. When the silver content is a high percentage of a native gold mass, the metal is called electrum, a natural alloy. Gold is also found in tellurides and ore containing quartz wherein it is either visible, or enclosed in particles of sulfide minerals such as chalcopyrite, pyrrhotite, pyrite, and arsenopyrite. In some high-production gold mines, the gold is not visible and can be seen only on a highly polished surface when viewed through a high-powered microscope.

Gold has no oxides and is not affected by oxygen in the atmosphere as are other metals. Chloride of gold is formed when the metal is attacked by aqua regia (4 parts hydrochloric acid to 1 part nitric acid).

Gold is malleable to the point that it can be hammered into a leaf or sheet of foil 3/1,000,000 inch thick (0.000003″) with an area approximately 6 square feet. The thin sheet is translucent and transmits a greenish light through the leaf.

When gold is alloyed, its ductility is diminished, but its malleability remains constant, except when large percentages of copper are added to the alloy. Nickel used in a white gold alloy has the same characteristics as silver. Zinc is added to the white gold alloy and lightens the color, but amounts in greater percentage than 14 per cent of the entire alloyed mass will change the color to red and make the alloy brittle. The reason for using zinc in gold alloys is to absorb the oxygen to prevent silver and copper oxides in the mix. Cheap "gold" jewelry is an alloy of copper and zinc with no trace of gold in the alloy. Any karat gold is called solid gold to distinguish it from gold-filled metals.

Skin discoloration by gold

Gold darkens the skin because of either skin secretions or perspiration, which contains chlorides and, often, sulfides that, coming into contact with the copper and silver molecules in a gold alloy, form dark-colored salts, either copper sulfate or silver chloride.

The seacoast and semitropical areas produce chlorides. These salts combine with the salts produced through perspiration to form a corrosive element that discolors the skin. The corrosive salts, when rubbed, turn to a smudge. Smog fumes filled with particles of silver dioxide and phosphate gradually attack jewelry and are evident as a tarnish that rubs off on the skin. Eighteen-karat gold does not produce a smudge as easily as 14k, and changing to white gold or palladium will usually eliminate the problem entirely.

Karat content of gold

The karat content and the color desired should be determined before alloying gold with other metals. Red or pink gold contains large percentages of copper and a small amount of silver; green gold is usually 14k or 18k gold alloyed with additional silver, or with silver that has a small percentage of copper; white gold is primarily 75 percent gold and the balance nickel, or both nickel and zinc. Gold alloyed with silver alone will be less hard and a lighter yellow color.

Copper alone added to gold makes the pure gold harder and more difficult to work; therefore, some percentages of copper and silver are usually combined in the alloy. White gold—formerly made of an alloy consisting of gold, silver, and/or palladium (from the platinum family)—is now also alloyed with nickel, copper, and zinc to produce more ideal melting characteristics.

A superior white gold contains 90 percent pure gold and 10 percent palladium. Palau, containing 80 percent pure gold and 20 percent palladium, is a platinum substitute (not of lesser quality) for chemical laboratory utensils.

Gold quality is determined by karat content or fineness, and each karat is 1/24th part. Pure gold is 24 karats, and as it is alloyed with other metals the karat content decreases so that 18k gold is 18 parts pure gold and 6 parts of alloy metals; 14k gold is 14 parts pure gold and 10 parts other metals. The calculation for changing the alloy to different karat designations, either increasing or decreasing the pure gold content, is important. See the Appendix for the following information:

1. Weighing metals for alloying (see Figs. 16 and 17)
2. Percentages of pure gold in various karat alloys
3. Determining percentages of alloy metals to produce specific karat golds
4. Weighing gold to determine cost per article (see Figs. 16 and 17)
5. Testing metal for any gold content (see Fig. 18)
6. Testing for karat quantity
7. Testing for the presence of white gold or platinum in metal
7a. Testing white metals with a blowpipe
8. Distinguishing between white gold, palladium, platinum, nickel, stainless steel, and dental alloy

Small amounts of different karat golds can be alloyed where a specific quality material is required and not immediately available. Large amounts should not be attempted for alloying. Melted gold must be combined with at least 50 percent new metal when the karat content is to be increased.

All metals must be free of impurities before being combined or alloyed with pure gold. The clean metals are heated in a crucible to their melting point, and then to a degree of heat approximately 200 degrees greater than the melting point so that the rolling metal can be poured into a mold to produce an ingot. The extra heat ensures that all metals in the alloy will be molten when poured. Graphite rods are used to stir the metals when alloying them.

Scrap metal containing any solder should not be used for alloying. The solder does not homogenize with the metals but concentrates in one mass and shows up as a discoloration, either hard or soft. A flux is necessary when melting metals; equal amounts of boric acid powder and household borax are used for this purpose. The boric acid powder retains the borax flux on the surface of the molten metal, preventing atmospheric oxygen from producing oxides. Scum or slag on the molten metal surface is skimmed off with an orangewood stick, and the molten mass is poured into a mold constructed in a charcoal block.

Gold-filled metal

The term "gold-filled" indicates the process wherein two thin gold sheets with a supporting piece of core metal such as nickel (approximately 1 inch thick) is placed between to form a sandwich, and then laminated with a brazing alloy into one inseparable sheet. After the fused ingot is made, it is placed in a rolling mill and rolled out to the required thickness. Gold-filled identification requires that the filling process must have been accomplished mechanically.

Gold-filled articles stamped "10k fine" indicate that the gold content of the sandwich is at least 1/20th of the total metal content by weight. Lesser amounts or thinner sheets of gold may be clad with the core metal but only if so marked. Thus, thinner gold sheets equal to 1/40th of the total metal weight would be stamped "1/40-14k" or "1/40-10k" depending upon the karat of gold used in the outer sheets.

Stamping metals with karat content

Gold articles *must* be stamped according to karat content. Severe federal penalties are imposed for misrepresentation. In addition to the karat content stamp, a hallmark (the craftsman's own insignia) should also be affixed in an obscure place on the inside or underside of the article. Articles so stamped with karat content indicate that all the metal used is equal to that karat marking. The alloy cannot deviate more than ½ karat in this claim of quality, and no more than 1 karat in the entire piece, which includes findings and solder. Articles of various metal combinations are not stamped according to karat quality.

Hallmarks are registered as trademarks with the U.S. Copyright Office in Washington, D.C.,

FIG. 18

by the individual craftsman. The same procedure for a copyright application is followed to register the hallmark.

Gold solders

Gold solders are alloyed to match the karat content and color of the metal. Solder for 14k gold is alloyed to approximately 13k with a resultant lower melting point. (See Chapter 9 and the Appendix for various melting points of karat golds and alloying.)

When purchasing gold, specific instructions and requirements must be stated including the karat content, color, square inches of area for sheets, millimeter thickness for sheets and some wires, gauge thickness for round wire and tubing, and linear inches for wiring and tubing.

Measuring and gauging karat golds

When determining the overall size or area of a design, one should remember that 14k gold alloys weigh one-fourth more than their counterparts in sterling silver. Gold thickness is measured in millimeters ($1'' = 25.4$mm) and surface area is measured in square inches (see Appendix). Round gold wire is measured by the standard wire gauge, and the length is measured in linear inches. Square, flat, and half-round wire are measured in cross section by millimeters and in length by linear inches. Tubing is measured by gauge for the outside diameter (OD) and by linear inches for length. Bezel wire is measured by linear length and identified according to a cross section of a specific type. Gold measured for specific requirements is sold by pennyweight (dwt.) and ounce (troy).

Silver

Silver, also called fine (pure) silver, is the queen of metals and, like gold and copper, is a versatile metal with thousands of different uses. In addition to its use in jewelry and decorative objects, it is an important electroplating metal. The manufacture of photographic film is dependent upon silver, and its use in dentistry is equally important. Other uses of silver include ecclesiastical and domestic plate, buttons, buckles, boxes, weapons, horse trappings, etc.

Silver has been held in esteem through the centuries. Silver hallmarks came into use in A.D. 1300, and Sheffield plate, an innovation of the eighteenth century, gave birth to an important plating industry which still flourishes in the United States and in England.

Formerly used for coinage, its value has increased as much as its demand for other uses. Silver is still worked as a native craft in Mexico, Thailand, the southwestern United States, and in Peru.

Silver occurs in the ore as a metal associated with other metals, especially gold. When it occurs as a constituent of large percentage on a natural gold/silver alloy, the metal is called electrum. It is usually a by-product of large mines producing gold, argentiferous lead, zinc, and copper ores, but is also found in cobalt and nickel, and in lead and copper ores. It is also a prominent constituent in gold tellurides.

In malleability and ductility, fine silver is second only to gold. When melted its color is milky white and a milky pink. Harder than gold but not as hard as copper, it is used in its pure state—fine silver; however, it is more often used as an alloy—sterling silver. Fine silver is used in articles where a higher melting point is desirable, and it is especially useful for enameling projects because of the absence of oxides formed by copper in alloys. Silver foil, used like gold foil, can be rolled or hammered to a translucent sheet measuring 0.000012″, which is so thin that a blue light can be transmitted through the metal.

Sterling silver

The standard alloy of sterling silver is composed of .925 parts pure silver and .725 parts pure copper. Mexican silver is alloyed with .950 parts silver and the remainder in copper. Prior to 1965, United States coin silver was .900 parts silver and the balance copper. Both types of silver are subject to oxidation when heated; however, in normal atmospheric conditions, the silver alloy reacts much sooner than the pure metal. The normal oxide occurring on the metal when heated is a sulfide film produced by the torch. Silver alloys also produce oxides, cupric and cuprous, formed by the presence of copper in the alloy. Tarnish on silver is produced by sulfuric oxides in the atmosphere and by certain foods or body salts.

The melting point of fine silver is 1760°F. and that of sterling is 1640°F. When the metal hardens, it is returned to a soft working stage by annealing. Silver is affected by both nitric and sulfuric acids.

Dental amalgam used for dental fillings or common silver fillings is 67–70 percent silver, 25–27 percent copper, and 0–2 percent zinc. Mercury added to the mix to produce the amalgam through trituration (kneading or vibrating) is in proportions of 45–53 percent. Excess mercury is squeezed from the mass as desired to produce a semidry amalgam paste. This is used in metal inlays and after curing is filed smooth and polished.

Silver solder

Hard solders are used for silver and are alloyed in four different grades or melting points for assembly soldering. Soft solder is also used to join silver. Metals can be tested for silver content and percentage of pure silver in the alloy. Silver is weighed to determine the amount of silver in a specific article using troy ounce standards. See the Appendix for the following information:

1. Testing for silver content
2. Determining amount of silver in an article
3. Constituents of silver solder

Measuring and gauging silver

Silver sheet is measured in thickness by the Brown and Sharp wire gauge, and the area is measured in square inches. Wire and tubing are gauged according to outside diameter (OD) and measured in linear inches. Bezel wire is identified according to cross-section types and measured in linear inches. Wire is usually sold by the running inch, and sheet is sold by the troy ounce regardless of thickness and area dimensions. Square, half-round, and flat wire are gauged on two sides and measured linearly.

Platinum

Platinum, rhodium, palladium—three of the six separate elements in the platinum family—are used for jewelry and decorative purposes. Platinum was in use for several centuries B.C., but a process to make it more malleable was not discovered until 1804.

The color of the metal is grayish white and resembles highly polished silver or white gold when finished. It is reasonably malleable and extremely ductile. The metal is softened with small percentages of silver or copper and is hardened when alloyed with iridium.

Like other metals, platinum work hardens and must be annealed to soften it to a malleable state. The metal does not oxidize when heated, or tarnish when exposed to the atmosphere. A long-wearing heavy metal, it has a melting point of 3223°F. It is attacked by aqua regia, but by no other acids. Platinum requires platinum solder with a definite metal content, and these should be purchased ready to use. Because of the high melting point of platinum, it requires solder with melting points of 2160–2912°F. Borax paste flux is required, and because of the extreme white heat of the hot metal, the use of goggles is mandatory when soldering to prevent eye damage.

In addition to its use as a precious metal for jewelry, platinum is used for electric wires, contact points, dentistry, and photography. It is the only metal that will fuse with glass without breaking the glass, hence its value for use in X-ray and other electronic tube manufacture.

Rhodium

Rhodium is resistant to oxidation and impervious to any acid or other solution. It is used almost exclusively for electroplating processes to ensure a permanent brilliance and long-wearing durability. Its melting point is 3560°F.

Palladium

Palladium is silvery white, is both malleable and ductile, and is much more fusible than platinum. Its melting point is 1652°F. and it is free of oxides. It is attacked by aqua regia and also nitric acid. The metal is alloyed with rhodium and iridium for a harder metal and combined with gold and platinum for jewelry, scientific instruments, and in its pure state for electroplating.

Osmium and iridium

Osmium and iridium are separate elements but they are also found in a natural alloy called osmiridium. Iridium is a silvery-white metal that is quite hard, brittle, and the second heaviest metal known. It is used by itself in electrical apparatus and contacts, and for standards of weights. Osmium is a bluish white metal and is one of the heaviest substances known. It is associated with iridium in alloys as mentioned above.

Ruthenium

Ruthenium, the sixth member of the platinum family, is very hard. It resembles osmium but it has no commercial importance. (See the Appendix for the test to determine platinum content in white metals.)

Copper

Copper is the oldest known metal. It is presumed to have been discovered as early as 8000 B.C. Three thousand years later it was alloyed with other metals, which initiated the

Bronze Age. Copper occurs in a native state also as a sulfide, carbonate, and oxide to produce in combination over 360 different minerals. It is a yellowish red metal turning to a lemon color when heated. The melting point of copper is 1979°F. It is used in its pure state, but is too soft for structural purposes unless hardened by alloying with nickel. The addition of small percentages of tin increases its softness. The metal, affected by nitric acid and slightly affected by sulfuric acid, is easily worked, and when work-hardened is restored to softness by annealing. It can be hard soldered with silver solders, brazed with copper or bronze rods, or soft soldered.

Copper is well-known for its electrical and thermal conductivity properties, which are second only to silver. Its use as an electroplating material cannot be minimized. It forms the base for many copper alloys such as monel metal, nickel-brass, and nickel-copper, and is a constituent in other metal alloys such as duraluminum.

Brass

Brass is an alloy of copper and zinc with the zinc in percentages of 10–40 for varying degrees of hardness. Though a hard metal, it is extremely malleable and ductile. It is a yellow color when cool, and a salmon color when molten. Its melting point is 1600–1849°F. It is soldered with silver solder, or brazed with bronze rods.

Another brass alloy called bath brass is used for restaurant table service of sugar and creamers, coffeepots and teapots, and individual services heavily plated with fine silver.

Brass is used mostly for inexpensive jewelry and other items such as trophies, novelties, and emblems, and is easily electroplated. Variations of the alloy constituent percentages produce other brass types which are used for wire, spinning, stamping, machined parts, shell casings, and brazing rods.

Brass with manganese added becomes manganese bronze.

Bronze

Bronze is an alloy of 90 percent copper and 10 per cent tin. It is harder than brass, less ductile, and moderately malleable. It melts at 1550 to 1850°F. and is a rich yellow-orange when cool and bright orange when molten. It is silver-soldered, or welded with bronze rods.

When aluminum is added to the alloy in place of tin, the alloy is called aluminum bronze; phosphorous added to the alloy produces phosphor bronze, and silicon, manganese, and/or tin added produces silicon bronze.

Bronze is used primarily for metal inlay, forging, metal sculpture, and casting.

Nickel

Nickel was first discovered in 1751. One of its first major uses was alloying with copper for coinage in many countries. Nickel is associated with nickel copper and iron sulfide ores, and is not found in a native state. It is the hardest of common metals. When refined, it is a highly malleable and ductile metal that can be forged, cast, machined, or worked by almost any method. It is used for electroplating and to produce anticorrosive surfaces. Its melting point is 2651°F. When cool, it is slightly yellowish, and when hot is a salmon color. It work-hardens and must be annealed and cooled slowly to prevent stress. It can be both hard-soldered and used with soft solder.

Nickel alloyed with copper (28 percent) produces an alloy familiarly known as monel metal. Nickel (36 percent) alloyed with chromium produces stainless steel. Additional nickel alloys are nickel copper, nickel copper zinc, nickel-iron, nickel bronze, and nickel aluminum.

Nickel silver

Nickel silver is a hard metal that is moderately malleable and ductile. Also called German silver, it is an alloy of 65 percent copper, 17 percent zinc, and 18 percent nickel. It is essentially brass (copper [65 percent] and zinc [35 percent]), but when ⅓ to ½ of the zinc percentage is substituted with nickel, it becomes nickel brass, commonly known as nickel silver. It can be soldered with either silver solder or soft solder.

There is no silver in this alloy, but it is easily electroplated with silver to produce high-luster pieces of hollow ware, food utensils, and costume jewelry. Variations of the percentages of constituents in the alloy produce other nickel silver metals that are used for furnace and heating elements, and watch and clock parts. It is used by itself in contemporary jewelry for articles that are not worn against the skin. It makes an excellent contrast in metal inlay techniques.

Aluminum

Aluminum was first discovered in the early nineteenth century, but the method of recovery required the extensive use of electrical current which was not discovered in the United States until 1886.

Aluminum is silvery white when polished and grayish silver when worked. There is no color change when heating the metal. Its melting point ranges between 900–1250°F. It is softer than tin or zinc and is malleable and ductile. Soldering is difficult except with special solders and flux. (See Appendix.)

Aluminum is worked in all techniques and processes in either of two alloys. One type is used for sand-casting and mold-casting and the other alloy with different working characteristics is used for spinning, stamping, forging, extruding, and rolling. It has excellent electrical and thermal qualities; hence, it is used for manufacturing cooking utensils.

Aluminum alloyed with copper, manganese, and magnesium produces an alloy with superior working properties called duraluminum.

Pewter

Pewter used in early New England was shipped to the United States from England the chief pewter center, either already fabricated, or as stock metal to be worked by colony craftsmen. It encompasses two metal alloys, both called pewter. The alloy known simply as pewter consists of 65–80 percent tin and 20–35 percent lead. The one most used by contemporary metalsmiths is called Brittania metal and is alloyed of tin (92 percent), antimony (5 percent), and copper (3 percent), with no lead. It

is excellent for all types of forging and wrought work, for spinning, casting, etching, appliqué, metal overlay, chasing, and hand engraving.

Pewter is extremely malleable, does not work-harden, and is not ductile due to the lead content. Because of the low melting point of pewter (490°F.), it must be soldered with a soft solder having a much lower melting point ranging from 360-420°F. Flux used with pewter is a mixture of 1 ounce glycerine and 10 drops hydrochloric acid and is used liberally in the soldering areas. Low heat is required and a Bunsen burner, alcohol lamp, or blowpipe is adequate for soldering steps.

Food vessels formed of pewter require a high tin content, otherwise the alloy will produce lead crystals as the molten metal cools. These crystals mixed with food acids will corrode the metal, contaminate food, and cause lead poisoning.

Lead

Lead is not found in a native state, but in the form of a sulfide called galena. It was used by the early Egyptians and Babylonians, and by the Romans who used it for pipes and for soldering. Lead is an extremely soft and malleable element, but with no ductility. It melts at 625°F. in its pure state and at 150–600°F. in alloys. It is used for casting, soldering, embossing (repoussé) stained glass, sealing joints, and as a constituent in pewter.

Modalloy and Sculpt-metal

Modalloy and Sculpt-metal, two fairly new materials, are available to the craftsman. Modalloy consists of a thin sheet of metal than can be hand-formed by crumpling, squeezing, and twisting to shape, and surface working it to fuse it into a solid covering with a structured interior section. Sculpt-metal, upon exposure to the atmosphere, hardens into a metallic mass that can be filed, sanded, buffed, and polished. It is similar to plastic aluminum and plastic steel products that are sold in squeeze tubes.

CHAPTER 3

Texturing

THE SMOOTH SURFACE OF THE METAL, BEAU-
tiful in itself, can be textured in many ways for
contrast to suit the taste of the craftsman.
Some of these texturing processes such as
hammering, or etching with acids in areas that
will be inaccessible after assembly, must be
done before the article is shaped. Other texturing processes such as sandblasting, florentining
(graving) and those produced with power-
driven wheels are always done atfer the piece is
completely formed and soldered, but prior to
the setting of any gemstones.

The metal surfaces can also be changed by
soldering small odd-shaped scraps of metal or
preformed sections to the article and then filing
the surface flat. Basically, this is an appliqué
technique, except that here the surface is al-
tered after soldering by filing it smooth (see
Fig. 19).

It is possible to get three basic texture patterns with any one hammer head (see Fig.
20). Of these patterns, random blows that
overlap are the most popular, but haphazard
patterns and those that go all in one direction
are often used.

Ball peen hammers of different sized heads
create the most common textures (see Fig.

400). Other hammer textures are created with
planishing, sinking, and forging hammers (see
Fig. 370).

Hammering techniques

The shape of the hammering surface will
naturally dictate the shape of the indentation
in the metal. The striking surface of the hammer should be checked to ensure that there are
no scratches, chips, or indentations that would
inadvertently be transferred to the metal. If
such marks are found, the hammer head must
be sanded with fine emery paper cupped in

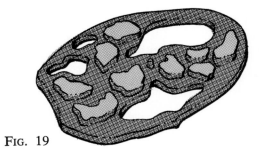

FIG. 19

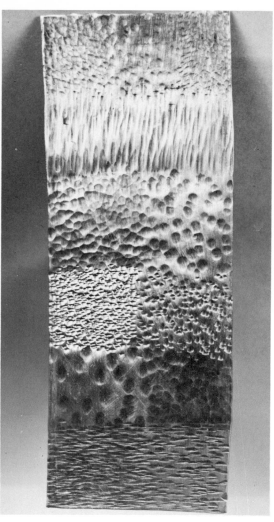

FIG. 20

the palm of the hand, followed by sanding with crocus cloth (a fine sanding paper with an iron oxide coating). When only the sanding marks remain, the surface of the hammer head is buffed and polished to a high luster. In order to protect this smooth hammer head surface, care must always be taken to avoid hitting any supporting base used under the metal that is being textured.

The force of the hammer blow determines the depth of the indentation in the metal surface. Blows should be even and the swinging action of the hammer should come from a wrist action, rather than an arm action. When the hammer blow is completed, the arm should be in a horizontal position.

Metals textured by surface blows require a smooth, hard metal surface as a support. A rough supporting surface would transfer to the underside of the textured metal and make additional areas to be reworked in the final buffing and polishing process.

A smooth piece of plate steel at least 1 inch thick with a flat surface 6 by 10 inches gives an ideal working area. Cast-iron plate with a smooth finished surface and the soleplate of any discarded household iron other than a steam iron also make suitable working surfaces for small metal sections.

Improvised textures can be obtained by placing nails, screws, metal lath or screen on the viewing surface of the metal. These, or any similar hardware hammered with an ordinary

FIG. 21   FIG. 22

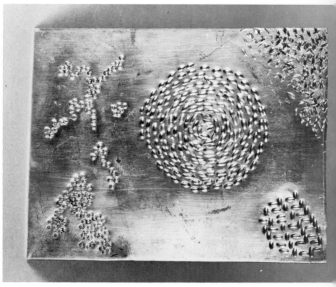

FIG. 23

hammer will produce various impressions in the metal (see Figs. 21 and 22).

Additional textures can be made by using a standard machinist's center punch or a nail set (punch with a flat end) (see Fig. 22).

During hammered texturing processes the metal tends to harden and become difficult to work, and it is necessary to anneal (soften) it often in order to keep it in a malleable stage (see Chapter 4).

Matting tools with textured working surfaces are used like punches to produce various design imprints on the surface. The tools may be purchased singly or in assorted sets, and if desired, they can be made in the workshop.

To make a matting tool, a steel rod or large building nail is filed flat on the end, heated to a cherry red and immediately pressed against a textured surface such as an old steel file. Holding the hot metal against the file for a few seconds will transfer the imprint of the file to the rod. The tool is quenched in water, reheated to a straw color to temper the metal, and then quenched again. The end of the rod can be filed to form various stamping patterns. The tool is held firmly on the annealed metal surface and hammered to produce the texture.

Chasing and Indian stamping tools are often used for texturing. Leatherworking tools (chasing tools without the finer surface) can also be used if the surface is sanded, buffed, and polished as directed when preparing hammer heads for texturing. These tools will provide many attractive beaded and crosshatched patterns that are usually associated with leatherwork (see Fig. 23).

Small sections of metal should be textured before sawing them out of the sheet because this gives the craftsman something to hold on to while texturing. Pieces that have been previously cut from a sheet or from small scrap sections can be held with a small block of lead that will not scratch or mar the metal.

CHAPTER 4

Annealing and Pickling

ANNEALING

WHEN METAL SHEET OR WIRE IS "WORKED" by texturing, hand-forming, filing, or by any other basic process, it tends to harden. This tendency to strain-harden is evident when a piece of wire is bent back and forth until it breaks apart. First the metal hardens, becomes difficult to bend, then grows brittle and cracks.

Metals are made up of tiny crystals that move into different positions when worked. Whenever these tiny crystals are moved too far, cracks develop in the metal. In order to prevent the metal from cracking, it must be annealed or softened to return it to a working condition. This annealing process consists of heating the metal until it reaches a dull red color, then air-cooling it slightly before immersing it in a pickling solution (acid and water) to remove the fire scale produced by the torch flame. The metal is then rinsed in running water.

Metal temperatures and colors

Gold (except red gold) can be heated to various temperatures and colors for annealing (see Appendix), then air-cooled and placed in a pickling solution brought to a near boiling point. The golds may also be quenched immediately in pickling solution as soon as they have lost the cherry red color. However, because of its high copper content red gold must be quenched immediately as it tends to harden and become brittle when air-cooled.

Silver, copper, and brass may be quenched immediately after losing the cherry red color or air-cooled and then pickled. Steel is air-cooled and quenched in oil to harden; *it is never put in a pickling solution.*

Metals to be annealed may be heated on an asbestos coil or sheet, or on a charcoal block. These are supported by firebricks placed on the workbench (see Fig. 97). A soldering pan two-thirds full of pumice chunks or charcoal lumps can also be used.

An ideal annealing pan can be made from a wok, a vessel used for Chinese cookery. This pan has a convex bottom and is easily rotated to direct the torch flame to all parts of the metal. Metal should not be heated directly on firebricks as this scratches the undersurface, necessitating additional finishing later on (see Fig. 24).

FIG. 24

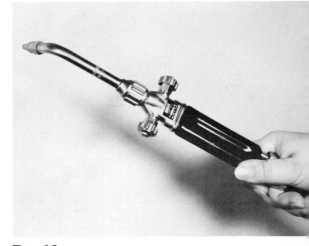

FIG. 25

Annealing wire

Wire lengths also need annealing before and as they are being worked (see Fig. 24). Smaller-gauge wires are wound into coils 2 inches in diameter; heavier-gauge wires are wound into 6-inch coils. The wire is wrapped with identical wire to hold it in a coil during the annealing process. Iron binding wire may also be used to hold the coil in position, but this must be removed while the metal is hot and before it is pickled to avoid contamination of the solution. To prevent melting, a soft flame is used when annealing wire. The wire coil need not be red hot all at one time. However, during the annealing step each part of the coil must have become red-hot at least once. The wire will be much softer if pickled immediately rather than air-cooled.

Torches

A variety of torches and blowpipes are available. It is well to keep in mind that blowpipes used with alcohol torches or Bunsen burners should be purchased according to lung capacity. Torches using specific combinations of compressed air and gas, oxygen and gas or acetylene and gas, butane or Prestolite tanks are available to the craftsman. The oxygen and natural gas mixture works very well (see Fig. 25 and 25A). The oxyacetylene combination is equal in heating capacity; however, the tendency when using acetylene gas is to increase the acetylene content of the mix and reduce the

oxygen to a minimum in order to prevent excessive oxidation (black discoloring from the torch flame) which creates overheat and often melts the metal.

Torch flame adjustment

The torch flame adjustment is very important. Only a certain area of the flame should be applied directly to the metal surface in a brushing manner. The preferred reducing flame uses a minimum amount of air to prevent oxides from forming, and to reduce previously formed oxides. An oxidizing flame, on the other hand, uses an excessive amount of oxygen which, combined with atmospheric air produces a heavy oxidation.

The metal should come in contact with the reducing portion of the flame which is the area from the tip of the light blue cone extending out 1 inch. The outer purplish cone, the oxidizing zone of the flame, is cooler than the reducing zone and should be avoided as the main contact point on the metal. The chart (see Fig. 26) shows the reducing areas of each air-gas combination and the oxidizing areas of the flame.

The position of the torch flame can be tested on a scrap piece of silver or copper. As the flame is applied with the dark blue inner cone in contact with the metal, a visible scum or oxidation will appear on the metal surface. As the flame is lifted so that the lighter blue cone tip is in contact with the metal surface, a bright clean appearance develops and the ox-

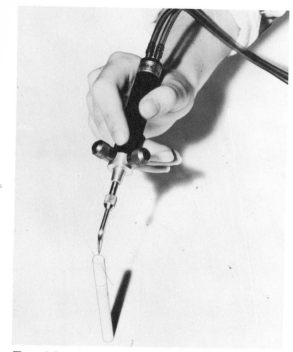

ide film disappears. When the torch is lifted a little farther away from the metal surface and the purplish blue outer cone comes in contact with the metal, the oxide scum reappears.

The torch flame should always be adjusted to obtain the best light blue cone possible (see Fig. 27). A loud hissing flame indicates either an improper adjustment or an oxidizing flame.

Torches that are difficult to light indicate too much gas. The gas valve should be merely "cracked" and only enough gas allowed to escape to light the flame. The air or oxygen is added slowly until the reducing flame appears, after which adjustments can be made in both air and gas to obtain the desired flame size.

Torches are supplied with graduated tip sizes that thread into the torch handle, from small tips and flames for the tiniest soldering job to large tips for the largest annealing job. Strikers for igniting the flame are available and should always be used instead of matches or cigarette lighters, as open flames are dangerous.

FIG. 25A

TORCH FLAMES—REDUCING AND OXIDIZING

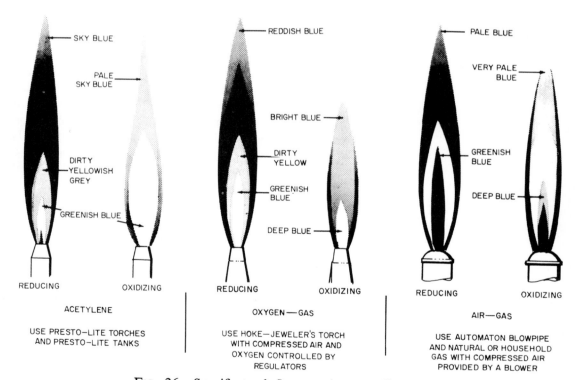

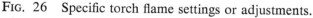

FIG. 26   Specific torch flame settings or adjustments.

Always obtain a reducing flame, never a noisy or hissing flame. A reducing flame is easily and quickly obtained by turning on the gas first, then adding oxygen or air until the yellow tinge just barely disappears. When the acetylene torch is used, a faint yellow tinge in the flame will be apparent.

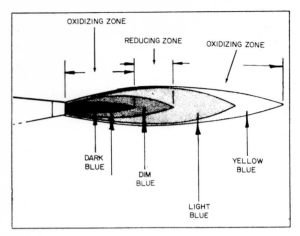

FIG. 27   Basic torch flame adjustment.

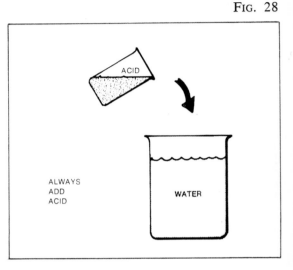

FIG. 28

PICKLING

After the metal is heated, either for annealing or soldering, it must be dipped into a pickling solution (a mixture of acids and water) to remove the oxides and flux. The mixture is used either hot or cold, i.e., cold metal in a heated solution, or heated metal in a cool solution.

Pickling solutions

Various pickling solutions can be purchased or formulated in the workshop for cleaning specific metals (see Appendix).

Removal of stubborn flux

Stubborn flux can be dislodged from metals if dipped in a stronger solution consisting of equal parts of acid and water. If any soldering is to be done, the metal should be boiled for five minutes in water containing sodium bicarbonate (baking soda) to neutralize the acid. The boiling is followed by rinsing under running water.

Mixing, using, and storing solutions

The acid is always added to the water, never the reverse. Water added to acid will boil violently and splatter, damaging both skin and clothing (see Fig. 28). The mixtures are combined in glass bottles that have ground glass stoppers or polyethylene bottles with similar caps.

The solutions should not be stored in bottles with metal caps. They are poured into a porcelain or copper pickling pan as needed. Porcelain pans are preferred because they do not contaminate the solution as do copper pans (see Fig. 29). The solution can also be used in any glass container, but when heated, porcelain or pyrex receptacles should be used. Large pieces of metal can be immersed in solutions used in a discarded battery casing.

As soon as the metal has been quenched in the pickling solution or pickled in any of the ways suggested, the solution is poured into another glass-stoppered bottle. This prevents contamination of the entire bath of liquid.

After the pouring step, the metal still remaining in the pickling pan is flushed with running water. Handling with the fingers should be avoided as much as possible. If the solution is to be used at short intervals, it should remain in the pickling pan and tweezers or tongs used to remove the metal from the solution. Tweezers with quartz tips (see Fig. 29), solid plastic tweezers, plastic-covered metal or wooden tongs are preferred to copper tongs. Copper tongs

FIG. 29

eventually contaminate the pickling solution with copper salts which will transfer to successive metals that are dipped into the solutions; this produces a thin copper coating on the metal surface.

Pickling pots

Commercial pickling pots, electrically heated, do an effective job of pickling. Sulfuric acid solution and Sparex #2 solution should be used exclusively in these containers. The small pot sits on the workbench and contains a stainless steel basket to remove the metals easily for rinsing and to prevent contamination of the solution with tweezers or tongs.

Pickling solutions should be used only as long as they are colorless; a greenish-blue tinge indicates that the solution is contaminated heavily with copper salts and should be discarded.

When pickling is completed, the metal is placed in a boiling solution of baking soda and water to neutralize the acid and then always rinsed under running water.

CHAPTER 5

Shaping Flat Metal

METAL CAN BE GIVEN A THREE-DIMENSIONAL form by twisting, bending, hammering the metal over various shaped stakes, and by hammering other tools into the surface.

Metal preparation and simple shaping

The metal must be annealed before attempting to shape it by any method. Large curves and bends can be made with finger pressure or by placing the metal over a horizontal or vertical stake and hammering it with a rawhide mallet (see Fig. 30). Wooden mallets can also be used; however, they tend to mark the metal if not struck flatly on the surface. Smaller convolutions or curves are formed on smaller stakes (see Fig. 31) or with special pliers designed for bending wire and metal strips without marking the metal.

Both raising and sinking of the metal can be done by hammering. Raising refers to forming the metal on the convex surface and is the goldsmith's method of forming metals (see Fig. 350). Sinking, which reduces the original outline, is the coppersmith's method. However, in jewelry the sinking process is most often used (see Fig. 351).

Ways to sink metal

Sinking can be done in hollowed-out areas of a hardwood block using a rawhide or wooden mallet. Either one of these hammers can be used, but they should be chosen for size to suit the design. Small maple blocks with hollows of various sizes can also be used. A rounded wooden peg, similar to a pestle that is used with a chemist's mortar, is supplied with the block (see Fig. 32). After the shaping is completed, the surface is bouged (rhymes with rouged) by placing the metal on a flat hardwood or metal surface and using a small rounded rawhide or plastic hammer to smooth out any surface bumps or lumpiness (see Fig. 353).

Sandbags

Sandbags, a double layer of heavy duck canvas filled with fine clean sand, are also used to a great extent in forming sections of metal. A small amount of lightweight oil may be added to the sand to prevent dust. The bag is approximately 6 by 9 inches and when filled with sand and sealed is about 2½ to 3 inches thick

FIG. 30

FIG. 31

either the embossing or the sinking hammer, or with the chisel or punchlike chasing tools that will give height or low relief. Small nails can be hammered into the surface to secure the metal during forming with chasing tools. Lead blocks (see Figs. 33 and 34) for forming metals can be made by partially filling a cast-iron skillet with lead chunks. Lead is available where most plumbing supplies are sold. Fish weights and skin-diving weights can also be used. The lead is heated and when melted the dross or scum is skimmed off the top with a smooth stick. The lead is allowed to cool in the pan and then turned over to release the lead cake. Sharp edges may be rounded off or peened over with a regular hammer. When the lead block is filled with hollows and is no longer usable, it can be remelted to create a new working block.

Metals formed on lead blocks should be checked and thoroughly cleaned with fine emery or sandpaper before annealing to ensure that no particles of lead adhere to the surface. When metal that has lead particles clinging to it is heated, the lead etches and pits the metal surface.

Repoussé and pitch bowls

Chasing tools define a line, sharpen up relief areas, and texture flat upper surfaces. Repoussé tools form high and low relief areas on

FIG. 32

in the center. This gives plenty of support and cushion for the metal when it is hammered into a hollow made in the sandbag. Smaller sandbags can be made of soft leather from discarded handbags, or from any other leather scrap. The sandbag can be held on the bench by drilling two holes directly underneath the edges and bringing a webbed or leather belt through the holes and up over the bag (see Fig. 288). This prevents any movement of the sandbag and helps to hold the work when chasing tools are used (see Chapter 18).

Lead blocks

Metals may be formed on a lead block with

FIG. 33

the reverse side of the metal (see Chapter 18). Using these tools requires light gentle overlapping blows with the hammer on the tool, starting from the center of the work.

Because chasing tools come in thirty-six assorted shapes and sizes, they can be used to the best advantage when forming delicate areas. All chasing tools are used with an 8-ounce chasing hammer (see Fig. 288). Metal is both sunk and bouged with the same chasing tool, except that the metal is placed on a hardwood surface instead of on a sandbag to smooth out any lumpiness.

In addition to the sandbag and lead block, pitch bowls or boxes can also be used to form the metal (see Fig. 289). Commercial pitch is used in a semispherical bowl (about 6 inch diameter) which nests in a hollowed-out base of hardwood or in a leather ring filled with sand. This permits the bowl to be tilted and rotated without moving the wooden base and allows the chasing tool to be used in a vertical position.

Using the pitch bowl

The metal is annealed before placing it in the pitch bowl. A corner extension in the metal is

usually bent downward from the working surface about ¼ inch to form tabs that will hold the metal steady in the warm pitch (see Fig. 35).

The pitch is warmed by playing a soft flame across the surface so as to not ignite it, or permit it to bubble. When it has reached a plastic state, the metal is placed on the pitch and pressed slightly so that the pitch contacts all of the underside surface. When the pitch is cool, the metal is worked with a chasing tool or small embossing hammer.

Usually in jewelry, the necessary amount of forming can be done without annealing more than once. There is no hard-and-fast rule except that annealing is necessary when the metal seems difficult to work.

FIG. 34

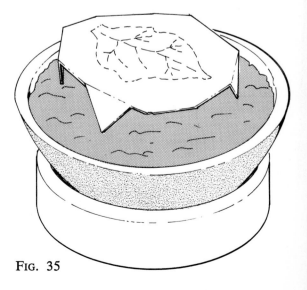

FIG. 35

To remove the metal from the bowl, the pitch must be warmed, just as it was before the metal was placed therein. The metal is lifted out with tweezers and placed on an asbestos sheet for heating to an annealing stage. It is then cooled to black heat and dipped in the pickling solution. This procedure removes the pitch, cleans the metal, and anneals it in preparation for any additional forming. The pitch could also be wiped off the underside of the metal with a cloth soaked in turpentine, or it could be heated to a soldering temperature to permit the flame of the torch to consume the pitch.

Some constituents of various pitch formulae help the pitch to adhere to the metal when dropped in pickling solution. Sampling on a small section of scrap metal will determine

FIG. 37

FIG. 36

which procedure works best. If additional use of the pitch bowl is necessary the metal is placed back into the warmed pitch.

Pitch box

A pitch box approximately 12 to 14 inches square often works better than the small bowl. A box 2½ inches deep, can be constructed of ½-inch plywood, and the commercial pitch heated in an enamelware pan and poured into the prepared box to within ½ inch of the top. The rim that remains in the pitch box permits the tools to be contained inside the box, thus eliminating the inconvenience of searching for them on the workbench.

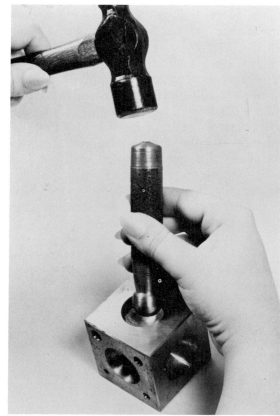

FIG. 38

Dapping-die blocks

Dapping-die blocks and matching punches are used to shape metals into small dished forms (see Fig. 36). Primarily used to form half-domes for bead making, the block can be employed to curve tubs that can be used as gem mountings, and also stacked on a sheet of base metal to simulate berries or grapes. The die-block and punches need not be limited to producing half-domes as they can also be used as an easy way to form metals for other purposes. The block, consisting of various-sized hollow depressions on all six sides, is sold with a series of ball punches that match the curve of each hollow in the block.

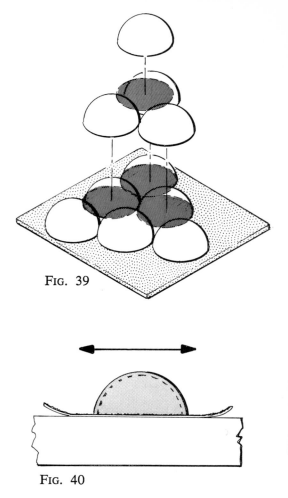

FIG. 39

FIG. 40

Forming half-domes

To make half-domes on the dapping-die block, circles or discs of metal are sawed out and the edges filed smooth. The diameter of the disc should be one-third larger than the diameter of the finished cup. A ¾-inch-diameter tub or cup will require a flat disc 1 inch in diameter. The flat disc is placed in a hollow in the block (all six sides are formed with various sizes of cups) which is larger than the disc (see Figs. 37 and 38). Because the hollows are half-circles, a half-dome will be perfectly formed regardless of the position of the disc in a depression. The disc is shaped with a dapping-die punch selected to fit the hollow closely. The punch is tapped with a hammer until the disc is formed as much as possible in that space. The disc is then transferred to the next smaller hollow and the smaller punch is likewise hammered on the disc. This procedure is continued until the disc is formed into a perfect half-dome.

Other uses for half-domes

Half-domes to be stacked for a grape effect or for beads are sanded on emery paper placed on a smooth metal surface (see Fig. 39). The half-dome edge must be flat to meet the sheet or the mating half-dome securely (see Fig. 40). When multiple layers of half-domes are used, a very small hole is drilled in the base metal under each half-dome to permit gasses that form during the soldering to escape.

A scribed line is made around the circumference of the half-dome on the base metal. The metal is cleaned, flux is painted inside the scribed line, and four or five small paillons of solder are added close to the line. The edges of the cup are fluxed, and the cup is placed on the scribed outlines. Heat is applied from underneath and occasionally from the top in a brushlike motion. Soldering is complete when a fine, bright, shiny seam is visible around the edge of the half-dome.

Half-domes as ring mountings

If a half-dome is used as a gem mount, a wire ring is soldered inside the concave tub as a bearing for the stone (see Fig. 41). The tub is soldered to its base, and the stone is seated; the area above the ring serves as a bezel. This area can also be sawed into prongs to hold the stone. When this is done the prongs are filed to points.

The dapping-die block can be used to form shallow areas in metal sheet, but the mark made by the edge of the hollow must be removed in the surface finishing steps. A sandbag, a pitch bowl, or a lead block can be used in place of a dapping-die block. A steel rod rounded on one end and polished, or a carriage bolt with the round surface sanded and polished smooth work equally as well as punches. If a lathe is handy, the bolt shaft can be turned on the lathe to remove the threads.

The semisphere will not be as deep as when formed with the regular dapping-die block and its mating punches, but often a deep perfect half-dome is not desired and the improvised tools will suffice.

Sinking larger metal sections

When sinking metals in symmetrical shapes, it is best to draw concentric lines on the metal. In asymmetrical sections, a series of lines are drawn in layers similar to contour map (see Fig. 42). The hammer blows start from the center and follow the lines around the perimeter of each marked section to maintain an evenly formed depression. Blows should always overlap and be of equal force. The metal should be hammered only when the supporting surface, whether stake, sandbag, or hardwood, is directly underneath. Thin metals gain rigidity through forming processes. There is always danger of cracking in areas sunk or formed too deeply, or too close to the edge of the metal (see Forging, Chapter 24).

FIG. 42

Planishing and bouging the metal

When a pass of the circle has been completed with the hammer, the metal should be bouged or planished. Planishing is done for the same purpose as bouging (previously explained) except that the metal is placed on a supporting metal stake and hammered on the convex surface with a planishing hammer to remove the irregularities.

Edge finishing

Both planishing and bouging are accomplished from the center out just as is the sinking process. Both of these processes are followed by strengthening the edge of the metal. This is done by placing the metal on a sandbag and hammering the edge in gentle overlapping blows with a cross-peen raising hammer, and with a chasing hammer for very small sections. Striking the edge too heavily should be avoided in order to prevent rolling it. The basic steps should be adhered to in the following order: sink, planish or bouge, reinforce the edge, anneal, and repeat until the metal is completely shaped.

Metal warping

Metal during shaping will often buckle and warp. This can be corrected only by hammer-

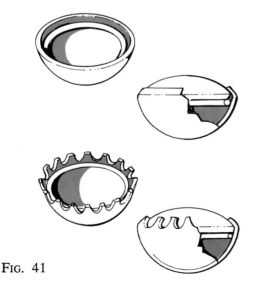

FIG. 41

ing the warped areas after annealing with a rawhide mallet on a hardwood block or on a wooden bench-top. After the forming is done, all hammer marks must be removed by filing, sanding, or simply by buffing away.

Pliers used for forming

Various pliers are used to bend and twist metal sheet and wire (see Chapter 12 and Figs. 198 and 198A). Round-nose, flat, and needle-nosed pliers are generally used. Ring-bending or chain pliers are best for very small curved areas (see Fig. 198A). Care must always be taken to make sure that the pliers do not mar the metal. Practice with round-nose and flat-nose pliers will enable one to choose the correct pliers for specific bending jobs.

The working areas of the pliers should be coated with a light film of oil to prevent corrosion from atmosphere or pickling acid fumes. Any corrosion on the jaws of the pliers will mar the metal. When using ring-bending pliers, it should be remembered that the curve of the metal should fit the curve of the jaws. Reversing the metal will mark the surface and require extra finishing work. Pliers are useful in adjusting assembled parts, in adding a curl to a leaf or stem (after soldering), and in adding an extra fluted section to an extension, etc.

Metal strips, rods, and bars may be placed in a bench vise and twisted by holding tightly at the opposite end. A clamping device called "visegrips" is best for this purpose because it does not release its grip on the metal until the pressure is mechanically reduced, which leaves the hands free to support and guide the metal as it is twisted.

CHAPTER 6

Sawing

THE JEWELER'S SAW IS ONE OF THE MOST important tools for the metalsmith. It can be used to bend areas, as a rasp, and as a file as well as for sawing. Often small areas cannot be filed by any known method and would have to be eliminated from the overall design of the article if it were not for such improvised uses of the saw.

Sawing accessories

The saw frame, available in various sizes and depths uses standard jeweler's blades. The blades range in thickness from size 14 (.0236 inch) to size 8/0 (.0063 inch) with tooth distances varying accordingly (see appendix).

A bench stake is used as a support for the material during sawing, and a carbide tipped scribe or ordinary scratch awl is used to make a sawing mark on the metal (see Fig. 43). There are three other methods of making a design on the metal. (1) Tracing the design onto a sheet of tracing paper and cementing it to the metal with a water-soluble glue makes removal easy after the sawing and filing are completed. (2) The metal surface can also be coated with an opaque white paint called Chinese white,

Artist's white, or Grumbacher white, a water-soluble opaque paint used for covering existing inked or typed lines or photo sections. After sawing, the paint is removed by scrubbing in warm water for a few seconds. (3) Metal surfaces coated with art material called white casein permit designs to be either drawn on the surface or transferred with pencil carbon when the paint is dry. The surface is then sprayed with clear plastic and dried. When sawing is completed the remaining design outline is removed by sanding the surface with emery paper.

A lap tray is necessary to catch the sawdust which is usually called filings. The tray is an integral part of a standard jeweler's workbench and can be improvised to suit the individual workshop (see Fig. 44). In due time the scrap metal and filings increase, and because of the value of this material it can be returned to the dealer for refining, or after it has been properly cleaned, can be used in the shop for casting projects. The tray also holds other tools such as the saw frame, files, hammers, etc., which otherwise fill up the work space on the bench top. Sawdust, filings, and scrap should not be mixed any more than

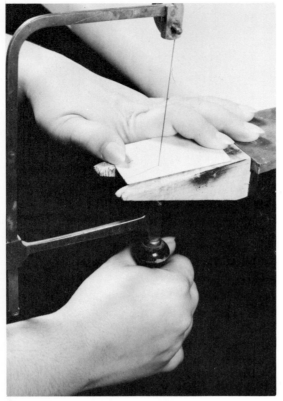

FIG. 43

(near the handle) in the same horizontal position as the opposite end, but only extending two-thirds of the distance across the clamp face. The saw frame is adjusted to obtain this proportion. Pressure is then applied from the chest against the saw frame handle, and the hands are used to guide the blade into the frame and to clamp it securely. The pressure applied to shorten the distance between the clamps creates the blade tension necessary when the saw is in use. A loosely clamped or too taut blade will be easily broken. Broken sections may be saved and used by shortening the saw frame extension or for use in the short frame.

Storing blades

An easy way to keep blades sorted and handy is to embed small pill bottles (plastic) in plaster of Paris or dental stone with a larger sized bottle in the center. The blade sizes and thickness in thousandths of an inch are marked on

FIG. 44

possible, and gold scrap is never mixed because of its high value. The tray can be lined with several layers of tissue paper or vellum paper. Silver scrap was at one time mixed with copper, brass, and other filings but, because of its increased value, it is best to keep it separate from other scrap as much as possible. A small soft bristled paintbrush should be used to brush the filings from the bench stake.

Loading the frame

The saw frame is loaded by placing it with the top end of the frame against the edge of the workbench, frame side down and with the handle pressed against the chest. The saw blade is selected and inserted teeth up, and always pointing toward the saw frame handle (see Fig. 45). The blade should be fully inserted into the clamp horizontally for best clamping action. If the clamp does not tighten on the blade tip, a small section of saw blade may be adhering to the clamp faces. After clamping the saw frame in the top clamp, the saw blade should lie, without tension, in the bottom clamp

the plaster in front of the smaller containers, and one blade size stored in each section. The center section is a catchall for unidentified or broken, but usable blades, which are gauged occasionally and sorted with a small micrometer (see Fig. 46).

Blades are selected for use not only by sight, but by correct size to ensure that the thickness of metal to be sawed is always greater than the distance between the saw teeth (see Fig. 47). Blades should not be used on metals that are as thin as 24 to 36 gauge. These should be cut with jeweler's snips for they tend to chatter and buckle if sawing is attempted. When using a saw as a file or rasp for hard-to-get-at areas or those inaccessible with a small file, the 4/0 to 8/0 blades are used.

Sawing the metal

The saw frame is held in a vertical position so that the top of the frame is parallel horizontally with the shoulder before the stroke (see Fig. 43). This means that the work surface should be elevated, or a short-legged stool or chair should be used when sawing. This enables one to get down closer to the work without the neckache or backache common to those sawing in an ordinary sitting position. This also keeps the saw blade in a vertical plane of travel which is necessary to preserve blades and the perpendicular walls of the metal section being sawed. The metal is supported on the bench stake a little to the right or left, depending on which hand is used by the craftsman, so that the scribed line can be easily seen during sawing.

The saw is always sawing directly in front of and away from the operator. The opposite hand, in a cuplike position, holds the metal as it is sawed and moves the metal so that the saw maintains the straight ahead direction of travel. The saw is pulled gently down through the metal (blades must be clamped so that they cut only on the downward stroke) using the full length of the blade in order to utilize the blade to its full capacity. Short strokes are used

FIG. 46

for closely defined areas. With a little practice it becomes evident that force is not necessary to saw the metal. A gentle pulling action with a firm hand to guide the saw on the line is all that is necessary. Clean lines are the result of light and proper use of the saw. Twisting and forcing and an improper position will break the blade.

The metal is sawed outside the scribed or drawn line in the portion of the metal that will not be used for the design. The line must re-

FIG. 45

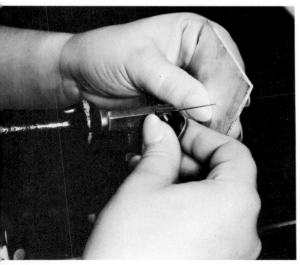

FIG. 47

FIG. 48   Pin, stone and metal inlay, sterling silver and brass with rhodonite, malachite, and lapis.
By Sharr Choate.

main, but a space should not be left between the cut (kerf) and the line. The material is filed to the scribed line. Beveled areas are sawed as close as possible to the scribed line with the angulation on an imaginary line. For inner areas, the metal is sawed inside the scribed line in the scrap or excess material.

Removal of inner areas of metals

Areas of metal which are to be removed, but which have no edge access, are reached by first drilling a small hole in the excess material slightly away from the scribed line. The drilled hole need only be large enough to insert the saw blade easily. The saw blade clamp closest to the saw handle is loosened and the drilled metal section is threaded onto the blade which is held continually by one hand to prevent saw breakage (see Fig. 45). The design section must always be facing the top of the saw frame. The regular clamping and alignment of the blade are then performed. It is necessary to support the metal strung on the saw blade so that it does not create any tension in the blade during tightening.

Turning corners and curves

Inside corners can be sawed in metal without drilling holes in each corner. Only a small hole is necessary in the inner area to thread the

blade through the metal. After the blade is clamped and the metal is placed on the bench stake, the sawing is directed to the scribed line and thence to the corner. The corner is turned simply by keeping the blade in motion as the metal is slowly rotated, fanwise, so that the saw makes an enlarged opening without any force applied to the blade, and without changing the direction of the saw. The opposite hand guides the metal around the curve. A little practice will permit this trick to become easy and natural. Another method of getting into corners is to saw along the side of the scribed line and, when reaching the corner, backing the saw off in its slot without cramping or twisting or removing the blade. A second cut is then made across the metal so that the blade comes to the corner from the opposite direction. This works well for all odd-shaped areas to be removed.

When sawing into an area and preparing to back off to turn a corner, or when coming to a junction point from an opposite direction, the saw frame is maintained in a moving vertical position to prevent breakage or jamming. Jammed blades which seemingly will not go in either an up or down direction can be freed by loosening the bottom clamp close to the handle and pulling the frame and blade upward.

Often larger areas of metal cannot be sawed completely around an outline because the metal

FIG. 49

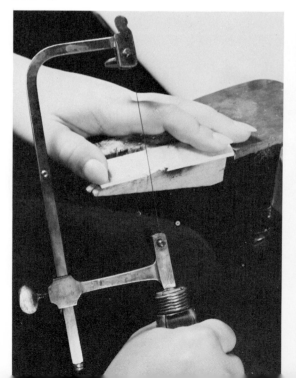

is larger than the depth of the frame. This makes it necessary to release the blade from the clamp closest to the saw frame handle to remove the blade from the sawed kerf or slot. The blade is then threaded through another area and clamped.

Decorative cuts

Single saw cuts are frequently used as an inlay of slim lines in contrasting metal, or simply as open decorative accents (see Fig. 48). It is necessary to become extremely familiar with the saw frame to reap the greatest amount of benefit from it. The finer the sawing job, the smaller will be the filing and sanding job.

Using the saw as a rasp

By careful use, a finer saw blade can be used as a rasp or file to "worry" away edges that need only a little filing but are impossible to reach with the smallest needle files. With slight side pressure, the blade will smooth off walls or small areas and prepare them for buffing (see Fig. 49).

Sawing metal strips

Long strips of metal may be sawed by using the saw frame with a rotated blade. Before inserting the blade in the bottom clamp,

the blade is twisted 90° with a pair of flat-jawed pliers (see Fig. 50). The blade is removed, the opposite end is inserted in the clamp, and the twisting action is repeated, but one should be sure that the twist is the same on both ends.

When completing the sawing step, or if the operation is interrupted for any reason, there will be less saw blade breakage if the saw is brought down through the metal so that the top clamp rests against the metal surface (see Fig. 51).

Large areas or notched edges of flowers, when rotated, tend to inhibit the sawing action. These areas can be trimmed close to the overall outline of the entire piece with jeweler's snips or bench shears. This brings the hard-to-get areas closer to the edge and permits easier sawing.

Saw blade lubricants

Lubricants for the saw blade are not necessary. Beeswax, often recommended, is difficult to remove and prevents the flow of solder wherever it remains on the metal. The only lubricant should be saliva, used infrequently and in sparing amounts. Usually the seeming need for a lubricant can be remedied by using a sharp blade and reducing the force applied to the saw.

FIG. 50

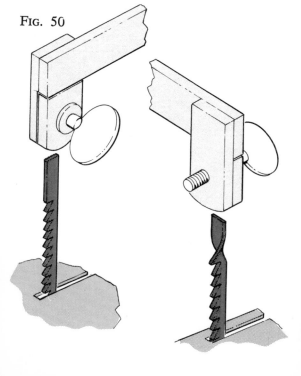

FIG. 51

CHAPTER 7

Filing and Sanding

FILING

FILES IN A GREAT VARIETY OF SHAPES AND types are used in numerous ways to smooth sawed or sheared edges, to remove metal quickly from surfaces, and for decorating purposes. Filing, especially on outlines for shaping, determines to a great extent whether the finished article will look professional or amateurish.

Filing time is reduced by the proper use of the jeweler's saw, shears, snips, and cutting pliers. Excessive and prolonged filing (except to reduce the thickness of metals) is an indication of poor planning or the improper use of tools in preparation for the filing step.

Surface scratches, blemishes, coarser filing marks, and unwanted hammer marks are removed from the metal by hand filing. Attachments used on machines to do this step provide a form of rough sanding.

File types

Standard American Pattern files in four basic types—mill, flat, half-round, and round—are the most commonly used for jewelry and metalsmithing. The files are available in any length and in three degrees of coarseness—bastard, second cut, and smooth as are various other types such as safe-sided, and uncut (smooth surfaces on some faces) and shapes such as knife-edge, triangle, square taper, and lozenge (see Figs. 52, 53, 54, and 55).

Files with surfaces covered with grooves cut on a 25° angle, all going in one direction, are called single-cut files (see Fig. 54). Only the smooth single-cut files are used for finish work. Crosscut files that have two sets of lines going in opposite directions but cut at the same angle on each working surface are used for rapid removal of metal from either a flat surface or an edge.

Swiss or Swedish pattern files (needle files) for smaller areas are also used for filing gemstone prongs and pierced work (see Figs. 56 and 56A). These files are made in many different shapes such as oval, knife, square, lozenge, cant, pippin, barette, crochet, and in both single and double cuts. They vary from coarse to extremely fine in seven different degrees. The degrees of coarseness and fineness are readily determined by referring to the illustration for comparison (see Fig. 53).

Generally, files have a cutting section (teeth) and a tang (smooth tapered end) that must

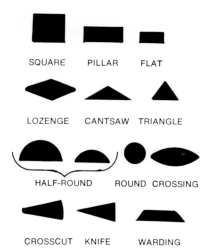

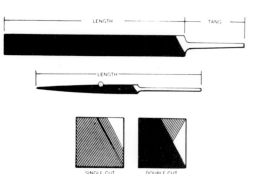

FIG. 52 Standard file shapes—available in various cuts and degrees of coarseness.

FIG. 54

FIG. 53

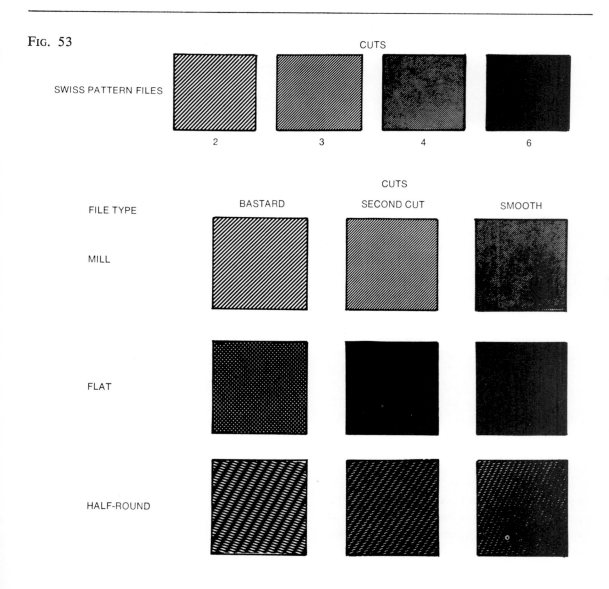

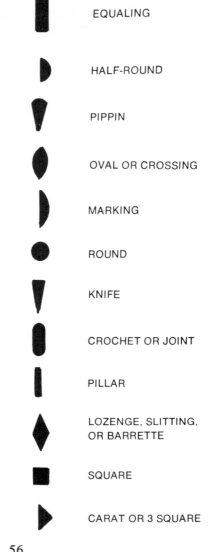

EQUALING

HALF-ROUND

PIPPIN

OVAL OR CROSSING

MARKING

ROUND

KNIFE

CROCHET OR JOINT

PILLAR

LOZENGE, SLITTING,
OR BARRETTE

SQUARE

CARAT OR 3 SQUARE

FIG. 56

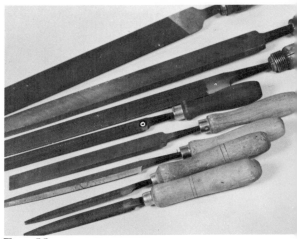

FIG. 55

FIG. 56A

always be fitted into a file handle (see Fig. 54). The length of the file is determined by measuring the cutting surface, but the tang is not included in this measurement. Needle files have a smooth round extension that doubles as a handle and are measured by their entire length.

Riffler files or die-sinker's files, in cross section, are shaped similarly to those previously described, but are curved at the tip ends and have a smooth center section that serves as a handle (see Figs. 56A and 57). They are not cataloged according to length, but to shape and cut. Riffles files can be made from needle files, using either the knife-edge or crossing shapes.

The file is heated to a reddish orange color, and while still hot is pressed against a metal block to bend the tip to the desired shape or curve. When bending is completed, the file is heated to a straw color and dipped in oil to temper it. If additional heating is required during the bending, the dipping step to temper the metal must be redone.

A separate set of files, especially the smaller needle and riffler files, should be reserved for working with gold. The best file for most uses is any style of American pattern file, smooth cut, 6 to 8 inches long, but files should be selected according to the best purpose for the work. This is not to be considered as a complete list, as there are many other kinds of files that are not used often enough to merit mention.

Power filing

Rotary files of carbon steel or tungsten carbide are used with flexible shaft and dental

FIG. 57

fore the backward or pulling stroke. The file should never be permitted to drag back across the metal and dull the teeth. The file should be used as much as possible in a general direction of the metal surface being worked. Right-angle filing is usually limited to small areas.

When filing, the work or metal is hand-held, supported on the bench stake, or on the sand-

handpieces, but should be used only by experienced craftsmen familiar with power tools (see Fig. 58). These files cut swiftly and can easily ruin a section of metal if not properly used. Metals filed with power tools must be held in some sort of clamping device.

Mounted carborundum stones—cylindrical or tapered cone, wedge or inverted cone, bud and ball shapes—should be purchased for specific areas that will need rough filing or sanding but cannot be easily worked with simpler hand-filing tools (see Fig. 59). These should be used on edges and contours, but not on flat surfaces. The smaller wheels (called stones when permanently mounted) are mounted on shafts or temporarily attached to small-sized mandrels. If the wheels are not immediately needed in a specific shape, it is best to purchase them in several large sizes and thicknesses and let them wear down to small sizes. This eliminates the expense of purchasing small wheels that have a limited life service.

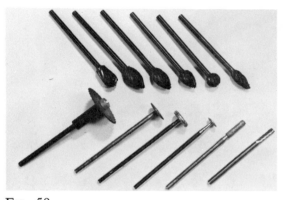

FIG. 58

Using the files

Ordinarily the file is held in the hand with the forefinger reaching out toward the tip end on the top of the file. This permits the worker to apply pressure to the file as needed in the push or forward stroke. Larger files are held in the same manner, but with the left thumb or first two fingers pressed against the tip of the file to stabilize the pressure in the whole file (see Fig. 60). *Files cut on the forward or push stroke in one direction only.*

Files are used diagonally, flush across a metal edge and a flat surface; parallel and flat around a contour; diagonally in a rolling motion across an inside curve. The file should be pushed with slight pressure across the metal its entire length wherever possible, rather than in short "fiddley" strokes. Pressure is released be-

FIG. 59

FIG. 60

FIG. 61

ing block (a short block of 2-by-4-inch wood with a slanted front bolted to the workbench). The metal can also be held in a hand vise, bench vise, ring clamp, welding clamp, or even vise grips if the jaws are covered with copper jackets to protect the metal against the serrations on the jaws (see Figs. 61 and 62).

Flat surfaces of metal that are to be filed are placed working-side-up on a wooden surface, and small brads are hammered into the wood around the edge of the metal and slightly below the metal surface (see Fig. 60).

Smaller flat pieces of metal can be placed on the cutting surface of the file and rubbed back and forth, using the thumb for pressure and to guide the metal.

Cross-filing is done after the rough filing is completed. This is used on very large pieces only. It is not necessary on the small jewelry-size sections of metal. The cross-filing produces lines which are diagonal to those made in the rough filing step. Draw-filing produces a fine line when the file is moved across the metal at right angles to the file length.

When filing a curve, a flat file is used for a convex or an outside curve, and a lentil or half-round file is used for an inside or concave curve. When filing inner areas that may require the file to be used at right angles to the metal edge, the file should travel in a rolling sideways stroke, not only to keep the contour, but to prevent cutting irregular flat spots in the edge of the metal.

Removing solder

If any soldering has been done on the metal, visible excess solder should be removed with a scraper before filing as this is much quicker and does not wear away the metal around the soldered joint (see Fig. 63).

Cleaning files

File teeth tend to clog easily with metal particles, and copper will fill them quickly. Therefore, they should be cleaned frequently with a file card (see Fig. 64) or wire brush, or by rubbing a section of copper rod across the teeth in the direction of the file cut (see Fig. 65). Blackboard chalk rubbed on the cutting

FIG. 62

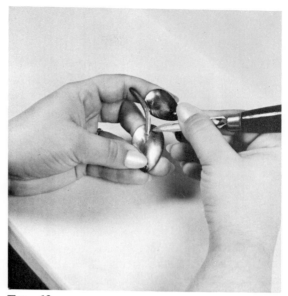

FIG. 63

FIG. 64

surface will prevent clogging to a great extent.

All files should always be kept in some kind of rack to prevent them from rubbing together as this dulls the cutting surfaces. Also, hands should not touch the cutting surfaces any more than necessary because body moisture creates corrosion on the metal.

SANDING

Sanding is necessary to remove filing marks, surface blemishes, and any visible solder. Like filing, it should be done only in the direction of any marks that are to be removed. Cross-hatching, or diagonally altering the direction of the sanding motion, will add more scratches that will have to be removed with finer sanding paper. Before progressing to a finer-grit emery paper, the metal should be checked to see if any file marks still show. A return to the coarser-grit paper first used, or perhaps even further back to a smooth file may be necessary to remove heavier file marks. It is time-consuming to proceed through finer grit sanding

FIG. 65

paper when heavy file marks remain to be
removed. All metal sections should be sanded
before soldering.

Sanding papers

Surfaces are sanded with garnet, carborundum,
emery (corundum) and aluminum oxide
coated papers and cloths in various grits ranging from coarse to fine. The grits on emery paper, for example, range from 4/0 (very fine),
3/0, 2/0, 0, 1, 1G, 2, to #3 (coarse). Crocus
cloth, which has an iron oxide coating, is used
for very fine finishing sanding. A similar paper for this use is called wet-or-dry sanding
paper.

Scotch stones

Water-of-Ayr or Tam O'Shanter hones (trade
names) are slatelike materials available in
sticks of various sizes from 1/8 to 1 inch
square. The stone, made especially for re-

FIG. 67

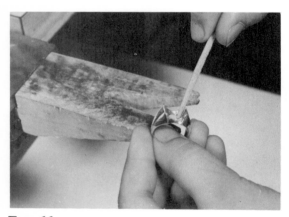

FIG. 66

moval of scratches, can be used in its original
shape or, if desired, a tip or wedge can easily
be filed on one end with any of the ordinary
shop files (see Fig. 66). The stone is dipped in
water and rubbed on whatever small scratches
remain on the metal surface. Large blemishes
or marred areas can be removed only by filing
and sanding.

Pumice sanding

Lump pumice may also be used for sanding
metal surfaces. The pumice block is dipped in

FIG. 68

water, rubbed over the metal surface in one
direction only, and lifted for the return stroke
(see Fig. 67). Water must be used at all times
when sanding by this method.

Stick sanders

A small wooden stick, slat, or a regular orangewood stick can be used for smoothing the metal
surface. The stick can be dampened and drawn
through the emery grit or pumice powder and
then rubbed on the metal surface. It may also
be wrapped with a small damp cloth, dipped
in emery grit or pumice powder, and rubbed
on the metal surface. Crocus cloth and fine
steel wool can also be used for this purpose.
Rigid plastic strips that have a metal clamping
device to hold a strip of emery paper are also
used for sanding flat areas and edges (see Fig.
68).

Flat surfaces of metal to be sanded are
placed, working surface down, on sanding
paper that is supported by a smooth flat
metal surface. Just as in filing, moving the
metal on the sandpaper in one direction only
leaves less work when going to a finer grit paper and in the final finishing stages.

FIG. 69

Power sanding

Small intricate areas of jewelry articles and
some areas of metalsmithing projects are best
sanded, buffed, and polished on small interchangeable wheels and buffs mounted on
mandrels (see Fig. 69). These are used in a
flexible-shaft handpiece powered by a small
electric motor capable of speeds up to 14,000
rpm. The dental handpieces are limited to
3/32-inch shaft sizes, the standard diameter
for small mandrels, (see Fig.70); however, the
Jacobs chuck handpiece used on the flex-shaft
setup will handle all shank sizes down to the
smallest drills. A slip-joint handpiece is available for either the flex-shaft or dental handpiece setup, but is also limited to 3/32-inch
shaft diameters (see Fig. 71). A smaller
chuck mounted on a 3/32-inch shaft is used
to hold the smaller drills (to size 80) and can
be used with any of the handpieces mentioned
(see Fig. 72). The small mandrels, used with
interchangeable sanding discs, buffs, and
wheels, are available in both regular and
heavy-duty shafts, but always in 3/32-inch

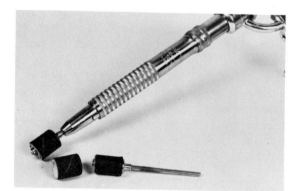

FIG. 70

FIG. 71

Small heatless carborundum stones sold by dental suppliers can be used for quick sanding and are especially good for sanding the inner surfaces of a ring. A wheel nearest in size to the inner diameter of the ring shank is selected, and then reduced by grinding (as previously mentioned) until the wheel just fits into the inner area of the ring. This surface is easily sanded with the stone by moving the hand in a circular motion as the stone turns.

FIG. 73

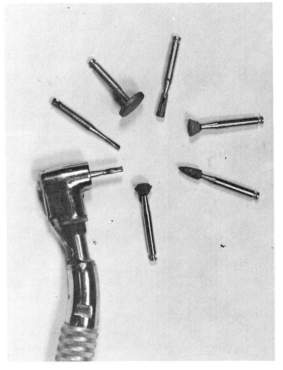

FIG. 72

diameter. The size of the hub or shoulder supporting the grinding wheel is the only difference between the two sizes. Many different choices of emery, carborundum, garnet, and cuttlefish-bone papers are available, in varying degrees of coarseness, in addition to stone wheels and rubber-bonded abrasive wheels in coarse, medium, and fine grits. Other small attachments are available for use, such as diamond or carbide saw blades, diamond abrasive cones, buds, wheels, carbide rotary files, and small wire scratch brushes (see Fig. 73).

Another type of mandrel used for sanding consists of a rubber cylinder bonded to a mandrel and having a setscrew in one end. A cardboard sleeve, coated in any of the different-sized grits, is slipped on the cylinder and held in place by tightening the setscrew to compress the rubber cylinder and spread it (see Fig. 70).

For longer service, carborundum and rubber-bonded abrasive wheels in coarse, medium, or fine should always be purchased in the largest-diameter size as they will gradually be reduced to smaller sizes through use. Different shapes such as concave or convex, knife edge, wedge, and round edge shapes in cross section can be produced by holding the rotating wheel against a coarse file (see Figs. 69 and 74).

FIG. 74

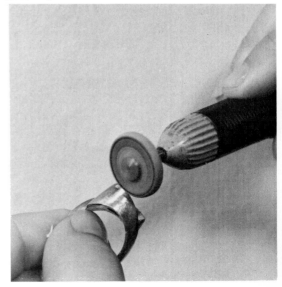

Diamond wheels and other shapes operate with optimum results if a small stream of water is directed to the sanding areas as a coolant. When water is not used, the heat generated by the tool rotating against the metal surface will loosen the bond that attaches the diamond particles to the shaft or wheel. The water supply can be maintained in a plastic container which is fitted with a small plastic hose attached to the nose of a handpiece or to the

straight mandrels with flanges and nut are attached to the straight spindles with setscrews (see Figs. 75 and 78). Tapered mandrels and basic tapered spindles have right- and left-hand threads so that the wheels can be removed by a forward motion on either end of the arbor. Sanding attachments are placed loosely on the tapered spindle end, and when the motor is switched on, the forward motion turns the wheels tight on the spindle. Wheels

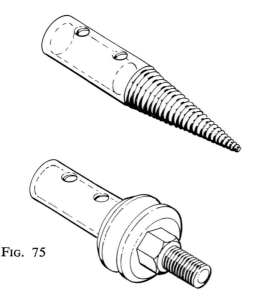

FIG. 75

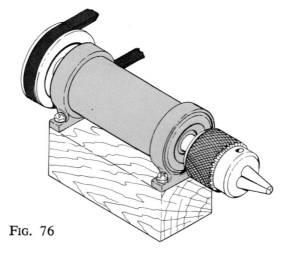

FIG. 76

outer shell of a small Jacobs chuck handpiece. The container is positioned above the work area and a small clamp is attached to the hose to control the water supply. Hose and container can be adapted from intravenous feeding bottles discarded by hospitals (see Fig. 174).

Heavy-duty power sanding

Power sanding equipment for large areas is done on a polishing lathe. The standard polishing arbor with a double-ended spindle and a two-speed switch is preferred to other setups. The motors are available in single- or double-ended spindle types. The spindles are either straight or tapered, but the straight spindles permit the craftsman to avail himself of many different attachments for sanding, buffing, and polishing. Tapered threaded mandrels and

without lead centers are placed on the straight mandrel, using flanges and nut for tightening.

A light-duty and inexpensive power-sanding arbor can be improvised by mounting a saw mandrel on a 4-by 4-by 8-inch wood block, or on two sections of wide channel iron placed on edge and firmly bolted to the workbench (see Fig. 76). A standard V type pulley is attached to one end of the arbor, and a Jacobs chuck attachment to the opposite end. Because speeds are important, the pulley size will be determined by the motor rpm rating, and the belt length is determined only by space limitations. Electric motors purchased new or salvaged from washing machines, etc., work well here as they usually operate at the basic speed (1725 rpm) required for buffing. By changing to a larger pulley on the motor, the chuck speed can be increased to 3450 rpm. Small mandrels, tapered, or straight with flanges and nut are inserted in the Jacobs chuck and used to turn smaller-size rubber-bonded abrasive wheels. The same arbor attachment can be used for the buffing and polishing steps that follow the sanding.

Special wheel shapes

Various wheels, cones, buffs, etc., normally used for buffing and polishing steps can be adapted for sanding special shapes. The adaptation consists of charging the wheel, cone, etc., with abrasive grit such as emery or carborundum. The wheels can be as small as 1¼-inch diameter up to 10-inch diameter. The working surface of the wheel is coated with a vegetable flake glue dissolved in boiling water. While the glue is tacky, the wheel is rolled on the working surface through a mound of the selected grit. It is then hung on a peg, or a protruding pin to dry before using (see Fig.

Fig. 78

Fig. 77

77). Rubber-bonded abrasive wheels should be operated at sfpm (surface feet per minute) or rpm as recommended by the manufacturer.

Holding the metal

Articles ground or sanded on the large wheels are held firmly with both hands below an imaginary center (the horizontal line from the center of the hub or shaft to the edge) of the wheel (see Fig. 78). The metal is moved downward, sideways, rotated, rolled, and positioned so that all areas requiring sanding will

be reached by the wheel. If any portion of the wheel outside the designated areas is used, the wheel will have a tendency to grab the metal from the hands. Working higher, lower, or behind the wheel with the resultant grabbing must be avoided, as articles can be damaged when grabbed and slammed against the workbench or dust cover.

Sanding rings

Round or tapered ring-sanding mandrels are used to smooth the inner surfaces of ring shanks after filing. The mandrel split through almost the complete length is thus made to permit insertion of a strip of sanding paper (see Fig. 88). The end of the strip is wrapped counterclockwise around the pin, and the mandrel is used to hand-sand the surface of the ring, or it is threaded onto the tapered spindle of the polishing lathe or sanding arbor. As the motor turns toward the operator, this will keep the paper tightly wound around its split wooden end. A minimum amount of strip sanding paper is used here, just so that the paper completes a single continuous wrap. Additional wrapping of the mandrel is wasteful and bulky, and takes

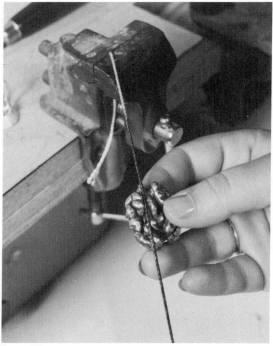

FIG. 79

ing pressure, guides the metal along the string (see Fig. 79).

Burnishing scratches

Heavy scratches, too deep to remove completely without damaging the surface contour, can be covered or obliterated by using an ordinary bezel burnisher. The surface of the metal is prepared by covering it with a thin film of lightweight oil or soapy water. The burnisher, used only when highly polished, is pulled over the surface to condense the metal. When the burnisher makes a squeaking noise and tends to grab, it is an indication that additional lubricant is needed to prevent scratching the metal. Any scratches on the surface of the burnishing tool must be removed and the tool buffed and polished to a high luster before continuing with the burnishing step (see Fig. 80).

time to rewrap after the ring has been removed for inspection.

The ring should never be run up the full length of a tapered cone when it is used on the polishing motor, because the ring will grab as it travels and become tight on the cone. Also, if there is a mounting on the ring, it will turn and be apt to injure the worker's hand or fingers.

String sanding

Strong string warp, nylon cord, or webbed tape coated with vaseline and various emery grits is used for sanding (called thrumming) small areas and curved surfaces inaccessible to regular sanding paper or power-driven sanding wheels. The string is held securely at one end by clamping it in a bench vise; the loose end is threaded through the opening in the metal and held with one hand as the other hand, us-

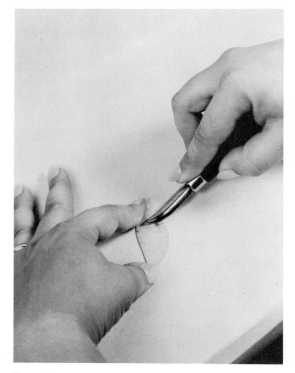

FIG. 80

CHAPTER 8
Buffing and Polishing

BUFFING AND POLISHING PROCEDURES ARE THE final steps required for finishing all metal articles. Buffing removes sanding marks and smooths out the metal in preparation for the final polishing. Any pits, scratches, or minute file or sanding marks overlooked when buffing are only accented by the polishing step. Polishing adds only color, brightness, and luster to the metal surface.

BUFFING

Buffing removes from the surface a thin film of metal equal to the depth of the scratch or mark, and therefore excessive buffing will only wear away precious metal, including any square corners that might be a part of the design.

Whenever possible, parts of any metalcraft assembly should be buffed before soldering so that all areas receive at least one buffing before the final stages of finishing. Areas which in the final stages may be inaccessible to buffing wheels require special buffing operations, and if a portion of the buffing is completed before soldering, then the total buffing time will be minimal.

Buffing speeds

All buffing and polishing methods use power equipment, except thrumming (string buffing) and stick buffing (flat wooden or plastic slats covered with felt, leather, etc.) Definite motor speeds are required for buffing and polishing; the important factor to consider for the most satisfactory job is surface feet per minute (sfpm). Motor speeds should be capable of producing at least 8000 sfpm on the buffing wheel, and at least 5000 sfpm on the polishing wheel. Speeds rated in rpm are used for rotating surfaces that do not change their diameter dimension, such as shafts, spindles, pulleys, etc. Buffing and polishing wheels, which wear to a smaller size through use, are calculated in surface feet per minute.

A motor rotating at 2400 rpm will turn an 8-inch buffing wheel 5025 sfpm, but as the wheel wears down to 7½ inches, the same motor speed produces only 4387 sfpm on the buffing wheel. Polishing lathes (see Fig. 82) should be purchased with a two-speed arrangement of 1725 and 3450 rpm, or a single-speed motor can be adapted for two speeds by installing a two-step pulley on the motor, and a single pulley on a polishing arbor. The motor and arbor setup, both equipped with 2-inch pulleys, will produce the basic motor speed. Identical sizes of any dimension, even of 5-inch diameter, will still produce the basic motor speed, but the perimeter of the wheel will be traveling a greater number of surface feet per minute. With a 2-inch pulley on the arbor, the speed of this wheel will increase approximately 280 rpm with each ¼-inch increase in motor pulley diameter. To illustrate, a 5-inch diameter motor pulley will turn an arbor fitted with a 2-inch diameter pulley approximately 5040 rpm, which would produce 2638 sfpm on a 2-inch-diameter buffing wheel with an increase of approximately 2635 sfpm for each 2-inch increase in the buffing wheel diameter, so that an 8-inch diameter buffing wheel will turn 10,553 sfpm with the same pulley arrangement.

If the same arbor pulley speed is used, but the buffing wheel size is reduced to 6-inch diameter, the sfpm total will decrease by approximately 2635 sfpm.

By checking the chart, pulley combinations and wheels with specified diameters, rpm and sfpm can be obtained (see Fig. 81).

Surface feet per minute is the distance traveled by the outer rim or working surface of a wheel rotating at X number of rpm. Surface feet per minute for an 8-inch diameter wheel rotating at 5040 rpm can be determined by the following example:

The wheel diameter (8 inches) is multiplied by π (3.1416) to obtain its circumference (25.133 or approximately 25⅛ inches). The circumference is multiplied

Fig. 81

APPROXIMATE RPM (REVOLUTIONS PER MINUTE) OF MOTOR PULLEY AND ARBOR PULLEY COMBINATIONS USING 1725 RPM MOTOR

Motor Pulley	Arbor Pulley												
	1¼	1½	2	2¼	2½	3	3½	4	5	6	7	8	10
1¼	1725	1435	1075	950	850	715	655	540	430	320	290	265	215
1½	2075	1725	1290	1140	1030	850	775	645	515	395	345	320	265
2	2775	2290	1725	1498	1325	1075	905	781	615	505	425	371	295
2¼	3100	2580	1828	1725	1525	1240	998	885	683	577	490	426	327
2½	3450	2870	2120	1875	1725	1405	1180	1020	795	655	555	485	372
3	4140	3450	2550	2260	2040	1725	1452	1254	980	810	685	595	416
3½	4670	4185	2990	2650	2380	1985	1725	1490	1162	960	815	710	460
4	5500	4575	3800	3300	2920	2360	2000	1725	1345	1100	940	820	545
5	6850	5750	4875	4230	3750	3040	2560	2205	1725	1425	1210	1050	835
6	8950	7475	5900	5140	4550	3700	3105	2680	2095	1725	1480	1250	1010
7			6950	6050	5340					2025	1725	1500	1190
8			8000	6950	6150	5000	4200	3450	2750	2120	1985	1725	1500
10			8620	7670	6900	5750	4300	3600	2825	2320	2150	1900	1725

BUFF DIA. (")	1725	3450		BUFF DIA. (")	1725	3450		BUFF DIA. (")	1725	3450
2"	877	1754		6"	2710	5420		10"	4517	9034
3"	1355	2710		7"	3162	6324		11"	4968	9936
4"	1807	3614		8"	3612	7224		12"	5419	10,838
5"	2258	4516		9"	4064	8128				

Surface Feet per Minute (SFPM) of Motor-Mounted Buffs Using 2-Speed Motor (1725–3450 rpm)

by the arbor pulley rpm (5040) to obtain the number of inches (126,670 inches) traveled by the outer rim of the wheel in óne minute. This sum is divided by 12 to obtain the number of surface feet per minute traveled by the rim (10,555 inches).

This method of calculating sfpm can be used for any size wheel providing the rpm of the motor or motor and arbor combination is known.

Many rpm and sfpm combinations can be worked out with various motor speeds and pulley arrangements. A two-step pulley with the largest pulley diameter of 4 inches, and the smallest 2¾-inch diameter will turn a 2-inch arbor pulley 4165 rpm and 2565 rpm respectively, and an 8-inch wheel 8723 sfpm and 5372 sfpm respectively, while using a basic motor speed of 1725 rpm.

Dust collectors and hoods

Dust collectors, shallow metal pans with hoods and cutouts to fit over motor shafts, serve as a catchall for buffing dust, and the metal article if it should suddenly be snatched from the operator's hands (see Fig. 82). Hoods, often equipped with a small incandescent bulb for greater visibility when buffing, can be attached to vacuum cleaning units. This eliminates much of the buffing and polishing dust that flies around the work area to be inhaled by the operator.

Buffing wheels

The various buffs, wheels, laps, and compounds for buffing and polishing are as numerous as their uses and are described here not in order of preference, but as general information.

Cotton flannel buffs with rows of stitching to make the wheel sturdy and fairly rigid are used for general buffing work. Muslin buffs, unstitched and attached at the center only, are usually reserved for polishing steps (see Fig. 83). As the buffs wear, the threads are cut so that the buffing edge can be used more effectively. The wheels can be trimmed with an ordinary kitchen grater held against the rotating wheel to shape the buffing surface to a new flat

FIG. 82

or tapered edge. Cotton (muslin buffs if preferred) can be charged with fine emery grit which is excellent when used to produce a scratch or satin finish. The grit-charged wheels are prepared in the same manner described for charging sanding wheels (see Chapter 7). Small buffs used on mandrels in the flex-shaft handpiece can be charged with grits in the same manner.

Separate buffs and wheels must be used for each compound used on gold and for each compound used on silver. One wheel can be used for each compound on all other metals collectively. The wheels should be clearly marked for their particular use near the center with a color code for identification. Wheels that have been inadvertently charged (coated) with a different compound should either be trimmed to clean the working surface, washed and dried (sometimes it takes a week to dry) or discarded. Substitute wheels can be made by tearing discarded fabrics such as cotton prints, old sheets, etc., into 6-inch squares. The center of each square is marked, and a small slit made so that the square can be placed on a threaded mandrel. (Tapered mandrels should not be used here.) The fabric squares are placed on the mandrel until the bundle is approximately ¾ to 1-inch thick, and the flange and nut added and tightened. With the motor switched on, the squares are trimmed to circular shape with a kitchen grater or sharp knife held parallel to the fabric edges. Cotton flannel and muslin buffs are used on textured and overlay (appliqué) surfaces. Felt buffs are used on plain flat surfaces.

Midget buffs, wheels, and brushes ⅞- to 1-inch diameter are used with the same compounds as their larger counterparts. Knife-edge buffs are used for smoothing bezels and any areas where a flat buff may cut a groove in the surface of the metal on a different plane (see Fig. 69). Cotton string buffs in different sizes and shapes are adaptable to any buffing and polishing job. Goblet, tapered cone, and cylindrical types with rounded flat or pointed ends are permanently attached to a mandrel that fits into the polishing lathe chuck or the Jacobs chuck attachment on a buffing and polishing arbor and are used with any buffing compound (see Figs. 88 and 89).

Brushes

Hard or soft bristle hog hair or nylon fibers are used in bristle brushes (see Fig. 84). These wheels are used with grease-base compounds for satin finishes. They are especially preferred when buffing chased, repoussé, engraved surfaces, and for square bezels to preserve the squared corners perfectly. They are also effective for buffing around prongs, mountings,

FIG. 83

clasps, and other fastenings and findings, besides working well on filigree, florentined, and scrollwork articles. The bristles carry the compound down into the undercuts and hard-to-get-to areas before the upper surfaces are worn smooth or rounded over.

A different bristle brush wheel must be used with each buffing compound. Bobbing compound is the preferred material for buffing when using this type of wheel.

Bristle hand brushes

Brushes with the same type bristles as used in the buffing wheels are used primarily with bobbing compound for cleaning and hand buffing filigree and florentined work (see Fig. 84A).

Metal scratch brush wheels

Steel, nickel, monel metal, and brass wire scratch brushes are used dry for cleaning metals, and for effecting a scratch finish on the

FIG. 84

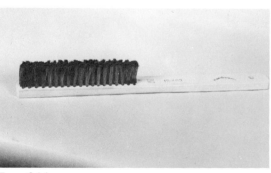

FIG. 84A

FIG. 85

FIG. 85A

FIG. 86

FIG. 87

metal (see Fig. 85 and 85A). Brass wheels produce a much softer finish, but are not used on silver as they leave a yellowish deposit on the metal. The wheels should be reversed on the shaft occasionally to keep the bristles from leaning too much in one direction. Very little pressure is exerted on the wheel so that the wire ends will not be burnished over. If this should occur the wheel is useless. The brushes should be operated at the slower speed of approximately 600 to 1200 rpm. If desired, pumice and water can be used on the wheels to produce a finer matte finish.

Leather wheels

Stitched leather wheels charged with fine grits or Tripoli buffing compound are used for buffing smooth flat surfaces. The wheels are also available in the small sizes ½ to 2 inches in diameter (see Fig. 86).

Rubber bonded abrasive wheels

Finer grit abrasive bonded in hard rubber is used to produce a satin finish when operated at medium speeds of 1500 to 2240 rpm. Higher speeds will put a light polish on the metal and also cut a groove quickly with very little pressure (see Fig. 87).

Tapered ring buffs

Tapered wood buffs covered with a thin layer of cotton or felt or tapered felt cones are used in conjunction with flat wheel buffs for ring finishing (see Figs. 88 and 88A). Any buffing compound is used with this combination. The tapered buff finishes the inner surfaces of the ring, the side of the felt wheel buffs the ring sides, and the face of the wheel finishes the outer surfaces, except the pronged stone setting which is buffed with a bristle brush wheel.

Rings should not be run all the way up the buff when the motor is running, for the buff will grab the ring and injure the operator.

Wood laps

Small wood laps with flat or knife edges are used on a tapered spindle. Abrasives, bobbing, and Tripoli compounds are used to buff sections where a sharp defined corner or area is to be retained (see Fig. 89).

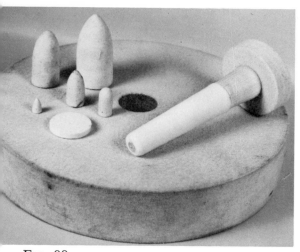

FIG. 88

lows in close order. They work well on most metals and types of surfaces, but the preferred use of each has been given for the craftsman's choice. Tripoli is generally used on gold, silver, and nickel silver and worked with buffs, brushes, and laps. Bobbing compound is used on any metal with a brush or lap, but not on buffs. White diamond compound is for general use on copper, brass, bronze, and aluminum, and worked on a buff, brush, or lap. Fine emery grit mixed with white vaseline (never yellow) is used for satin finishes on any metal. Pumice and water paste is used for a satin finish on silver because it gives a higher luster than those produced otherwise. The work is done with a bristle brush or wooden lap.

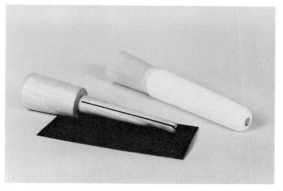

FIG. 88A

FIG. 89

String buffing (thrumming)

String, firmly held at one end in the bench vise, is threaded into areas that are inaccessible to buffing wheels and brushes. Any type of buffing compound can be used on the string. Small-size string used with excessive pressure will cut a groove into the metal. Large areas to be string-buffed should be done with a large cord, such as heavy warp used for carpets, or with various widths of webbing tape such as that used for dressmaking. By using a heavier cord for buffing in large areas that are inaccessible to buffing wheels, more surface area is reached and the buffing is completed much faster (see Fig. 79).

Buffing compounds

Tripoli compound is the most generally used buffing material and bobbing compound fol-

When the metal section or article is ready for buffing it is scrubbed with warm soapy water, rinsed, and then placed in pickling solution which is brought to a near boiling point to remove any oxides and any remaining flux if soldering has been done. It is then rinsed again in running water and dried.

The buffing wheels are charged with a scant amount of compound, not only to keep the shop clean, but because buffing compounds leave a black deposit on the metal if an overabundance of compound is used. The compounds are applied to the wheels as they are running slowly. This is accomplished by turning on the motor and then switching it off before it has had a chance to gain momentum. At the switch-off moment the compound is applied to the wheel, acting as a brake to slow it down. This procedure prevents an excess of material from loading the wheel, thus hindering the buffing action. It also leaves less compound to be thrown onto the workbench or into the dust cover. The corners of the wheel are charged with compound so that they too will buff the metal as it is worked across the face of the wheel.

Tripoli compound will adhere more readily to the buffing wheel if the stick is dipped in kerosene before coating the wheel. Overloaded wheels can be cleaned by holding a short length of hacksaw blade at a 90° angle to the wheel face as it rotates. This will slightly decrease the diameter of the wheel. The wheel can also be cleaned with the grater used for trueing wheels.

Holding the metal

When buffing the metal the article must be held firmly in both hands, and just below the wheel center (an imaginary horizontal line from the shaft or hub out to the edge of the wheel; see Fig. 78). The article is then moved downward, sideways, rolled, rotated and positioned so that the buffing wheel reaches all possible areas of the metal. If the wheel portion, either above, or too far below center is used, the wheel will grab the metal from the hands. The tendency to work lower on the wheel with its resultant grabbing must be avoided, for many almost completed pieces are damaged when grabbed and slammed against the bench top or the dust collector.

If metal being buffed becomes too warm to handle comfortably, it should be held with small leather finger stalls that fit separately over each finger. The use of gloves or a holding cloth is dangerous as either can be grabbed by the machine. Goggles should be worn to protect the eyes from the buffing dust, and the possibility of flying metal if it should not be held in the proper position on the wheel. Small inhalator masks with replaceable filters which cover only the nose and mouth can also be used to prevent inhalation of the dust.

Sanding scratches are most easily removed if the buffing is done on the surface across the scratches and from different directions, rather than with them. Because buffing wears away the metal slightly, buffing in line with a mark may tend to deepen it, which would necessitate additional work on the surface.

Buffing soldered joints

Soldered joints should be buffed across, rather than with, the joint. Because solder is softer than the metal it connects, it will buff away quicker than the surrounding metal. This is called cross-polishing, and considerable time is saved with less metal wastefully removed if this rule is followed.

Buffing findings

Articles requiring pin-backs (pin swivel and latch) should be buffed before soldering the findings onto the metal. If buffed after soldering, the pin is kept closed. Excessive buffing around findings rounds them off so that they do not work properly. Buffing or polishing with the pin open will permit the wheel to grab the metal out of the hands, not only damaging the parts, but with possible injury to the operator.

Holding chains for buffing

Chains, necklaces, and chokers should not be held in the hand when buffing or polishing. These metal parts should be wrapped around the ring clamp, around a section of 1-inch dowel wood (an old broom handle section can be a substitute), or around a short thin board with rounded edges (see Figs. 90 and 91). This will prevent them from being grabbed out of the hands when the chain is held against the rotating buffing wheel. Chains grabbed by the buffing wheel usually wrap around the wheel and arbor with resultant damage to equipment, the chain, and the operator.

Cleaning buffed metal

When buffing is completed, the metal is scrubbed in warm detergent suds with a small amount of household ammonia added. A soft bristle brush is used to dislodge any evidence of buffing materials in overlapping areas, draws, or other detailed areas of the metal form. The article must always be thoroughly dried before proceeding with the polishing step.

Ultrasonic cleaning

Ultrasonic cleaners are an added adjunct to regular metalworking equipment. The machine

FIG. 90

matter from ring mountings and other intricate settings too detailed to be scrubbed with the finest bristle brush. The articles emerge bright and clean, and gemstones cleaned along with the metal have a new brightness unobtainable with other cleaning methods.

POLISHING

Polishing, like buffing, is done primarily with power equipment, and with various shapes and types of wheels, brushes, buffs, etc., but with different compounds.

Polishing speeds

Surface feet per minute requirements for polishing wheels are as important to polishing as to buffing. Polishing requires less speed than buffing, therefore motor rpm, pulley arrangements, and polishing wheel sizes should be computed so that the polishing wheel runs as close as possible to 5000 sfpm.

operates at a high rate of frequency to create a vibration that dislodges dirt, filing, buffing, and polishing particles adhering to the metal from investment soldering steps, and it is equally effective in loosening clogged filigree or florentine surfaces that have become loaded with either buffing or polishing compounds. The cleaner consists of an electronic vibration circuit which is enclosed in a stainless steel or (in inexpensive models) plastic case. The container holds a small recessed glass tub or glass beaker. Some inexpensive models clean the article in the machine itself without a beaker; however, the machine must be tipped to inspect the article being cleaned and also to change the solution.

Different solutions are used to clean different metals, glass, plastics, and even dentures. The object is placed in the recessed container partially filled with the proper cleaning solution and vibrated accordingly as the timer is set on the machine. Cleaning time varies from 2 to 15 minutes, according to the manufacturer's instructions. The machine is extremely useful in removing debris and accumulation of foreign

FIG. 91

Special buffs are used for each polishing compound, and extreme cleanliness is important. The polishing buffs should be stored when not in use in plastic bags to prevent contamination with buffing or sanding materials. Wheels are color coded, cleaned, and shaped in the same manner mentioned for buffing wheels. The compounds are applied to the wheel and the metal is held in the same manner and position as when buffing. The standard polishing wheels, brushes, etc., that follow are for general information and are not listed in order of preference.

Muslin buffs

The most common polishing wheel is the muslin buff, loosely stitched or center attached only (center attachment is also called a lead center) and used with rouge polishing compound. The loose flexible folds of the fabric permit the polishing compound to adhere readily to the inner folds so that the fabric quickly reaches all portions of any textured or formed surface. These buffs are also available in the small sizes, 7/8 to 2 inches diameter (see Fig. 83).

Flannel buffs

Used in the same manner as muslin polishing buffs (see Fig. 83).

Felt buffs

Hard wheels used with all rouges produce the best polish on smooth flat surfaces. Knife-edge buffs are used to polish sharply defined corners without rounding them. Various shapes of felt buffs such as tapered cones, ball, cylinder, and goblet are used with various compounds for a high-luster finish on the inside surfaces of metal objects (see Fig. 88).

Leather (chamois, buckskin) wheels

Unstitched leather polishing wheels, similar to muslin buffs, are used with the different rouges for fine finishing on textured, formed, and smooth surfaces (see Fig. 86).

Bristle brushes

Fine bristle brushes are used with pumice and water paste to polish filigree and florentined textures and any other complicated or intricately detailed surface (see Figs. 84 and 84A).

Wood laps

Small wood laps are used with all polishing compounds to polish square and sharply defined corners. They can also be used for polishing flat enameled surfaces (see Fig. 89).

Stick buffs

Stick buffs are wooden slats covered with felt, chamois, or buckskin. They are charged with the polishing compounds and used to hand-rub surfaces to a high polish (see Fig. 92).

FIG. 92

String polishing

String polishing is the identical method described in the buffing section except that polishing instead of buffing compounds are used (see Fig. 79).

Rouge polishing cloth

A soft flannel-like fabric impregnated with a rouge compound is used for hand polishing. This cloth is usually sold with an uncharged fabric section used for the polishing after the surfaces have been rubbed with the rouge-charged portion.

Polishing compounds

Rouge polishing compound in bars or peel-away tubes is the most generally used polishing compound. Various rouges, identifiable by colors, are used with specific metals. For instance, red rouge is used on gold, silver, and copper but not on burnished surfaces. The compound will load up on a burnished surface, creating a discoloration, and will be impossible to remove in minute compressed areas. It is not objectionable if a light film of the compound remains in cuts and grooves on chased and engraved surfaces; however, if a dark color is actually desired, it is best to use an oxidizing solution or some other type of surface-coloring agent.

Brown rouge is used on softer metals, such as pewter and lead. White rouge is best for polishing platinum and white gold. Platinum rouge is used primarily for these two metals. Green and yellow rouge create a high luster on stainless steel.

Any rouge should be used sparingly. Excessive amounts applied to the wheel will pile up on the metal surface, causing these areas to remain dull when the compound is scrubbed away; also, excessive pressure or overly slow surface speed on the wheel will cause a pileup of rouge and the same blotchy finish.

Pumic and water paste gives a rich luster to silver. This paste can be applied with a brush, felt buff, or with the finger and by hand-rubbing.

A combination of whiting and water is used dry to highlight oxidized surfaces. The dry powder is picked up with a finger dampened with water and then rubbed on the metal surface. It can also be used with a bristle brush if mixed with water to make a paste; however, this is usually only used on filigree or florentined pieces.

Chrome oxide

Chrome oxide is a compound that comes in either a powder mixed with water to a paste, or in a bar as a grease-base compound. It is usually used to polish certain gemstones, but it can be used on a flannel buff to give a mirror finish to nickel silver.

Tin oxide

Tin oxide is another useful lapidary polishing material. It is mixed with water to form a paste and is used only after other polishing compounds have been meticulously scrubbed from the metal surface. Tin oxide preserves the high polish, especially on tarnish-prone metals, and adds an even greater luster to the metal than does a regular polishing agent. It should never be used in place of the regular polishing compounds required for specific metals.

Linde A

Linde A is a compound used in the same manner described for tin oxide, but it should be used in a hand-rubbing operation rather than with power equipment.

Polishing compounds are scrubbed away in the same manner as described for buffing compounds. All traces of the compounds must be removed or they will eventually discolor and tarnish the metals. After scrubbing the polished metal and rinsing it in running water, the article is placed in a box of hardwood sawdust such as maple, birch, mahogany (not Philippine) or boxwood to avoid its streaking or spotting as the metal dries. (Other woods contain soluble matter and resins that can tarnish metals and therefore are not recommended.)

The metal article is removed from the sawdust with cotton-gloved hands to prevent leaving any fingerprints on the surface.

CHAPTER 9

Soldering

METALS ARE ATTACHED WITH AN ALLOYED metal called solder which is of a lower melting point than the metals that are to be attached, but similar to them in color and content. A correctly soldered joint will be as strong as the metal it connects.

The right torch is essential to good soldering. Various tip sizes permit the worker to choose the proper one for each job. A reducing flame is always used for soldering.

Solders

Hard solder is alloyed into varying percentages of metal combinations in order to obtain a cohesive quality and for better wear and strength. The largest metal percentage is gold or silver. All hard solders must have a minimum melting point of 800° F. By altering the various percentages of metals in the formula, hard solder can be modified so that it has different melting points (see the Appendix).

Gold solders range in color and karat content to match the gold colors—yellow, white, green, pink, and red. A large amount of silver in yellow gold solder gives a greenish tinge; a small amount of silver lightens the gold color.

A large amount of copper changes the yellow gold color to red or pink; a small amount of copper makes the gold color a deeper yellow. Platinum or palladium changes yellow to white.

Each karat grade of gold solder has various melting points in order that multiple soldering steps may be accomplished with the same karat gold. Commercial gold solder is alloyed to be close in color and karat content to the particular gold sheet, bar, and wire used, but well below the melting point of the gold. A 14-karat solder does not mean that the material is 14-karat gold, but that it is alloyed to 12–13 karat (see the Appendix).

Solder should melt at temperatures that are 150° to 250° F. below the melting point of the metals to be joined. The flow point of most solders is 45° to 85° F. higher than their melting points, according to the type of solder being used.

The gold solder most generally used is 14k yellow, and the melting-point range for this color and karat is practically standard among most manufacturers.

The melting points for 14k are hard—1450° F.; medium—1410° F.; easy—1360° F. The melting points for 18k gold solder are hard—1520° F.; medium—1485° F.; easy—1390° F.

When working with gold the solder must be matched in karat content with the gold being soldered. Articles to be soldered are stamped 18k, 14k, 12k, which denotes the metal content of the article; only a small amount of variance (1 percent) in karat content is allowed for the solder. Metals of less than 50 percent gold content should not be stamped at all.

Silver solder is an alloy of silver and brass in varying amounts, depending on the melting point desired (see the Appendix). The various melting points of silver solder are hard #1 —1460° F.; medium—1390° F.; easy-flow —1325° F.; low—1175° F. for soldering findings to articles.

Greater intricacy and detail can be obtained in fabricating jewelry and other metalcraft articles by using the various grades of solder, because the lower melting-point solders when heated do not loosen previously soldered joints.

When combining gold and silver, silver solder should be used because the melting point of the gold solder being greater than that of silver, the silver portion of the article

of tin and lead by weight. It is seldom used on quality jewelry. The melting point of soft solder is always below 700° F.

Solder is sold in thin narrow strips approximately 1 inch wide and 2 inches long. Each strip when sold is marked with its identifying melting point. Because the solder will be cut into small squares (paillons) when used, it is necessary to keep solders of different designations separate from the very beginning. Silver and gold solders must never be mixed. There is no way to identify the solder after it is cut

FIG. 94

FIG. 93

would melt. Copper, brass, and bronze may be silver-soldered, but joints must be extremely close fitting to avoid evidences of the solder. Copper solder consists of 5 parts copper by weight to 1 part lead by weight. Brass solder is an alloy of 50 parts copper to 50 parts zinc, both by weight.

Soft solder, used only for the attachment of findings, etc., is usually alloyed of equal parts

from the marked sheet. Small plastic boxes legibly marked with melting point, or hard, medium, etc. (and karat content if gold solder) should be used for storing solders (see Fig. 93).

Strips approximately 1/32 inch or 1 mm wide are cut lengthwise, in from the end of the solder piece, with soldering shears or jeweler's tin snips. These strips are hammered out flat on a smooth metal surface with a rawhide mallet. The solder strip is then cupped in the palm of the hand, and the soldering snips cut across the strips to produce paillons of solder. The crosscut is made according to the size of pallion desired (see Fig. 94). Only enough solder for the job at hand should be cut to prevent having an excess of the same size squares.

Alloying solder

If the craftsman runs out of solder at a crucial point, or if time is essential, small amounts of solder could be alloyed to finish the job. To do this, check the tables in the Appendix which give solder constituents and their percentages. The metal percentages must be determined by weight alone.

The method of determining the amount of constituents in gold alloys of specific karat content is illustrated in the following examples: one pennyweight (dwt) of 18k gold contains 18 grains of 24k gold and 6 grains of alloy. By increasing the alloy content to 9 grains, the gold content is two-thirds of the mixture. Two-thirds of 24k is 16k, and this is the karat content of this mix. The metals must be measured by weight only. (See the Appendix for instructions for raising and lowering the content of gold in alloys and the conversion tables of dwt, grains, and grams.)

When gold solder is being alloyed, a small amount of borax sprinkled over the surface of the molten mass aids in the removal of oxides and any other contaminants. The metals are melted in the hollow of a charcoal block or in an asbestos-lined crucible. When the molten metal forms a ball, it is rolled out onto an asbestos sheet and gently flattened with a hammer as it cools. It is immediately dropped in the sulphuric acid pickling solution (see Chapter 4) and rinsed in running water. It is then rolled out to standard solder thickness (28 gauge).

Soldering bases

Metals are soldered on tripods with webs, charcoal blocks, magnesium blocks, on asbestos sheets, or rounds (tightly wrapped asbestos strips approximately 1¼ inches wide held together in a shallow metal rim) placed on firebricks for bench-top protection (see Figs. 95, 96, and 97). A charcoal block is preferred for it can be heated before the metal is placed on it, and it retains the heat. The torch flame heats the metal from the top and equalizes the heat temperature throughout the metal. Charcoal blocks do not last very long when used extensively for soldering, but their life can be extended by holding them together with several wrappings of binding wire to prevent splitting

as they cool. Electric soldering machines are also used for fine soldering (see Fig. 98).

Cleaning the metal

Metals to be soldered and the solder itself must be absolutely clean and free from grease, dirt, grime, wax, oil, and oxides. They may be scrubbed in soap and water and rinsed, then heated and quenched in the pickling solution, and carefully sanded with fine emery paper or rubbed with steel wool. A fiber glass eraser sold in stationery stores works nicely to clean

FIG. 95

off oxides and tarnish. After the metal has been cleaned, the fingers should be kept off the areas that are to be soldered.

Fluxes

Solders require flux, which is a substance applied to the metal before heating to keep the metal clean and to prevent oxides from forming. This allows the solder to adhere to the metal. The flowing properties are in the solder, not in the flux, so that the flux coating permits the solder to smooth out or flow along a seam.

The flux should become fluid at a temperature just below that of the melted solder. Both metal and flux arrive at the correct soldering temperature at the same time.

Commercially prepared fluxes that work well are available; however, the best flux is made of boric acid and borax combined in equal parts, either in liquid or paste. This flux becomes fluid at 1400° F. Water or alcohol can be used to thin the two constituents as desired. Flux paste should be mixed and used in a thinner consistency on thin-gauge metals and a thicker consistency on heavier-gauge metals. The ratio of boric acid and borax can be varied to produce fluxes that melt at different temperatures. By increasing the boric acid content to 75 percent, the fusion point is lowered considerably for soldering at a lower heat. Lowering the boric acid content to 25 percent produces a high fusing flux. Solders alloyed in gold content to match a high karat content metal have a higher fusing point which require a flux with a high fluidity point. Gold solders with a melting point of 1450° F. or less require a flux with a lower fluidity point. All metals can be soldered using the boric acid–borax flux, although such divergent metals as platinum and pewter should be soldered with commercially prepared fluxes because of additives that are required to produce satisfactory results.

Holding fluxes

A special holding flux used on vertical, curved, and otherwise hard-to-hold areas where the solder paillons may drift away from the joint consists of borax glass and white vaseline (petroleum jelly). A small amount of borax is placed in a small crucible and heated until it becomes a glassy bead. When cool, the bead is ground to a powder and mixed with the petrolatum. The organic substance which will not interfere with the soldering is eliminated in the air or flame. Gum tragacanth (used for enameling) can be added in small amounts to the boric acid–borax flux mix for the same purpose.

Holding devices

When the torch is applied to the metal, it may sometimes warp the metal if proper support is

FIG. 96

not provided underneath. The torch flame may push the metals apart or move them slightly. Because of this, metal sections or parts to be soldered should be held together with some sort of clamping device, or with iron binding wire called soldering wire. Clamping devices, besides wire and other standard soldering aids, include tweezers with tension locks, cotter pins, staples, clamps, or other improvised aids (see Fig. 99). The tweezers, which are automatically locked, except when squeezed to open, are best for holding the metals together. They are also used equally well to hold a section of metal in midair so that it can be heated from all sides. The tweezers may be held in the hand or in a third-hand base, thus leaving both hands free to hold the torch, and to rotate the

FIG. 97

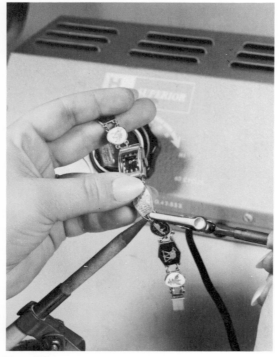

Fig. 98

metal during heating (see Fig. 100). The tension tweezers are also available in a double arrangement that will permit even greater clamping action. Wire, cotter pins, small nails or brads, and staples used to hold metals in place during soldering must be removed before plunging the hot metal in the pickling solution.

Often metals hold together by tension alone. Rings, jump rings, chain links, and bezels are formed so that the ends when brought together are bypassed side by side. When forced open with finger pressure they snap into place with the filed ends butted tight against each other. Rings formed with this tension need no wire or other clamping device to hold them during soldering.

Sheet metal clamps and hi-fi alligator clips are also used, but the alligator clips lose their tension if overheated. Iron binding wire is an important basic item for the metalsmith as it can be used many ways in soldering. The wire is wrapped around the metals after they have been fluxed at the contact points. Larger pieces of metal may require several wrappings of wire. The ends are twisted gently with flat-nosed pliers as close to the metal as possible (see Fig. 101). Wire twisted from the ends will break long before it is tight enough to hold the metals together. Iron binding wire, though excellent for holding metals during soldering, must be removed before plunging the heated soldered metal into the pickling solution to remove the oxides from the torch heat. If the wire is left on, it will contaminate the solution and deposit a thin layer of metal on subsequent pieces immersed in the same solution.

Excessive use of solder and flux may weld the iron binding wire to the soldered piece. When this occurs, the metal is allowed to cool, but is not dropped into the pickling solution until the wire is removed. The binding wire is pulled gently with pliers while the metal is securely held with the opposite hand to prevent

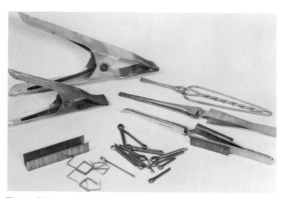

Fig. 99

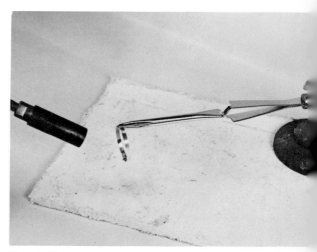

Fig. 100

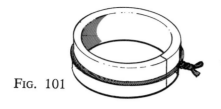

FIG. 101

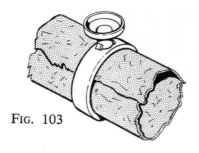

FIG. 103

any distortion. Rings and bezels can be slipped back onto a ring mandrel to hold them as the wire is being removed with the pliers. If the wire is securely attached, it is cut off with end cutting pliers as close as possible to the metal, and the remainder is gently filed and sanded away. When the wire and solder have been removed, the metal is placed in the pickling solution, and the solution is heated to cleanse the surface of any oxides. It is then rinsed in running water. Containers of water used for rinsing are discouraged because the contaminants of the pickling solution remain in the water, causing a problem in subsequent soldering steps.

Another soldering aid is made by bending a

FIG. 102

length of ⅛-inch drill rod to form a Z. One end is flattened into a narrow spatula shape. The opposite end is embedded in plaster of Paris or dental stone poured into a shallow container to form the base. Rings bound with wire, or rings held by their own tension may be suspended from the flattened end and soldered easily with heat applied to all areas. Other metal sections may be suspended by the binding wire wrappings to permit the even application of heat to all areas (see Fig. 102).

Though in most cases it is necessary to clamp or wire the parts together, if adequately supported, weight alone will hold large sections of metal in proper position during the soldering process. An annealing pan two-thirds full of fine sand can be used for this purpose. After fluxing, the metal pieces are placed in the pan and the sand is pushed under them for support.

Small bits of asbestos strip are folded and used to lift up the metal where it is not possible to use sand. The metal pieces should be well supported, not just resting or balanced precariously one on another (see Fig. 103). Before clamping devices were known, Mexican silversmiths used this method. The pan may also be filled with lump charcoal which disperses the heat more evenly above and below the metal than sand but does not give as much support.

When soldering, the heat should be directed to the thicker metal as thin metal heats quickly and extra precaution is necessary to keep it from melting. All areas of the metal must be watched constantly so that the torch flame does not dwell on any one area too long. This is especially important when soldering bezels, gallery wire, prongs, clasp mountings, and wire ends.

An article that is to be repaired can be completed by embedding the stone in a raw potato to protect it while it is being soldered. The solder step must be finished as soon as possible, for prolonged heating with the torch will affect the stone.

Joining the metals

Sections should be soldered in sequence, the solder with the highest melting point being used first. Several separate sections may be joined with high melting point solder and attached to another section with a lower melting point solder, continuing down to the lowest melting point solder for the final assembly stages.

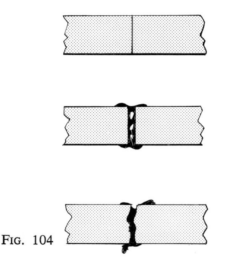

FIG. 104

All metal sections to be joined together must meet perfectly. Flat surfaces must be absolutely flat; curved areas must match exactly curve for curve; walls or edges must be parallel and perpendicular respectively, and ends must butt together tightly. When a joint is held up to a light, no light should be seen through it, and the metals must fit together without being held under tension. Clamping methods or binding wire are used only to hold the parts from slipping when soldering.

Solder will not bridge a gap or fill in a low spot or a crack (see Fig. 104). Contoured surfaces must be checked to see that all contact points meet without any need to rock them to make them meet.

The following types of contact points must be minutely inspected and held to the light to be sure they meet perfectly: wire soldered to wire, wire soldered to flat sheet, tubing seams, and tubing soldered to wire or flat sheet.

A soldered joint will be stronger where a minimum amount of solder flows through an area of contact. When the joints are properly fitted, the solder will flow freely, alloy with the metal, and freeze smooth and clean without any pits or pinholes.

If a gap or separation appears in a soldered joint, no effort should be made to fill the area with additional solder. Instead, a piece of metal sawed from scrap (identical in karat content, if working with gold) should be fitted into place. This may necessitate drilling a small hole in which to insert an 8/0 saw blade so that a smooth clean area can be sawed out for refitting. This fine saw blade is also used to cut the small piece of scrap metal to be fitted into the opening. The metal is fluxed, soldered as before, and the excess solder removed. This hard-soldered joint, unlike soft-soldered joints, will be as strong as the metal it holds together.

The metal should be evenly heated so that a cold area cannot draw the heat away from the area to be soldered, as solder will only flow to the hottest part. Small sections to be soldered to larger ones should never be heated first. Much of the heat will transfer from the larger to the smaller section so that it will need only last-minute direct heat in order to aid the flow of solder to the desired area. This is especially true when soldering small rings to pendants, etc.

Observance of the colors of heated metals will reveal the metal temperatures (see Appendix). The first visible red tinge appears at approximately 900°F., an even dull red at 1200°F., a cherry red at 1400°F., and a pink glow at 1600°F., the danger point. It is best to heat all metals in shaded light, but it is particularly important when heating gold, because gold changes color only momentarily and very close to the point when it melts and collapses completely.

A soft flame is used to heat the metal and the flux. Heat dries out the water in the flux which, when borax is used, becomes a fine powder as soon as the correct temperature is reached.

To equalize the heat, the flame is brought closer and moved over and under the metal wherever possible. When the metal reaches a dull red it is close to the solder melting point, and the solder is applied by dipping a small camel's-hair brush in the flux and then using the damp brush tip to pick up a square of solder and transfer it to the area being soldered.

The solder can also be transferred to the heated metals with a pusher rod made from a 12- 14-inch section of ⅛-inch drill rod (see Fig. 105). The rod, filed to a long taper on one end, must be kept clean. The point is sufficiently sharp to prick the solder so that it can be lifted and carried to the heated metal. The pointed rod is also used to push solder into place and to spread it on a flat surface so that it will flow to all desired areas. As flux bubbles when heated, solder placed before heating the metal may lift and move to an undesired area. If this should occur, the rod is used to flick the solder quickly from the area, but should this be impossible, the rod can be used to transport a new piece of solder immediately where desired. After the metal cools, the misplaced solder can be removed.

The heat of the metal itself will heat the solder. The flame is directed to the area enough to melt the solder so that it flows. The torch is lifted, as soon as a bright thin line of flowing solder is visible, and played over the entire area to equalize the flow of solder. If the solder becomes overheated before the metals are sufficiently hot, it will roll up in a ball and will not flow until the metals reach the correct temperature. Whenever the area to be soldered and the solder are not fluxed properly, the solder will oxidize and will not flow at all. Balling of solder also occurs if the area surfaces have not been cleaned properly.

Solder may also be placed on the cold fluxed metal before heating, but the flame should be kept away from the area until the entire piece is evenly heated. After the water evaporates, the flux will form a glassy puddle that will hold the paillons in place. With the flame moving at all times, heat is brought closer to the joint. The solder will ball up, then smooth out and flow into place. If the solder paillons move during the period of evaporation, they can be returned to the proper position with the pusher rod.

After the soldering is completed, the metal is dipped in the pickling solution, rinsed in run-

Fig. 105

ning water, and dried. The pieces are then carefully checked to see if they are adequately soldered together. If they are not, more solder must be added at the risk of loosening the joint.

Smaller flames should be used for the subsequent soldering steps to avoid overheating previously soldered areas. When the entire piece is heated during subsequent soldering, the previously soldered joints must be free of flux to prevent the flow of solder which would permit these joints to loosen if they should be heated excessively.

When soldering subsequent joints, an antiflux (antioxidizer) is applied to all areas where solder should not flow, especially adjacent joints already soldered. The metal is first pickled, rinsed in running water, and dried. The antiflux is then applied to the appropriate areas. Commercial preparations can be purchased for this purpose, or the area can be covered with a paste made by mixing either yellow ocher (artist's material) or red polishing rouge with alcohol. Another antiflux is boric acid saturated in alcohol which can be painted on the surface. The surface is ignited with an ordinary match to consume the alcohol and leave a dry coating that prevents oxidation. A commercial antiflux sold by dental suppliers can be used as a pickling solution. It will protect the surface against oxidation through five or six subsequent solderings. On the other hand, paste mixes must be scrubbed off the metal after it cools and before it is dipped in any pickling solution.

Oxides can be prevented when soldering gold if areas which are not to be soldered are coated with a paste made of 1½ ounces of sesquioxide of iron, 1 ounce of calcined borax, and ½ ounce of ammonia. After soldering, the paste is removed by boiling the article in a sulphuric acid pickling solution.

Cuprous oxide, the black residue left after soldering, can easily be removed by pickling the soldered metal. Cupric oxide, a reddish purple spotting caused by overheating the metal, discolors the metal far below the surface. This will become evident as a dark gray area during the buffing and polishing steps. Often a piece may have to be either heated to a dull red and immediately quenched in pickling solution to remove the surface copper of the alloy, or discarded. A thin layer of pure metal remains on the surface and must be left as is. Polishing, buffing, sanding, etc., would break through the pure metal coating exposing the discoloration below the surface.

In appliqué or lamination projects (layers of metals), eutectic solder can be used effectively. This consists of a flux and powdered or filed solder (that have identical fusing points) mixed together or applied separately to both mating surfaces. The surfaces are heated from underneath to coat them completely. They are then mated and heated to fuse them.

Soft soldering is usually done with a soft flame torch, but a soldering iron or gun can also be used. Excess solder is removed with a bearing scraper and file reserved for this purpose. Soft solder flux is usually zinc chloride in commercial form. It is made by placing hydrochloric acid in a glass jar and adding small pellets of zinc to the acid. Because a violent boiling action takes place, this must be done outside in the fresh air. When the boiling subsides, additional zinc pellets are added, and as the gas subsides more pellets are added. This procedure is repeated until the solution no longer produces any gas. The solution is either used as is or is formed into a paste made from one ounce of the solution mixed with one pound of white petroleum jelly (vaseline).

Soft soldered joints are never immersed in pickling solution, but are cooled in the atmosphere because the joint must not be moved until it is cool. Cooling may be speeded by dropping water onto the warm joint with a

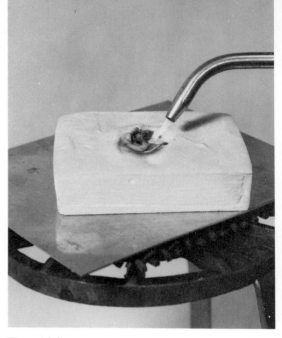

FIG. 106

toothpick or pipe cleaner.

The soft soldering flux must be thoroughly removed after soldering by boiling the metal in a mixture of sal ammoniac and water. A common household equivalent for this is a commercial product called Oakite.

Soft solder must always be completely removed before any joint is hard-soldered because soft solder when heated at high temperatures will burn into the metal and etch the surface.

Brass solder can be made by adding to the brass one-fourth of its weight in zinc. Copper solder is alloyed from 80 parts of copper, 5 parts of phosphorous, and 15 parts of silver. Regular flux (borax) is used for both brass and copper solder.

Bronze, copper, and brass can be soldered with silver solder, but the metal contrast will be evident if the seam is not fitted extremely close. It is best to use a lower-heating hard solder to prevent overheating the metals because overheating would cause their collapse. Steel and iron are soldered by using brass for a solder and borax for a flux.

Investment soldering

Investment soldering is a method of holding small parts when any other clamping or holding procedure will not work. This is especially good when working with small pieces that are to be soldered in one operation.

A thin sheet of dental wax is placed on a smooth flat surface. Small loops of soldering binding wire are cut and wrapped under the cleaned and pickled metal sections as the sections are placed on the wax (see Fig. 331). The sections are pressed into the wax so that they are just visible. When all parts have been looped with the binding wire and are in correct position, the area is enclosed with a wax border of softer consistency, and the entire assemblage is covered with a thin layer of plaster of Paris mix, dental stone, or dental investment mixed with water. When the investment has set up and hardened, usually in 8 to 10 hours, it is removed from the wax frame. The wax base is also removed exposing the metal parts held in place in the investment with tiny loops of binding wire. The wax must be completely removed by placing the entire unit in boiling water for a few minutes. The plaster should then be dried and checked for excess investment in areas where soldering is to be done. These areas can be cleaned with a small darning needle embedded in the end of a short length of dowel wood, or with dental instruments. The joints are fluxed in the usual manner, solder is applied, and the metals are joined together. The binding wire loops are cut with small end-cutting pliers, and the metal is removed, pickled, and rinsed in running water.

Larger sections that require investment soldering but cannot be held without additional support are completely embedded in investment plaster as described in the following procedure.

Buffing and polishing compounds and any oxidation are removed by scrubbing the metal in soap and water, rinsing in running water, and pickling and rinsing again. The metal parts are joined with wax, then embedded in investment and set aside to dry so that only the joints are exposed (see Fig. 106).

Because it is compounded of ingredients with cristobalite at a minimum proportion, soldering investment is preferable to casting investment. The ratio of water to powder should be in accordance with the manufacturer's recommendation. It must be a thick viscous mass that will hold together on the glass slab without

being confined in a ring or boxed frame. This mass, when dry and hardened, will hold the sections together during the soldering.

The Bunsen burner or torch can be used to dry and heat the investment which must be placed on an asbestos sheet on top of a wire grid on the soldering tripod. To prevent contamination of the metal solder the investment must not be heated excessively.

All wax must be completely removed from the joint. This is done by dipping the exposed section in boiling water. The clean joints are fluxed at the joint areas only. Soldering flux paste made by combining boric acid and borax powders with petroleum jelly or white vaseline will stay on the metal best. The organic petrolatum protects the surface from air and is eventually burned away in carbon.

Antiflux, applied in the form of rouge and alcohol paste, confines the flow of solder to critical areas. Ordinary graphite lead pencils can be used to mark off an area for solder containment, but if temperatures soar too high any marks are ineffective.

A reducing flame, adjusted to its smallest possible cone, is applied gradually to the exposed joints so that only these areas are heated. When the flux begins to flow, the torch heat is increased to soldering temperature, and the solder is added without removing the flame so that it flows smoothly and quickly into the joint area. Whenever the solder does not flow freely, the flame must be removed and the metal allowed to cool, so that it can be recleaned of oxides or other contaminants. Continual heating of the flux will fuse the solder with the metal and make it difficult to get a flow of solder in the joint. Soldered joints will be weak and porous if the distances between the sections are not minimal. To remove the soldered article after completion, the heated metal in its investment case is dipped immediately in water to disintegrate the investment. When all remaining particles of the investment are scrubbed from the metal, the article is ready for the pickling and finishing steps.

Electric soldering

An electric soldering machine may be the best method for soldering in some instances, but it cannot be made a complete substitute for torch soldering. It should be used according to the manufacturer's instructions, and some experimenting may be necessary to prevent burning the joint. The machine solders very quickly with extremely high concentrated heat and the adjustment of the control is crucial (see Fig. 98).

The metals to be soldered must be cleaned thoroughly. The carbon point must be cleaned after each soldering to remove a glaze of old flux that will prevent good contact. The carbon point should be pressed against the joint just enough to make contact. It should not be removed when the solder flows; only the foot control should be released. Regular fluxes and pickling solutions used for other soldering methods are also used here. Various carbon tips, available with the machine, permit soldering of ring shanks with stones intact, chain soldering, etc.

Removal of solder from gold

Gold articles should not be soldered with soft solder, especially if they are to be sold and therefore stamped with the karat content as required by law. Articles for personal use only can be soft-soldered if desired.

Visible soft solder is removed from gold by first eliminating it with a scraper. Care must be taken so that the gold is not damaged. The soldered piece (up to 12k) is immersed in a cold solution consisting of 4 ounces of ferric chloride, ½ ounce of hydrochloric acid, and 1 pint of water, which is brought to a boiling point. The metal is taken from the solution, and the area brushed to remove any evidences of solder. The article is rinsed in running water, rebuffed, and polished as necessary. A solution for articles of more than 12k is made by combining 2 ounces of iron sulphate, 1 ounce of potassium nitrate, and 10 ounces of water. The mixture is brought to a boil and then set aside to cool. As it cools, crystals form that are dissolved with 8 parts hydrochloric acid and 4 parts boiling water. The solution is used hot. After immersing the article in the hot solution it is brushed, rinsed, and the surfaces refinished accordingly.

To unsolder a joint, the piece must be fastened securely on an asbestos sheet or held with clamps to prevent it from lifting when the metal section is removed. The entire piece could also be suspended from the soldering aid (see Fig. 102) so that it falls apart at the joint when heated. After separation, the pieces are pickled and the solder is removed.

Solder can be removed from silver by scraping and filing, but it is best removed by placing the article in a hot strong nitric acid solution of 1 part acid to 4 parts water. The article is left in the solution just long enough to dissolve the solder. The nitric acid should be pure and free of hydrochloric acid which would attack any gold contained in the article. After the removal of the solder, the article is taken from the solution and rinsed in running water. It is then boiled in a sulfuric acid solution (pickling) if additional soldering is required.

CHAPTER 10

Metal Coloring and Finishing

METAL COLORING

Colorings consisting of oxides, patinas, and metal coatings such as gilding and silvering are performed as the final treatment after the article has been buffed and polished. Delicate colorings and finishes should not be attempted on articles requiring a considerable amount of stone setting because of the subsequent buffing and polishing steps that are necessary to remove the marks of bezel and prong burnishers and other stone-setting tools.

Metal must always be completely free from contamination of any kind before the surface is colored. The metal is cleaned by scrubbing it with warm detergent suds and then rinsing in running water. From this point the article should not be touched with the bare hands because any body moisture contaminates the metal so that the coloring will not be even on the surface.

Coloring Gold

Black and gray

Because gold is the most beautiful of all precious metals, and because it does not discolor in the atmosphere, oxidation is seldom used ex-

cept for unusual contemporary pieces, and then only for contrast in recessed areas. Gold can be oxidized by applying the heated liver of sulfur potassium sulfide solution given for silver with a steel rod or a common nail instead of with a brush or by immersion. The chemical action of the steel nail and the solution on the heated metal forms the oxide coating. Gold can be oxidized with commercial solutions used in concentrated form for the very dark shades or in a diluted 2-ounce solution to 1 pint of water for the gray casts. The heated gold article can also be colored by applying a warm solution of ammonium sulfide (sal ammoniac) with a small camel-air brush.

The metal is heated slowly by heat transfer (see Chapter 26) until a black oxide forms on the surface. Buffed highlights on the metal will reveal the gold color through the surface coating.

Coloring Silver

Dark gray

Silver is oxidized by dipping the article in a near-boiling solution of liver of sulfur (potassium sulfide). A small lump of potassium sulfide ½ to ¾ inch is dissolved in a quart of water to which is added 1 ounce of ammonia. The article is suspended in the heated solution on a copper or brass wire until the desired color is reached, and then immediately removed and rinsed under running water to halt the coloring action. If certain areas only are to be colored, the solution may be applied with a wisp of cotton on a toothpick, a cotton swab, or with a small camel-hair brush.

If the article is not absolutely clean before the coloring steps are begun, the color will be blotchy and uneven and if the solution has been overheated, the coloring will flake off in some places. In either case the article must be pickled, scrubbed, and rinsed before recoloring. Though this is the most common method of coloring silver, commercial oxidizing solutions can be used if desired.

French gray

A French gray finish on silver is effected by oxidizing clean metal in the liver of sulfur solution until a black shade is reached. After drying, the surface is buffed evenly with a bristle brush to cut through the dark coating so that a uniform gray color appears. This color is preserved with a light coating of clear lacquer.

Crimson, purple, and brown

To obtain the colors crimson, purple, and brown, which occur in this sequence, the article is dipped in or painted with a near-boiling solution of ammonium chloride (sal ammoniac) made with 2 to 3 lumps of the ammonium sulfide dissolved in ½ pint of near-boiling water. This concentrated solution is diluted 1 part solution to 6 parts water for the coloring process. When the article has reached the desired color it is taken from the solution and rinsed immediately in running water to halt the coloring action.

Jet black

To produce a black color the same concentrated ammonium chloride solution given for crimson, purple, and brown is mixed 1 part of solution to 2 parts water and used at near-boiling temperature. The article is rinsed in running water when the color is reached. The concentrated solution and the dry chemicals must be stored in a dark place because they deteriorate when exposed to light for an extended period.

Yellow (gold-colored)

Silver can be given a "gold" coating by immersing the article in a solution consisting of one part iron oxide (micronized umber) dissolved in one part diluted sulfuric acid. When the desired color is reached, the article is rinsed in running water.

Green

A green patina on silver is produced by immersing the clean article in a solution consisting of 3 parts hydrochloric acid, 1 part iodine, and 1 part water. The article is removed from the cool solution as soon as the desired color is reached; it is then rinsed in running water.

Steel blue

A steel blue color is obtained by placing the article and two or three small lumps of sulfur in a tight-fitting covered metal container which is heated with a torch. The metal must not be allowed to touch the sulfur as it will stain the silver. Sulfer fumes produced by the heat will color the metal. Additional sulfur and heat may be required in order to reach the color desired.

Coloring Copper

Dark gray

Copper is oxidized in the same manner in the same heated liver of sulfur solution given for the coloration of silver.

Crimson, purple, and brown

The same procedure is used as given for silver.

Black

The article is immersed in the same heated solution of ammonium chloride given for coloring gold and silver.

Blue-black

The metal is suspended on a copper wire in a heated solution consisting of 4 ounces of lead acetate (sugar of lead) dissolved in 8 ounces of sodium thiosulfate (antichlor). When the color is obtained it is removed from the solution and rinsed in running water.

Blue-green-black combination

The article is immersed in acetic acid for two to three minutes and then placed in a closed container large enough to include a small uncovered dish of ammonia. The exposure of the metal to the ammonia fumes for several hours will produce the three-tone color.

Green

A patina is produced on the metal by brushing the surface with a solution consisting of 1 gram each of copper nitrate, ammonia chloride, calcium chloride, and 1 ounce of water. When the color is reached the article is set aside to dry.

A patina can also be produced by pouring a hot solution consisting of 1½ grams of copper nitrate and 6 ounces of water onto the metal and allowing it to dry.

In both methods the metal surface is highlighted by rubbing desired areas with a fine paste of pumice mixed with water or thin oil.

Heat coloring

Oxides, cuprous and cupric, are formed on a clean copper surface as the metal is slowly heated with a low-heat brush flame such as that produced by a Bunsen burner. If a large object is being colored, the metal should be rotated on a swivel base to equalize the heat. The metal changes colors from yellow to various shades of red, to violet and then to brown as the heating continues. Color retention at any state is accomplished by withdrawing the heat as the color nears the desired tint. The heat remaining in the metal will complete the coloring to the desired shade.

If the metal is overheated, or quenched in water while hot, the oxide coloring will flake off, thus requiring recleaning and recoloring.

Coloring Brass and Bronze

Black

The surface of the metal is coated with an antimony chloride solution (butter of antimony) and set aside to dry. The metal is highlighted in the same manner described for patina finishes.

Green

The same method is used as described for patinizing the copper.

Blue-green-black combination

The same method is used as described for coloring copper.

Blue-black

The same methods are used as described for coloring copper.

Gray-yellow-orange

Liquid soldering fluid with a low melting point, heated with a household candle for soft soldering purposes, is used to obtain this color range. The fluid is usually used on chased pieces and is applied on the chased lines. The liquid flows when heated from underneath and when cool is rubbed with steel wool for highlights. A minimum amount of the fluid should be used in order to retain the basic metal color.

Coloring Nickel Silver

Black

The metal is immersed in a satured solution of copper sulfate dissolved in water. The solution will be a green color. Any sediment will be dispelled by adding ammonia slowly until it disappears, and the solution turns blue. The metal is either painted with the heated solution or immersed in it. It is then rinsed in running water and highlighted by buffing as described for other colored metals. The same procedure can be used on brass and bronze articles. When oxidizing or coloring is completed and highlights brought out, the area should be rubbed with wax to preserve and protect the color. The entire article can be sprayed with clear lacquer instead of waxing it; however, bright shiny areas will tend to tarnish from atmosphere even under the lacquer coating which would have to be removed to restore the piece to its original beauty. Lacquering should be limited or confined to articles that have no coloring on the surface.

Metal surfaces with discolored areas that have been caused by oxidizing or by other surface coloring methods can be cleaned with a scratch brush or by rubbing the spots with a paste made of whiting and alcohol. The paste is rubbed on the surface with a finger, or with a small cotton-tipped stick, and then gently scrubbed with a soft nylon bristle brush in warm detergent suds and rinsed in running water.

Gilding Contrasting Metal

The metal surface is scratch-brushed and the gild is spread over the surface with a copper rod embedded in a wooden handle. Gild is made of 1 part gold to 8 parts quicksilver (mercury) by weight. To mix the two elements, they are placed in a heated crucible and rotated while held with tongs. The rotation should be continued only long enough to amalgamate the two ingredients, else it will become too thick. The mass is poured into a container of cold water and washed under running water until the water is clear.

When the surface is completely covered with the gild, the metal is heated over a slow flame to eliminate the mercury that will burn away in fumes, leaving a gold coating. These fumes are extremely toxic even in a well-ventilated room and this operation should be performed outdoors. When the mercury has burned away the article is left to cool slowly. It is then inspected to see if any areas require additional gilding. If it is necessary to regild the metal it must be cleaned with tartrate of potash and water before repeating the gilding operation.

Other Gilding Substances

The same color on the metal can be obtained without using the toxic mercury substance by

FIG. 107 Pin, pierced appliqué with florentine finish, 14k gold.
By Sharr Choate.

immersing the metal in either of the solutions as follows:

Solution #1   1 pint chloride of gold*
3 ounces sodium carbonate crystals
3 ounces cyanide potassium
1 quart distilled water
The solution is used at nearboiling point.

Solution #2   1 pint chloride of gold*
2 pints distilled water
16 ounces potassium bicarbonate
The solution is mixed and maintained at near-boiling point for one hour before immersing the metal.

When using either formula, as soon as the color is reached the article is removed, rinsed in running water, and dried.

Silvering Contrasting Metals

A silver coating for accent on contrasting metals is produced by completely covering the article with a paste coating consisting of 1 ounce pure silver dissolved in 1 ounce nitric

---

* Chloride of gold is made by dissolving 6 dwt. gold in 1 pt. acid consisting of 8 oz. each of nitric and muriatic acids.

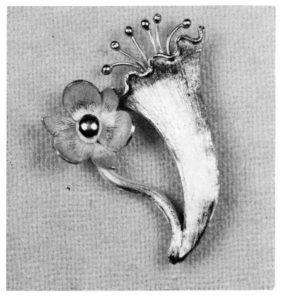

FIG. 108 Pin forged with florentine finish, sterling silver.
By Sharr Choate.

acid. Cream of tartar is added to the solution to form a thin paste. The paste is rubbed onto the metal surface (brass, copper, or bronze) with a small cloth pad. The rubbing is continued until the silver color appears on the surface. The excess paste is wiped off, and when the surface is dry it is rubbed with a damp cloth charged with 400–600 grit emery powder. The gritty substance will remove the coating from the surfaces, leaving a silver color in the undercuts and recesses. The rubbing operation is similar to the buffing operation used to highlight bright metal underneath.

Different gold colorings on gold and contrasting metal coatings on other metals are accomplished by electroplating (see Chapter 28).

FINISHING

Various surface finishes, done last so that no damage will occur during the metalworking, are effected by the use of florentine-lined gravers, power-driven wheels, and sandblasting equipment. Hand-burnishing tools are used to attain a bright shiny finish. Metal articles are surface-treated after all other work except the setting of gemstones has been completed.

Florentine gravers

Lined gravers are used in the final finishing stages to give a fine-lined texture called a florentined finish. Those portions of an article that will be inaccessible after assembling should be florentined before the soldering step. Areas where excess solder has been removed and which are visible in the finished piece can be touched up with the graver in the final stages (see Chapter 19 and Figs. 107, 108, and 109).

Satin finish

A satin finish on metal surfaces can be obtained by using any one of the following methods:

1. Dipping the article in a "satin" finish solution consisting of one part hydrofluoric acid and three parts water used in a rubber or hard plastic container, followed by rinsing in running water. This is the simplest method.
2. Wire-brushing the surface with a steel or brass wheel (see Fig. 86) charged with a paste of pumice mixed with a thin oil. When using this method it should be kept in mind that the ends of the bristles do the work. Too much pressure applied against the wheel tends to curl the bristles, thus producing a poor surface. A brush thus damaged should be discarded. Brass wheels are never used on silver as they leave a yellowish tinge on the surface.
3. Brushing the surface with a hog bristle-

FIG. 109 Pin forged with florentine finish, sterling silver.
By Sharr Choate.

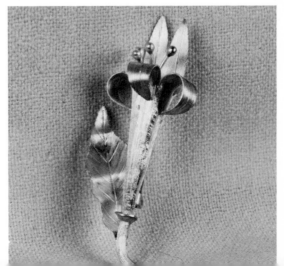

brush wheel of soft bristles (see Fig. 85) or with a nylon bristle-brush wheel, both of which can be charged either with Tripoli or an emery grit and vaseline paste. This method is particularly effective when contrasting metals are used in one article because the different colors immediately become more apparent.

4. Using muslin buffing wheels (including the small ones used with a flex-shaft handpiece) charged with fine grit emery. This method is best used on flat areas because the wheels will not get into all the small undercuts of an assembly.

5. Using fine steel wool (000) to produce a sanded finish on the metal. The wool is rolled into a ball and used in one direction only. The fine grades of steel wool will produce a softer satiny finish.

6. Using small squares of crocus cloth or 600 grit emery paper and hand-rubbing the surface. Small squares (approximately one inch square) of the paper are turned up slightly at one corner so that they can be held by the thumb and forefinger (see Fig. 110). The side of the thumb acts as a pressure plate as the paper is moved in one direction only across the metal. Pressure is released for the return stroke, and the paper is lifted away from the metal because it is impossible to retrace the same pattern.

7. Sandblasting with a small bench-top machine (see Fig. 111). The machine is operated with air pressure at 18–20 psi (pounds per square inch). The blasting mix is usually 85 parts sandblasting quartz (200 mesh) and 15 parts washed silica sand (100 mesh) by weight. Blasting sands are sold in various grits, depending upon the degree of satin finish desired. For a frosted surface, a heavier mesh sand is used.

Burnishing

Burnishing is a method of brightening metal surfaces with tools made of either steel or agate. The tools are round or flat in various shapes (see Fig. 112).

Circular or back and forth strokes are made on the metal surface with the tool that has been dipped in a slurry consisting of liquid soap and

Fig. 110

water. The burnisher should "bite" into the metal but not drag or scratch it. The burnishing process pushes the metal down and over by a rolling pressure (see Fig. 80). The edges of an article can also be rolled over and burnished to a bright luster with this tool. As soon as the burnisher begins to slide over the surface, it must be honed on a strip of leather which has been impregnated with crocus dust.

The burnished article is polished with green rouge mixed with glycerine. Red rouge should not be used for polishing because it is worked down into the metal with the burnisher, thus contaminating the metal surface.

Coating the tools with a thin film of oil will prevent rusting when not in use.

Bright dip for gold and silver

Matte surfaces can also be produced by immersing the metal in Bright Dip solution. The metal is heated to produce cuprous oxides on the surface. After it is cool, it is dipped in the strong Bright Dip solution for two or three seconds only. This dissolves the alloy in the metal which has come to the surface in the form of oxides.

The solution consists of either one part sulfuric acid and one part water for gold or one part nitric acid and one part water for silver, and is used at room temperature. The article is dipped in the solution and then rinsed in running water. Glass-tipped tongs, string, etc., should be used to dip the metal in the solution. A bright pure layer of the base metal remains on the surface. The thin layer of pure frosty metal is easily lost if the article is buffed or polished.

Matte finishing

A matte finish is a frosted texture that can be produced on metal articles by scratch-brushing the surface in one direction only with steel wool (000) or with a nickel or monel metal wire wheel. Either kerosene, or soap dissolved with water to a thick cream can be used as lubricants on the wire wheels which are operated between 800 and 1200 sfpm.

Matte dip

A heavier frosted finish can be produced on metals with a matte dip. The article is bright-dipped, rinsed, and dried, but the burnishing step is omitted. The metal is dipped for two to three seconds in another solution consisting of one part each of sulfuric and nitric acids and one part water, and then rinsed and dried.

The layer of pure base metal on the surface can be thickened by repeating the burnishing step three or four times. After each burnishing the metal is heated, pickled, and rinsed in running water.

For a contrasting finish on the metal surfaces, specific areas can be masked off with an acid resist such as wax or lacquer until the matte dip step is completed. As the resist requires very little rubbing to remove, the matte finish will not be damaged.

FIG. 111

FIG. 112

CHAPTER 11

Mountings and Findings

MOUNTINGS

THE MAIN PURPOSE OF ALL THE VARIED mounting devices available to the craftsman is to feature and enhance the stones, precious or otherwise, that are to be mounted. The method of attaching or holding gemstones must be determined when articles are designed. Stones may be elevated above the finished surface, recessed, inlaid, or placed directly on the metal to give the appearance of being an integral part of the article.

Many mountings such as bezels, baskets, pronged boxes, delicate wire prongs, and twisted filigree wire cages are used to hold the stones in position. In addition, there are other types of mountings such as tension or pressure, slotted or V grooves, domed settings, burnished feather edges, diamond-drilled stones attached with jump rings, and stones inlaid on a flat or slightly convex surface.

Gemstone mountings are usually added after the metal working, including the first buffing and polishing, is complete. However, when a stone is the main part of the design, the mounting is constructed as the work progresses.

Gemstones

Gemstones can be selected from opaque, translucent, and almost transparent gemstone material of varying degrees of hardness and cut into various shapes as follows:

1. Cabochons with polished convex surfaces that can be round, square, oval, cushion, octagonal, flat-slabbed, heart, triangular, cross, kite, teardrop, rectangular. The surfaces can be high, low, medium, or equally convex (lentil-shaped) laminated shapes of two layers (doublets) or three layers (triplets) of material (see Figs. 113 and 114).
2. Two-dimensional flats (in any regular geometric outline or freeform—no equal sides).
3. Spheres.
4. Carvings.
5. Tumbled "baroque" nuggets (see Fig. 115).
6. Single natural crystals (see Fig. 116).
7. Crystal clusters (see Fig. 116).
8. Small crystal-lined geodes (sliced to reveal their hidden beauty).
9. Faceted stones in various shapes and forms (see Figs. 117 and 118).

In order to obtain as nearly as possible identical sizes and shapes for a definite design, baroque stones must be carefully selected from gem stock. Tumbled stones, always in baroque or nugget shapes, usually require wire prongs to hold the stone securely in the metal. There need be no more prongs than are actually necessary or as many as desired to create a design. Gem material can be inlaid with other gem materials, or in cloissons of metal, as well as cut into definite shapes as listed, or it can be reduced to a gravel or fine powder for other applications. Bezels with irregular outlines can also be used.

Bezels

In contemporary pieces, a bezel mounting appears to be the most popular method for stone setting (see Fig. 119). A bezel usually refers to types of mountings such as boxed, circular, and oval which are formed of flat wire, gallery wire, or commercial bezel wire in karat golds, sterling, or fine silver (20 to 26 gauge) to match the main portion of the article.

Because of its higher melting point, fine metal bezel wire is preferred. Commercial wire may be purchased with beaded and other type decorated surfaces and with a shoulder or bearing for the support of stones. Bezel wire with a bearing is used primarily where the bezel is not attached to a solid metal backing. The open area also permits a reflection of light through translucent gem material. This type of bezel is also used to elevate shallow or low-profile stones (see Figs. 120 and 121).

Transparent stones should be set with as little metal as possible remaining under the

FIG. 113

stone. The metal shows through the stone and detracts from its beauty. Silver mountings with an excess of metal under the transparent stone, if not kept bright, will make the stone seem dark and unpolished on its undersurface. Opaque stones do not require a bearing in the bezel unless they need to be elevated in the mounting.

Bezel wire with a bearing (collar) can be either purchased or constructed from flat wire or metal strips. The bearing height should not be more than half the height of the bezel. The remainder of the bezel which extends above the bearing should be no higher than one-third the height of the gemstone. Some high-domed stones will require a slightly higher bezel than normal because the curvature of the stone requires more metal to hold the stone. The bearing is always fitted into a soldered flat wire bezel and soldered at the base (see Fig. 119).

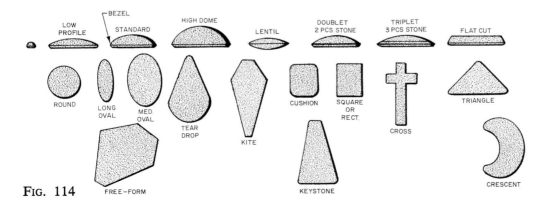

FIG. 114

FIG. 115

FIG. 116

All gemstones, if cut correctly, will have a chamfer (under-beveled edge) which provides clearance for the stone should a solder fillet remain in the joint between the bezel and its bearing (see Fig. 121). (The beveled edge on the stone is sometimes referred to as a bezel but this should not be confused with the metal mounting called a bezel.)

Bezel lengths for round or oval gemstone cabochons are cut to match the circumference of the stone. Two different methods of determining the lengths are possible.

1. The circumference of a round stone is found by multiplying the diameter of the stone by π (3.1416) to obtain the exact length of bezel wire. To determine the circumference of an oval cabochon, both the longest and the narrowest diameters of the stone are added together. The sum of these two dimensions is divided in half and then multiplied by π to get the circumference of the stone. The decimal inches are converted to fractional measurements for easy marking on the bezel material (see Appendix). The metal is cut approximately 1–2 mm longer

Fig. 117

than required and filed to fit.

Example: A round circle with a 1-inch diameter $\times \pi = 3\frac{9}{64}$-inch circumference. An oval stone with a long dimension of 1 inch and a narrow dimension of ½ inch = 1½ inches. This dimension is divided in half, which is ¾ inch and then multiplied by π, which indicates a circumference of $2\frac{23}{64}$ inches.

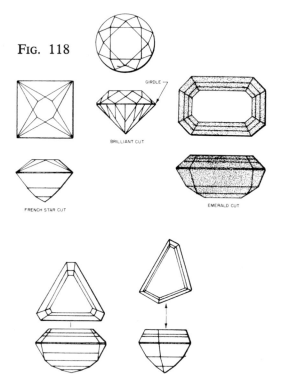

Fig. 118

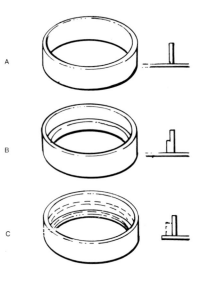

Fig. 119

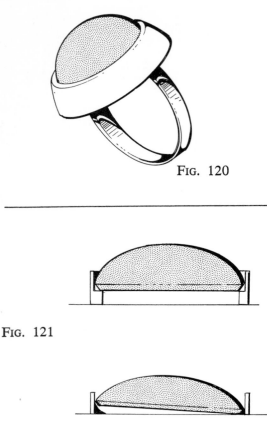

Fig. 120

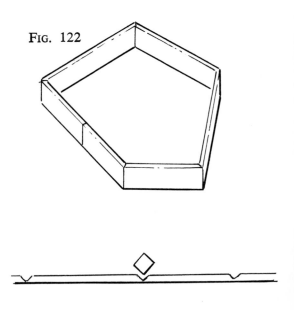

Fig. 121

The bezel, if properly annealed, can be bent easily with ring-bending pliers, round-nosed pliers, with finger pressure, or by hand-bending around a ring mandrel. The bezel joint is placed on the long side of a rectangular or oval stone.

It is not necessary to form the bezel to the shape of the stone before soldering if the stone is round or oval. Other shapes require definite forming as corners must be filed to bend correctly.

Bezels can be made from bezel wire with or without a bearing or of a strip of flat wire mitered to make various geometrical figures the sides of which do not have to be equal. Free-form shapes having five or seven sides can also be constructed to give a wide variety of bezel shapes. After measuring, small V-notches are cut in the top edge of the wire, halfway through the metal or down to the bearing. The metal that remains below the notch is then filed with a square file to a depth equal to three-fourths of the thickness of the metal so that the metal will fit tightly at the corners when it is shaped around the girdle or bezel of the stone. The V-shaped notch in the corner is absolutely necessary when using bezel wire with an inner bearing (see Fig. 122).

The bezel wire, after filing, is bent with flat-nose or snipe-nose pliers to a 90° angle for the corners. Ends are filed and fitted and the bezel soldered. The bezel ends are brought together by passing each other slightly so that

2. The circumference of a stone may also be found by wrapping a round wire around the stone at its girdle or bezel and twisting it snugly. When removed, the wire is cut with pliers and spread out straight so that the length of the wire can be measured to determine how much flat wire or strip is needed to form the bezel for a specific stone.

Square, rectangular, triangular, and free-form shapes are measured along the sides for a total measurement. A Rathbun jeweler's saw can be used to saw the bezel wire squarely. The small saw is placed in the bench vise and the bezel strip is placed squarely on the saw for cutting (see Fig. 218).

As previously mentioned, the width of the bezel wire should be kept to a minimum—one-third of the height of the stone, or just high enough to hold the stone in place. Because there is some shrinkage when soldering bezels held together with binding wire, a space equal to the thickness of the bezel is left between the bezel and the stone.

Fig. 122

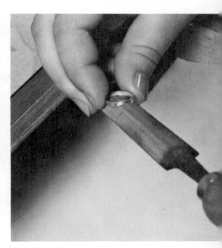

FIG. 123   FIG. 124   FIG. 125

when brought back into position, tension will hold them together without binding wire during the soldering step. This method saves time by eliminating the necessity of removing the binding wire before dipping the bezel in the pickling solution after soldering. Binding wire can be used if desired to hold the bezel together firmly, but not to squeeze it.

Bezel ends which are rounded, sawed but not filed, filed on an angle, or cut with pliers will not solder properly because the solder will not fill in the voids. Therefore, it is imperative that the ends of the bezel meet. They must also he aligned so that there is no tension pulling on the piece when brought together.

Soldering the bezel

The surfaces of the bezel ends are fluxed, and the bezel is placed with the joint down on a carbon ring soldering mandrel, held in the locking tweezers of a third-hand soldering aid, or on an improvised soldering stand. Solder is placed inside the bezel, and the joint hard-soldered together (see Fig. 102).

If after the soldering the bezel is too small to fit the stone, it can be stretched to fit by tapping it lightly on the outer surface when it is placed over a steel ring mandrel. Hard blows will flatten the metal or destroy any design detail which is a part of some manufactured bezel wires. Square or rectangular bezels which may be too short on one end or side after soldering are placed on a square mandrel and hammered

in the same manner. Small bezels can be worked on a chasing tool (either round or square, according to the bezel) which is placed horizontally in a bench vise (see Fig. 123). If too large, the bezel must be sawed apart, the section with solder removed, and the ends resoldered. The bezel edges, top and bottom, are filed so that they are parallel and uniform in height when soldered into position.

Bezels joined with hard solder are attached to the main base of the design with medium solder and, therefore, are best added at a time when other medium soldering may be required on the main article. If multiple soldering steps are required to assemble main portions of the design before attaching gem mountings, then naturally the bezel or type of mounting will be attached with the next lower melting-point solder.

The bezel itself can be soldered and attached to the metal in one soldering procedure, but this takes practice to be successful. After the bezel is soldered, the hollow scraper is used to remove excess solder from the inner surface and the bearing, if used.

Finishing the bezel

The bezel is shaped to fit the stone on the ring mandrel (see Fig. 124) on small oval mandrels or on a small round bench stake. When much bending and manipulating are required to get the bezel in shape after soldering, it is necessary to heat, anneal, and pickle before completing this step.

The bezel is checked with the stone for fit, and also checked on a smooth flat surface to see that it is level. Some sanding on fine emery paper should be done to smooth off the base surface of the bezel.

Bezel mountings are fitted to curved surfaces by filing the lower edge of the bezel with a half-round file. As the work progresses, the bezel section must be tried out often on the metal to determine what part needs to be removed (see Fig. 125). Small rotary grinding stones will speed the fitting process.

The bezel is filed on the outer surface to thin it out slightly for easier burnishing. To maintain a flat edge around the stone, it must be filed up to the edge that will be next to the stone. The bezel should never be filed to a knife edge. When buffing and polishing the bezel, care must be taken not to apply excessive pressure in order to avoid the danger of cutting a groove in the metal at the base of the bezel.

Bezels, when properly soldered to their base, do not leave excess solder. If any excess solder is visible it must be removed. Stones used for mountings should be ground properly on the lower edge with a small chamfer. This is done especially to prevent the inner radius of the bezel from cramping and chipping the stone as pressure is applied to seat it (see Figs. 121 and 126). If commercial stones are used, these should be selected carefully to ensure that the small chamfer or bezel on the bottom of the stone is present.

Bezels are easily soldered to a flat piece of metal if done on a charcoal block. The charcoal block is heated to a bright red, and the plate is placed on the heated area. Heat is applied to the plate around the bezel and in the center of the bezel, but not directly on the thinner metal. Because the metal is more evenly heated this way, the solder heats faster and flows easily without direct contact with the torch flame.

Gallery wire bezels

Gallery wire, a fancy detailed commercial bezel material, must be heated from underneath. The metal is held with locking tweezers, clamps, or tongs. If the bezel is to be attached to a base, the metal surface is coated with flux, and

FIG. 126

the gallery wire bezel is placed in position. Small squares of solder are added around the inner joint, and the torch is moved back and forth, or in a figure eight motion from underneath. The metal must be heated and soldered as quickly as possible to prevent sagging when overheated.

Stone fitting

A stick coated with dop wax, as used by lapidaries when grinding a gemstone, can be used to hold a stone for try-in in a mounting or setting (see Fig. 127). The wax on the wooden dowel stick is heated along with the stone. The stone is placed on a stand above an alcohol

FIG. 127

lamp or household candle to heat. A small speck of dopping wax placed on the stone will melt when the stone is sufficiently heated to apply the holding stick. The wax-coated dop stick is heated in a candle or lamp flame in a rolling motion to soften the wax and melt it, but not to volatilize it. The wax end of the dop stick is placed against the stone table or dome and held in a vertical position until it is cool and rigid. The stone is removed later by dissolving the wax in acetone, or placing it for a few minutes only in the freezing compartment of the kitchen refrigerator. The dopped stone enables the craftsman to hold the stone in position in the mounting when determining bezel depth, prong notches, etc.

If for any reason a bezel must be removed or unsoldered, the piece is clamped down or held with a third-hand soldering attachment. The joints of the metal section to be removed are painted with flux in order to permit the solder in the joint to flow. When the metal is heated to a dark pink, and the solder appears bright, the damaged bezel section can be lifted or slid off to one side with pliers, tweezers, or the soldering rod. Bezels removed for repositioning or repair should usually be discarded and a new bezel used in its place.

Setting stones in bezels

After the stone is placed in the bezel (or pronged setting), a straight or curved burnishing tool is used to press the bezel against the stone (see Figs. 128, 128A, and 129). The tool is never used unless its surfaces are highly polished to prevent marring the metal. The tool is pressed lightly against one side of the stone and then on the opposite side. This procedure is repeated, crisscrossing the stone surface to burnish alternately all sides of the bezel down over the stone.

Another bezel burnisher is a rocker-type tool that compresses the metal bezel around the stone gradually, eliminating crimping (see Fig. 129A).

Bezels can also be set around stones by using a setting punch instead of a burnisher, and a graver to clean out the bearing instead of a hollow scraper. The stone should always be checked to see that it fits in the bezel snugly

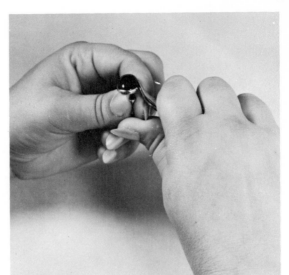

FIG. 128

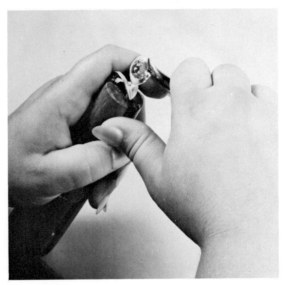

FIG. 128A

FIG. 129

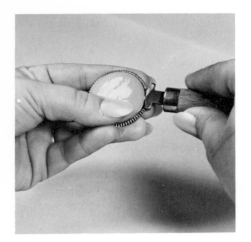

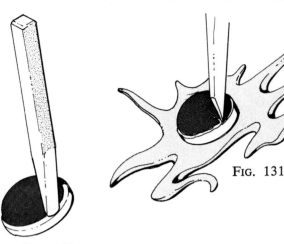

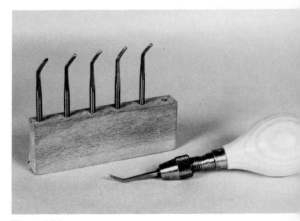

FIG. 131

FIG. 129A

FIG. 130

without grabbing. Stones fitted too tightly, or forced into undersized bezels, will crack or chip when pressure is applied during the burnishing.

The ring is fastened in a ring clamp while cleaning out the bezel and setting the stone. The setting punch is borrowed from the set of chasing tools; however, any tool with a fairly flat surface can be used. The tool is placed against the bezel and tapped gently with the chasing hammer, forcing the bezel down around the stone (see Fig. 130).

A notch made on each outer surface of the ring clamp will help to steady the tool against the bench edge or stake when used to hold a mounting while setting the stone or filing the prongs.

Burnished bezels often have a wavy uneven edge where the metal meets the stone because unequal pressure has been applied with the burnishing tool. The pointed graver, with its sharp cutting edge, is used to follow the edge of metal around the stone and level it (see Fig. 131). This is much more practical than buffing the metal edge, which often discolors the stone or "burns" the metal if excessive pressure is used.

The edges of the bezels can be trimmed with a milgrain tool that has been dipped in light-weight oil to make it roll easily. This tool has a small wheel set in the end of a steel shank which follows the bezel or metal rim around the stone, making a beaded edge on the metal (see Figs. 132 and 133).

Bezel trim

A common trim for any bezel is a beaded twisted wire around its outer base. Thin wire ends of a loop are held together in a bench vise. The loop is threaded on a small eye hook which is placed in a small bench drill, and turned to twist the wire as desired (see Chapter 12). The soldering operation is done at the same time the bezel is attached to the plate. Solder squares are applied to both the inner and outer joints. Careful attention must be paid to make sure that the ends of the twisted wire meet. During soldering, it may be necessary to hold the wire ends together with a pair of locking tweezers.

FIG. 132

If the remaining metal edge around the bezel is symmetrical, it can be easily marked with a pair of dividers such as are used by machinists and draftsmen. The dividers are set with one point directly inside the bezel, and the other at any desired distance outside the bezel. The point of the dividers scribes a line on the metal as the inner point follows the curvature of the bezel. This gives a line to follow when sawing (see Fig. 134).

Various bezel mountings

There is no end of possibilities for attractive mountings that can be improvised from the basic types that are detailed in the remainder of this chapter.

Fig. 135

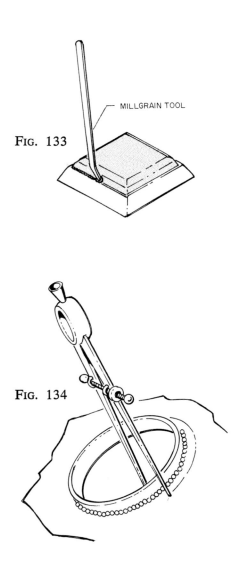

Fig. 133

MILLGRAIN TOOL

Fig. 134

Picket bezel

Small "pickets" instead of a solid bezel can be made in a solid bezel box. The pickets are slit as deeply as desired and about 1/16 of an inch apart with the jeweler's saw. If a bearing is used, the metal is slit down to it. Careful use of the saw when making the slits eliminates sanding, which is almost impossible to do in the very fine cuts produced by the thin blade. The tiny pickets are easily burnished over the stone and buffed and polished (see Fig. 135).

Mitered prong bezel

Narrow bezel wire can be used to construct bezels with mitered corners. Wedge-shaped prongs are soldered onto the outer surface to hold the stone (see Figs. 136 and 137). The bezel box, which becomes the bearing, is soldered to extensions on a ring, or on the surface of any other article. The prongs, notched on the inner surface to fit the stone, can be extensions of the piece, and the bezel frame set evenly inside them and soldered into place. The bezels can be constructed with perpendicular or angular walls.

Free-form bezels

Free-form faceted stones are frequently mounted in soldered partial bezels of V-grooved metal. These mountings need not encompass the stone completely, but they must surround it enough to prevent the stone from

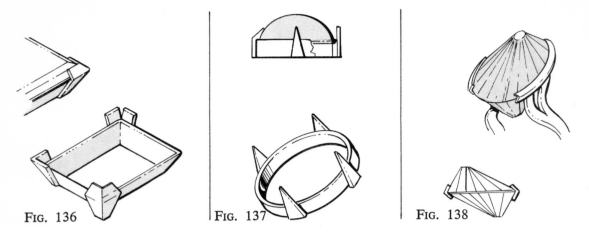

FIG. 136   FIG. 137   FIG. 138

slipping out of the mounting in any direction (see Fig. 138). A V-groove mounting can be curved around one side of a stone leaving the other side to be secured with a prong, which is an integral part of the article, or which has been previously soldered onto the metal surface. The prong is grooved to fit around the bezel or girdle of the stone, but is not burnished down over the stone—only held against it by tension.

Bezel inserts

Stones can be mounted down in the metal itself by enlarging the opening in the metal to fit a regularly constructed bezel. The bezel, shaped to fit the stone and held in position by tension of its ends, or with iron binding wire, is inserted into the opening and soldered. The only protruding portion of metal is the bezel and, when it is burnished down, buffed, and polished, the separation or seam between the bezel and metal is no longer visible (see Fig. 139).

Prong mountings

Oval or rectangular cabochons and/or free-form polished sections require four to six prongs to hold the stone securely. These prongs are plotted out for sawing according to the specific stone used in the design.

Prongs can be made from a single bezel strip. Bezel strip must be cut or sawed wide enough for the shallow base of the bezel and the required length of the prong (see Fig. 140). The width will depend on the curvature of the stone. All soldering is eliminated except to attach the bezel ends to make the form and to attach the bezel to the article.

Self-prongs for irregular gemstone shapes

Irregular shapes can be held in a pronged or picket-type mounting, if the mounting is constructed from one piece of metal. The stone outline is drawn on the metal and an extra line outside the first line drawn. This space is the height of the prongs, and should be marked

FIG. 139

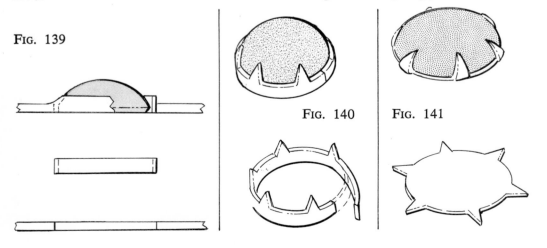

FIG. 140   FIG. 141

only after determining how much metal is needed to come up over the stone edge to hold the stone securely. The prongs are marked around the periphery, sawed out into triangular shape, and filed smooth. The prongs are then bent up so that they are at right angles to the main area of the mounting (see Fig. 141). The prongs will bend easily if the bend line is filed with a small needle file, scored with a graver, or ground with a thin grinding wheel used in a flex shaft handpiece.

the stone, the prongs are marked with a scribe. The stone is removed and another mark is made on the prong just below the first mark (approximately $\frac{1}{32}$ inch). A notch is sawed with the jeweler's saw or filed with a square file to one-third of the prong thickness at that point. It is then lengthened either all the way, or partially out to the end of the prong (see Fig. 142). A flat graver or small file is used to remove the burr (made by the tool) from each side of each prong. The prongs are filed to a

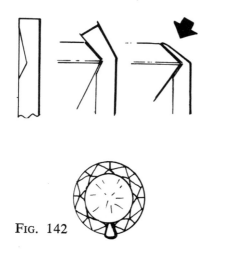

FIG. 142

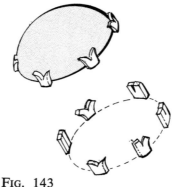

FIG. 143

Because the scoring of the bend area weakens the metal, a small amount of solder should be fluxed and added to the groove inside the prongs. Small squares of solder $\frac{1}{32}$ inch are added at each prong and heated until the solder flows into the area (see Fig. 142).

Setting stones in prong mountings

To seat the stone in a prong mounting, the prongs are notched with a square file (see Fig. 142). The position of the notch inside the prong can be determined by placing the stone inside the mounting and leveling it. When set, the stone should not protrude through the underside of the mounting. A ring can be held on a ring mandrel which has been wrapped with a strip of "wet-or-dry" or crocus cloth sanding paper that prevents the ring from slipping sideways. At the point of contact with the girdle of

taper above the girdle notch, but not on the surface that will touch the stone when set.

Instead of filing them to a tapered point, the prongs can be slit down the center with the jeweler's saw to three-fourths of the distance between the prong point and the gemstone notch. The slit prong is spread to make a double prong on each side of the stone (see Fig. 143). Square-cornered prongs and corner prongs are slit in the center down to the filed notch with the saw. The tops of the prongs are filed on an angle so that the edges meet when the prongs are burnished or set over the stone (see Fig. 142).

After filing the prongs, they are buffed and polished. Each prong is then bent slightly inward with snipe-nose pliers. The stone is seated, and the prongs are burnished over with a two-sided pusher, burnisher, or prong-setting pliers. They can also be tapped down over the

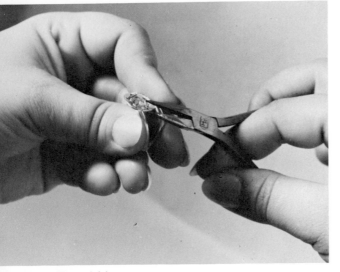

FIG. 144

Holding small stones while setting

Small stones can be held while setting prongs with a quickie holder made by wrapping a small scrap of silk fabric around a swab stick. The end of the swab is coated with wax, and this is then pressed against the table of the stone to hold it securely while burnishing the prongs.

Wide prong settings

Wider prongs can be used to hold a stone. These are made from half-round wire, or short flat sections of metal which are soldered into

stone by placing a small wedge-shaped flat-ended tool (highly polished on the working end) on the prongs, and gently tapping them down over the stone with a small hammer. The prongs must fit flush without any space between metal and stone. The prong points are filed to a rounded point with a small needle file. Soft stones can be damaged when the prongs are filed, but this can be eliminated if the edges of the file are first smoothed on an Arkansas stone before filing the prongs.

Prongs bent over stones often do not come flush with the stone. After all prongs have been burnished or pushed over the stone equally, and as tightly as possible, a pair of flat-nosed pliers is used to bend the tip ends into contact with the stone with positive tension. Care must be taken that no arching of the prongs is visible (see Fig. 144).

Flat gravers used for prong setting

Flat gravers can be used for prong pushers. The graver is ground off smooth on the end but is not highly polished, as this would cause it to have a tendency to slip off the prong. The graver is used with a regular graver handle instead of using the tool as a punch (see Fig. 145). Prong pushers can also be made from discarded round gravers inserted into a handle. The graver is filed on the end into two angles similar to an L or 7, depending how the tool end is viewed.

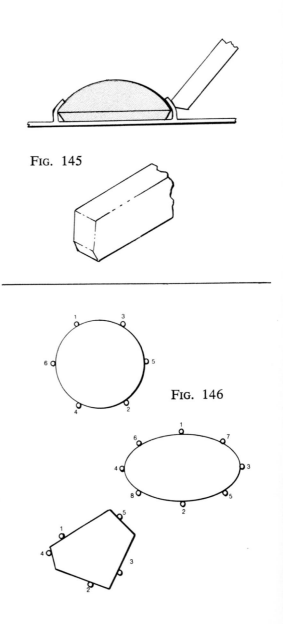

FIG. 145

FIG. 146

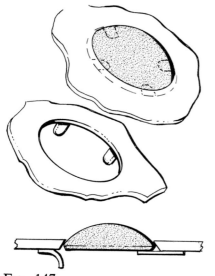

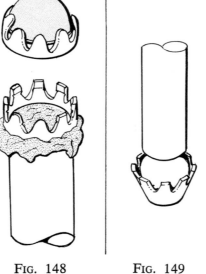

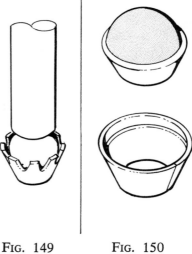

FIG. 147   FIG. 148   FIG. 149   FIG. 150

place, filed to a long taper, and buffed and polished. The stone is placed inside the prongs and the prongs burnished down lightly over the stone by setting the end prongs first, then the side prongs. This is followed by burnishing any remaining tabs. The prongs are seated firmly by applying pressure in the same order as when first burnishing the tabs. If the tabs are burnished down consecutively in rotation, the stone will not seat properly and it will be impossible to level the stone (see Fig. 146).

Tab prongs

Stones are set in the surface of metals by soldering tabs or prongs to the underside. These are bent up to permit an exact fitting. The angle of the contoured walls of the opening is filed to fit the curvature or angle of the stone perfectly when it is positioned. After buffing and polishing, the stone is placed in the opening from the underside, and the tabs or prongs burnished down over it (see Fig. 147).

Tube settings

Prong settings can be made from tubing. A short section of tubing is attached to a wooden dowel stick with dopping wax (used for holding stones when grinding them to shape). After attaching the tubing to the stick, a line is scribed inside the tubing and a ledge is cut on the line with a narrow pointed bearing scraper. This support for the stone can also be cut with

a scorper graving tool. The tubing is marked on the outside with the desired number of prongs and these are sawed to three-fourths of the depth of the mounting. The prongs can be filed or sawed in various widths or shapes, but should be narrow enough to bend easily over the stone (see Fig. 148). The notches are buffed with thread or string coated with Tripoli (see Chapter 7).

The buffing should be checked continuously because the action of the taut string will soon produce a groove impossible to remove. The bottom of the mounting may be notched also, but this leaves only small points of contact for the soldering step.

After the prongs are made and buffed, a round-ended tool such as a dapping-die punch can be inserted and used gently to spread the prongs slightly. The stone held on the dopping stick (see Fig. 149) is placed down in the mounting and the prongs are checked for depth. The mounting is removed from the waxed stick, cleaned, fluxed, and soldered to the article.

Collet mounting

A collet mounting can be made from a strip of metal curved into a ring and soldered together (see Fig. 150). It is shaped to a slight taper on a round or oval ring mandrel. Smaller collets are shaped on a short length of drill rod which is placed in a bench vise. The prongs, or coronets, are spaced as desired and sawed or filed down to a depth of three-fourths of the distance between the top and the bottom of the collet.

Tapered collet mounting

This type of mounting can also be made from a curved or angular strip of metal soldered to make a tapered ring (see Figs. 151, 151A, and 151B). The stone is placed in the mounting and a line scribed where the girdle meets the metal as previously mentioned. The prongs are sawed and filed away on the inside so that a

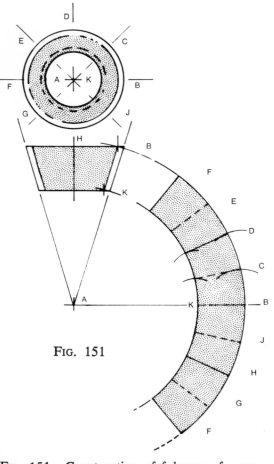

FIG. 151

FIG. 151 Construction of fulcrum of a cone. Using A as a base or pivot point, construct an arc equal in radial distance of AB and a second arc equal in radial distance of A*k*. From point AB*m* intersect the outer arc with distance equal to BC, CD, DE, etc. Draw a straight line through the outer intersections to point A to obtain divisions on the inner arc.

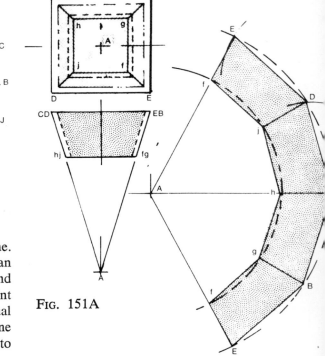

FIG. 151A

FIG. 151A   Construction of fulcrum of square pyramid.

Using A as a pivot point, construct an arc equal in distance of AE (side view) and an arc equal in distance of A*h* (side view). Intersect outer arc from point AE equal in distance to BC on top view, etc. Draw lines from these intersections to point A to obtain divisions on the inner arc.

fine taper remains. The collet mounting is placed on the article and soldered into position. After pickling, rinsing, buffing, and polishing, the stone is inserted and the prongs are burnished down over it. The section of the prong that is bent over the stone should not be less than $\frac{1}{32}$ inch and can be increased according to stone size and its surface angle or curvature (see Appendix for curved strip layout).

Cone mountings can also be made from tubing that has parallel walls. By tapping or forcing a tapered wooden pin through the short

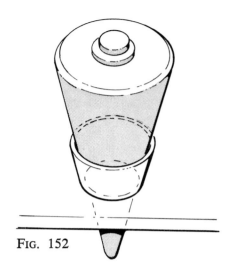

FIG. 152

length of tubing the cone shape can be obtained (see Fig. 152). The wooden pin can be forced as deeply as desired by placing the metal in a tapered opening that has been made in the workbench. The metal must be annealed before it is formed or it will crack and split. Prongs are sawed in the edge as previously described.

Star mounts

Star mountings are formed from a sawed and filed five- or six-point metal star (See Figs. 153, 153A, and 153B). A small hole is drilled in the center of the star large enough for a fine jeweler's saw blade, and a slot is made from the center out toward each star point to within about 1/16-inch from the end. The points are turned up into a basket, and the edges are filed smooth, buffed, and polished. The mounting can either be soldered to a small disc the same diameter as the bottom star points, or it can be soldered directly onto the metal. The mounting, which stands upright without support, can easily be soldered.

Various methods of holding small stones on stems are possible. Regular mounting heads which are soldered on the end of the wire can be used, or four small strands of wire can be attached as a cage (see Figs. 154 and 154A). The cage is compressed slightly to permit en-

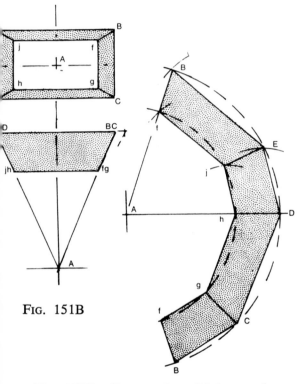

FIG. 151B

FIG. 151B   Construction of fulcrum of a rectangular pyramid.

Using A as a base or pivot point, construct an arc equal to the distance of AD (side view) and a second arc equal to the distance of AH (side view). On the outer arc, draw a line to intersect the arc from AD with length equal to ED in top view. From this point, intersect the outer arc with a line equal in distance to EB. Draw straight lines through intersections BE, ED, CD, CB on the outer arc and a straight line on the inner arc from FJ, JH, HG, FB.

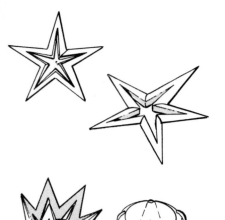

FIG. 153

Belcher mounting

This mounting is a modification of the gypsy setting and is detailed in Chapter 14 (see Fig. 238).

Flat-topped stones, or those with a faceted table, must be set deeper in the mounting to compensate for the curve of the mounting. Oval or rectangular stones set in this type mounting should, if possible, be cut and polished to fit the opening in the metal, rather than preparing the opening to fit the stone.

Pavé mountings

Pavé mountings are usually done on a domed surface to enable the setting tool to reach easily

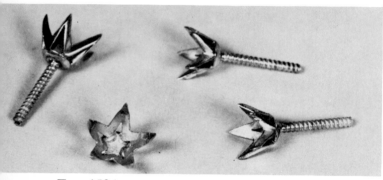

FIG. 153A

FIG. 153B

try of stones, and then twisted with small needle-nosed pliers to hold the stones in the cage. Smaller star mountings can also be constructed and soldered to the wire ends.

Small bezels on stems

Small bezels, metal parts, sections, and domed or star prong settings can be attached to threaded stems (see page 106) and inserted through drilled holes in the metal (see Figs. 153A and 153B). A mating nut as small as 3 mm in diameter made from a small circle or square of metal is drilled and threaded with a tap to fit, after which it is fastened tightly to the post. A drop of soft solder, applied after cutting off the excess threaded stem, will prevent the nut from loosening.

Gypsy or flush mounting

A gypsy mounting with the stone recessed in the thick upper portion of a ring is detailed in Chapter 14 (see Fig. 155).

all of the small stones. The stones, faceted rather than cabochon types, are set in small conical depressions made by drilling into the surface of the dome, but not completely through (see Fig. 156). The conical shapes, made with a stone-setting bur, support the stones held in place by small prongs. The prongs are either raised with a scorper (graving tool) from the domed surface, or are made from small wires soldered into drilled holes around the periphery of each stone. The mounting, when completed, should have a minimum amount of metal showing around the stones so that the effect is a surface paved with sparkling gems and small beads of metal.

Half-dome mountings

Convex-curved tubs for gems are half-domes of thin sheet metal made with the dapping-die block and punches (see Figs. 36, 37, 38, and 41). The bearing or seat is a wire ring curved to fit inside the half-dome. The lip above the ring becomes the bezel, which is burnished or sawed and filed into prongs that are bent over the stone to hold it in place. The half-dome is soldered to the base and buffed and polished afterward.

Metal half-domes are sawed and filed or ground to produce three or more prongs with small mounted grinding stones which are used in the flexible shaft handpiece.

Tension mounts

Stones can be mounted on, or in the metal without using any extra metal or soldering. (see Figs. 157 and 157A–D). A small depres-

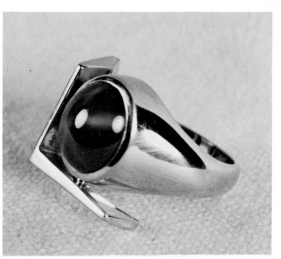

FIG. 155   Ring cast showing stone set in gypsy mounting, 14k white gold with star sapphire. By Sharr Choate.

FIG. 156

FIG. 154

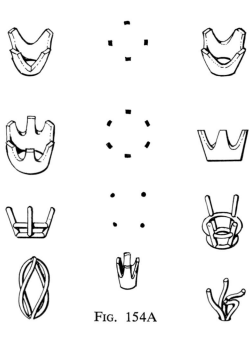

FIG. 154A

sion is ground into the surface with small grinding stones used in the flex shaft handpiece, or a hole slightly smaller than a pearl or bead (if these are used) can be drilled in the metal. Diamond-setting bur may be used to form the crater-like base for the stone. An extension or arm that is part of the design is brought over the stone, and positioned to hold it with proper tension in the depression or small hole. Small beads or tumbled stones can also be held in a long tapering triangular section sawed with a 6/0 blade in the jeweler's frame. The long taper is bent up slightly to file the edges, after which it is wrapped around a stone previously grooved with a knife-edged diamond or carborundum wheel. In order to hold the stone in place, the wire is wrapped around the stone and worked to tighten it.

Cabochons and faceted stones can be held in a three- or four-prong arrangement by drilling a small hole in the center of the mounting area (see Fig. 157C). Three tapered-prong

FIG. 157

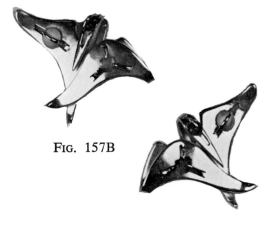

FIG. 157A

FIG. 157 Pin, single-piece construction with tension mounts, sterling silver with pearl, coral, and natural emerald.
By Sharr Choate.

FIG. 157A Pin, single-piece construction with tension mounts, sterling silver with alexandrites (synthetic) and star sapphires (natural).
By Sharr Choate.

FIG. 157B Single-piece construction with tension mounts, sterling silver with pearl, coral, and natural emerald crystal.
By Sharr Choate.

FIG. 157B

sections radiating out are sawed outward from this hole. The prongs after sawing are bent up, and the outer surface filed so that the prong is tapered on all sides except the inside. The stone is positioned between the prongs, and the notch for the girdle is marked on the inner surface of each prong. The notches are filed with small needle files, and then the stone is tried in the mounting before proceeding further. The prongs are filed and adjusted until the stone fits correctly. It is then buffed and polished. If a cabochon is used, the notch preparation is omitted. The stone is placed in position and the prongs are burnished over the stone with a regular burnisher. If necessary, the prongs are buffed and polished to remove any burnishing marks.

Wire mounts

Wire mounts are a standard scrollwork type of gemstone mounting (see Chapter 21). Two lengths of wire are curved into a half-circle,

and a straight length of wire is placed between them. The wires are soldered at their junctures. The stone is placed on the soldered wire, and the wires are cut to length. The lower end of the straight wire can be cut so that it does not show below the stone outline or it can be wound into a spiral. The opposite end is bent to form a bail for a necklace cord or chain (see Figs. 158 and 158A). If used for a pin or bola, the pin-back or slide is soldered to the underside and all six wire ends are bent up over the edge of the stone, cut to length, burnished, buffed, and polished where required.

This type of mounting can also be used to mount stones on any flat or curved surface. A small hole is drilled in the metal and the wires for prongs (four to six) are inserted in the drilled hole and soldered to hold them in place. The wires are then bent down flat and parallel with the metal, the stone is placed in the wires, and the setting procedure is followed as outlined above.

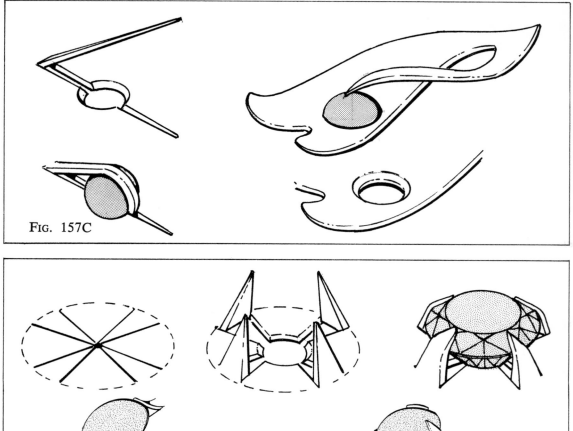

FIG. 157C

FIG. 157D

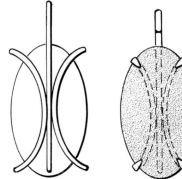

FIG. 158

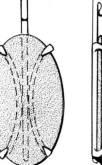

FIG. 158A Cuff links, wire mounts, sterling silver with thulite.
By Sharr Choate.

Wire can be used to mount stones in different ways, such as looped wire to hold a lentil-shaped cabochon in place or strung across an open area. Small beads are strung on the wire before insertion in the metal frame, and spheres are added on the extensions (see Figs. 159 and 14).

Leaf mounts

Wires with small leaves or balls on the tips can be used effectively for prongs (see Fig. 160). The wire end is fluxed and held in the flame until the wire melts into a ball. It is pickled and either left in the ball shape, or the balls are hammered flat and filed into small leaf shapes. The flattened sections can also be filed to an outline of small crystals to match any natural mineral specimen used in the design. This method is much easier than attempting to file small leaves, or construct small balls and soldering them to the end of a wire. The wires, after forming, are inserted in drilled holes in the metal, cut to length, and soldered in place. They are twisted into pinwheels and bent over the gemstone with round-nosed pliers, burnished, and buffed if necessary, to remove any tool marks.

Prong mountings for irregular shapes

Mountings for natural crystals and baroque or tumbled stones are easily made by first placing the stone on a sheet of 22-gauge metal (see Fig. 161) and scribing a line around the periphery of the stone onto the metal; those areas where a prong would be appropriate are marked out from the line. Usually six prongs are sufficient for a mounting, but as few as three or four may be used. The prong positions should be selected in small areas of the stone where the outline may curve inward in an indentation or small bay. The outline or side view of the stone should be studied to determine whether or not the prong can be bent over that particular area enough to hold the stone securely. It is also necessary to view the stone at different points to determine the length of the prong. The prongs must hold the stone securely so that it cannot be budged.

When the outline, prong locations, and length have been determined, the metal outline is sawed out, filed smooth, and the prongs filed

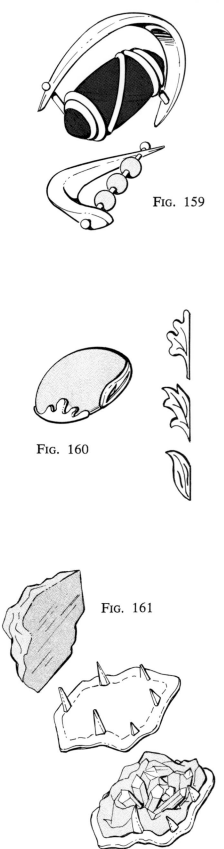

FIG. 159

FIG. 160

FIG. 161

to a flat taper. The prongs are bent up to a 90°
angle from the main portion of the mounting,
and the stone or crystal cluster is tried in the
upright prong border for size. The prongs can
be bent to the upright position with a minimum
amount of marks on the metal by placing a
clamp on the metal, parallel to the scribed line
across the base of the prong. The prongs are
peened over the side of the clamp to the 90°
angle with a small hammer. The prongs are
checked to see if they are long enough and any
which may be too long are filed to a shorter
taper. A scribe is then used to make a mark ⅛
inch in from the edge of the base and all
around the outline. The metal is drilled and
the saw inserted so that this inner area can be
sawed out, leaving just a pronged rim to serve
as the mounting for the stone. The inner edge
is filed smooth, and the entire piece is buffed
and polished.

Because of the frailty of the metal when
buffing, it is best to support the mounting on
a thin section of wood to prevent bending (see
Fig. 91). Polishing is done in the same way.
The findings, such as a pin back or bola slide,
are now attached to the underside of the
mounting. Pin backs should be mounted above
the center of the mounting to prevent the entire
piece lopping over when worn (see Fig. 162).
Earrings and cuff links are soldered to the back
of the mounting which is left solid without the
sawed-out inner section.

Natural crystal settings

Crystal specimens are usually more attractive if
the specimen is recessed rather than placed on
a flat surface (see Figs. 163 and 163A). The
general outline of the specimen as it will appear when mounted is drawn on the metal
sheet, and the scribed areas are sawed out.
Short lengths of metal wire or strip are sawed
and filed for prongs. These pieces are soldered
to a backing sheet at the same time the sawed
section is soldered. The prongs will stay in
position during soldering if they are inserted
in predrilled holes. The mounting, which will
extend beyond the outline of the specimen, is
scribed and sawed to remove.

Natural mineral specimens, crystal clusters,
and drusy crystals (tiny crystal coatings) that
form on another mineral or a base rock called

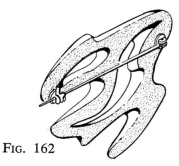

FIG. 162

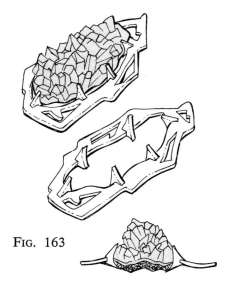

FIG. 163

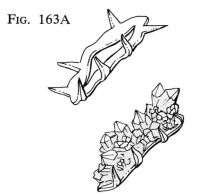

FIG. 163A

a matrix can be mounted in solid metal sheet, in impressions in the surface, or suspended in open areas of the metal.

Prongs or forklike supports are made to fit the curvature or outline of the stone as closely as possible. They are placed on the edge of the opening or inserted in a slot made by the saw blade (see Fig. 163). After the stone has been partially inserted in the mounting, one or two of the prongs are gently bent sideways, then returned to the correct position after the stone has been seated properly. The prongs can also be soldered parallel with the surface of the metal and bent up to allow the stone to be inserted.

of the hook. The hook end is run around the stone inside the bezel several times so that the stone can easily be lifted out of its bezel (see Fig. 165). A small amount of dopping wax, heated and placed on the end of a small stick, can be applied to the stone while the wax is still hot. When the wax has cooled the stone can be lifted up out of its snug mounting (see Fig. 166). Care should be taken so that the bezel is spread only enough to remove the stone, otherwise the bezel will be enlarged and must be removed and replaced. If the setting has a milgrained edge on the bezel, the beads must be removed with a knife-edge graver before opening the bezel.

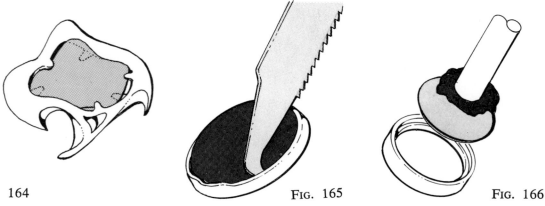

FIG. 164   FIG. 165   FIG. 166

Supporting prongs are an integral part of the mounting, though this is not readily apparent. They can be soldered on the underside of the metal opening and aligned with an upper prong, or they can be spaced alternately so that one prong is on the viewing surface and the next projects from the undersurface of the metal (see Fig. 164). The prong may also be an outside loop or yoke-type mounting made as a part of the article or soldered on during the finishing step. The ends, flattened to enhance the design, hold the stone securely so that it cannot move in the mounting.

Stones can be removed easily from a bezel with a tool made by grinding a section of a discarded hacksaw blade or thin piece of steel (such as a fingernail file) with a slight hook or wedge on the end and reducing the thickness

Settings with prongs instead of a bezel are opened to remove the stone by inserting the edge of a small pocket knife blade between the prongs and the stone and gently lifting them. The stone is eased out with a minimum of clearance.

Stone setting

When setting a stone in a plain surface or a flat top mounting, the center of the stone location is marked, and a hole slightly smaller than the diameter of the stone is drilled through the metal. If the stone has a culet (a small flat facet on the bottom of the stone) the hole is drilled through the metal (see Fig. 172).

To determine the position of the prongs for a setting, a standard drafting circle guide is

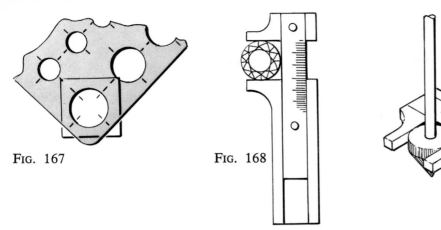

FIG. 167   FIG. 168   FIG. 168A

used. The circle of the guide which corresponds to the diameter of the stone is placed over the metal, and the horizontal and vertical center lines become markers for the prongs (see Fig. 167). A six- or eight-pronged arrangement can also be plotted on a circle. Oval stone prongs are set at 30° and 60° from the vertical center line for a six-prong mounting, and at 45° and 90° for an eight-prong mounting. Angular markings are determined with a standard or machinist's protractor. The stone-setting bur is used to make the correct conical base for the stone.

The correct size of a stone-setting bur is determined by first measuring a stone at its girdle or widest part with a stone gauge (see Figs. 168, 168A, and 168B). The dimension of the bur at its widest point should be the same as the stone, or slightly smaller. The rotation of the burr when drilling the setting will enlarge the opening enough to seat the stone

correctly without any problem. The bur should be rotated at a medium speed (5,000 to 6,000 rpm); excessive speed will create a vibration that will enlarge the hole too much. The bur is sunk into the mounting to a prescribed mark on the metal which indicates the position of the girdle of the stone when mounting is completed (see Fig. 169). Where it is impossible to see the depth of the setting, a white lead pencil mark is made on the circumference of the bur to act as a depth guide.

Beads of metal cut from the mounting hold a stone in place. The length of the bead cut for a stone with 3-mm diameter is approximately $\frac{1}{16}$ inch. The cut varies with the stone size. Enough metal should be raised to form a bead large enough to go over the stone facets, and strong enough to hold the stone adequately. Large beads detract from the beauty of the stone, and undersize beads permit the stone to slip out of the mounting, and the beads wear away quickly

FIG. 168B

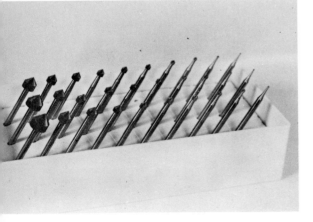

FIG. 169

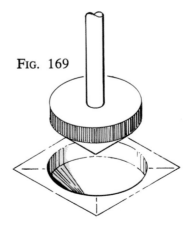

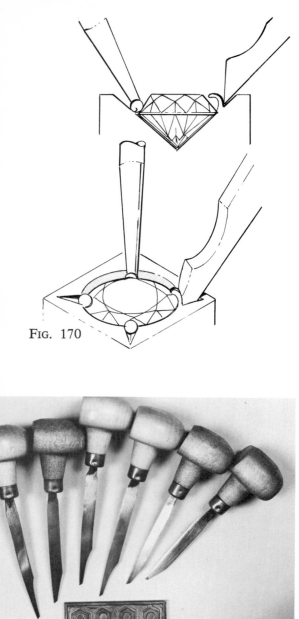

FIG. 170

FIG. 170A

The tool is rocked from side to side with a very gentle pressure forward and, as the tool cuts deeper, the wedge of metal is curled up over the edge of the stone. The tool should not "dig" into the metal.

The tip of the tool should be in position directly below the stone's girdle when the cut is complete. The tool is then raised to a 45° angle, which lifts the wedges even higher, directing them over the edge of the stone (see Fig. 170). A beading tool is used in a circular motion to complete the forming of the bead down over the facets of the stone in a single operation (see Fig. 171). The correct size of beading tool is mandatory to form the small bead perfectly in one operation.

Beading tools are small metal rods in assorted sizes tapered with a flat end. In this portion of the tool there is a small hollow which is necessary to form the bead, ball, or grain from the wedge of metal that has been raised by the graving tool. The small hollow in the end of the tool must be burnished so that the metal slides smoothly while being formed into the ball shape. The tool is rocked from side to side to form the bead as it is gently pushed toward the stone. Beads should be set in opposing positions around the stone. If one is set in a corner, the bead diagonally across from that corner is set next, etc., until the stone is secured. The bead is pressed firmly against the stone, leaving just enough movement in the stone so that it can be adjusted for position before giving the bead its final push. Round or oval settings require that the first bead be set, followed by the second which will be set approximately 180° from the first.

because of their small mass. All cuts are directed to the center of the stone. The first cut is made with a knife graver starting at the halfway mark of the planned length of the cut. The tool is directed as mentioned to the center of the stone and to a point below the girdle of the stone, not directly toward it (see Figs. 170 and 170A). When the small cut is completed, the round graver is used to make the final cut at its farthest point from the stone in the same angle and direction toward the stone.

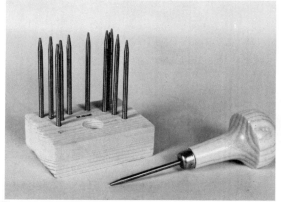

FIG. 171

After the beads have been completed, the area between the beads can be cut away with a sharp polished scorper to produce a sparkling finish around the stone (see Fig. 172). Scorpers (short gravers) used for setting stones can be made from drill rod. The rod is heated to a bright red color, and hammered flat while still hot. When cool, it is filed or ground to a round graver shape, reheated to a bright red, and cooled again. The tool is then ground on the tip to the correct angle using carborundum stone and emery paper. This is followed by grinding on the Arkansas stone to remove any grinding burrs. The tool is heated again to a bright red and quickly immersed in a container of water that has just been stirred so that the water is traveling in a circular motion when the tool is immersed. The cooling process returns the hardness to the metal. The tool is reheated at a lower temperature away from the ground tip and should be watched closely as it passes through the color changes to the brownish yellow color which occurs at 480°F. The tool is immersed in cold water as soon as the correct color has been reached. This tempers the metal so that it is not brittle. The final step is to strop the tool, especially its cutting surface, on a strip of leather to burnish it.

Prongs and beaded settings are buffed with a stiff bristle brush wheel (see Chapter 8). The bristles get into intricate areas and undercuts which are impossible to reach with even the smallest cloth buffing wheels.

Setting pearls

Pearls can be placed in a mounting without drilling when a cage-type setting is used (see Fig. 173). When purchased with holes drilled through, they are used on a thin wire and when partially drilled they are placed on small pins or posts.

The pearl is held for drilling in a small jig consisting of a flat strip of metal ½ inch by 8 inches, bent into a springlike clamp. In one end, a hole is drilled to hold the pearl. The opposite end of the metal supports the pearl. A small rectangular wire loop can be slid onto the holder to hold the ends together during the drilling procedure.

To drill a pearl or gemstone, a tiny indentation is made first with a small ball-shaped dia-

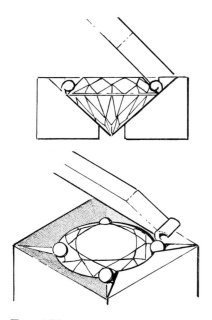

FIG. 172

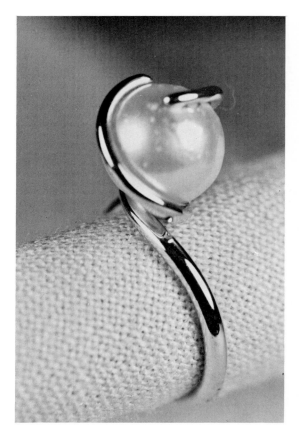

FIG. 173 Ring, tension mount, no solder, 14k gold with pearl.
By Hakon Jonnson.

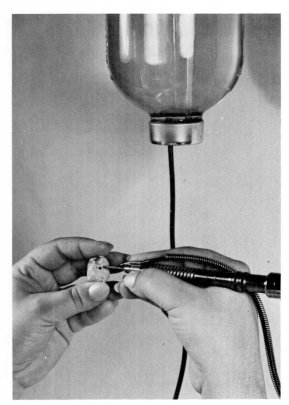

FIG. 174A Detail of drilled stone necklace with beads of sterling silver and turquoise. By Sharr Choate.

mond point. This acts as a center-punched hole to guide the large diamond point as it starts to drill.

Small diamond-charged burs or drills such as are used in dental work are operated at high speed to drill pearls. Water must be used as a coolant and to wash away the grindings during drillings (see Figs. 174 and 174A). The water must be used copiously in order to prevent fracturing the stones (translucent stones especially) as the speeds used to rotate the diamond, and the friction created, produce great heat.

A small metal pin, slightly smaller than the diameter of the drilled hole, is soldered into place. The metal pin is split at the tip with an 8/0 saw blade to permit the insertion of a thin metal wedge. The drilled hole is partially filled with pearl cement, and the pearl is placed on the pin. The pearl, eased into place, forces the wedge down into the split pin so that it remains secure (see Fig. 175). Small pearls are attached by simply bending the wire into an S-shaped curve that wedges the pearl firmly. The hole is partially filled with cement, and the pearl is then pressed on the pin. Pearls are easily dislodged if placed on a straight peg.

Drilled pearls and gemstones can also be mounted by threading them onto jump rings or lengths of wire that require soldering. An electric soldering machine, if available, works well as the heat of the torch can damage the stones if great care is not taken (see Chapter 9). Wrapping the stones in dampened asbestos or embedding them into a raw potato will protect them if a torch is used.

Attaching wood and stone sections

Exotic woods such as ebony, osage orange, and rosewood, and gemstone flat sections are held onto metal areas with bezels or small pins or rivets. The rivets are usually 20- to 22-gauge wire soldered into a hole in the base metal, which is drilled at the same time the wood is drilled so that the holes are aligned properly. The rivets are peened over with a small peen or chasing hammer and filed or sanded smooth (see Fig. 176). Small concealed pins to hold the wood in place are soldered in predrilled holes in the metal base, and the mating holes for the wood are drilled only partially through the wood from the underside. Epoxy adhesive is used to hold the wood on the small tapered pins (see Fig. 177).

FINDINGS

Findings are all kinds of jewelry attachments, such as pin backs, earring screws and clips, cuff link swivels, pendant bails, box clasps or catches, spring rings, sister hooks, bola slides and tips, tie tack studs and clutches (see Figs. 178, 178A, 178B, and 179). Findings with no moving parts include necklace and guard chains, jump rings, bell caps, and bezel cups or prong mounts. Metalcraft findings include hinges and locking devices.

Except for bezel mounts and jump rings, which are primarily constructed by the craftsman, findings can be purchased ready for as-

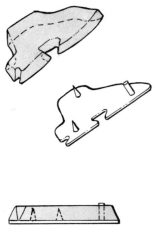

FIG. 177

sembly on articles. As they vary in design and kinds of metals with each manufacturer, there is a wide range of possibilities from which to choose. Of course, it is possible for the craftsman to construct many of the findings if he so desires. However, before soldering, the findings should be fitted to the article to be sure they are operable.

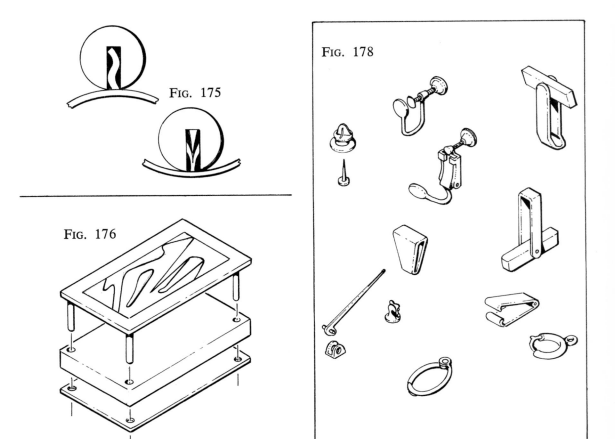

FIG. 175

FIG. 176

FIG. 178

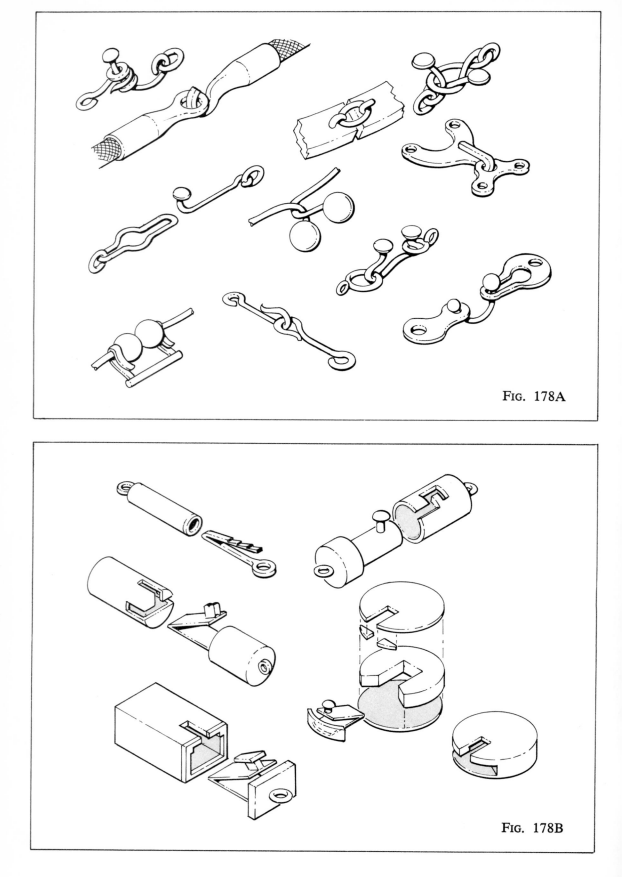

FIG. 178A

FIG. 178B

Findings are available in different price levels according to the metal used. Most inexpensive findings are nickel or brass plated with a yellow or white metal. Nickel silver findings are available, but only sterling silver and karat gold findings should be used on the best pieces, especially if the article is to be stamped according to its precious metal "Sterling Silver," "14-Karat Gold," or such.

Soldering the findings

The location of a finding on an article is marked on the metal with a carbide scriber. Pin-backs and bola slides should be soldered in the upper third of the article to hold them upright when worn. The contact points between the findings and the article are cleaned and coated with flux. Soldering is usually done with medium, easy-flow, or soft solder, and must be done before adding any gemstones.

The solder in very small paillons approximately $\frac{1}{32}$-inch square are placed against or close to the base of the finding and heated with a soft flame. The findings can be coated with flux and solder and heated to "tin" the parts before placing them in the mating area. *The article is heated—not the finding.* The heat transfer will reach the finding very quickly so the torch need be held only a very short time at the juncture point. As the torch brushes the area, pressure must be applied to hold the parts in place to prevent drifting. Various clamping devices are available for this (see Chapter 9). The torch flame is removed as soon as the solder turns bright. The soldered parts are allowed to cool before moving them. Cooling may be speeded up by dropping cold water on the soldered joint from a small paintbrush, toothpick, or pipe cleaner.

When soldering pin-backs or broches, the hinge should be offset slightly so that the pin always has tension on it. This will hold the pin in the clasp when the article is worn even though the safety catch may be turned to an open position (see Fig. 179). The clasp is soldered in a closed position, and care must be taken to prevent any melting of the finding during soldering.

Pin-backs without a safety lock can be made of a single section of wire or of several pieces as desired. The single piece of wire is bent to shape as shown (see Fig. 180), the center area flattened slightly with a hammer to give a better

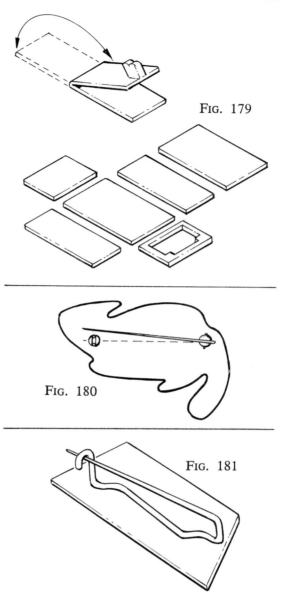

Fig. 179

Fig. 180

Fig. 181

soldering area, the pin end filed to a taper, then buffed and polished.

Pendant bails are constructed in diamond shape of 26-gauge metal sheet. The ends are brought together and soldered. The bail, soldered to a short section of small diameter tubing, can be used to convert a pin to a pendant. The tubing is cut to fit between the safety clasp and swivel of a pin-back. The bail is strung on a necklace cord or chain when worn (see Fig. 181). Permanently attached pendant bails are soldered to the article (see Fig. 182A).

Earring screws are attached primarily with easy-flow solder. The screw is bent open

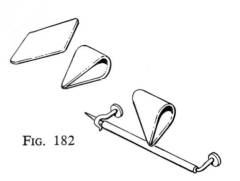

FIG. 182

of two parts—a ring made of wire or cut from metal, and a T-shaped bar which is slipped into the center and then turned at a 90° angle to retain itself in the ring. The T-bar can be made of metal, stone, or wood to match the material used in the article. Hook latches constructed of flat metal or wire can also vary in design and type. Beads on ends of wire are used for retainers as are half-dome cups (see Fig. 178A).

to a 45° angle to prevent the heat of the torch from melting the threaded shaft (see Fig. 183). The attachment area is fluxed, the cup is filled with solder and, if a pad is used, it is tinned and the finding is placed in position.

Box clasps and safety locks

Box clasps are simple to make once one has become skilled at working with small parts. This type clasp is the best one for the beginner to make before proceeding to more intricate clasps that require many soldering steps (see Figs. 178B, 179, and 184).

Safety locks for box clasps are made from 18-gauge wire. A small pin with a bead on one end is soldered into a predrilled hole in the side of one clasp section. A short length of small-diameter tubing is soldered to the side of the remaining clasp section. A short piece of wire is threaded through the tubing and bent to a figure eight shape. The ends are not cut to complete the curve, but are left bent to produce a small tang for lifting the lock. The wire is soldered at the ends to prevent spreading. When the wire catch is forced over the pin-head, the pin must protrude up through the wire catch to hold properly (see Figs. 184 and 185).

Hinge locks consist of two sections of small-diameter tubing with each section soldered to a mating edge of metal links or sections. The tubing sections are notched, sawed, and filed to mate with each other. A pin slightly smaller than the inside diameter of the hinge is filed to a taper and a jump ring, or bead and jump ring combined, are soldered to the opposite end. The pin is attached by a small section of chain to the article to prevent its being lost.

T-bar fasteners can be made in different ways (see Figs. 185 and 178A). The fastener consists

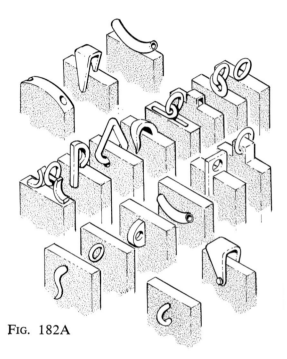

FIG. 182A

Threaded stems and nuts

Though usually purchased, threaded stems and nuts for earring screws or prong mounting posts can be made from metal sheet and round wire if a small tap and die are used. The threading sets are available in very small sizes of taps mated to dies, which come as separate small dies or in a plate (see Figs. 186 and 186A).

Holes are threaded with taps, and shafts or pins are threaded with the small dies. A small hole is drilled in metal sheet from which a nut will be sawed after tapping the hole (see Fig. 187). The drill size for the hole should be slightly smaller than the inside diameter of the

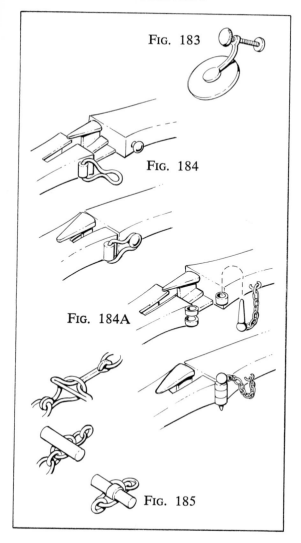

FIG. 183

FIG. 184

FIG. 184A

FIG. 185

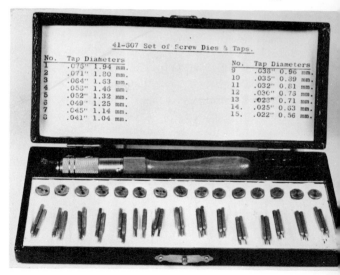

No.	Tap Diameters		No.	Tap Diameters	
1	.075"	1.94 mm.	9	.038"	0.96 mm.
2	.071"	1.80 mm.	10	.035"	0.89 mm.
3	.064"	1.63 mm.	11	.032"	0.81 mm.
4	.058"	1.46 mm.	12	.030"	0.75 mm.
5	.052"	1.32 mm.	13	.028"	0.71 mm.
6	.049"	1.25 mm.	14.	.025"	0.63 mm.
7	.045"	1.14 mm.	15.	.022"	0.56 mm.
8	.041"	1.04 mm.			

41-307 Set of Screw Dies & Taps.

FIG. 186

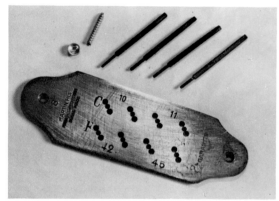

FIG. 186A

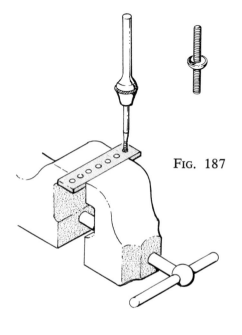

FIG. 187

tap threads (the root). Metal used for the nut section should be thick enough for at least three complete threads. The hole is drilled in stock metal sheet marked for drilling. Small nut-sized discs should not be sawed before drilling and tapping as these are difficult to hold in the vise. The tap is placed in a tap handle and a small amount of thin oil is added to the tap. After insertion in the drilled hole, the tap is turned gently about 1½ turns in a clockwise motion. It should not be forced, but turned firmly and held absolutely vertical while in use. To remove any chips or burrs, the tap is reversed for a ½ turn and then turned again for another 1½ turns.

The same procedure is continued until the tap has emerged through the metal beyond its tapered tip. The tap is then turned in a counter-clockwise rotation for removal from the metal which is scribed for an outline and sawed to shape, followed by sanding.

Pins or shafts are threaded with the small dies which are matched with the different taps. Both mating parts are numbered according to the size thread that is produced. The wire diameter should be slightly larger than the outside dimension of the threads on the mating tap. The wire is placed horizontally in a bench vise and only a short section is threaded at one time. The die is placed in the die stock (handle) and gently started on the wire in a clockwise motion. A small amount of oil is added to the wire to make the die work easily. The die is turned 1½ turns on the wire,

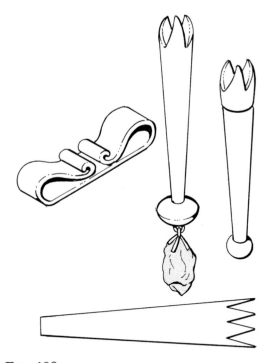

Fig. 190

and then reversed ¼ turn to remove the chips, and then rotated clockwise another 1½ turns. These two procedures are continued until the wire length is threaded. The threaded pin or shaft must be slightly longer than needed to go completely through the nut when the two parts are assembled. The threaded wire is cut square with end-cutting pliers, filed smooth, and attached with medium or easy-flow solder to the article.

Ear clips

Ear clips are simple to make out of two parts of metal—one part slit in two places and the other bent to shape (see Fig. 188). A small pair of pliers is needed to make the necessary tension adjustment on the spring section of the clip. The base is tinned with solder and attached to the article. The clip is added after the soldering is completed.

Tie tacks, bola tips

Tie tack studs can be made of round wire, filed, buffed, and polished to a taper. The clutch section must be purchased, and often the price of the clutch includes the stud. Tie clips are easily made by bending the metal to a spring-

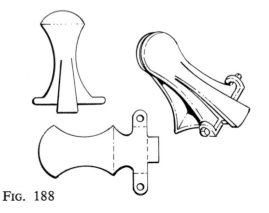

Fig. 188

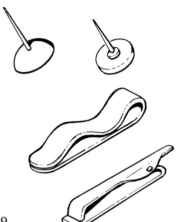

Fig. 189

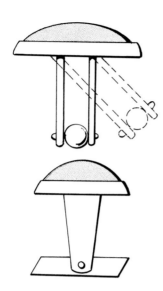

Fig. 191

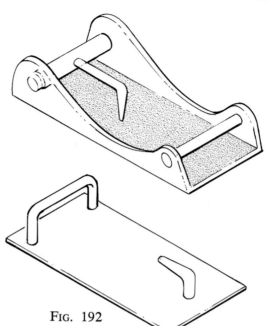

Fig. 192

type tab or by soldering a small "alligator" clip to the underside (see Fig. 189).

Bola tie slides are easily made by bending a ³/₁₆-inch-wide strip of 24-gauge metal to the shape shown in the illustration (see Fig. 190). Tips are made from tubing filed and flattened and then filled on the end with solder, or by constructing a tapered tube from 26-gauge metal and later installing a bead at the base. A small jump ring can be soldered at the tip end to be used as a hanger for a bell cap (small pronged caps which fit over irregularly shaped stones).

Cuff link swivels

Cuff link swivel frames can be constructed out of a sheet of 18-gauge metal sawed to shape or made from square or half-round wire (see Fig. 191). The swivel is made of 8-gauge metal or two lengths of 14-gauge metal soldered together and filed to shape. Pivot holes are drilled partially through the sides to mate with the lugs on the swivel frame. Cuff link swivel frames are attached with medium or easy-flow solder to the link without the swivel.

Belt buckle swivels and tangs

Belt buckle swivels are constructed of heavy wire with tubing fitted over the wire. Belt buckle attachments can also be made without the hinging action (see Fig. 192).

CHAPTER 12

Wire

WIRE IS A VERSATILE METAL FORM, READY TO use as purchased for complete units of jewelry, or worked into links and chains, pendant frames, ring shanks, gemstone prongs, necklace, bracelet, and ring inserts, and decorative trim. Wire is also used for filigree, scrollwork, appliqué, inlay, and for enameling cloisons as described in other chapters.

Even though wire is flexible and easy to handle, especially when annealed, some practice in winding, forming, and drawing copper or soft solder wire should be done before more expensive wires of precious metal are used.

Drawing the wire

Wire, available from suppliers in a few standard shapes and gauges, can be reduced in size and changed in shape by pulling it through a drawplate. Drawplates are available in various combinations of holes such as all square, all round, and in a combinaiton plate of round, half-round, square, triangular, diamond, knife-edge, and pear-shaped holes. The holes range in size from 2-gauge (.257 inch) to 28-gauge (.012 inch), each plate having at least twenty different holes (see Figs. 193 and 194). In addition to reducing or altering a single wire, two wires of one shape may be drawn through one hole at the same time, thus eliminating the need to purchase a large number of expensive plates.

Single lengths of wire, such as round, can be drawn through a smaller square hole, and square wire can be drawn through a smaller round or oval-shaped hole. Two lengths of square wire of the same gauge drawn through a round hole will produce two sections of half-round wire, and two lengths of half-round wire drawn through a square hole will produce triangular-

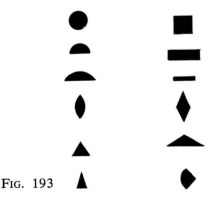

FIG. 193

shaped wire. When drawing wire to a triangular shape, it is necessary that the mating flat surfaces of the half-round wire align with opposite corners of the square hole.

Generally, 12- to 18-gauge wire is used for drawing, but, of course, when wire is to be drawn to very small gauges, much smaller wire can be used to start with.

Most wire will draw easily if annealed first. Fine wire is wrapped in coils ¾ to 1 inch in diameter and larger sizes wrapped in coils 1½ to 2 inches in diameter (see Fig. 24). The coils, even for large-gauge wire should never be larger than 4 inches in diameter when annealing. In preparation for heating, the wire ends are tucked in the coil to prevent melting, and the coil is held together in several places. Iron binding wire can be used for this, but it must be removed before pickling to avoid contaminating the solution. Clips made from scraps of the same metal, or of the same type wire as the coil, can remain on the coil during pickling. The wire coil is heated with a brush flame that is continuously rotated. The entire coil need not reach a dull red color at the same time, but every part of the coil must reach that stage at least once during the heating.

After pickling and rinsing, the wire is unwound and one end of the wire is filed to a long tapered point in preparation for drawing.

The drawplate is placed in a bench vise with the small sides of the holes or the numbered side facing the worker. The wire is first drawn through a piece of beeswax or, if desired, a drop of light-weight oil can be placed in the tapered side of the hole to lubricate the wire as it is drawn. The first hole the wire is drawn through should be slightly smaller in size than the wire to be inserted. If there is too great a variance between the wire size and the first hole selected, it will be very difficult or even impossible to pull the wire through. The wrong choice of size is made evident if the tip end of the wire breaks off.

The wire, grasped with the draw tongs, is pulled in one continuous draw. Plenty of room should be allowed around the vise so that the wire can be drawn out at right angles to the plate face (see Fig. 194). Because large gauges of wire require a good hard pull, it is necessary that the workbench be firmly attached to a wall so that it will not move when the wire is

FIG. 194

drawn. By drawing the wire in one long continuous pull it emerges equal in size, whereas stops and starts will produce unevenness. Jerking the wire will as a rule cause breakage. Small-gauge wire should be annealed after drawing it through two holes in succession, and in large-gauge sizes it should be annealed after each draw.

Square wire, which has a tendency to twist when it is pulled through the drawplate, can be kept in perfect alignment by clamping two boards across the wire, just loose enough to permit the wire to be pulled through. The clamp is placed against the backside of the drawplate, and is held in place by the wire as it is pulled through the holes. Small boards screwed together with barely enough clearance for the wire can also be used for this purpose (see Fig. 195).

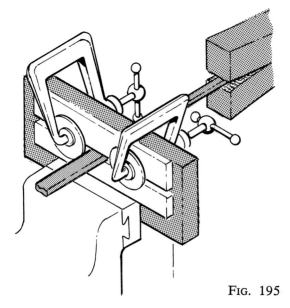

FIG. 195

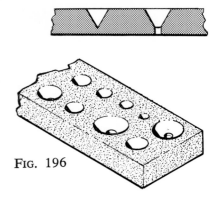

FIG. 196

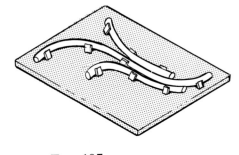

FIG. 197

To save time when reducing wire to a smaller size, small paper adhesive discs sold for indexing can be applied as markers on the front of the plate. A ready reference of wire requirements can be compiled by measuring the length and gauge of a section of wire, and then noting the length after drawing and the new gauge size. The wire must be measured before drawing through the first hole and checked when all drawing is finished. By maintaining a list of the different wires produced one can soon determine in advance how much wire is necessary for any certain length.

Additional holes for drawing wire can be made in a drawplate. The metal plate is heated to a bright red and left to cool slowly without quenching. The hole location is centerpunched on the backside of the drawplate, and a deep tapered hole is drilled into, but not through, the plate. This should be a long taper rather than a flat standard countersunk hole. The hole for the size of the wire is then drilled through the plate (see Fig. 196). The drawplate is then reheated to a bright red and immediately plunged into cold water to cool it quickly and evenly. This hardens the metal but leaves it brittle. It is then reheated to a brownish yellow or straw color which occurs at approximately 470°F. Color changes are evident as the heat rises. The tool is quenched in cold water or oil to temper the metal as soon as the color is reached.

Soldering

Wire which is to be soldered to a flat sheet must be perfectly flat, as the solder will not fill in any wide spaces left between the two metal pieces. When soldering, the solder should be placed on the outer curves of the wire, lean-

FIG. 198

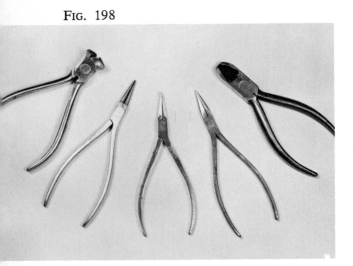

FIG. 198A

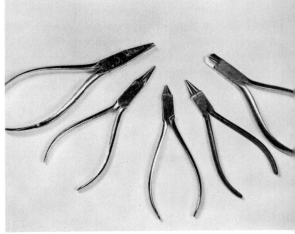

ing against the wire (see Fig. 197). The heat will draw the solder along the seam and leave less of it to remove than if it were laid flat on the plate. The heat should be directed to the sheet away from the wire to prevent melting the wire. In addition to the probability of melting the wire if the wire is heated directly by the torch, the solder will travel up the wire (making it larger in some areas) rather than flowing along a fine seam where wire and sheet meet.

Soldering is started with hard solder if additional soldering is to be done, otherwise the wire is soldered to a flat sheet with medium solder.

Wire is soldered to wire by first fluxing the contact points and then adding a small square of solder on top of the juncture of the two wires. As the solder melts, it falls into place and flows over the fluxed areas.

Wires or long tapered metal sections used for gemstone prongs that are to be soldered in an upright position on a flat surface should be placed in position in a predrilled hole whenever possible. In this way, the soldered joint is below the surface so that the wire or tapered section will not be bent at the soldered joint when burnished over the gemstone.

Wire soldered to a tube should be seated over a small groove filed in the tube. This gives the solder something to travel in and also helps to hold the wire in place.

Pliers used for bending

Five basic types of pliers—round-nose, needle-nose, flat-nose, and both side and end cutting pliers—are required to start with. Other specialty types can be added as needed for a particular technique (see Figs. 198 and 198A).

Methods of bending

Wire sections, bent, shaped, and soldered are also used as pendant frames. Corners or curves are flattened for a forged effect (see Figs. 199 and 199A). Smaller soldered sections flattened on the corners or around the circumference can be used as large links in a necklace or bracelet design. Holes are drilled in the flattened areas. Sections can also be constructed and interlaced. Soldering is done after all assembly work is completed.

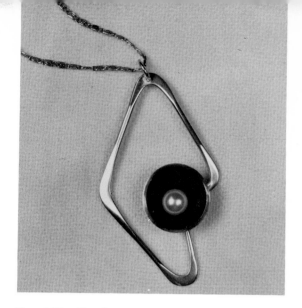

FIG. 199 Pendant, wire-forged with half-dome sterling silver and pearl.
By Sharr Choate.

Round or square wire can be used as a necklace by itself or as a hanger for pendants. The wire is cut to length, determined by bending a length of soft solder wire or copper wire around the neck and allowing for a decorative twist or curve at the end in addition to the interlock used as a fastener (see Fig. 200). Cabochons in bezels, hollow spheres, or solid beads of metal can be soldered to the ends.

Heavier wire can be formed into nonobjective articles by bending and curving annealed wire. Fourteen- to sixteen-gauge wire is used for this type of work. Portions of the wire may be

FIG. 199A Pendant, single-piece construction, 14k gold wire with pearl.
By Sharr Choate.

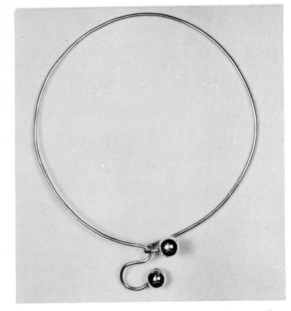

FIG. 200   Necklace, wire with beads, sterling silver.
By Sharr Choate.

FIG. 201   Necklace, box construction, sterling silver with gold-sheen obsidian.
By Sharr Choate.

flattened with a flat, polished hammer to give more character to the form.

Large-sized flat links constructed for necklace sections can be contoured after soldering by placing them on a bracelet stake and hammering gently with a rawhide mallet (see Fig. 201).

Winding aids

Wire to be formed or wound into a pattern is made on a jig. These improvised tools are absolutely essential if multiple identical sections are to be made. The jig is constructed of a flat hardwood section. Small blocks and circles cut from particle board (used in formica-covered sink tops) make excellent jigs. The smooth flat surface is easily marked with the design and is much smoother to work on. Metal pins or wooden posts are inserted in holes drilled partially through the board (see Figs. 202 and 202A). The diameter of the pin must correspond to the inner radius of the curve planned for the wire. Small pins will make sharp corners or kinks rather than gentle sweeping curves. Additional bending of the sections can be made by hand or with pliers after removing the wire from the jig.

Making identical wire loops

Links for jump rings and chains are made by winding annealed wire usually 18- to 20-gauge, on a mandrel or rigid shape. The mandrel can be a small section of drill rod, nail, dowel wood, knitting needles, square- and hexagonal-shaped bar stocks, etc., in various diameters or sizes. The cross section of the mandrel will indicate the shape of the individual ring or link. The wire is held against the mandrel, and both are tightened in a bench vise in a horizontal position. This clamping of the wire end prevents slippage of the wire as it is wound. If the wire is wrapped on a metal mandrel, it should first be wrapped with several layers of heavy paper

FIG. 202

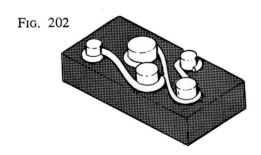

FIG. 202A Necklace, wire cage construction with frosted beads, sterling silver.
By Sharr Choate.

(see Fig. 203). After winding, the paper is ignited to destroy it. When the paper disappears the wire is easily removed from the mandrel. The coil is placed in the vise or hand vise for sawing into rings. One end of the saw blade (4/0) is fitted into the saw frame with the teeth pointing toward the handle, facing in toward the frame. The remaining end of the saw blade is threaded through the coil and tightened in the frame. The sawing is done from the inside out, and at all times is sawed at right angles to the coil (see Fig. 203A).

If a wooden mandrel is used for winding, the wire may be left on the mandrel which continues to be held in the bench vise. The saw is then used in the normal manner to saw lengthwise through the coil. If desired, the mandrel may be slotted lengthwise for the saw blade. This sawing is best done with a metalsmith's saw, also called a metal back saw.

Wire can be wound around any shape that will produce the form required to match the design. Oblong or oval links should be sawed at the end so that the joint will not be easily visible after soldering.

Links are always opened by twisting the ends in opposite directions to maintain the link shape (see Fig. 203A). The ends are filed flat before closing them. Links should never be spread, for it is difficult to close them again to their original shape.

Wire is twisted into two strands by placing both ends of a length of annealed wire in a bench vise. An eyehook is looped through the wire and inserted into a hand drill. The wire is held taut in a horizontal position and twisted with the hand drill. In place of the drill a short (4-inch) section of dowel wood may be inserted in the wire loop and used as a handle to twist the wire.

Twisted and flattened wire ring shanks are made by first soldering parallel wires together. These might consist of two wires of 14-gauge material; 2 of 16-gauge; 3 or 4 of 18-gauge wire. After soldering, the wires are cleaned again and fluxed before twisting them tightly. The wire is then placed on the soldering block, and a tiny snippet of solder is added to each twist and the twist is soldered. The section is

FIG. 203

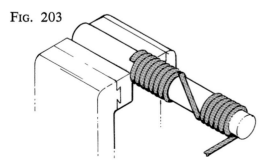

FIG. 203A

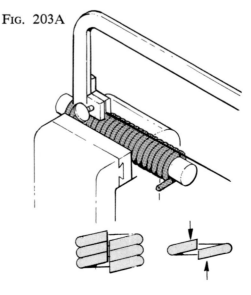

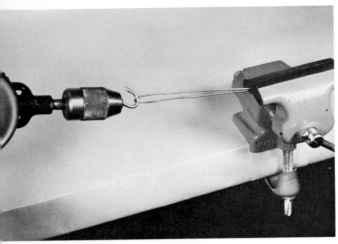

FIG. 204

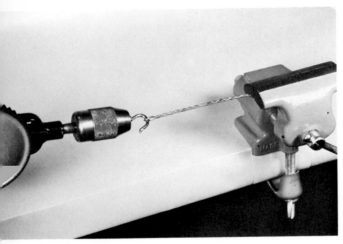

FIG. 204A

section of the wire remains in the vise. A small crescent wrench is placed on the wire against the jaws of the vise to prevent the wire from twisting inside the vise. A second wrench is placed on a scribed mark equal to the length held in the vise and the wire is twisted 360° or one complete turn (see Fig. 205). With the wire remaining in the vise the wrenches are moved out on the extending wire, and the twisting operation repeated. The square section of wire between the twists can be varied in length as desired.

There are at least seventy different attractive wire-twisting combinations. Interesting arrangements can be worked out in the same piece by twisting a double strand of wire and, after twisting, unwinding it gently into single strands (see Fig. 206). The separated wires can be cut to length and soldered into loops for use as stone hangers with the twisted curves flattened slightly with a hammer for a different effect. A small bail is added at the top for the bezel loop.

Other effects can be obtained by threading wires of different metals into wound wires of various types or by twisting three wires together and then rewinding one strand and in its place inserting a small square wire.

Small-gauge strands of wire can be twisted with a larger-diameter wire. Single strands can be twisted in either direction and used singly or in a combination of opposing twists. Wire twisted first to the left and then to the right in

flattened to the width desired either with a hammer on a smooth metal surface or by rolling it in a mill. If the metal is hammered to flatten it, the surfaces should be filed to remove any hammer marks. The metal is sawed to length, formed, sized and soldered to the bezel or other gem mounting.

Single strands of square or half-round wire are twisted by first making a loop around a section of dowel wood and winding the end around the wire for a handle. The other end of the wire is held in the bench vise while it is being twisted (see Figs. 204 and 204A). Square wire can be twisted at intervals by placing the wire in the bench vise (with the wire placed between protective jaw covers) so that only a short

FIG. 205

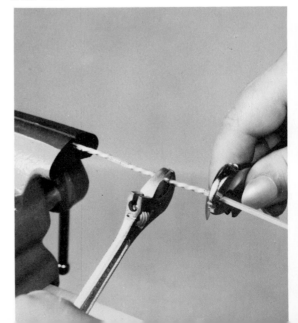

one strand is also attractive. To do this it is necessary to hold the wire in the center of the twist with a small wrench or vise grips.

After twisting, the wire, supported on a smooth flat metal surface, is flattened with a flat polished hammer. It can also be slightly flattened by running it through a rolling mill. The wire should be annealed again after twisting, and before working it further to prevent it from becoming brittle and breaking. The twisted wire can also be drawn through the wire drawplate for additional effects. If two or more wires are drawn through the plate, the ends must be hard-soldered together, and then filed to a tapered point so that the wires can be threaded through the plate.

Twisted wires used for inserts in bracelets, rings, and necklaces are sawed on the same angle as the twist, so that the ends will meet properly when soldered in the main section of the assembly.

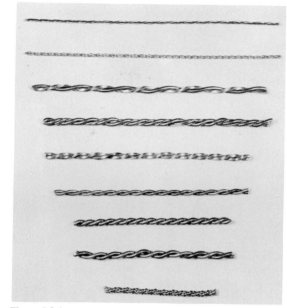

FIG. 206

Whorls or pinwheels

Whorls are made by twisting annealed wire around a mandrel which is positioned upright in a hand vise or a bench vise. As it is wound, the wire is supported on a small disc placed over the upright mandrel.

The mandrel is placed in the vise so that one end of the wire is held firmly when tightened. The length of wire protrudes through a small center hole in the disc next to the mandrel, and is bent at a 90° angle and started in a wind tightly around the mandrel base (see Fig. 207). The second revolution of wire is guided around the outer edge of the first wind and kept flat on the supporting disc. The wire is wound continuously until the desired whorl size is reached. Wire whorls may be wound with a hand vise also. The mandrel and disc are set up the same way as when the bench vise is used, but, during the winding operation, the hand vise is rotated to wind the wire which is held taut with the other hand (see Fig. 208).

Beads from wire

Beads or grains can be used as decorative accents. These are made of wire coiled around mandrels in accordance with the size balls desired. The links or sections, equal in length, are melted into identical balls. After winding and separating, the individual links are fluxed and melted on an asbestos coil, charcoal block, or in a container filled with powdered charcoal. They are then pickled and rinsed in running water. To keep the beads or grains in position when soldering them to a flat sheet, a small indentation is made in the surface of the sheet and filled with solder. The fluxed bead is then positioned in the depression and heat applied from the underside.

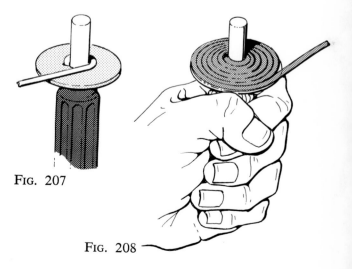

FIG. 207

FIG. 208

CHAPTER 13

Chains, Tubing, and Hinges

CHAINS

CHAINS PLAY A VERY IMPORTANT PART IN creating articles of jewelry. Commercially offered chains are usually easily recognizable stock designs, and besides being expensive, matching the exact metal color of a handcrafted piece is usually very difficult, if not impossible. Also, commercial chains often have plated protective finishes such as rhodium, which makes it difficult to shorten, lengthen, or repair them. Therefore, when a chain is required as a part of the design, it is essential that it be handwrought so that it will compliment and enhance rather than detract from the beauty of the article.

Chain combinations

Various kinds of chain combinations are possible such as all rounds, squares, ovals, hexagonals, and free forms of different sizes, rounds and ovals mixed, ovals of different sizes or mixed with solid sections, small rings connecting larger round or square sections of wire, square wire constructed in random length, rectangular links, and many other combinations depending on the ingenuity of the craftsman (see Fig. 209).

Chains made with jump rings

Chains formed of any size links are constructed by soldering pairs of rings together. After sawing the wound coil on the mandrel (see Chapter 12), the rings are opened slightly by twisting them sideways, filing the ends smooth, and reclosing the links. A small amount of flux and hard solder is applied to each link. In the same manner, the links are then joined with a connecting third link (see Fig. 210). Each set of three connected links is then joined with a single link to produce a seven-link section. The length of the chain or necklace will determine how many seven-link sections are needed. Often a three-link section may be required to complete a chain to the desired length. When soldering the single links, either initially or in an assembled section, the heat is always directed to one spot. It is necessary to watch continuously one join at a time in order to avoid overheating and melting.

Links can be flattened after soldering by placing them on a flat steel surface and covering them with a small steel block that is hammered with a heavy hammer. The links can be flattened for a sculptured effect by eliminating the steel block and using a dome-faced forging hammer.

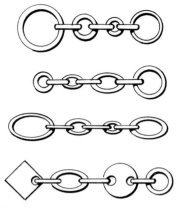

FIG. 209

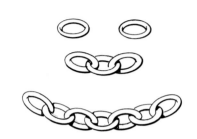

FIG. 210

Flat soldered links can be used as appliqué patterns in different arrangements. The links can be soldered onto flat plates that will serve as necklace or bracelet sections (see Fig. 211). All soldered sections can be identical and symmetrical or the links can continue across the plates to form a connecting design.

Flat chains for necklaces and bracelets must be fitted so that the individual units are flexible and all the links work freely. Links that have an inclination to twist must be adjusted by reversing or reconstructing them. After the connecting and soldering process chains may be flattened in a rolling mill to give a different effect.

Forming links

Oval links can be made from round links after soldering by inserting round-nosed pliers in the ring with the soldered join positioned over the outer curve of one side of the pliers. The pliers are forced apart to form the oval ring; a well-soldered joint will hold during this forming step (see Fig. 212). Changes in the oval can be made by pressing the center of the oval ring together while it is still held on the round-nosed pliers. The two sides of the link can meet in the center or at one side (see Fig. 212A). By positioning the soldered joint at the end of the link, it is covered by the next link when assembling the chain.

The drawplate has other uses in addition to wire size reduction. Soldered links (jump rings) assembled in a chain may be pulled through holes on the plate to elongate the links, making them either oval or uniformly oblong.

Rings other than jump ring combinations

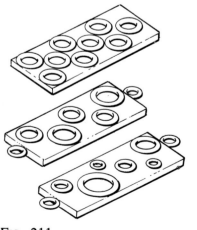

FIG. 211

FIG. 212

FIG. 212A

can be used in many ways to make interesting chains. Here are some suggestions:

1. Small or large rings nested together and connected with an oval ring of flat wire.
2. Oblong loops with a smaller ring nestled inside and connected with a flat wire loop or a smaller jump ring.
3. Oblong rings squeezed together to resemble an hourglass and connected with flat rings or round rings.
4. Oblong rings soldered and then twisted in the center 180° and connected with a smaller jump ring.
5. Very large oblong rings twisted one way and then the other with an adjustable wrench by inserting a small rod in the end of the loop and gently turning it.

In order to have identical sized loops, it is important to hold the flat center part of the loop in the wrench when twisting the loops at the end.

Use of tubing for chains

Hollow tubing, round, square, and hexagonal can be sawed in thin sections either straight or obliquely across the tube to produce links for chains. The links are attached to each other with jump rings or by hinges that can be constructed in several different ways, as described later in the chapter.

TUBING

Tubing is used for hinges on articles, clasp sections, decorative necklace links, and in large sizes as gem mounts. It is available in various gauges and wall thicknesses. Small sizes of tubing are more easily purchased than constucted. The correct width for the flat metal strip used to make the desired size of tubing can be determined by making it three times as wide as the diameter the tubing is to be when finished plus the thickness of the metal gauge.

Forming tubing

Tubing is formed by pulling a narrow strip of metal through a wire drawplate (see Fig. 213).

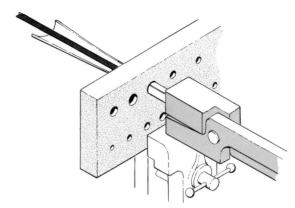

FIG. 213

The strip is snipped and filed to a tapered point at one end, then placed over a groove in a wooden V block, and a length of dowel wood the same size as the groove in the block is placed over it. The dowel wood is hammered to partially bend the metal strip to a U shape as an aid in forming it before using the drawplate (see Fig. 214). A V block can be made by drilling holes of different sizes through the side of a block of wood. The block, when sawed through the center of the drilled holes, will produce two blocks with half-round grooves in the surfaces.

Machinist's steel swage or V blocks can also be used to bend the tubing for drawing (see Fig. 215). A steel rod is hammered with a rawhide mallet to form the strip into a U shape. A creasing hammer may be used for the same purpose.

The tapered end of the partially formed metal strip is inserted through the hole in the drawplate and grasped with drawtongs (see

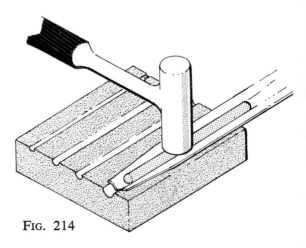

FIG. 214

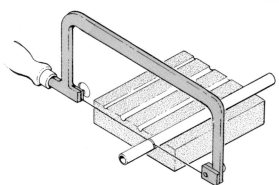

Fig. 215

Fig. 217

Fig. 213). The strip is pulled through the plate and progressively through smaller holes to form the tubing. The tubing is then strung on a longer length of piano wire and pulled through the drawplate so that the edges are brought together to form a crease or seam. The piano wire prevents an overlapping that would be difficult to correct. The wire is removed from the tube by inserting it in a drawplate hole slightly larger than its size but smaller than the tubing size (see Fig. 216). The wire is pulled through the drawplate and out of the tube which remains on the backside of the drawplate.

Cutting the tubing

Tubing is cut to length by placing it in a V groove made in a block of hardwood or the groove of a regular machinist's V or swage block (see Fig. 217). It is absolutely necessary that the tubing ends be sawed and filed flat and perpendicular to the axis or center line of the tubing. Such a block makes it possible to align the tubing properly for sawing or filing. Tubing may also be sawed on a jeweler's small Rathbun saw; however there is no V joint or groove to align the wire properly (see Fig. 218). Small burrs inside the sawed tubing sections are easily removed with a needle file, but care must be taken to avoid flaring the ends, as this would result in a loose hinge.

Bending

Tubing can be bent without creasing or kinking if filled with beeswax before beginning the bend. The tubing is filled with the melted wax, and after bending, is remelted in boiling water to remove the wax.

Soldering

The seams are easily held together for soldering if a length of binding wire with knots tied

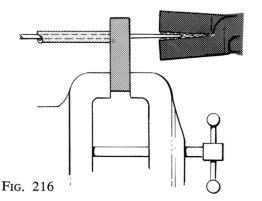

Fig. 216

Fig. 218

at intervals (to avoid slipping) is wrapped lengthwise around the tubing. Other wires are then wrapped around the perimeter of the tube. This works especially well on tapered cones used for gem mountings or bola tips (see Fig. 219).

When soldering tubing to a flat sheet, either hard or medium solder is used, depending on any subsequent soldering requirements.

Necklaces can be formed by stringing random lengths of tubing on a small chain or by connecting short sections of chain with larger jump rings to hold short lengths (see Fig. 220).

Using tubing as a clasp or closure

Tubing is used to make clasps by fitting interlocking sections called knuckles or cheniers which are soldered to the ends of a necklace or bracelet (see Fig. 184). The joint pin is soldered to a small jump ring for attachment to a safety or guard chain. The opposite end of the pin is filed to a long blunt taper for easy insertion through the knuckles when locking the necklace. The end of the joint pin may be soldered to a small solid metal ball and the jump ring attached to it for embellishment.

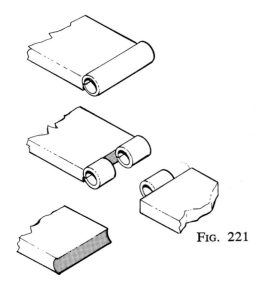

FIG. 219

FIG. 221

FIG. 220

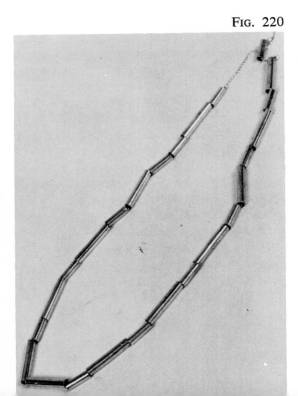

HINGES

Hinges can be attached to links as a complete tube section which is then sawed into separate knuckles and the excess metal filed away during fitting, or the knuckles can be cut and fitted separately before soldering (see Figs. 221, 221A, and 221B). Knuckles constructed from a complete section of tubing soldered onto the link or hinge area must be fitted with a limited amount of filing. Close attention must be paid when marking and sawing the knuckles so that the sawing is done in the tubing portion which is to be completely removed from the assembly. The knuckle is then filed to the scribed line for fitting.

A better alignment of the knuckles is possible if the complete hinge is constructed with an

FIG. 221A Locket, appliqué with hinge construction, chain from Guatemala, sterling silver. Locket by Sharr Choate.

FIG. 221B Locket pendant opened to show hinge and inner surface detail, sterling silver with Guatemalan silver necklace chain. Locket by Sharr Choate.

odd number of knuckles. Three sections are usually sufficient for small jewelry items, but knuckles are added as the link size increases. If one section is stationary, it should have the single knuckle attached to its edge. The moving section will then have the two outer knuckles for support. The central knuckle should always be longer than the two end sections.

Hinges mounted on one side of a metal section are placed in a groove with the tubing seam positioned in the bottom of the groove (see Fig. 221). The seam is fluxed and a small amount of solder is placed in the groove. The link section is fluxed, placed next to the hinge,

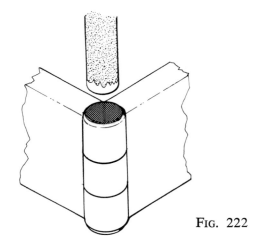

FIG. 222

and additional solder added. By placing the hinge seam in the bottom of the groove, one can be reasonably sure that the seam will be well soldered. Any excess of solder inside the hinge can be removed with a small reamer.

Knuckles can be cut separately and soldered to the hinge sections at one time by stringing the parts on an oiled steel rod to hold them in correct alignment while soldering. Oil prevents any adherence of the solder to the rod.

Links can be soldered flat on an asbestos sheet, coil, charcoal block, supported in a third hand, or suspended on the improvised soldering stand.

Knuckles may also be soldered to a link edge with a closer fit if the link edge is filed to a concave surface to match the diameter of the tubing (see Fig. 221).

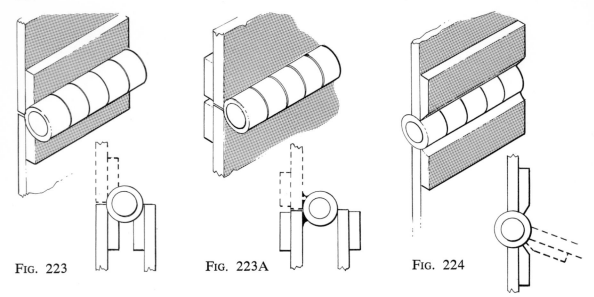

FIG. 223   FIG. 223A   FIG. 224

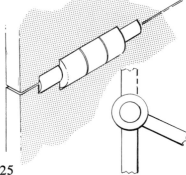

FIG. 225

Joint pins

Joint pins, which hold the hinges together, are usually constructed of nickel silver; however, silver or gold wire may be used if preferred. The pin is cut to a length slightly longer than the assembled hinge section and placed upright by the hinge sections on a hard metal surface. The pin is cut to length and hammered gently to peen or slightly "mushroom" the end (see Fig. 222). Some trimming of the pin may be necessary if it was left too long at the beginning.

Box hinges

Hinges constructed of tubing should have one more knuckle to form the section that will swing or hinge over the stationary section. This applies to boxes, etc. When there is equal action, either section can have the greater number of knuckles.

Hinge sections, especially when attached to boxes, should be well thought out before they are soldered. A reinforcement strip is used to prevent buckling or bulging at the hinges when the lid is opened. These strips are placed above and below the hinges either inside or outside the box, depending on which side the hinge is to be attached (see Figs. 223 and 223A).

A hinge can be mounted both outside and inside the box in the same manner except that when the hinge is mounted on the inside surface, the lid edge and the box edge must be relieved (filed on an angle) to give clearance to the two sections when the box is opened. A hinge mounted in this way is not visible from the outside (see Fig. 224).

Another method of attaching hinges is to mount the hinge between the lid and the box section (the reinforcement strip remains inside). Both the box section and the lid are notched the length of the hinge and as deep as the radius of the hinge (see Fig. 225). If the two parts are not notched sufficiently, there will be a gap at the back indicating an improper fitting.

All the reinforcing strips are soldered flush with the edges of the box and lid sections. The edge of the strip, which will be attached to the knuckles, is filed on a concave curve with a small round file to match the knuckles (see Figs. 223, 223A, and 224).

CHAPTER 14

Rings

A PROGRESSIVE STEP TOWARD THE CREATION of original rings demands the breaking away from standardized piece assembly procedures which use the ordinary bezel or prongs on a shank method of ring construction.

With a little imagination, a simple design, and the necessary technique, a craftsman can make a ring that may appear to have been constructed by means of casting even though it has been sawed, filed, hammered, bent or formed to shape, and often hard-soldered before being combined with other constructed sections.

According to the technique used, some designs are made while the metal is flat and others are done after forming into a ring. These techniques are covered in separate chapters except for the carving method. This is done with engraving tools to alter the surface with various tools to give a bas-relief or low sculpture profile effect.

Gemstones in the ring

Gemstones incorporated into rings are unlimited in size, shape, and material. These can be purchased ready-cut to standard stone size in millimeter dimensions or custom cut by the craftsman to the same shapes, or in free-form styles which are usually custom cut to the design specifications. If possible, the stone should be selected and purchased before beginning the metal work. If the stone is to be cut by the craftsman, it can be done before or after the metal construction because of the availability of lapidary equipment necessary to alter the stone size in the event that the metal cannot be easily reworked to fit the particular stone.

Ring shank construction

Ring designs in simple or complicated form can be constructed first in wax, available in thicknesses comparable to sheet metal and wire gauges. The wax is softened over a household candle to render it easier to manipulate. After the form has been satisfactorily modified, the sections are flattened for design outlines and transferred to the precious metal sheet. Thin copper sheet, plus other workable materials such as toothpaste and shaving cream tubes split and flattened, can be ultilized to perfect a design before using the precious metal sheet and wire (see Fig. 5).

Small manicuring, embroidery, or surgical scissors are used to cut the copper sheet into

FIG. 226 Ring, double bezels with forging 14k gold with amethysts. By Sharr Choate.

FIG. 226A Ring-cast to show bezel attachment, 14k gold with Mexican fire opal. By Sharr Choate.

FIG. 227 Ring, wire, and half-domes, sterling silver. By Sharr Choate.

small curves and angles. One may start out with a strip of metal or wire with no previously conceived design and bend, loop, dish, and otherwise form the metal into a nonobjective original shape. Ring shanks can be made of plain, twisted, and braided wire (see Figs. 226, 226A, and 227).

A variety of ring ideas is possible when flat metal is used for the ring. The surface can be chased and embossed, etched, inlaid, or overlaid with contrasting metals or stone, pierced, enameled, embellished with scrollwork, and carved with engraving tools (see Figs. 228 and 228A).

Channelwork settings filled with stone or enamels, recessed areas with small stones mounted on pegs or pedestals, asymmetrical arrangements of multiple mountings, swirls and scrolls of metal accented with filigree or scrollwork, tension-type rings holding spheres or

natural crystal specimens in suspension, heavy-gauge wire twisted to shape and accented with faceted stones set in the wire ends, intertwining loops accented with small faceted stones, wires tied in various knots and the ends soldered together as the shank are but a few suggestions of ring variations (see Figs. 229 and 229A–G).

Ring design improvisations

There are many possibilities for creating ring shanks besides the standard types with the various familiar mountings and settings. Shanks can be constructed of formed sheet metal in patterns of flower petals, leaves, pods, etc. (see Fig. 230). Multiple layers of sheet metal can be soldered at the base and spread to hold a gemstone or bezel cup (see Fig. 231). Heavy-gauge metals held in a ring clamp can be carved

FIG. 228 Three silver rings made from demitasse spoons. *Left:* blue stardust (synthetic) *Center:* amethyst crystal (natural) *Right:* pink sapphire (synthetic) By Sharr Choate.

FIG. 228A

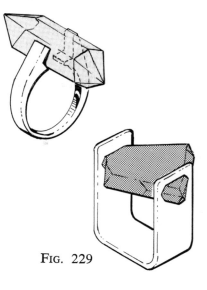

FIG. 229

FIG. 229A

FIG. 229B

FIG. 229C

FIG. 229D

FIG. 229A   Ring, sterling silver with emerald (synthetic).
By Sharr Choate.

FIG. 229B   Ring, scrollwork, 14k gold with peridot.
By Sharr Choate.

FIG. 229C   Ring, wire and cup construction, 14k gold and aquamarine.
By Sharr Choate.

FIG. 229D   Ring, bezels, and scrollwork, 14k gold and opal.
By Sharr Choate.

FIG. 229E   Ring, set stones in single circle, 14k gold, topaz, diamonds, rubies. By Alberta Best.

FIG. 229F   Ring, forged, sterling silver and 14k gold with ruby. By Wayne Smith.

FIG. 229G   Ring, bezel, bead and wire construction, sterling silver and turquoise. Zuñi Indian design.

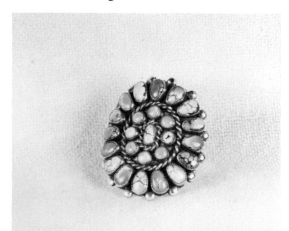

with gravers to form a bas-relief design and in the final stages textured as desired with matte tools.

Also, two identical rings can be constructed and soldered separately, then soldered together at the bottom at a point opposite the joint, gently separated, and bent out to form two flared sections. Binding wire can be wound around the rings to hold them as they are joined with medium solder. The rings can be used "as is," soldered only at the base, or soldered partially up the curve, depending on the amount of spread desired in the prongs or in the extension. From two to five rings can be used in this manner by reducing the size of the wire as the number of rings is increased (see Fig. 232).

The spread sections of the rings are sawed

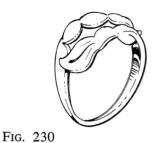

FIG. 230

open at the center tops and bent to fit either a stone or a bezel. Rings of various sizes may be assembled to form prongs of different lengths. The ends of the sawed wires are filed on angles to fit the particular gem mounting used in the assembly.

Split or double rings

Split or double rings are a recent innovation in jewelry design. They are made by constructing one plain wide shank or two narrow ones. The single wide band is sawed into two parts parallel with its circumference and equal in width or otherwise if desired (see Fig. 233). The mating edges are filed and notched in a variety of cuts and then realigned irregularly to form an attractive decoration (see Fig. 234).

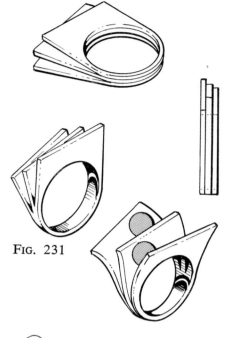

FIG. 231

FIG. 232

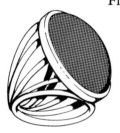

FIG. 233

The two parts are held in position with soldering wire and reattached with solder.

The ring can be marked for parallel sawing by using a small improvised scribe. The scribe consists of a small block of wood with a short section of metal rod inserted in the hole that has been drilled in the edge. Holes may be drilled at various levels for wide and narrow rings. The rod is filed to a sharp taper on the protruding or scribing end. Both the ring and the scribe are placed on a smooth flat surface, and the ring is rotated against the point of the scribe to mark a sawing line.

When the edges have been notched and worked to suit, one ring is fluxed on the sawed surface only and small bits of solder placed thereon. The ring section is heated to melt the solder, thus coating these surfaces alone. The

FIG. 234

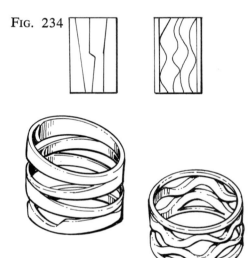

remaining ring half is fluxed only on the sawed surfaces and remated with the first ring section. The ring is wired and heated to permit solder to flow. The soldering wire is then removed and the ring is pickled, buffed, and polished.

The shanks can also be sawed irregularly in a curving or angular design and, when soldered, the sections aligned so that the ring has an irregular shape (see Fig. 234).

Prongs

Pronged settings are easily adapted to the shape of the stone if concentrated study of the stone is made before beginning the mounting. The prongs usually need pressure to hold the stone

FIG. 235

filed to shape. The outer surface can be rounded smooth, filed to flat tapering sides, filed with "faceted" sides, pierced, accented with appliqué or scrollwork, or embellished with graving tools. The gemstone opening is enlarged to the stone diameter (at the girdle) with a diamond setting bur (see Fig. 239). A line $\frac{1}{16}$ inch from the edge is made around the opening with a scribe and deepened with a graver. The stone is placed in the recess, and the lip is pushed from the groove over the stone with a blunt-end punch. When the stone is se-

securely in place. The position of the prongs must be determined in advance.

Side prongs are soldered on the edge of the ring and bent up over the stone. Flat tabs the thickness of the ring shank can be soldered onto the shank and brought up around a stone. If preferred, the prongs may be used to hold bezel cups (see Figs. 235 and 235A). Coiled wire attached to the ring shank and the bezel cup give support, are also decorative, and can be used as prongs if a bezel is not used.

Single crystals of natural gemstones may be mounted in a simulated suspension above the ring shank. The prongs (usually two) are soldered to the ring shank on the upper curve or halfway down the shank.

Tiffany-type setting

A Tiffany-type setting which consists of a pronged setting mounted on top of a ring shank can be made of any one of the various round pronged setting suggestions given, or by using a commercial head purchased to hold a specific stone. This type of setting is usually used for rings with transparent stones, as this permits the maximum amount of light to pass through the stone to show its beauty (see Fig. 236).

Gypsy mounting

Rings may also be constructed of two layers of different gauges of metal to build up one area for thickness. This type is usually called a gypsy mounting (see Figs. 237 and 155) or when modified, a belcher mounting (see Fig. 238).

The two sections of metal, homogenous after soldering, are drilled with a small hole for the gemstone opening. After soldering, the ring is

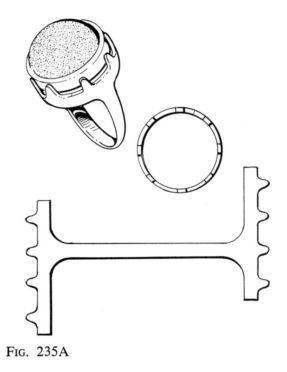

FIG. 235A

FIG. 236

FIG. 237

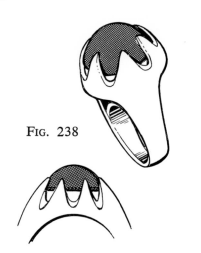

FIG. 238

seat or bearing for the stone (see Fig. 239). Additional filing can be done now to remove excess metal from the prongs before setting the stones. If desired, the ring may also be filed partially down the shank to give an added effect. The stone is tried in the opening for proper fit, and any adjustments necessary to seat the stone made with a graver. The prongs are burnished over the stone and buffed and polished. A flat graver can be used to cut small facets (called bright cuts) on each prong.

The main portion of the ring is the shank, which is usually constructed first. The bezel,

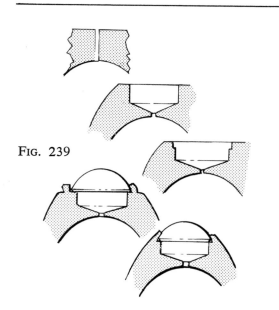

FIG. 239

FIG. 240

curely set the metal around it is filed smooth so that the groove is completely removed. After filing and sanding, the entire piece is buffed and polished.

Belcher mounting

For a belcher mounting, the thick portion of the ring, after drilling an opening for the gemstone and forming and soldering the ring to shape, is marked around the drilled hole with four, six, or eight marks for prongs. The metal is then filed away so that the desired number of prongs remain (see Fig. 238). The small Swiss files are used here, especially the knife-edge, lentil, and half-round shapes. When the filing is completed, a stone setting bur is used to cut the

prongs, or other mounting types are constructed separately and then added to the shank. By constructing a complete ring shank, it is easy to determine the appropriate size of the mounting.

Determining ring sizes

Ring sizes are determined by measuring the finger with a short length of string, strip of paper or flexible metal, or with a ring gauge (see Fig. 240). The ring gauge consists of a series of rings marked according to standard sizes used by the jewelry trade. The rings marked off in full and half sizes permit the craftsman to ascertain easily the correct ring size. When the size has been determined, it is compared with the ring size chart (see Appendix) for the length of wire, shank metal, or metal strip necessary to construct the ring to the chosen size. The chart lists ring sizes, diameter of the ring, and the flat length of a complete shank.

Metal requirements

The diameter chosen for the ring size plus the thickness of the metal to be used is multiplied by 3 (see Appendix). It is usually best to make the ring a half size smaller than desired to allow for buffing on the inner shank surface. Wide bands should be constructed one half-size larger than necessary to permit them to be removed easily from the finger.

When measuring the shank metal it should be cut 2 mm longer than required to allow for filing, etc. A complete shank should be constructed even though a portion may be removed for a mounting. As one becomes adept at measurements of metal, the shank length can be shortened to save sawing out a section later on. Of course many types of ring construction require a complete shank and the outer surface, and the ring sides are much easier filed to thinner shape if a complete shank is constructed regardless of ultimate use.

Forming and soldering the ring

The shank metal, whether wire, sheet strip, or formed shank stock, is formed in a circle with finger pressure, with shank bending pliers, or by hammering the metal gently with a rawhide mallet over a ring mandrel (see Fig. 240). The metal may be initially formed to a U shape by placing it on a swage block and with a mallet the pin is hammered, forcing the metal into a groove in the block (see Figs. 214 and 215). The swage block works well with flat metal such as that used for pierced rings or gypsy mountings. The rest of the metal is then formed on the mandrel with the mallet. It need not be a perfect circle at first. The important part is that the shank ends, filed flat, should meet. The ends are bent slightly past each other so that when brought back to a mating position they will stay together with spring tension, thus making it unnecessary to use binding wire when soldering the shank.

FIG. 241

Rings are usually soldered in steps or sections; therefore, the use of the various hard solders with their individual melting points is essential for such construction.

Rings are held for soldering in a third-hand soldering aid, on an improved soldering stand, or in a depression in a charcoal block (see Figs. 241, 102, and 103). After soldering the shank, it is placed on a ring mandrel and tapped with a rawhide mallet to true it.

Finishing

Ring shanks are filed with half-round and round files, small carborundum discs mounted on

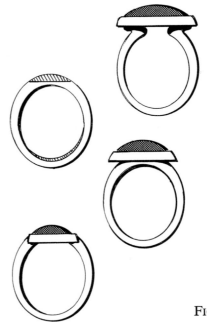

FIG. 242

mandrels, or on mounted grinding stones in various shapes that are used with power-driven handpieces.

After the shank is soldered it is placed joint down in a small bench vise to file the outer surface so that the portion of the ring opposite the joint will be thinner (see Figs. 242 and 242A). This part will be inside the hand at the finger joint and should not be too thick to be comfortable. The taper should start at least one-third of the distance from the top. The file is held at right angles to the ring surface when filing.

When the thinning is completed, the sides are

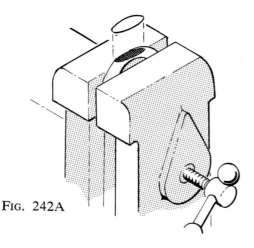

FIG. 242A

filed to a taper at the bottom of the ring with the file held parallel with the ring sides.

Ring sizing to fit

Rings that have been sized and are too small even after filing and sanding can be corrected by sawing on each side of the soldered joint and completely removing it so that a larger section of metal can be inserted and soldered into place. The parts should always be filed to fit perfectly before soldering.

Rings can also be enlarged a size or so without the sawing, fitting, filing, and soldering steps by using a ring mandrel (see Fig. 124). The center of the ring shank, between the two sides of the mounting or top, is hammered lightly with a rawhide mallet while in position on the mandrel that is held in a bench pin, vise, or hole drilled in the bench edge. This stretches

the metal slightly. When tapping, the hammer travels out a short distance from the shank center and then returns to travel outward to the other side of the shank center. In order to gauge the ring size as the stretching progresses, the ring is tapped onto the tapering mandrel with gentle side blows with the mallet so that it fits snugly.

If the ring is oversize, it will require sawing the shank and removing a section of metal to bring it to the correct size. The joint must then be soldered together again.

Adding prongs or bezels to the shank

After the mounting has been constructed, the shank is sawed and a section removed for the mounting. If a bezel or prong box is to be used, it should be ready to assemble to the shank before the shank is sawed. When using bezels, they must extend above the supporting metal to permit the bezel edge to be burnished over the stone (see Fig. 235A). Shanks fitted to bezels are filed to fit the outer curve of the bezel or are filed on an angle to fit flush with the bezel underedge or flat surface (see Fig. 242).

Ring shanks that are to have a bezel cup or flat plate attached to the top or viewing surface should be finished with a flat section on the shank. The soldered ring is placed in a hand vise with just the amount of shank to be removed protruding from the jaws. The protruding portion is filed flat and level with the jaws of the vise (see Fig. 242A). It is then ready for the attachment of the bezel cup.

Additional support for the cup is possible if the shank is sawed open and the ends bent back over the shank slightly, and up around the bezel to form the trim. The shank is soldered on both sides under the cup (see Fig. 242).

Bezels mounted on the curved surface of a ring made of sheet metal must be filed on a half-round file to match the curve of the metal. The bezel cannot be soldered in place on the flat metal and then bent to ring shape (see Fig. 125).

Commercial heads and other prong boxes should be obtained or made before sawing an opening in the shank. The mounting or setting is measured and the distance marked on the ring side equally on each side of the soldered joint. The cut should be inside the scribed mark

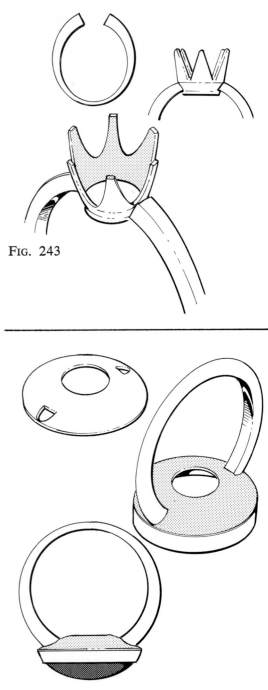

FIG. 243

FIG. 244

on the ring, so that the ends can be filed to a snug fit. Tapered shank ends must be determined for the correct angle before sawing through the shank. The opening must be sawed straight through the shank at the narrowest part and the ends then filed to a snug fitting angle (see Fig. 243).

A small groove can be made around the base of the head so that the shank is held with slight tension and does not slip off of the head during soldering (see Fig. 243). When soldering, the head is placed upside down on the charcoal block with the shank looped above the head so that the torch does not melt the prongs before the sections are soldered.

Underbezels

Instead of a mounting simply perched on or inserted in a shank, underbezels can be added to rings to give a more substantial appearance. The underbezel is a flat section of metal which is domed or otherwise formed to a shallow dish shape. Its outer circumference must equally match that of the bezel (see Fig. 244). If the stone is opaque, a thin plate of metal may be used to separate the two bezels as an aid to soldering. Translucent stones require an open area under the stone for light to be refracted through the stone. The bezel is constructed and then mated with the underbezel. The undersurface of the bezel and the edge of the underbezel must be sanded on a flat surface to be sure that they will make perfect contact when soldered. After soldering, small holes are drilled in the underbezel for the shank. These should be just large enough to permit tight insertion of the shank ends. If preferred, the shank can be filed to fit the outer undrilled surface of the underbezel and held in place by tension while soldering. When the soldering is completed, a half-round file is used to make an opening in the center of the underbezel. The curve of the opening should match the curve or radius of the inner ring opening.

CHAPTER 15

Appliqué

APPLIQUÉ CONSISTS OF LAYING ONE METAL ON another to give an added dimension (see Fig. 245). The appliqué may be of wire, silver, shot, scrap pieces of metal, or sawed and filed sections of metal—plain, textured, or domed. Pieces may be applied flush with the surface of the baseplate, partially overlapping open sections, standing on edge or wrapped around the baseplate before attaching underneath (see Figs. 246, and 246 A, B, and C). The shape of the appliqué sections may be as varied as the outline of the baseplate. Layers or plates of contrasting metal, treated in various ways such as texturing, doming, or piercing can be used in one article if desired.

Appliqué articles can be made by sawing out a central or inner portion of the metal and filing the edges of the opening smooth. The edges of the section removed are also filed. The piece is then placed over the opening but in a slightly rotated position, reversed or as desired. Where the sawed piece overlaps the opening, flux is applied, and the removed section is soldered in this position (see Fig. 247).

Appliqué sections may also be partially assembled with higher-melting-point solder and then attached to the baseplate with solder of a lower melting point. This makes possible more intricate fabrications.

Twenty-gauge metal is preferred for the appliqué section; however, in some abstract articles the possibility of using varying gauges of metals in one article should not be overlooked. The baseplate metal gauge may be any desired thickness.

Wire used as the appliqué material can, before applying, be twisted, coiled, or flattened with a hammer in different areas for unusual effects.

Soldering

Domed or formed sections should be sanded so that the contact points have a flush instead of a knife-edge contact on the surface. This permits the solder to have a larger attachment surface and removes the possibility of melting small extensions when soldering (see Fig. 248).

Solder must be applied to the underside of flat sections, or to the sanded flat surfaces of formed sections before they are attached to the baseplate (see Figs. 249 and 249A). In this process, called sweating or tinning, the undersurface is sanded, cleaned, and coated with

FIG. 245 Pin appliqué, sterling silver and Chatham emerald crystal.
By Sharr Choate.

FIG. 246 Necklace and earrings, appliqué, sterling silver.
By Sharr Choate.

flux. Small squares of solder are placed at random on the metal, which is then heated so that the solder flows over the entire surface, leaving it completely coated with a thin film of solder.

The tinned section is placed, tinned side down, on the fluxed second section. The outline is scribed lightly on the second section for alignment and the two sections clamped or wired together. The second section should be fluxed only inside the scribed line; this prevents the flow of solder on any extending or protruding areas that are part of the design. The two

sections are placed together on a section of metal sheet such as steel, thick aluminum, copper, or brass wide enough to support the entire piece. The metal sheet should be heavy enough so that it will not sag from heat when suspended from two firebricks.

When the torch flame is applied from below, the tinned section will settle in place as the proper temperature is reached. The sections may be placed also on a soldering web or tripod for support during the soldering step. If the metals are not held with clamps or binding wire during soldering, but simply permitted to

FIG. 246A Pin, appliqué, sterling silver.
By Sharr Choate.

FIG. 246B Pin and earrings, appliqué, sterling silver.
By Sharr Choate.

FIG. 246C Pin, appliqué, 14k gold and rubies.
By Sharr Choate.

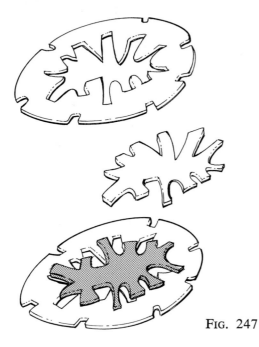

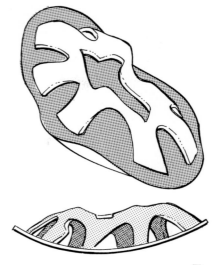

FIG. 248

FIG. 247

settle into place, it may be necessary to use the pusher rod to move the upper section into an exact position while the solder is at the flowing stage. Binding wires and clamps must be removed before dipping the soldered piece in the pickling solution.

Contact points of shaped or domed sections can be tinned before attaching or, if desired, the solder can be applied to the contact points at the time of attaching. The main purpose of coating the underside with the solder is to eliminate the time-consuming and surface-marring job of removing excess solder from the

seams that will be visible when the article is completed.

Soldering to gold sheet

If silver is to be appliquéd on gold or vice versa, silver solder is always used, as gold solder melts at a higher degree of temperature than silver sheet. If yellow and white golds are to be combined in one article, the yellow gold solder, which has a lower melting point and same karat content as the article, is used. The solder coating should be even and not lumpy under the plate so that the plate will lie flat. Uneven sur-

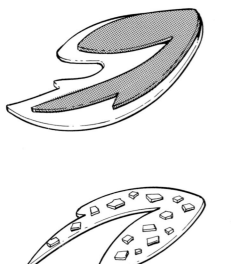

Fig. 249

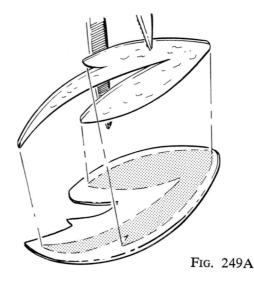

FIG. 249A

faces are always sanded before soldering to the baseplate. Whenever possible, appliqué sections should be clamped or wired to the baseplate for soldering in order to prevent shifting of position as the torch flame is applied.

Soldering to curved surfaces

Metal sections to be attached to a curved or domed surface can be held in position for soldering with a small amount of gum tragacanth (a substance used to hold enamels in position during firing). The mixture should be used sparingly with just enough to hold the metal in position. When soldering wire, the solder is placed along one side of the wire and the torch applied from either side or from underneath.

Domed sections soldered into dished or sunken sections should have the contact points filed flat to match. When two convex sections are soldered together, the edges of both sections

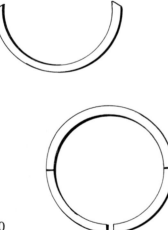

FIG. 250

should be filed flat for greater contact (see Fig. 250).

Finishing

The baseplate should be completely finished before soldering the appliqué sections to it. After the soldering is completed it will be impossible to buff and polish small intricate areas without damaging the appliquéd sections. Only light touch-up buffing and polishing are necessary.

Adding gemstone mountings

When gemstones are added to the appliquéd article, appropriate mounting devices for the stones, such as bezels, prongs, cups, etc., should be planned in advance and soldered along with the appliqué sections or subsequently with a lower melting point solder. Bezels may be prefabricated with a hard solder and attached to the baseplate with medium or easy-flow solder.

Extra caution must be used when burnishing bezels or prongs down over gemstones so that the surrounding metal is not damaged by the burnishing tools. Small intricate areas are difficult to rework without damaging adjacent areas with the finishing tools.

Removal of sections

If a section must be removed for any reason, the entire piece is first coated with flux so that solder will flow easily, and while the torch is applied to the metal the section can be lifted up off of the baseplate. Sections which are soldered flat or flush with a baseplate need not be fluxed, but simply heated and slid sideways for removal.

CHAPTER 16

Metal Inlay

MARRIED METALS, EVEN UPON CLOSE EXAM-
ination, give the impression that various metals
are merely etched into a basic metal, but in
reality the same saw-and-fit technique is used
as for wood inlay. However, there are several
techniques especially for metal inlay as follows:

Basic metal inlay

Thick metals, 12- to 14-gauge, are required for
the basic metal inlay technique. A metal section
is scribed, sawed, filed to shape, and placed
on a second section of metal. The outline of
the portion to be mated is scribed onto the
second section, sawed outside the outline, and
filed to form a perfect fit with the first section.
The remaining portion of the design is then
sawed out and filed (see Figs. 251 and 251A).
The second section of the metal is placed on a
third section, and the mating area of the pieces
is scribed in the same manner until all the pieces
are completed. Each section, one at a time,
must be sawed outside the scribed lines and
filed to fit. Because joints require a very close
fit, it is impossible to stack metal and saw it in
one cut with the idea that the pieces can be
counterchanged. The design may be started

in the center or at the edge, as long as each
section is fitted to the preceding section.

The sections must be filed to form matching
perpendicular edges (see Fig. 252). The edges
are then coated with flux and the sections
placed together on an asbestos sheet and held
with small steel pins. Flux is added on the
surface along all the joints and small paillons
of solder are placed in the flux approximately
¼ inch apart (see Fig. 253). As the metals are
heated, the soldering rod is used to keep the
solder close to the joints and to spread it into
areas where it is needed. This very important
tool is also used to turn the metal assemblage
over to check for any areas on the reverse side
that may require additional solder.

When the soldering is complete, the soldered
section is held in place on the wooden surface
or bench top by placing small brads around
the outer edges and below the surface of the
metal just enough to prevent slippage of the
metal as the file makes contact (see Fig. 254).

The metal is filed down on both sides to a
16- to 18-gauge thickness. Large files 12 to 14
inches long are used in the coarse cuts to remove excess metal and solder quickly. The
larger files take a bigger "bite" with each

FIG. 251 Pin and earrings, metal inlay, sterling silver, nickel silver, brass, copper, and lapis lazuli (eyes).
By Sharr Choate.

pass over the metal and thus minimize the filing time considerably.

If stone inlay is to be used a backing sheet is necessary for support of the thin stone sections (see Figs. 255, 280, and 280A). For this purpose either a sheet of metal soldered to the underside of the inlay section, or a layer of gemstone inserted between the backing sheet and the inlay section can be used. If a gemstone layer is used, the parts are riveted to-

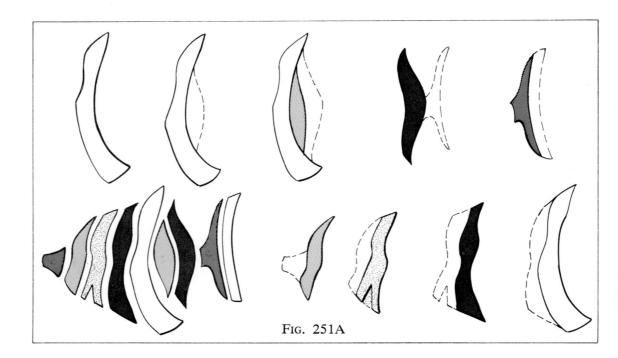

FIG. 251A

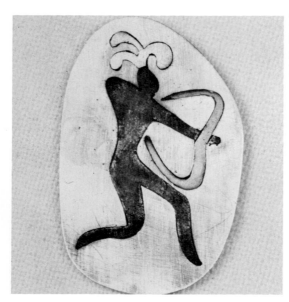

FIG. 252 Sample metal inlay (unfinished), approximately 1¼ by 1 inch, showing fit of metals, sterling silver, copper, nickel silver.
By Sharr Choate.

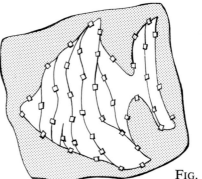

FIG. 253

gether, giving added weight and bulk (see Figs. 279 and 279A).

The sanding, buffing, and polishing steps all follow the basic silversmithing procedures.

Fitting metal into metal

A metal section is removed from the center or other areas of a metal sheet by drilling and piercing the metal with a jeweler's saw. The section left with the opening is then placed over another piece of metal, and the sawed and filed outline of the opening in the top piece is transferred to the undersection. The scribed area on the undersection is then sawed and filed to fit the opening in the first piece (see Fig. 256). At this point the piece can be left as is and soldered, or drilled and pierced for a stone inlay section. The same step may be repeated for additional contrasting sections of metal as desired.

FIG. 254

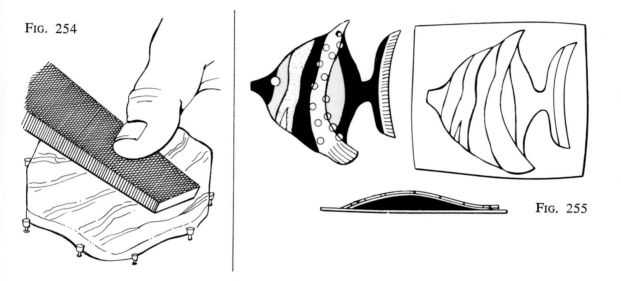

FIG. 255

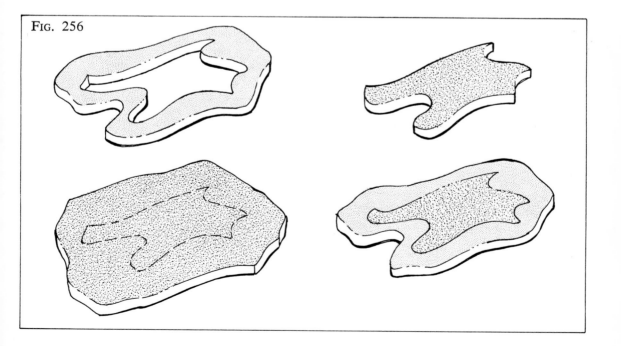

FIG. 256

Inlaying metal strip

A metal strip may be inlaid in another metal by making a single saw cut in a piece of metal and inserting the strip on edge (see Figs. 257, 258 and 259). The smallest hole possible is drilled to accept a jeweler's saw blade. The blade size, determined in advance, dictates the drill size. A single saw cut is made on a scribed line and finished with the saw as necessary, for there can be only a simple single forward cut as filing is impossible.

The thickness of the saw blade is measured and a contrasting metal is rolled to a dimension slightly less than that of the saw blade. If a dealer's stock of metals is depended upon, it is necessary to check the chart to determine the optimum combination of sawblade and metal gauge required to fill the saw cut properly. For this purpose a chart is furnished in the Appendix which gives pertinent information as to the saw blade sizes and metal gauges that work well together for the best fit (it also gives wire and drill sizes).

The metal is cut into strips a little wider than the thickness of the metal to be inlaid, and a strip is inserted edgewise down into the saw cut (see Fig. 259). Small pliers are necessary to push the metal down into the saw cut, and to bend the strip around any curves and corners in the design. This technique is especially valuable when making small lines, monograms, and any other fine line detail.

Inlaying contrasting metal strips

Metal inlay with crossing lines of contrasting metal may be accomplished by first soldering one metal into a saw cut. The saw cuts for the other metal are then made and soldered into place with a lower melting point solder. This procedure prevents the pieces from falling apart (see Fig. 259A). The same technique may be used for inlaying the metal into wooden sections; however, very little of the metal strip should protrude above the wood surface which would be damaged by considerable filing of the metal.

The hardwood surface is incised with a sharp knife to a depth slightly less than the width of the wire so that the section is not weakened. The wire is bent by finger pressure or with

FIG. 257   Belt buckle, metal strip inlay, sterling silver with copper.
By Sharr Choate.

round-nose, flat-nose, and snipe-nose pliers to match the shape of the design on the wood. It is cut to length with end-cutting pliers to make a square cut. The wire, placed on edge along the wood cut, is hammered down into the wood until flush with the surface. No cement is used. The wood is sanded smooth, followed by finer sanding with steel wool, and then stained, oiled, and waxed.

Wood and stone sections can be inlaid with small rounds of metal appearing as circles or dots on the surface (see Fig. 278). The wood and stone are drilled, and wire, purchased in sizes (gauges) to match the drill sizes, is cut into short lengths and inserted in the drilled holes. These are cemented in the base with epoxy adhesive. After drying, the surface is filed and sanded until the slight protrusion of wire is flush with the base surface. The small inserts can be varied if tubing is used in place of a single solid rod. A contrasting metal rod or wire is inserted into the tubing, and both parts inserted and cemented as a unit. Tubing by itself can be used; however, the inner portion will have to be filled with sanding dust and epoxy mixed into a paste.

Fig. 258 Pin, strip and rod inlay, sterling silver, copper, nickel silver.
By Sharr Choate.

Inlaying wire

Holes for inlaid circles of metal are drilled according to the wire diameter to be used, and short sections of wire are inserted into the drilled holes (see Figs. 259 and 278). The drilled holes in the metal may also be plugged with a ground-up grout of gemstones.

When selecting wire sizes they should be matched as closely as possible to drill dimensions to ensure a snug fit. Drills are available in a greater range of sizes than can be obtained in wire. A small inexpensive ½-inch micrometer is very handy for checking drill sizes, wire diameters, and saw blade thicknesses.

Solder inlay

Metals can also be inlaid with solder alone. Silver solder is used in gold, copper and steel, and brass solder is used in copper, steel, and iron. The inlay areas are chased into the surface (see Chapter 26) or etched (see Chapter 20). Large areas should be avoided and the inlay confined to small areas and lines. If a large area is required, sheet solder, preferably slightly thicker in dimension than the depth of the excavation, is used. Thin narrow grooves or lines, etc., are fluxed and the solder paillons placed along them. The steel soldering rod is used to spread the solder and to assist in pushing it into its proper place. After pickling and rinsing in running water, the surface is sanded

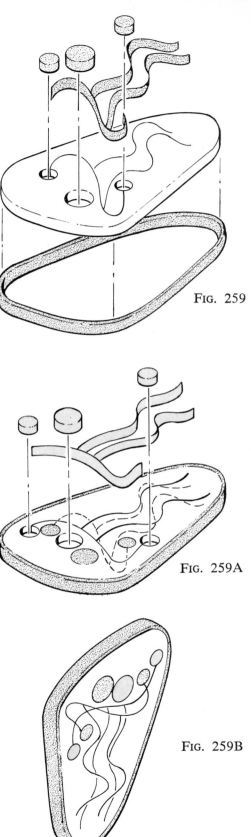

Fig. 259

Fig. 259A

Fig. 259B

to remove any excess solder before proceeding to the regular metal finishing steps. The inlaid metal will stand out in sharp contrast.

Surface metal "inlay"

A surface "inlay," giving the appearance of true inlay, can be produced by coating the design areas on the clean metal surface with soldering flux. The flux is applied in the desired areas, either with a small camel-hair brush or with a rubber stamp dipped in flux and pressed against the metal surface. Special designs on the rubber stamp are made by carving one surface of an ordinary pink eraser (see Fig. 401). Solder is placed in each fluxed area and the entire metal article is heated from underneath. The solder will be contained in the fluxed areas and will buff and polish to a bright contrast with the metal surface (see Fig. 400).

FIG. 260A   Pin, metal inlay, Toledo, 14k white gold.
Toledo, Spain.

FIG. 260   Cuff links, Toledo metal inlay, 14k gold.
Toledo, Spain.

Toledo wire inlay

Gold and silver wire hammered into grooves is the same as damascene work except that damascene applies to steel and iron only and is never used for jewelry (see Figs. 260 and 260A).

The inlay consists of filling minute grooves in the surface of annealed 16- to 18-gauge silver or copper sheet with finely drawn wire (see Figs. 261 and 262). The grooves are made extremely close together in one direction only with a fine-pointed or line graver if a solid mass of contrasting metal is desired. The

grooves on pieces executed in Toledo, Spain—which is famous for this type of metalry—are as close as 5 lines to $\frac{1}{32}$ inch, similar to the grooves cut with a #8-12 line graver.

Single grooves of any size may be cut in the metal for one wire inlay (see Fig. 262). The grooves for the wire are always cut in the metal surface before assembling any sections. The order of procedure is forming, grooving, assembling, soldering (including findings), buffing, and polishing all except the grooved surface.

After cleaning the buffing and polishing compounds from the metal, the grooved surface is oxidized to a dense black color for greater contrast with the wire inlay. Metal borders, undersides, and findings should not be oxidized; only the grooved area is painted with the solution using a small camel-hair brush.

The fine wire is usually drawn to 34-36 gauge. It fits the groove properly if it is slightly larger than the depth of the groove (see Fig. 262). The wire coil is held in front with the wire extended back toward the work (see Fig. 261). With a small planishing hammer, the wire is gently burnished or tapped into the grooves to the desired length. Because of the small size of the wire, it can be easily cut by holding it under the hammer head with one hand and tugging at the coil with the other; a slight tension snaps the wire quickly, but if the hammer is tilted the unworked surface will be damaged.

Hammering on a piece of steel placed over the wire in the groove will prevent marring the surface of the metal. Should marking of the oxidized surface inadvertently occur, it can be touched up with a Scotch stone and reoxidized by applying the coloring solution with a paintbrush.

When the grooves have been filled, a few decorative cuts with a round or lozenge graver can be made in the concentrated inlaid portions (see Figs. 263 and 260).

An alternate method of inlay consists of piercing a metal sheet and sawing out on an angle the section that is to be inlaid with wire. This section is soldered to a backing sheet and, following the proper procedure given previously, the wire is hammered into the grooved areas (see Fig. 264). The grooved section may be made separately and inserted in a polished bezel or prong mounting when completed.

FIG. 262

FIG. 263

FIG. 261

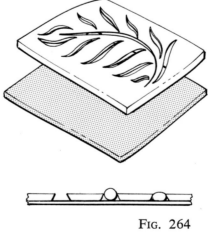

FIG. 264

FIG. 265 Cuff links, mokume, metal lamination, four bars soldered together and sliced, sterling silver, nickel silver, copper.
By Sharr Choate.

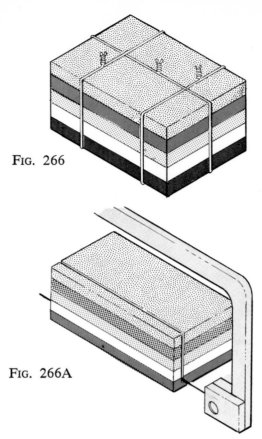

FIG. 266

FIG. 266A

Mokume (wood grain)

Mokume is a Japanese technique for metal inlay in which two to six different metals (of equal or different gauges as desired) are stacked to form a sandwich (see Fig. 266). After soldering the metal layers into a single stack, the sandwich is sawed into thin slices across the layers (see Fig. 266). These thin slices can be treated in various ways to give effects that are unattainable by means of the regular metal inlay technique.

Gold, silver, copper, brass, bronze, and nickel silver can be used all together or combined in contrasting sets. Usually, small strips of 14-gauge metal approximately 1 by 3 inches are used to form the sandwich (see Figs. 265 and 265A).

The metals are cleaned and placed in a warm pickling solution which is brought to near boiling point. The fingers should not be allowed to touch the metal as it is removed from the

pickling solution and rinsed in running water. To ensure a clean, greaseless surface so that the solder will adhere completely, the metal is scrubbed in warm detergent suds and checked under running water to see that the water covers the surface in a solid film, not in small spots or bubbles. Each strip must be carefully held by the edge, so that fingers do not contaminate the surface as they are dried.

Before stacking for soldering, one surface only of each strip is completely covered with flux and solder filings sprinkled on this surface. It is then set aside to dry. An excess amount of solder is not a problem when soldering the metal layers as it tends to appear as a thin layer of metal giving added contrast.

When the strips are completely dry they are stacked together so that the metals alternate in contrasting colors. A metal with a higher melting point should be placed on the top so that the heat from the torch will not break down this metal before the others have heated sufficiently.

The complete stack is held together with

FIG. 265A Cuff links and bar, mokume, metal lamination set in nickel silver border, sterling silver, copper.
By Sharr Choate.

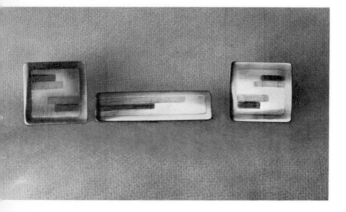

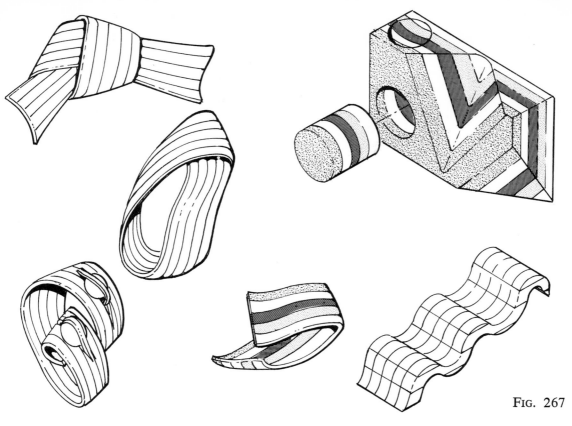

FIG. 267

iron binding wire, and as it is heated, pressure is applied to help settle the metals down into a closely welded sandwich. Heat is applied uniformly by continually sweeping the stack with a brush flame until the bright solder seam between each layer indicates that the solder is flowing. When the stack has cooled, it is dipped in the pickling solution and rinsed in water.

Thinner contrasting layers of metal, approximately 22 gauge and 2 by 4 inches in size can be used to give an entirely different effect if two stacks, after soldering, are stacked one on the other and soldered again with medium solder.

The stack is sliced with a hacksaw into strips $\frac{1}{16}$-inch thick (16-18 gauge) which are rolled out to approximately 20-gauge ($\frac{1}{32}$ inch) thick (see Figs. 266, 267, and 267A). The strips are sawed, filed, and used singly, soldered to each other, or to other layered sections, then twisted, rolled, folded, grooved, domed, or sunk from the underside with dapping-die blocks, punches, and sinking hammers into irregular lumps which are standed or filed through the

FIG. 267A

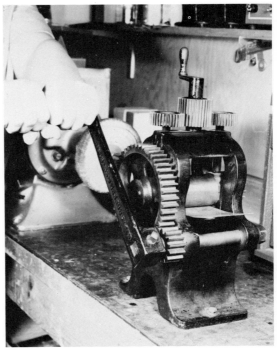

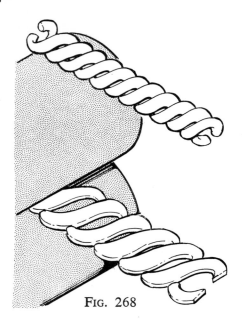

FIG. 268

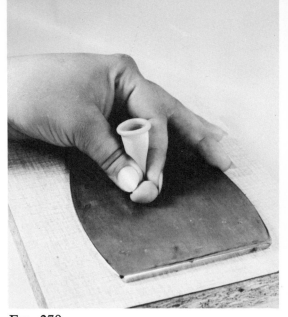

FIG. 270

layers to show wavy or concentric metal patterns. The piece can also be filed to a long taper along a side or an edge or across an end to show the metal combinations, and when heavier stacks are sawed on an angle, the slices will also give interesting effects.

If a rolling mill is not available, regular forging hammers, cross or dome-faced, will flatten the metal and force it into different directions for additional variations.

Various shapes of metal burs and grinding wheels are useful in finishing the metal. They integrate the laminated surface, giving many different effects.

The thin-layered metal sandwich, used unsliced as a laminated sheet, can be worked in several ways to reveal the different metals (see Fig. 267. Holes can be drilled, either straight or angularly through the thin pieces, and conical

FIG. 269   Cuff links, amalgam inlay with jasper as base, sterling silver.

depressions can be made in the surfaces with large drills or mounted grinding stones. When drilling holes through the metals, the drill will not grab or "hang up" if lubricated with white vaseline.

Wires of various metals can be soldered together and then twisted, braided, and coiled, after which they are hammered or rolled. The small coils are used "as is" and larger ones are sawed into sections and re-formed in various ways (see Fig. 268).

The completely worked and assembled article is buffed, polished, and oxidized as described for other metal articles. Because the various metals react differently to oxidizing and patinizing solutions, additional effects can be produced by the finishing processes.

Gold amalgam inlay

Gold inlay in silver is accomplished by filing fine gold into a powder, and then mixing or triturating it with an equal amount of mercury by weight. Trituration is a method of blending another element with mercury. This can only be done with force within a closed container. The two ingredients can be placed in a large capsule and vigorously shaken or placed in a rubber finger stall (used for finger injuries) that is twisted to prevent leakage, and kneaded on a smooth hard surface (see Fig. 270). *Mercury vapors are extremely toxic and must be handled in a well-ventilated area.*

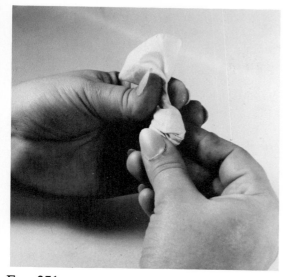

FIG. 271

The amalgam must be applied to the metal surface with a carrier so that it is handled as little as possible with the fingers. Carriers can be plastic or wooden tweezers or sticks that have a flat surface on which to carry the mix to the metal surface (see Figs. 272 and 273). The mixture is spread over the grooves that have been made in the surface with graving tools or over the excavations that have been made with etching solutions. After the article is allowed to set for several days it is placed on a rigid metal sheet and heated slowly from underneath to evaporate the mercury. The metal is then gradually heated to the regular annealing color. Excess inlay material is sanded

off after cooling. The surface is burnished and then gently polished.

Silver amalgam inlay

Amalgam filling material, similar to dental amalgam, contains finely powdered silver and is mixed with mercury (5 parts silver to 8 parts mercury by weight) and burnished into a surface groove or etched indentation (see Figs. 269–273). The powdered silver and mercury can be mixed into a paste with a small mortar and pestle, or the ingredients can be placed in a small rubber finger stall. To mix the two ingredients, the end of the finger stall is twisted and the bulbous section is rolled on a bench top (see Fig. 270). (The ingredients could also be placed in a large capsule and shaken vigorously.) The mix is then transferred to a small circle of cotton called a squeeze cloth which in turn is twisted to hold the paste and to squeeze the excess mercury out through the threads of the fabric (see Fig. 271). The amalgam is transferred to the metal in the same manner as described for inlay in gold (see page 148). The metal is then set aside to harden for several days, after which it is sanded (if necessary) and buffed and polished.

Niello

Niello is another surface inlay often found in silver jewelry made in Thailand. The charcoal black inlay is a metal alloy mixed with sulfur

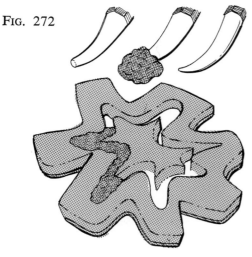

FIG. 272

FIG. 273

FIG. 274   Pin, metal-stone inlay, niello, sterling silver.
Siamese (Thai) design.

to a grainy consistency. It is spread over the metal in excavations made either by etching, graving, or unit construction such as cloisonné (see Fig. 274). After the areas are filled with the mix, the metal is placed in a furnace, and heated until the niello mix has melted. The surface is smoothed over with a metal rod and removed to cool. It is filed smooth, the metal is reheated slightly, and then burnished with the regular steel burnisher which has been dipped in oil. The final finish is accomplished by buffing.

The niello mixture consists of 1 ounce of fine silver, 2 ounces of pure copper, and 3 ounces of lead. The silver and copper are melted in a crucible, after which the lead is added. The molten mix is poured into a ceramic or earthenware vessel containing approximately 8 ounces of sulfur. The mixture is covered until it cools.

The action of the constituents will permit the sulfur to absorb the metal so that a grainy metallic powder is produced. The grains should be crushed to a smaller size before adding them to the prepared metal. They are then spread over the clean prepared metal to approximately the thickness of the back edge of a pocket knife or 16-gauge metal. The inlay material is sprinkled with borax and placed on a section of thin sheet iron which is then put in a heated furnace until it melts. It should never be allowed to become red-hot because this overheats the lead which will corrode the silver or gold base metal. While the niello is melting, it should be smoothed out with a steel drill rod similar to the pusher rod used for soldering. When melted, the metal is removed from the furnace and cooled. The inlay area is leveled with fine files until the inlay is flush with the surrounding metal. The article is returned to the furnace and heated until slightly hotter than can be borne by the bare fingers. It is then removed from the furnace and quickly burnished with the burnishing tool. A little oil on the burnishing surface of the tool will aid in closing up any bubbles in the niello. The final finish is made by gently buffing the surface with Tripoli and, if desired, polishing with tin oxide or rouge.

JEWELRY CREATIONS
BY SHARR CHOATE

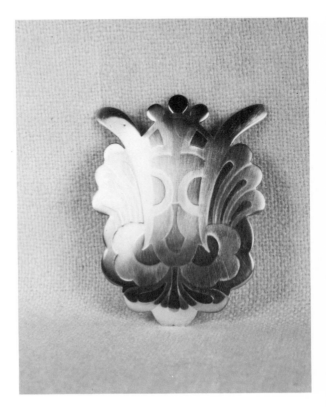

Above

Pin, sterling silver and copper strings.

Right

Pin, metal inlay, sterling silver, copper, bronze, nickel silver.

Above
Pin, repoussé, sterling silver.

Left
Pin, repoussé and stone inlay, sterling silver and turquoise.

Below
Pin and earrings, chased and repoussé, 14k gold.

Left
Pendant, abstract Christmas tree, single-piece construction, 14k gold with jelly opals.

Below
Pin, appliqué sterling silver.

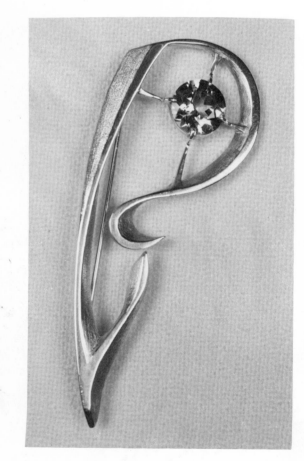

Above
Pin, forged-assembly sterlg silver with ruby corundum.

Left
Pin, contour-shaped from 8-gauge metal, sterling silver with aquamari.

Color Plates

PENDANT. Pierced contoured 14k gold and sterling silver with Chatham emerald crystals and rutilated quartz.
By Sharr Choate with free-form stone cut by Gus Mollin.

RING. Forged, 14k gold with amethysts.
By Sharr Choate.

CHESSMEN. Sheet construction with ebony bases, sterling silver with enamel.
By Ellen Brøker.

PIN AND EARRINGS. Metal inlay, sterling silver, nickel silver, bronze, brass, copper.
By Sharr Choate.

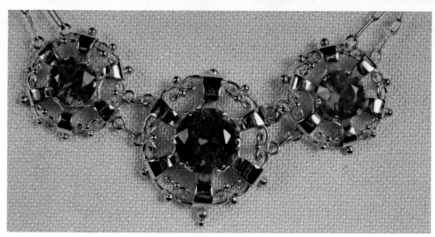

NECKLACE. Scrollwork with faceted ruby corundum, 14k.

By Hakon Jonnson.

PIN. Scrollwork, 14k, Montana gold agate and black jade.

By Alberta Best.

PLATE. Pierced and forged, feather inlay to transmit light (inlay area sealed with resin), brass.

By Sharr Choate.

PIN. Florentine shapes, 14k gold.

By Sharr Choate.

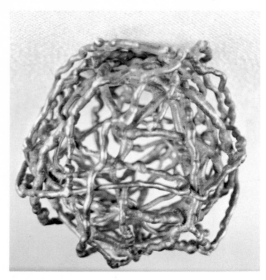

DECORATIVE BALL. Fused wire, silver.
By Hakon Jonnson.

RING. Sheet and bezel, 14k gold
and Australian opal.
By Ellen Brøker.

HAIRPIECE. Half domes on wire and
sheet, sterling silver and enamel.
By Ellen Brøker.

PIN. Chased, repoussé, 14k gold
and diamonds.
By Ellen Brøker.

PENDANT. Wire, beads and bezel, 14k gold with Austra-lian opal cabochon.
By Hakon Jonnson.

NECKLACE. Wire, 14k gold, jadeite.
By Alberta Best.

CANDELABRA. Various types of metalwork, sterling silver with various faceted stones.
By Hakon Jonnson.

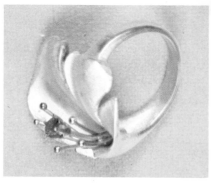

RING. 14k gold and sterling silver with ruby.
By Wayne Smith.

JEWEL BOX. Various types of metalwork, sterling silver, agate.
By Henrietta Norton.

BRACELET. Filigree, silver.
By Hakon Jonnson.

RING. Flat wire and beads, 14k gold with man-made emerald faceted.
By Hakon Jonnson.

Above
Pendant, chased sterling silver.

Left
Bracelet, pierced and forged,
sterling silver.

Above right
Pin, forged sterling
with alexandrites
(synthetic).

Right
Pin, chasing and
repoussé, sterling
silver.

Above
Pin, repoussé and
half-domes, sterling
silver.

JEWELRY CREATIONS
BY LEADING CRAFTSMEN

Necklace, spider, wire construction and cast, 14k gold with free-form amethyst.
By Alberta Best.

Above
Necklace, scrollwork, 14k gold with plume agate.
By Alberta Best.

Left
Pendant, doublet ruby-blue sapphire cushion stones in 14k gold, double bezel.
By Hakon Jonnson.

Opposite above
Pin, wire construction, 14k gold.
By Wayne Smith.

Opposite below
Pin, pierced and domed, sterling silver and jelly opals.
By Wayne Smith.

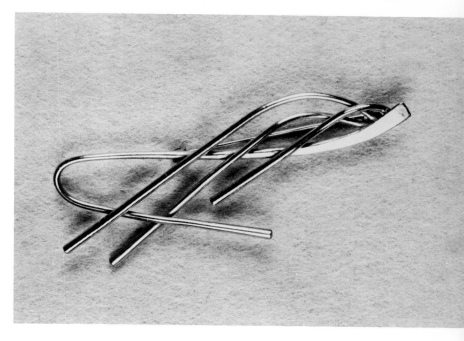

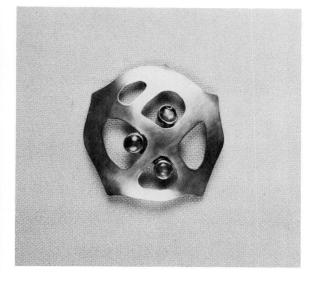

Necklace, scrollwork wire and metal inlay, sterling silver and coral.
By Wayne Smith.

Pin, scroll and pierced metal, sterling silver with sapphire.
German design.

Pin, filigree, sterling silver.
Chilean design.

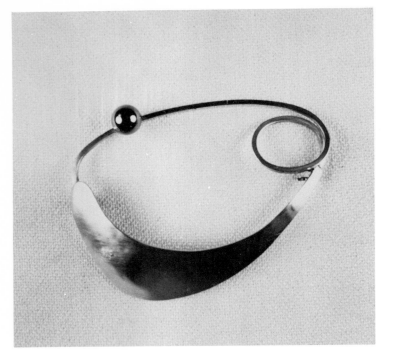

Above
Pin, penguin, forged and scrollwork, sterling silver
and black pearl.
By Wayne Smith.

Above right
Pin, scrollwork and forging, sterling silver.
Danish design.

Right
Ring, piece construction, 14k gold with pearl,
ruby (synthetic), and blue spinel.
By Hakon Jonnson.

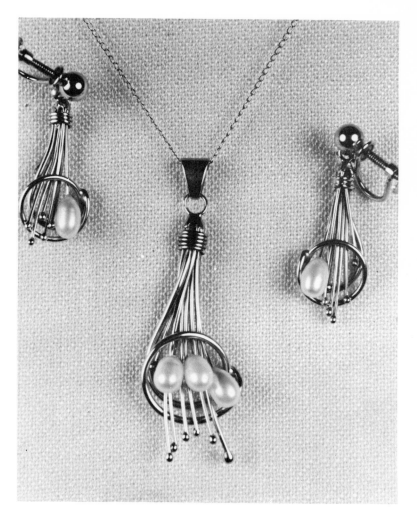

Above
Pendant and earrings, scroll and wirework, 14k gold with seed pearls.
By Hakon Jonnson.

Left
Pin, 14k gold with jade.
By Hakon Jonnson.

Left
Necklace, textured metal, 14k white gold and topaz.
By Wayne Smith.

Below left
Ring, piece construction, 14k gold with amethyst.
By Hakon Jonnson.

Below right
Ring, florentined and inlaid gold in ruby (synthetic), 14k gold.
By Hakon Jonnson.

CHAPTER 17

Stone Inlay—Channel Work

METAL SURFACES CAN BE INLAID WITH THIN sections of gemstone or with prefabricated sections of contrasting gemstone materials. The inlay is usually surrounded by a grout made from small chips and dust of the same material mixed with a bonding substance such as epoxy.

Stone selection

The stone selected is usually in direct contrast to the metal. Abalone shell, used extensively in Mexican inlay articles, is effective on curved surfaces (see Fig. 12).

Stones with a hardness of 4 to 5 on Mohs' scale are best for inlay. Translucent stones should not be used unless they can be ground to fit an area without using grout for a fill-in. Translucent crystalline materials will turn to a powdery white when crushed for grout mixture, regardless of the original color of the stone. When grout is required the material should be opaque.

Open areas between the stone inlay pieces and the metal border are filled with a grout made from the same inlay material. Small chips and pieces of the stone are hammered into a fine powder and mixed with a waterproof cement. A small amount of waterproof writing-ink, close in color to the inlay stone, is added to the grout. The grout is mixed and immediately transferred to the open areas. The hammer head is used to push the grout down in the open areas, thereby compressing it. When the grout has hardened, it is ground off smooth with the surface of the metal and inlay stone. Pumice blocks or India grinding stone are used to grind the stone surface while the inlaid article is held under running water. The stone is polished when the metal is polished.

The stone does not require a high polish as a satin finish is desired for contrast with the highly polished metal.

Stones usable for inlay and grout are available from lapidary dealers and include lapis lazuli, turquoise, shattuckite, malachite, jaspers, chrysocolla, travertine, and massive azurite.

Areas that can be filled with a single section of stone that has been ground to fit the opening perfectly can be filled with almost any kind of gemstone material. The most popular are jade, opal, amethyst, agate, chrysocolla, and small crystal-coated sections of natural material.

Mineral crystal specimens may be used for inlay if a slight bas-relief effect is desired. Small crystal coatings should be selected for the inlay, such as drusy coatings on a matrix or base mineral. The matrix or crust is ground away on the wet carborundum wheels as much as possible to reduce height, and then trimmed with a small lapidary trim saw to fit the area (see Figs. 275 and 228).

Various applications

Mating sections of stone such as intarsia types of lapidary may be joined together and then fitted into the opening in the metal surface (see Fig. 322B). The stone sections should be joined together with the edges perpendicular or angular if contours are small and varying. The gemstone sections should be completely fitted, cemented, and surface-finished prior to embedding them in the metal. Varying hardness

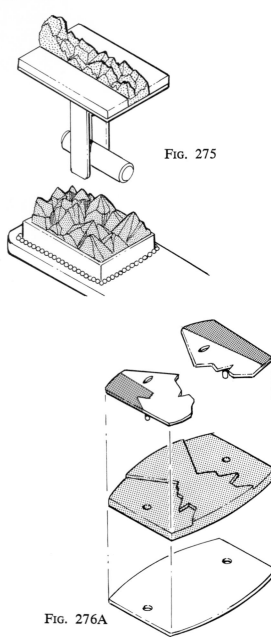

FIG. 275

FIG. 276A

Another method of stone inlay is to fold over partially a section of metal that has been previously filed and sanded so that a wedge of gemstone material can be inserted in the opening. The stone, before cementing in place, is ground as closely as possible to the metal outline to eliminate any excess grinding on the metal (see Figs. 278 and 278A).

All metalworking, including soldering of the findings on the metal backpiece must be completed before adding the gemstone inlay. All stone inlay requires a metal backing or a stone slab sandwiched between the front and back metal sections (see Figs. 279 and 279A). Because the extra support is essential, it is not feasible to attempt to inlay stone in open areas without a metal backing. The metal section is first drilled and pierced to remove unwanted areas, and the openings are filed smooth. Both surfaces of the metal and all edges are filed and sanded to leave as little metal finishing as possible to be done later on (see Figs. 280 and 280A).

Any stone similar to slate is slabbed in sections and used to separate the metal design from its backing sheet. This material must be sanded perfectly flat to the desired thickness before it is used with the metal to form the sandwich. The design section and the backing sheet are either cemented or riveted together with small sections of tubing soldered to the underside of the design section. The stone sandwich section and the meal backpiece are drilled to match the small tubing sections, and after assembling and cementing together, the

FIG. 276   Cuff links, stone-metal inlay, sterling silver and 14k gold with *piedra negra.* By Sharr Choate.

of the combinations of stones makes it impossible to delay any finishing of the stone until after it is placed in the metal.

The effect of metal inlaid in stone can be achieved by using the sandwich method with this same stone used as the inlay in the surface of the metal. The metal sections are cemented or riveted to the core stone and the metal back piece, and then the surface is filled with thin sections of the same gemstone material. This gives the appearance of etched stone with metal inlay (see Figs. 276, 276A, 277, 279, 279A, and 280).

FIG. 277   Pin, sandwich construction, sterling silver with malachite and *piedra negra*. By Sharr Choate.

small tubing is flared over the backpiece and filed smooth.

Wood and other inlay materials

Exotic woods such as ebony, rosewood, osage orange, and the more common hardwoods such as walnut, birch, mahogany, or any other wood chosen for grain or color can be used as a backing for metal fabrications or inlaid in the metal surface. The wood sections are glued to the metal surface or secured with small rivets made of small-diameter tubing soldered to the metal. Small tapered pins made by filing 22- to 24-gauge wire to a point after soldering to the metal are used to hold the wood to the surface. The wood is pressed against the pins until flush with the metal and, if desired, epoxy adhesive may be used as additional assurance that the wood will not separate from the metal.

These same hardwoods reduced to a fine sawdust and mixed with an epoxy adhesive into a paste can be used to fill in cavities, depressed areas, or cloisons in the metal. When the mixture has hardened, it is sanded down

FIG. 278A

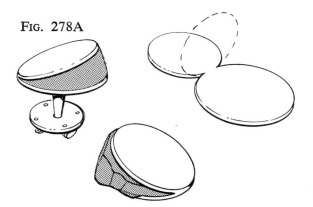

FIG. 278   Cuff links. *Left:* sandwich, sterling silver and lapis lazuli *Right:* metal and stone inserts in *piedra negra*.

has hardened, which takes an hour or so. The Plastic Marble is first mixed with a chosen color and when it has set slightly in three to four hours, it is kneaded and shaped. In another six hours it will have set up sufficiently to be cut to rough shapes with a knife or razor. When completely hardened. which requires approximately fourteen hours in all, it is sanded, and polished *by hand* because the heat generated by power wheels will soften the base. After sanding, it is polished with 4/0 emery paper.

FIG. 279 Pin, sandwich construction with inlaid metals with stones, sterling, nickel silver and bronze with turquoise and *piedra negra*. By Sharr Choate.

CHANNEL WORK

Channel work or stone inlay in metal frameworks is accomplished by constructing cells of

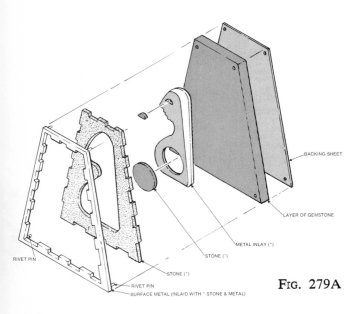

FIG. 279A

FIG. 280 Pin, stone inlay, sterling silver with malachite. By Sharr Choate.

to the metal surface, fine finished with steel wool, then oiled and waxed.

Other decorative inlay materials include random or free-form shapes of composition stone, resin fabricated pieces and small mosaics of stone, glass, or plastic segments. The composition stone consists of small pebbles (⅛ inch or smaller), bits of glass, etc., which are embedded in sealing wax, or wax used by the lapidaries. Another similar material is called Plastic Marble. The composition mix can be sanded to shape and polished as soon as it

FIG. 280A

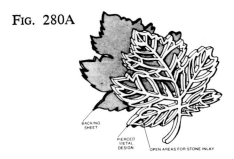

flat wire similar to those used in the cloisonné enameling technique.

Building the framework

The border is bent, curved to shape and stood on a pre-scribed line on a section of flat metal backing sheet (see Figs. 281 and 281A). Smaller lengths of flat wire are cut, filed, sanded, and bent to shape. When the wire sections have been formed, all the pieces are cleaned thoroughly, and the parts coated only on the contact edges and ends with a mixture of gum tragacanth adhesive, powdered flux, and solder filings.

The coated pieces are assembled on the metal backing sheet and carefully placed on a wire grid. Heat is directed to the underside of the metal and to the design side with a torch used in a brushing motion. The framework can also be soldered on a porous refrac-

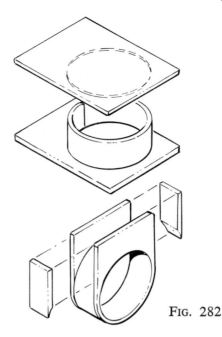

Fig. 282

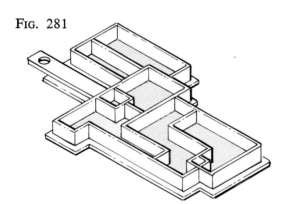

Fig. 281

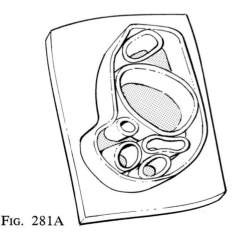

Fig. 281A

tory brick. When solder has flowed to the joints, the metal is pickled, rinsed, and checked for any sections requiring additional solder.

Constructing a channel ring

Finger rings constructed for channel work are made by forming a ring shank of 16-gauge flat wire or 18-gauge strip metal. Before soldering, two rectangles of 20-gauge matching metal are cut to fit over one half of the ring, extending above the curve of the ring approximately ⅛ inch (see Fig. 282). The ring shank and one sheet section are cleaned and fluxed. The ring shank is then placed with its joint on the flat metal, and the two parts soldered together. The half-round section is sawed out of the center of the ring, and the second flat piece is soldered to the opposite side of the ring shank in perfect alignment. The second half-round section metal is then sawed out of the ring center and the inner shank filed smooth and sanded (see Fig. 282).

Small pieces of 20-gauge strip metal are sawed and filed to fit the ends of the channel, and to form sections within the channel as desired. These pieces are fluxed and soldered into place. They are held in place with gum

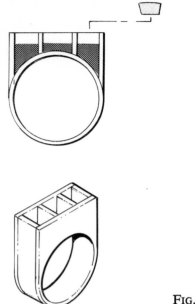

FIG. 283

tragacanth adhesive to prevent any movement when heat is applied.

Smaller sections can be formed by cutting a long strip, and notching it at intervals to fit a mating notched strip. The notches should be cut to a depth slightly beyond half the width of the metal, and narrower than the thickness of the metal, so that they can be filed slightly to provide a tight fit for each of the crosspieces (see Fig. 283). The assembled piece is coated with a flux and solder filing mix before it is placed in the channel and soldered. Angular compartments can be made by filing beveled ends on the crosspieces.

The flux and solder mixture combined with gum (see Chapter 27) will hold the pieces during soldering. To ensure that the adhesive is dry before soldering, the pieces may be placed under a heat lamp or in a moderately heated. oven for 10 to 15 minutes.

Filling the channels

Before grinding the inlay stone to any height, the compartments are partially filled with freshly mixed dental stone or casting plaster (see Fig. 283). This filler material provides a level base to support each stone, and eliminates the need to grind the stones to fit the curved bottoms of the compartments.

After the plaster has hardened, the stones are ground to fit the compartments or sections. There must be a slight taper toward the bottom which is ground flat. This is necessary in order to leave room for the cement that will hold the stone inlay in place.

Thin sections of gemstone, such as turquoise and chrysocolla, can be elevated to correct height by first filling areas with thin slab sections of plastic, inexpensive unpolished gemstone, as well as with dental stone. Such material is not visible, but it gives set stones the appearance of being much thicker.

The surface of the gemstone is not ground flush with the surrounding metal until after it is cemented in place and thoroughly dry. Clothespins or any other small clamps can be used to hold the stone with light pressure during the drying process. The stone and the metal are polished at the same time.

CHAPTER 18

Chasing and Repoussé

CHASING

CHASING AND REPOUSSÉ ARE DIFFERENT TREAT-ments of metal surfaces, though both refer to varying degrees of indentation. Chasing is the use of a short chisel-like tool which indents a prescribed line on the surface of flat metal to stress the main aspects of a design, and to define detailed areas. Repoussé forms the design from the underside, raising the metal into high or low relief which gives the appearance of shallow metal sculpture (see Figs. 284 and 284A).

Although both terms mean chasing, one term or the other is used to refer specifically to the particular technique used. Repoussé is also referred to as embossing. By using the tools for the two different techniques in surface design, outlining, detailing, decorating, and forming from the underside, various effects, either simple or complicated, can be achieved.

Metal preparation

Designs are transferred to the metal surface, which has been sanded but not buffed or polished. The surface is painted with artist's white casein or show card white paint (other coatings are called Grumbacher white or Chinese white) and, after the coating has dried, the design is drawn on the surface or transferred from tracing paper. The design is scribed into the metal surface and the coating scrubbed away with soap and water. The tools will move smoothly over the surface only if the metal is clean.

Chasing the viewing surface is done before the metal is domed or shaped. The metal is worked on a flat smooth metal base held in place with lead weights, small sandbags (3 inches square) or with any material that will not mar the surface (see Fig. 285). The metal could also be held by attaching it to a wooden board with small brads driven into the wood, approximately $\frac{1}{16}$ inch from the metal edge. The heads are removed from the brads with end-cutting pliers, and the small nails bent over the metal edge to hold it without marring or indenting the metal. Thin 20-gauge metal is preferred for chasing, though 18 to 24 gauge can be used.

Chasing tools

The tools used for both chasing and repoussé are available in a set of twenty-four assorted shapes which includes liners, tracers, planish-

FIG. 284   Pin, quetzal bird, chasing and repoussé, sterling silver.
By Sharr Choate.

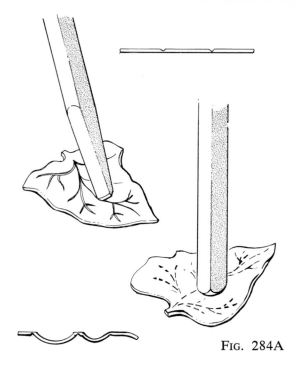

FIG. 284A

FIG. 285

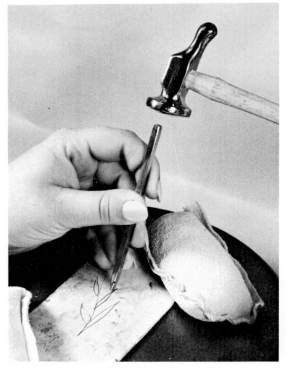

ers, raisers, and matting tools (see Fig. 286). Tracers are blunt chisels and are used for tracing or outlining the design. Curved tracers are necessary for curves.

Cushioning or embossing tools are used for raising bumps and ridges in varying sizes from wide to narrow, from square to round, from rectangular to pear-shaped. Matting and lining tools that produce textures have detailed texture patterns on the tip ends of the tools to fit different-sized areas.

Ring tools, as the name infers, are simply tools with a concentric ring on the end which, when hammered into a metal surface, leave an indentation of a small ring. Tools not included in the assorted sets of chasing tools (which come in seventy different tips) can be made from blank steel.

Making chasing tools

Chasing tools may be constructed from small cold chisels or from carbon steel bar stock.

The metal, ³⁄₁₆ or ¼ inch square, is sawed into 4-inch lengths and heated, one length at a time, to a light straw color which is approximately 430°F. (see Appendix for temperature color scale). The tool is allowed to cool without dipping in any solution in order to soften the metal. The softened metal is then filed to a long taper approximately one-third of the length on two sides. For narrower widths the remaining two sides are filed. The tip end is filed to a bevel with a slight curve (see Fig. 287). Other shapes—half-rounds, V-shape, and S-shape, etc.—can be filed according to the particular need or desire. The sanded surfaces are buffed and polished to an extremely smooth finish. Embossing tools are made in the same manner, but the ends are simply sanded off to whatever flat dome shape is preferred.

Matting tools with various textured tips are worked in the same way. After the tool is buffed and polished, it is reheated by applying the torch to the unworked portion. By watching the color changes, which gradually extend down to the working tips, it can easily be determined when the dark-brown straw color appears. As soon as this color becomes evident,

the tool is quenched in lightweight oil or room-temperature water to return the temper to it. Tools heated above this color stage (480°F.) will be very hard, quite brittle, and not suited for use as chasing tools.

Many tools used for leatherworking can be adapted for both the chasing and repoussé techniques; however, the sharp edges on the chisel-like points must be rounded and polished smooth (see Fig. 23). In fact, all the tools used must have a smooth surface and be highly polished for use on metal.

Using the tools

The first three fingers hold the chasing tool with the thumb placed opposite the second or middle finger. The little finger is used as a support and guide for the tool as it moves over the metal surface (see Figs. 288 and 285). The tool is held at an angle which, if too high, will dig into the surface and if too low, will slip off the scribed line.

The metal is placed so that the chasing tool will always travel toward the operator. The tool is slanted backward so that the top of the

FIG. 286

FIG. 287

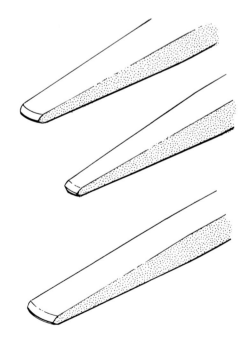

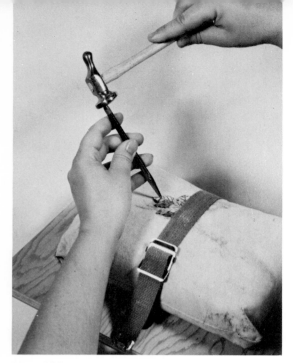

FIG. 288

FIG. 289

tool tilts away from the worker and only the corner of the tool is used to chase the line. Tilting the tool makes it possible to see the line and know that the hammer is hitting it squarely.

The chasing hammer has a flat enlarged head that gives plenty of surface to make contact with the chasing tool. As the work progresses, the working end of the chasing tool is watched, not the hammer striking on the opposite end. It must be remembered that the tool does not cut a groove in the metal as it does in engraving, but simply indents a line.

The tool should be used in the inner portions of the design and then worked to the outer open parts. In this way the tool can be lifted as it reaches the end of the line, which is tapered out to nothingness. The first cut, and the blows with the hammer on the tool, produce a small mound of metal in front of the tool. This can best be removed in the inner portion of the design rather than at the fading end of a design such as leaf vein.

REPOUSSÉ

Repoussé technique is used to give a sculptured effect to metal formed as leaves, petals, or any other three-dimensional shape that may be

used for a design. Geometric patterns and interlacements such as knots can be effected with repoussé and chasing techniques, both of which must be drilled and pierced to remove excess metal. Appliqué sections using either of these techniques can be formed and joined to other metal sections.

Holding the metal

The metal used for the repoussé work is not cut to the exact design size, but left with a slight edge to aid in holding the work. The metal is placed in a container of warmed soft pitch to hold it while it is being worked, and also to act as a cushion for the formed areas as they are hammered down into the pitch. The cushioning material consists of a combination of plaster of Paris, rosin, and pitch, and is best when purchased already prepared. This substance is used in a wooden box, tray, or in a cast-iron semispherical bowl resting in a hardwood block or leather ring (see Fig. 289). The box or tray with a larger working area than the bowls (usually 12 to 14 inches

FIG. 290   Pin, forged-chased and bead construction, 14k gold.
By Sharr Choate.

square) is preferred. It will hold the tools neatly so that any tool is easily available.

Before placing the metal in the pitch, the corners of the metal are bent at a 90° angle downward to prevent movement on the pitch (see Fig. 35). The metal may be coated with a thin layer of oil or vaseline to aid in removing it; however, the continued use of these substances will affect the pitch. The pitch is heated with a brushlike motion of the torch so that it softens, but does not burn (burning causes flaking when it hardens).

Holding the tools

The embossing tools for repoussé are not used the way chasing tools are used. The main distinction is that tools are not placed on the metal and hammered into it, but are held vertically between the first three fingers and the thumb. The little finger acts as a stabilizer and a support to hold the tool up off the metal about $1/16$ of an inch. When the tool is tapped with the chasing hammer, the springlike action of the tool works like a tiny drop hammer forming the metal held in the pitch base.

Removing metal from the pitch

From time to time metal will require annealing. Metal is removed by heating the pitch and lifting the metal up and out with tweezers or with a steel soldering rod. It is then heated on an asbestos sheet to a dull pink, and dipped in pickling solution to remove the old pitch and the fire scale, or oxidation from the torch. Old pitch may also be removed from metal after it is taken from the bowl or box by rubbing it with a cloth soaked with turpentine or alcohol.

When embossing has been completed, the metal is removed from the pitch, and the reverse side of the piece is checked for irregularities. It may be necessary to return the metal to the pitch for further smoothing and working of the raised areas. If the metal is worked from the viewing surface, and is placed back in the pitch with this surface up, sufficient pitch must be used to support the hollow underneath before the metal is worked. Metal should not be left in pitch because it becomes extremely hard in three to four hours and is difficult to remove.

When all the embossing or repoussé work has been completed, the metal is cleaned by heating, dipping in pickling solution, and rinsing in running water.

Additional embossing

After embossing, large areas of metal can be bouged—smoothed out on small stakes called snarling irons that are held firm in brackets or in a bench vise. Snarling irons are bars having small, smoothly polished anvil-like sections to support the metal as it is bouged with a small hammer.

Final chasing accents

Any additional chasing or other accents to be added can be made on areas that are placed flat on a supporting metal or hardwood surface. Small veinings in leaves may be done with a fine graver, but chasing must be limited to flat areas. After all the forming and decorating is complete, the design is sawed from the metal and subsequent metalsmithing procedures are followed (see Fig. 290).

CHAPTER 19

Engraving and Gravers

ENGRAVING IS A METHOD OF PRODUCING raised lines, characters, and patterns on a metal surface. The use of gravers for complete surface decoration on plates, trays, bowls, cups, etc., and the technique of producing complicated initials, ciphers (intertwining letters), and monograms are a specialized trade.

Because engraving is a special field that requires an art background, individual instruction, intensive study, and practice, the instruction given here will be limited to methods used to effect a texture and accents on metals. (See Chapter 11 for mounting gemstone with gravers.)

Metals

Ten metals—gold, silver, copper, brass, bronze, steel, platinum, palladium, aluminum, and pewter—are normally used for engraving. The hardness characteristic of each metal when worked is as follows:

Gold	Hard (hardness increases as the karat content or percentage of pure gold is decreased in the alloy)
Silver	Soft
Copper	Soft (slightly harder than silver)
Brass	Hard
Bronze	Hard
Steel	Hard and brittle
Aluminum	Soft and flaky
Platinum & palladium	Hard (without a bright finish in the cut)
Pewter	Soft

Gravers

Gravers are made in various sizes and shapes. Round and flat pointed gravers are used for large cuts and for the removal of metal (see Fig. 291). Flat gravers are used for trimming settings, for accents, alphabets, and flat-lined gravers are used for texturing. Flat gravers can be used like line gravers to produce a texture under transparent enamel sections. They can also be used for a wriggled final surface finish.

Round gravers and knife-edge tools are used for shaping beads when setting stones. Diamond (or square) and onglette gravers are used for intricate detailing, fine lines, and shading. Tapered lozenge and tapered square gravers with angular faces are used for patterns and

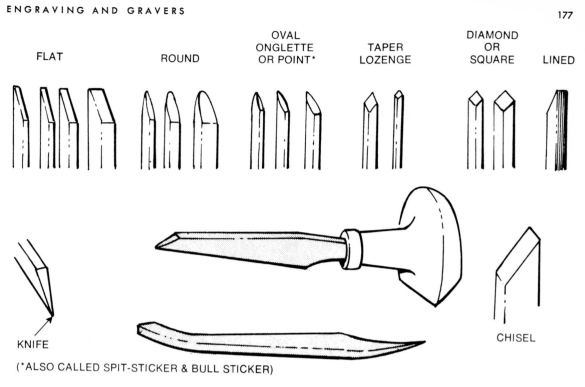

FLAT ROUND OVAL ONGLETTE OR POINT* TAPER LOZENGE DIAMOND OR SQUARE LINED

KNIFE

CHISEL

(*ALSO CALLED SPIT-STICKER & BULL STICKER)

FIG. 291

FIG. 292 Pin, rose, chasing and repoussé, 14k gold.
By Sharr Choate.

will turn a curve more easily than those that have faces at right angles to the tool shaft. Line gravers, also called florentining tools, used extensively and exclusively for texturing metal surfaces, are employed in the final stages of assembling and finishing, but areas that will be inaccessible after soldering should be textured before soldering (see Figs. 292 and 293). The cutting surface of the tool is grooved in fine lines running lengthwise on the belly (see Fig. 291). Like all other gravers, the length is shortened so that it can be handled with ease. The tools are available in twenty different sizes with from two to ten lines on the cutting surface. The varying width of the tools and the density of the lines gives the craftsman a choice of heavy or delicate surface treatments. The lines can be made in the metal in any direction according to the whim of the craftsman. Straight, wriggly, wavy, crosshatched, basket weave, and random scatter are some of the different patterns used.

A sharp graver needs very little pressure to push it across the metal surface, but it should be held firmly to prevent skidding. A deep bite into the metal must be avoided. Florentined

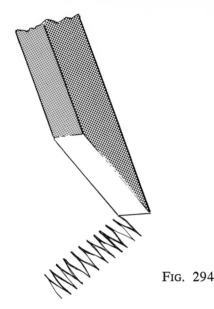

FIG. 294

FIG. 293   Pin, chasing and repoussé, florentine
finish, sterling silver.
By Sharr Choate.

surfaces cannot be buffed and polished but the
surface should be buffed prior to texturing to
remove any scratches or other marks. Polishing
is superfluous as the polished surface is lost in
the texturing process. The line graver can also
be used to cover up blemishes or marks in the
surface left by the removal of visible solder.
Discolorations in the metal because of overheating during soldering can also be diminished
visibly with this tool. When using a line graver,
it must be remembered that an overabundance
of texturing can spoil a pleasing design.

Standard flat gravers are used for accenting
details on a leaf, a border, and around a setting, etc. The wriggled effect previously mentioned is produced by lifting a flat graver to increase the angle between it and the metal and
then "walking" it across the surface (see Fig.
294). To texture an outlined area, the tool is
first walked around the inner edge of the area,
and the space is filled in by continuing the
same procedure in parallel rows.

Flat gravers are also used for Gothic and
block lettering; square gravers are used for
script letters. A combination of both tools is
used for Old English letters (see Fig. 291).
Types of lettering should be understood before

attempting to use graving tools, even on inexpensive copper sheet. Letters, monograms, and
ciphers should be sketched freehand to give the
hand and wrist freer movement and a feeling
for the direction of travel of the gravers in rela-
tion to the letters and numerals. The letters
can be practiced on paper with a drawing pencil sharpened to a wedge point and pushed
ahead of the hand across the paper to form
letters, strokes, circles, and curves.

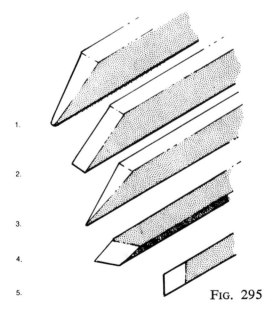

1.

2.

3.

4.

5.

FIG. 295

Although the primary use for gravers has been mentioned, they can be used for several other purposes such as: raising beads to hold gemstones in place, reaming out a shoulder or bearing as a support for a gemstone in a mounting, removing excess solder from hard-to-get-at areas or from those areas too small to be reached with a hollow scraper (see Chapter 11).

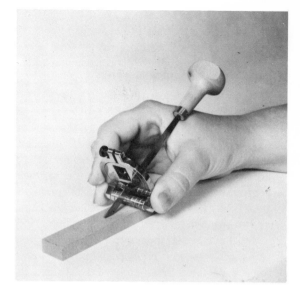

FIG. 296

Sharpening the tools

Gravers are sold in full lengths (approximately 6 inches); however, this is too much length to give accurate control over the tool. The length should be shortened to 3½ to 4 inches by breaking off a portion of the tool from the tang or handle end only.

The tool can be broken easily by placing the part to be retained in the bench vise and allowing the unwanted section to protrude above the jaws of the vise. A sharp tap with a hammer will readily make the break.

Tools are never sold sharp. Sharpening must be done by the craftsman who should keep them so sharp that they will cut the moment they touch metal.

Whenever considerable pressure is necessary to cut a line, remove metal, shade an area, produce a texture, or follow a line for veining, for detail and for making any other cuts, the tool should be resharpened.

Different kinds of gravers require individual sharpening treatments. Round and pointed gravers have two side faces, a top, and a cutting face. Flat and line gravers are the same but also have a belly or heel surface (see Fig. 295).

When grinding flat gravers, the belly is sharpened before the cutting face. On all other gravers, the cutting face alone is sharpened. Gravers made from drill rod are usually shaped and sharpened only a portion of the way back from the point. When resharpening, the belly is ground first, followed by the faces and the top; the cutting face is ground last.

Gravers hand held for sharpening require experience and a steady hand; therefore, the beginner should restrict himself to a mechanical graver sharpener until the sharpening process is mastered. Mechanical sharpeners (which

provide the greatest degree of accuracy on graver faces) are small jigs designed to hold the tool securely at the proper angle for grinding (see Fig. 296). Experienced engravers and stone-setters usually sharpen their gravers by hand, as it is time-consuming to set up the tool in the sharpener. Because jig designs vary with manufacturers, the operating instructions packed with the tool should be carefully followed.

When sharpening a graver, the first step before grinding is to heat the tool to a bright red color, after which it is allowed to cool. It is not quenched in water or oil until the grinding and polishing are completed.

The graver is ground on a carborundum or India stone that has been soaked in oil. Thin oils such as those used for precision machinery and rifles, are used for the stone. The stone is saturated until no more oil can be absorbed. The best method is to submerge the stone in a shallow pan filled with oil and then allow it to saturate overnight. A stone can be used only when saturated; a dry surface will become glazed with metal particles from the grinding.

Unless the angle of a face or the belly is to be changed, the cutting face remains parallel with the stone during the sharpening process. The belly should be ground to an angle of 8 to

12° from the bottom of the tool with 10° being the optimum angle. The angle should be checked at the back portion, rather than at the tip. A regular machinist's protractor is an ideal tool to use here. The cutting face is ground to a 45° angle from the straight top edge.

As the upper portion of the tool is not used for graving, it can be ground away to give better control and better viewing, and leaves less surface to be ground when the tool requires resharpening (see Fig. 297). When the surfaces are ground and edges checked for burrs, the graver (still fastened in the sharpener) is transferred to the Arkansas stone, and the fine grinding on the face is then completed. The tool face should be checked occasionally to see if it has been held absolutely flat against the stone. If facets are visible on the cutting face of

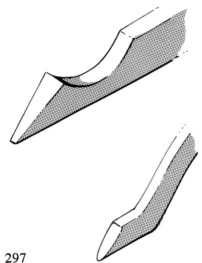

FIG. 297

the tool, the tool has been tipped as it was being ground. Such facets must be removed from the face of the tool before it is used, or an imperfect cut will be left in the surface of the metal being engraved.

After grinding the tool on the Arkansas stone, the face is sanded on a strip of 4/0 emery paper supported on a section of heavy plate glass. Several strokes are all that is required to polish the surface; overpolishing will round the edges. The polishing is followed by a stropping which consists of pulling the face of the polished graver the length of a leather strip that has been rubbed with Tripoli buffing compound.

The line graver is sharpened in the same manner described for the other gravers, except that the lined surface (belly) is left untouched and only the tip end of the cutting face is smoothed to remove small burrs which will form between the lines. These can be removed easily by stabbing the graver into a wooden block.

When the grinding and polishing steps have been completed, the tool is heated to a bright red and completely immersed in water which is stirred in order to cool the metal as quickly as possible. The swirling action of the water cools metal faster than still water. Quenching hardens the metal, but if the tool is used in this state it would be brittle and break easily. Therefore, the tool must be tempered to lower the hardness. Too much tempering will soften the metal so that the tool will require frequent resharpening.

Tempering the tool

Fire scale is first removed from the tool with a wire brush, and the tool is reheated in a low flame. The tool is heated until the color changes are brought up through brown to brownish yellow (approximately 480°F.) after which it is immediately immersed again in the water or oil to halt the softening process. As the steel is heated, the following color changes are observed in order to obtain the desired maximum temperature of the metal according to the ultimate use of the metal or tool.

No color	200°F.	Scrapers
Pale yellow	390°F.	
Bright yellow	430°F.	
Straw yellow	450°F.	Punches, chasing tools
Dark yellow	470°F.	
Brownish yellow	480°F.	Engraving tools
Brownish red	500°F.	Hammers, drills
Purple	520°F.	
Violet	540°F.	
Dark blue	550°F.	Cold chisels
Cornflower blue	570°F.	Screwdrivers, knives, saws
Bright blue	600°F.	Springs
Bluish-green/gray	630°F.	

Determining tool sharpness

Sharpness of gravers is quickly determined by touching the cutting face edge of the tool against the thumbnail. If the tool slips over the surface it is dull; if it catches or bites into the surface it is sharp and ready for use.

Tools can be curved slightly so that they do not have to be held at a high and awkward angle to keep them from dragging on the metal. To curve the tool, the area back of the tip, approximately 1 inch from the end, is heated, and while still hot the tip is pressed with slight pressure against an asbestos soldering sheet or firebrick. The tool will bend easily when heated sufficiently (indicated by a bright red color). After heating, the tool is immediately quenched in water or oil to harden it.

After quenching, the fire scale is removed with a wire brush and sanded and polished if desired. To put the temper back into the tool, it is reheated to a brownish-yellow color—480°F.—and then quenched in water or oil to stop the tempering process.

Graver handles

Following the initial grinding and hardening, the gravers are inserted into wooden handles in any of the available shapes such as round, pear, mushroom, oval, or half-head (see Fig. 298). The half-heads are preferred as they fit the palm and can be gripped comfortably and securely. A drilled hole, slightly smaller than the tang end of the graver, is made in each graver handle. The handle is pounded gently with a mallet onto the tang end of the graver, which is held upright in a bench.

The engraving process is done after the piece has received its final buffing and polishing. This will permit retaining the brightness of the cut rather than obliterating it with heavy buffing. The design is drawn on the metal surface, already coated with Chinese or Grumbacher white (artist's colors used here for layout). When the white coating has dried, the lines of the design and other markings are drawn on the surface with a hard lead pencil and then scribed very lightly with a steel point. A fine line, not a deep mark, is needed on the surface. The line need not be scribed, as pencil lines can serve only as a guide; however, they

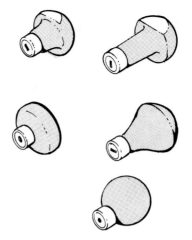

FIG. 298

should not be made directly on an uncoated metal surface. Steel-point scribed lines can be made directly on bare metal.

Holding the metal

Metals are held in an engraver's block when engraving. The block is a threaded clamp with a rounded base that rests for support in a hardwood or leather ring (see Fig. 299). The support permits the block to be moved easily into any position as the metal is engraved. The upper portion of the block rotates around the vertical axis of the block while the lower portion remains static, if preferred. Various clamping attachments are provided with the block for special purposes. Metal placed in the block should be protected with small metal jaws, chamois leather, or flannel strips to prevent nicks in the edge of the metal. Metal sections too small to be clamped adequately and firmly with the attachments supplied with the block can be cemented to a heavy sheet of copper or brass held in the block. The small section is cemented with water-soluble glue or a sodium silicate (water glass) solution, both of which may be removed by soaking the metal in water. The metal may also be cemented to the support with dopping wax used by lapidaries. Metals can also be held in a pitch bowl or box and in hand vises and ring clamps. Jeweler's sandbags are also used to hold metal for texturing or decorating with the graving tools (see Fig. 288). Two holes are drilled in the

should overextend or slip off the metal. The thumb contacts the other thumb tip to help steady and support the graver as the block is turned (see Fig. 299). Most of the movement is turning the block as the graver travels across the metal with little more than slight wrist action.

Engraving the metal

As the graver moves to cut the metal, the thumb of the hand holding the graver retains contact with the other thumb tip and acts as a steady support to guide the tool. Single or parallel lines without shading are cut while the firm pressure of the tool against the thumb is exerted; the thumb stays in position on top of the metal, and the tool glides along straight up in its cut with sides vertical. Shaded cuts are made similarly, except that the tool is tipped

FIG. 299

workbench about 6 inches apart. The sandbag is placed between the holes, and a webbing strap is threaded through the holes to hold the metal in place on the sandbag. The straps are cinched at one side of the bag or underneath.

Holding the tool

The graver is held in one hand as if holding a short-handled screwdriver with the index finger pointed toward the tool tip for steadiness (see Fig. 300). The thumb extends along the side for stability and support and the tool extends ½ to ¾ inch beyond the index finger. The graver should be held high enough so that the fingers can wrap around the handle.

The gravers are held so that the face is tilted at a 45° angle from the metal surface. If the tool is raised so that the angle is greater than 45°, a deep cut is made in the metal (see Fig. 300). A low tool angle makes a shallow cut, and often the tool breaks at the point, except when used on pewter. Holding the tool at this angle will permit the tool accidentally to skid off the scribed line, damaging the metal surface.

The opposite hand is positioned around the block, but below the surface, to prevent injuring the hand in the event that the graver

FIG. 300

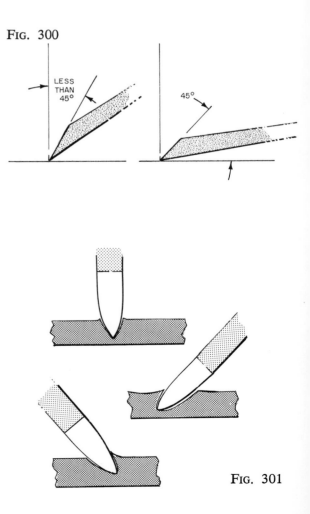

FIG. 301

practice to make the two shaded sections meet perfectly.

Accent cuts, small flicks, or nips with a tool in tear-drop or long triangular shape can be made only with a sharp tool that has a high polish (see Figs. 302, 302A, 302B, and 302C). Care must be taken that the cutting surface of the tool is not rounded off and dulled during the polishing.

Constant practice alone will enable the craftsman to perfect making cuts without slipping off lines or gouging the metal beyond repair. Gravers can be lubricated for easy movement across the metal by touching the cutting face on a small piece of sponge or cotton swab moistened with oil of wintergreen.

Decorative cuts for jewelry should be practiced before attempting them on precious metals. These and other practice cuts, lines, circles, etc., should be made on 22-gauge cop-

FIG. 302 Pendant and earrings, pierced and engraved, sterling silver.
By Hakon Jonnson.

to the side so that one portion of the cutting face is used more than the opposite side (see Fig. 301). Circular and curved lines or cuts are made while the tool is supported by the thumb; however, here the thumb rotates as the tool arcs on the surface to give continuing pivotal support. The gentle curve of a design can be made in the rotating metal in a single well-controlled stroke if the tool cuts the surface with a slight downward pressure and a firm movement forward.

Near the end of the cut or stroke, the tool is curved up toward the surface again. As this is done, a small curl of metal is formed. When the end of the stroke is reached, a slight lifting of the tool and a quick flick will loosen the curl and separate it from the metal sheet. If the metal cannot be removed easily, a vertical cut with the graver on the other side of the curl will release it.

Broader shaded cuts on curves or parallel lines are made by leaning the graver to either side. The shading should spread out gradually to its widest point and then taper off until it merges with a single line. If preferred, the shading can be made from one direction to a midpoint where the metal is rotated and the shading done from the opposite end with the tool tipped accordingly. It will require a little

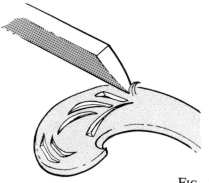

FIG. 302A

per sheet cut into 2- by 2-inch squares which are annealed before using. One can test agility with the tools by cutting short straight lines with a graver, and then trying out other types of cuts with different gravers. Gentle curves should be practiced until one can engrave a circle with one continuous line or cut.

Removing engraving errors

Engraving slips or scratches, if not too deep, can be eliminated by burnishing (see Fig. 81). The highly polished curved-tip burnisher (the same as used for burnishing bezels over stones) is dipped in a soapy solution and then worked over the surface of the metal in a circular motion. When the tool begins to grab, more of the soapy lubricant is needed to prevent the metal from being scratched by the tool. A gentle buffing usually covers up a completely burnished blemish. Surfaces, other than plated, filled, or gilded, when damaged by a slip that is too deep to be removed by burnishing, can still be reworked. The surface is ground or filed, sanded, buffed with Tripoli compound, polished, and then reengraved.

FIG. 302C Pendant, pierced and engraved, sterling silver.
Japanese design.

FIG. 302B Pin, engraved pierced metal, sterling silver.
By Sharr Choate.

Tool storage and care

Gravers, when not in use, are coated with a thin film of fine oil as a rust preventive, and stored with the point up for easy identification or selection. If gravers are used frequently (or the work is interrupted) they can be left on the workbench without damage to the points if the cutting faces are pressed into a small cork.

CHAPTER 20

Etching

ETCHING IS A METHOD USED TO DELINEATE A design upon metal by means of a corrosive agent. The corrosive agent is an acid that reproduces depressions that can be left as is, or filled with another metal, stone, or fine enamels (see Figs. 303, 303A, and 303B). Etching can also be used to texture metal.

Preparing the metal

The metal, with the areas masked out that are to be left unetched, is placed in an acid bath to erode the surface into depressions. The depth of the depressions will depend on the length of time the metal is immersed. Before the masking is done, the metal surface must be sanded smoothly so that it is completely free of all irregularities and ready for the buffing and polishing steps. Any effort to remove surface blemishes after etching will result in a general decrease in the thickness of the raised or unetched portions of the metal.

Transfer of the design is made by first painting the metal with artist's or showcard paint called Grumbacher white, Chinese white, or casein. After the coating has dried, the design is drawn on the surface or transferred from tracing paper and scratched into the metal surface with a scriber or awl. The coating is scrubbed away with soap and water.

Masking

Masking is done by coating all areas that are to be left unetched, including the metal back and edges, with a resist called **black asphaltum varnish** (see Fig. 304).

Only one surface of the metal should be painted at a time, and it should be allowed to dry thoroughly before proceeding. If the resist is too thick to paint on the metal easily, it may be thinned slightly with turpentine; however, an extremely thin coating will require additional coats of resist to prevent the acid from eating through. If the resist extends over the scribed line, it can be removed with the point of a small knife. Chipping can be avoided by heating the metal slightly. After the resist is painted on, it must be completely dry before the metal is immersed in the acid bath.

Etching

Etching solutions, called mordants, consist of various combinations of water and acid mixed by pouring the acid into the water—*never* the water into the acid. The mordant is mixed in a glass tray, pyrex baking dish, or discarded battery box in a well-ventilated area, and stirred with a glass rod. The metal, face up, is placed in the solution with copper or quartz-tipped tongs. Approximately ¼ inch of solution must cover the metal at all times (see Fig. 305).

The mordants used for etching are mixed in these suggested formulae:

Gold	Aqua regia solutions consisting of:	
Formula #1	Hydro-chloric acid	8 parts
	Iron per-chloride	1 part
	Nitric acid	4 parts
	Water	40 to 50 parts

Formula #2	Equal parts of nitric and sulfuric acids mixed in a solution and diluted 1 part solution to 1 part water. (Hydrochloric acid may be substituted for the sulfuric acid.)	
Silver	Nitric acid	1 part
	Water	2 parts
Copper, brass, etc.	Nitric acid	1 part
	Water	1 part
Steel	Hydro-chloric acid	2 parts
	Water	8 parts
	or	
	Sulfuric acid	1 part
	Water	8 parts

FIG. 303   Zodiac pendants, etched, sterling silver.
By Sharr Choate.

FIG. 303A   Pendant, etched, sterling silver with Icelandic jasper.
By Hakon Jonnson.

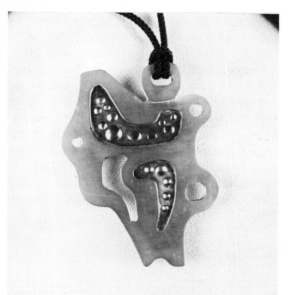

FIG. 303B Pendant, pierced, etched, granulation sterling silver and 14k gold. By Wayne Smith.

subsequent coating is dry, the metal is returned to the solution for further etching. When the final depth has been reached, the metal is removed, rinsed, and dried, and the asphaltum removed with a turpentine-soaked cloth. The metal is then scrubbed with pumice or household cleanser and rinsed clean. Edges of the depressed area can be trimmed or trued with a round graver; however, one should be careful not to cut a groove in the corner of the depression with this tool (see Fig. 308).

FIG. 304

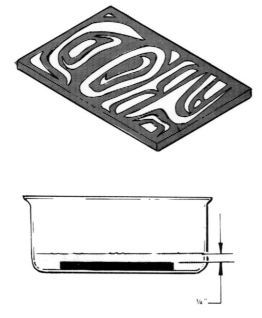

FIG. 305

The reaction of the acid on the metal should be observed in order to detect whether the solution is too weak or too strong. Tiny gas bubbles should rise slowly to the surface if the solution is right. If no bubbles rise the solution is too weak, and if the bubbles rise too rapidly it is overly strong. Bubbles that cling to the edge of the resist on the metal surface should be removed by gently rocking the dish or by brushing away with a small cotton wisp or a small feather (see Fig. 306). If the bubbles are permitted to remain on the edges, they will pit or notch the edge of the metal (see Fig. 307).

The metal is to be left in the solution until the desired depth of the etched area is reached, but it may be removed with the tongs, rinsed under running water, and checked for depth at any time.

The usual depth of the depression is $\frac{1}{32}$ inch which occurs in 1 to 4 hours. Deeper depressions require longer immersion times and heavier-gauge metals. If certain areas are to be etched deeper than others, the metal is removed from the solution and rinsed in running water, dried, and the additional areas masked out with the resist. As soon as this

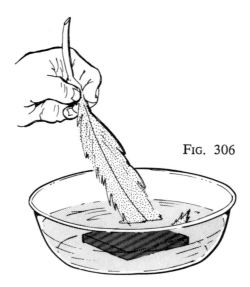

FIG. 306

Inlay materials

If desired, the etched areas may be filled with inlay metals by simply fusing the metal or by soldering. Solder, such as silver solder which can be used with gold, copper, brass, and steel, may also be used as an inlay metal. When regular silver solder is used as an inlay material in etched pieces, the area to be covered with

solder must be clean and painted with flux so that the inlay material will adhere to the metal. The flux must not be allowed to extend beyond the etched areas because the finished surface would have to be reworked to remove it.

If the depressions are to be filled with enamels, 18k gold or fine silver should be used, as other metals such as lower karat golds, sterling silver, and copper tend to oxide under transparent enamels (see Chapter 27).

Electroetching is a quick method of etching using electroplating equipment (see Chapter 28).

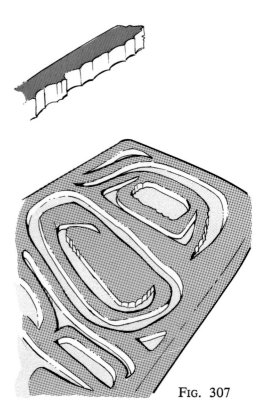

FIG. 307

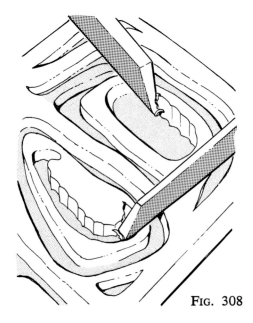

FIG. 308

CHAPTER 21

Scrollwork

CERTAIN GEMSTONES OFTEN REQUIRE A DELI-cate mounting to enhance the beauty of a cut stone. The fine tracery of wire that forms the mounting is an assembly of various scrolls bent with pliers, by hand, or wound on small jigs. The combination of various S and U forms interspersed with circles and question mark shapes is further enhanced with small beads, grains, or leaves (see Figs. 309, 309A, and 309B). The wire shapes may be assembled without plans for a gemstone in the design; however, if the gemstone is to be used, a bezel mounting or some other type of prong mounting must be added.

Wire

Round, half-round, and square wire 16 to 20 gauge are used for the forms. Round wire is the preferred choice as the other two wires are easily damaged with the pliers and are difficult to bend into shape.

Designs are usually a combination of the various forms previously mentioned, and it is best to practice making scrolls with 18-gauge copper wire before attempting to bend and twist the gold or silver wire.

When the technique of winding the wire is mastered one will be able to determine in advance how much wire is needed for each scroll. Until then the wire should be cut into 2-inch lengths for S or U scrolls, and 1-inch lengths for single scrolls. When there is no difficulty in forming identical scrolls, shorter lengths may be cut to form smaller U shapes (see Fig. 309).

Round rings or jump rings are used for circular sections. The wire should be annealed in a coil before cutting to length for forming. Round-nose pliers are used for the scroll forming, and the jaws should be polished and free of any nicks or grooves.

If a ball, bead, or grain is to be used, it should be added before the scroll is formed. The wire may be wound first if preferred; however, in soldering a decoration to the scroll there is a possibility of melting a section of the wire with the torch.

Copper wire is inexpensive and is easily annealed and straightened so that it can be used over and over for patterns for scroll sections.

Designs for symmetrical assemblies are best planned if drawn on quadrille-lined paper (drafting paper marked in 1/8- or 1/4-inch squares). The squares make it quite simple to arrange the scrolls in attractive designs that balance perfectly.

The basic scroll patterns are a single scroll, double S stretched; double S regular, or deep U-shape long, regular, or shallow; question mark, and circle (see Fig. 309). Scrollwork designs are made up of combinations of these basic forms, and there is no end to the different arrangements that can be made alone or in conjunction with gemstones.

Beads and leaves

Beads to be added to the scroll ends are made by melting small jump rings on a charcoal block

Fig. 309

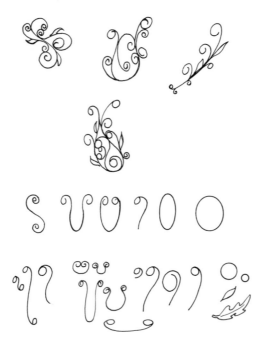

Fig. 309A   Pin, scrollwork, chasing and repoussé sterling silver with fairy plume agate. By Alberta Best.

torch and the wire one can see a very tiny to medium-size bead form on the end of the wire (see Fig. 310). After pickling and rinsing, the wire is either formed into a scroll, or the opposite end is fitted with a bead before bending.

Small leaves are made in the same technique described for making beads on the end of a wire. Round wire is selected which is the proper size for a stem to go with the leaf. One end is dipped in borax flux and melted in the same way as for beads. When the bead has formed, the wire is dipped in pickling solution and rinsed. The bead is hammered flat and filed to a leaf shape (see Fig. 310). This is much easier than filing small leaf sections and then soldering them to stems.

or asbestos sheet. When the fluxed metal melts and forms a ball, it is rolled away from its melting place with the pusher rod as soon as it cools to a dull red so that the melted flux (used to bring impurities to the surface) will not cement the ball to the block or sheet. If the ball or bead becomes attached to the block, it is simply reheated and moved again. The small balls or beads are fluxed and soldered to the wire ends. Beads can be formed on the wire to eliminate a soldering step by holding the wire downward about 6 inches from the end and placing the end about 1 inch from the blue tip of the torch flame. By watching the

Bending the wire

To bend a scroll, the annealed length of wire is grasped at the end with the round-nose pliers held vertically. The left hand holds the wire for support, and the left thumb is used to apply pressure as the wire is bent. The pliers are twisted in a counterclockwise direction as far as the hand will turn comfortably. Without releasing the firm grip on the wire, the right hand can readjust to a normal position and another counterclockwise turn be made. The coiling of the wire is continued (with the pliers holding the wire in the same place as when the twist was started) until the end of the wire makes a complete circle and comes back against itself.

The result is a complete single scroll that may be cut to any length (see Fig. 311).

All the other scroll types are made by repeating the same procedure on the opposite end of the wire and, as stated before, to ensure the correct length of the scroll after winding. It is best to practice making the shapes first with copper wire before attempting them in gold or silver.

Scrolls can be combined in endless ways to form interesting arrangements (see Fig. 312). Designs combining gemstones and scrolls should be planned in advance in order to visu-

brushing motion with the torch. The wires are then cooled and refluxed. Solder is added under the junctures, and the torch again heats the wires. The torch must be kept moving to avoid concentrating the heat in one area and melting the wires. The solder will rise up through the joints when it flows. The piece is pickled and then buffed and polished while supported on a thin section of wood.

Scrolls can be made to frame forms in any technique—pierced, chased, and formed (repoussé), etched, and enameled work as well as for bezel mountings.

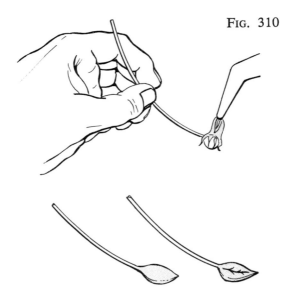

FIG. 310

FIG. 309B   Pendant, scrollwork, chasing and repoussé 14k gold with chrysoprase.
By Alberta Best.

FIG. 311

alize the best arrangements. The ends of single scrolls must be filed to a flat taper where they make a juncture with another wire (see Fig. 313).

Soldering

When all scrolls have been completed, they are cleaned and positioned on a charcoal soldering block or a pumice block that is sold by restaurant suppliers as a grill cleaner. Flux is added to the joints and the wire is heated in a

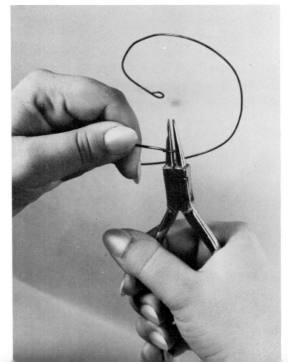

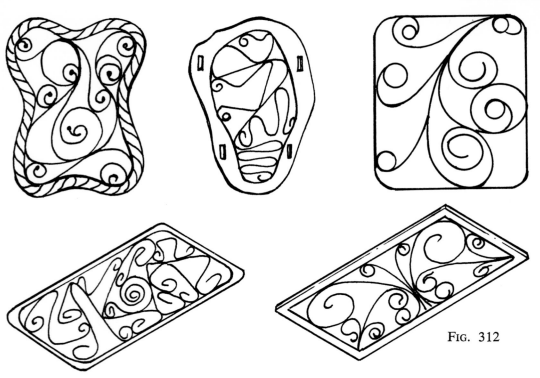

FIG. 312

Jump rings

Jump rings are used in making beads, balls, grains, and leaves, and they are also used when a design calls for small circles. To determine bead sizes, one, two, or three rings can be melted into balls and set aside. These small beads can be glued to a card and the number of rings required for each size bead noted. If preferred, a bead size reference can also be made by cutting and melting 1/8- or 1/4-inch lengths of wire.

Jump rings in short coils are easier to make and separate than when formed in long coils. The wire is wound on a mandrel consisting of a nail, drill rod, or section of dowel wood placed in a small bench vise. The rod is bent at a 90° angle at one end so that it will not turn in the vise and can act as an aid when sawing the rings. The wire, annealed before winding, is wrapped approximately five or six times around the mandrel to form a set of rings. The set of rings, with a long loop left between each set, will appear as though stretched in about 5/16-inch spacings on the mandrel. The complete coil is removed, and the short sets of rings are separated with the end cutters, and placed, one

coil at a time, on the mandrel and sawed through parallel with the mandrel (see Fig. 314).

The bent end of the mandrel can be placed in the V cut of the wooden bench stake, or a small hole can be drilled in the bench stake for insertion of the mandrel. Pressure on the mandrel against the stake will hold the wire coil as it is sawed (see Fig. 314).

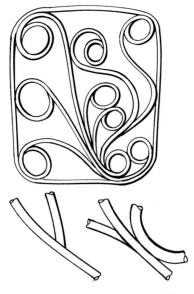

FIG. 313

It is much easier to saw short coil lengths than those which are 5 to 6 inches long as it is difficult to guide the saw in a straight line to cut all the rings evenly. The saw is used with short strokes, approximately 1 to 2 inches at the most, and should be at least halfway through the wire before the strokes are lengthened. This will eliminate saw marks that will occur if the saw blade jumps out of the groove during sawing. (Scratched or nicked rings can be saved for melting into beads.) After sawing, the rings are bent sideways with the flat-nose pliers to close the ends. They are opened in the same manner, never spread open, as this would change their shape (see Fig. 203A).

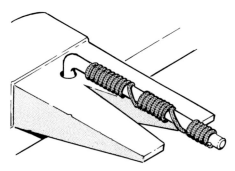

FIG. 314

Large leaf forms

Leaves used in a design should be shaped in a curve on the flat sheet, and after sawing, formed from the underside to add dimension. It is difficult to curve and form the leaf from a symmetrical flat design without resistance from the metal (see Figs. 315 and 318). Leaves are formed in the dapping die block or on a sandbag if large sizes are used. The patterns are made in reverse for opposite sides of a ring, pin, pendant, earrings, or necklace links. The design is drawn on a sheet of paper that is folded over and cut through both thicknesses to make an exact duplicate of the design in reverse.

Leaf sections are made of 22-gauge sheet which, after forming, are soldered to the stem

wire. If the stem wire is to be fitted with a small bead, the leaf is placed under the stem when soldering the two together. Veining depressions are made from the viewing side, and the leaf is cupped or formed from underneath.

Leaves are soldered to a stem with the solder placed at the heel of the leaf. Heat applied with the brushing action of the torch is directed primarily to the leaf and occasionally to the stem after the flux melts. As the solder melts, the torch is used to pull the solder along the stem. Solder naturally flows toward a flame; however, the metals must be absolutely clean and adequately fluxed for it to travel in this manner and to eliminate the little patches of solder stain which would have to be removed from the leaf.

Previously soldered joints will not loosen if covered with antiflux paste; however, the paste must be scrubbed off the metal after cool-

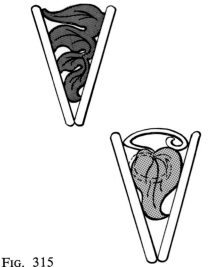

FIG. 315

ing and before pickling to keep the pickling solution clear.

Rings

Rings made of wire with scrollwork ornamentation are constructed of 16-gauge wire. Two sections of wire slightly longer than needed are cut from an annealed coil and joined with solder at each end only. The center top of the ring is marked on the inside surface of the wires with the edge of a small file. When the wires are spread for the bezel, the opening can

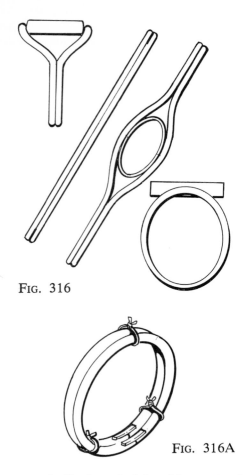

FIG. 316

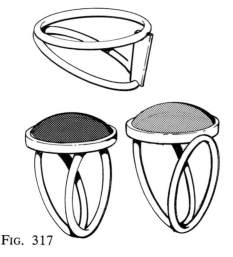

FIG. 317

FIG. 316A

FIG. 317A

be symmetrically shaped. A bezel is constructed to fit a preselected stone and, after soldering, the center ends and center sides of the bezel are marked for alignment in the spread wire frame (see Fig. 316). The wires should be spread enough to permit the bezel to sit down in the frame rather than on top of it. The parts are cleaned, fluxed, and heated to melt the flux and then cooled. The solder areas are fluxed again and solder is placed under the joints. The torch will pull the solder up into the joint. If preferred, the ring can be formed, sized, and soldered before adding the bezel. In this case after soldering the bezel, it is necessary to file the bottom of the bezel that protrudes through the curved portion of the ring.

After soldering the bezel in the wire frame the wires are squeezed together with the round-nose pliers. Some protective covering such as a strip of cloth or thin leather should be placed on the nose of the pliers to prevent marking the metal.

The wires are fluxed and soldered together the length of the extensions. The wire framework is placed on a ring mandrel, formed into a ring, and the overlapping ends are sawed through after the correct size has been ascertained. The ends of the soldered wire shank should be filed flat so that they butt against each other in a tight joint. Two small narrow snippets of solder are placed lengthwise on the two wires of the shank, and, with the bezel down on the soldering block, the ring shank is soldered together. The solder is placed on the inner surfaces of the wire, and the flame is directed to the joint from outside the ring (see Fig. 316A). By placing the solder in this manner, instead of across the two wires, an invisible join is produced giving the effect of two parallel wires without a joint.

The amount of spread left on each side of the bezel down to the ring shank will determine the size of the ornamentation. Wire size for stems or other scrollwork should be 20-gauge round. Small leaves or other shapes are made from 22- to 24-gauge sheet. The forms are sawed to shape, filed, sanded, and dished. The stem is soldered to the underside of the leaf, and a bead is added to the opposite end of the stem. The two parts are fitted to the open area on the ring, and the stem is bent to fit inside the space (see Figs. 315 and 319). Both ends of the stem may be coiled and soldered to the underside and, if this is the case, the wire should be completely formed before it is attached to the leaf. Ornamental sections when added to the ring assembly are soldered on one side of the ring, and when secure are soldered on the other side.

Soldering aids

Ornaments are soldered to the ring with an asbestos support when needed. This support consists of a tube of asbestos paper cut from

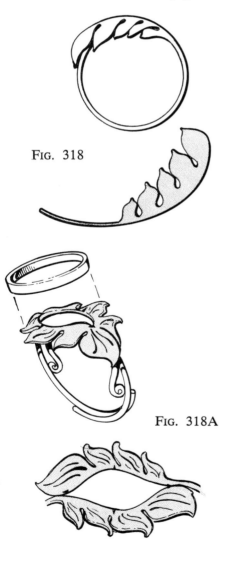

FIG. 318

FIG. 318A

a roll. The asbestos strip is dampened, placed on the ring mandrel under the ring, and pinned to hold its shape. The ring is removed, and the asbestos roll is heated with the torch to dry it out. This removes the carbon which otherwise smokes during soldering (see Fig. 103).

Small sections that require even more support during soldering are held in place with the asbestos strip material dampened and wadded into a mass. This is applied wherever needed and is dried before soldering is begun.

The leaf or any section of the stem should not extend up on the outside of the bezel any higher than an imaginary line level with the inner bearing of the bezel. Ornamental sections soldered above this point will make it difficult to burnish the bezel over the stone (see Fig. 317). Bezels used without a bearing require that ornamental attachments be no higher than $\frac{1}{16}$-inch above the base of the bezel.

Leaf ring assembly

Large leaves can be used as the main structure of a ring. The stem running almost the complete length of the leaf is extended so that it meets the stem from the opposite side to complete the shank (see Figs. 318, 318A, and 319). Leaf sections are made in exact duplicate pairs. The leaf is designed in a curve, and a pattern should be cut first out of thin copper or brass and bent around a ring mandrel. The dishing of the leaf areas requires that the basic curved outline be established in the flat metal section. The actual leaf is cut from this pattern, filed, sanded smooth, and dished. The stem is shaped to fit the outer curve of the leaf. Both parts are

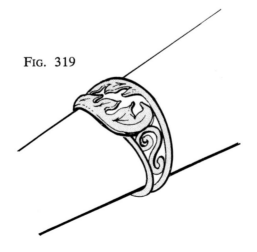

FIG. 319

FIG. 320

onto the solid metal base. The bezel must be soldered after forming and sizing, and is filed on a half-round file to fit the curvature of the ring at the top (see Figs. 320 and 125).

Ornamental wire sections with small leaves can be soldered to solid ring shanks. These are held with binding wire and are soldered on after the ring is formed on the ring mandrel and the bezel and shank have been soldered. The bezel is cut to the length required for the stone that is to be used in the design, and the ends are filed and soldered together. It is then filed on a half-round file to produce a curve in the base to match the curvature of the ring, after which it is cleaned, fluxed, and soldered in place.

Necklace and bracelet link frames can be made out of square or round wire. The frame

cleaned and fluxed, and solder is placed at the base of the leaf and heated to attach it.

The soldered leaf, stem, and ornamental scroll wires are then formed on the ring mandrel. The stem extensions will overlap underneath, but will be cut only after alignment of the two leaf sections is completed. These are held in place temporarily on the mandrel with wax or solder binding wire (see Fig. 318A).

Small single scroll sections are formed to fit on the inner curve of the stem and on top of the leaf. The ends are filed to a flat taper to fit the curve of the stem. The bezel is constructed to fit the leaf assembly. Center end and center sides are marked on the bezel and the leaf extensions for alignment during soldering. The ornamental wires are still coiled down close to the stem. The bezel is soldered to the leaves only, followed by cutting the wires of the shank, sizing the ring, and soldering the shank together. The ornamental wires are now uncoiled and arranged so that they come up to the base of the bezel to match the design. They are then soldered to the base of the bezel making the ring ready for buffing, polishing, and stone setting (see Fig. 317A).

Other scrollwork uses

Rings can be made of sheet with bezel mounting and scrollwork ornamentation soldered

FIG. 321 Bracelet, scrollwork, bezels, sterling silver and opal (synthetic).
Mexican design.

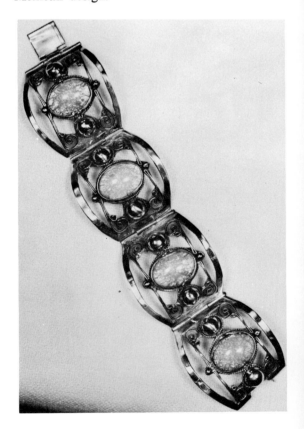

or border can also be made from a section of metal sheet that is pierced and sawed to remove the inner section (see Fig. 321). The scrolls are fitted along with any bezels or other types of mountings to be used for the gemstones. Small jump rings are soldered at the upper and lower corners on each side for connecting to identical links. The links in turn are connected with small jump rings or narrow flat loops of thin metal strips which need not be soldered unless desired (see Fig. 312).

Findings are soldered in position, or the article is attached to a necklace with a pendant bail or jump rings. Earring findings are screwed out as far as possible and the loop is opened to approximately 45°. The underside of the pad that will be attached to the metalwork is coated with flux and tinned with solder. It is positioned on the scrollwork, fluxed, and heated so that the solder flows to the wire.

Baroque stones are easily mounted with an assembly consisting of one stretched S and two regular U forms. The coils are wound after soldering. A baroque stone is placed on the wires, and the bending point is marked with a small file on the top of the wire framework. The coiled wire ends are bent up to 90° and the stone tried in the space. If no adjustments are needed to ensure a solid fit for the stone, the coil ends can be burnished down over the stone (see Fig. 158).

A cluster of small bezels or bezel boxes can be arranged to serve as the focal point of a scrollwork border. They need not be arranged symmetrically, but in any pleasing setup. The scrolls are constructed around them.

CHAPTER 22

Filigree

FILIGREE CONSISTS OF A NETWORK OF TWISTED fine gold or silver wire formed into spirals, whorls, curves, etc., and fitted into a framework of flat ribbon wire. This is one of the most ancient and widely used of all metalsmithing techniques (see Figs. 322, 322A, and 322B).

The wire constructed into an assemblage of lacy networks is soldered together to form designs. The framework alone can also be used as an enclosure for cloisonné or plique-à-jour enameling (see Chapter 27). When used for enameling, the framework is filled with enamel and the spirals, coils, etc., are not only a part of the design, but act as separators for the different colors. Ground stone, when reduced to a finer powder in a mortar and pestle can also be mixed with epoxy adhesive and used to fill in the spaces or networks. When the stone has hardened, it is ground off level with the wire design. The filigree can be soldered to a backing sheet if desired, and the open areas drilled and pierced with the jeweler's saw (see Chapter 6).

Wire preparation

Round wire, 26- to 32-gauge can be used, but 30-gauge is preferred for the windings, though other shapes may be drawn and used. Craft suppliers will draw the wire to the preferred size, or it can be done by the craftsman himself (see Chapter 12). The wire framework or outline is made of 26-gauge flat wire approximately $\frac{1}{16}$-inch wide. Metal wires other than gold and silver can be used and plated after completion.

The wire should be annealed before winding it into the different spiral and coil patterns (see Chapter 4). After annealing, the wire is straight-

FIG. 322   Pin, filigree, sterling silver. By Sharr Choate.

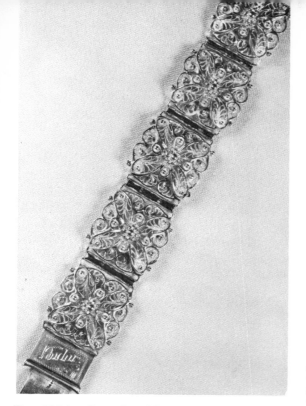

FIG. 322B Pendant, filigree mounting for florentine stone intarsia, sterling silver.
By Sharr Choate.

FIG. 322A Bracelet, filigree, sterling silver.
By Hakon Jonnson.

ened by a slight stretching. Since the fine strands break easily, this must be done with extreme care. One end of the wire is placed in a bench vise, and the opposite end grasped with the drawtongs (or a small pair of vise grips) and a gentle tug is given to the strand of wire. It can also be pulled across a bench stake, bracelet stake, or ring mandrel.

After straightening the wire, the two ends are placed in a bench vise, and the center loop of the wire is hooked onto a curved nail held in the chuck of a hand drill (see Figs. 204 and 204A). The strand, twisted gently until evenly wound, can also be woven or braided for different effects. It is removed from the vise and flattened in a rolling mill or hammered gently on a smooth hard surface (see Fig. 323). The wire should be flattened only until it is as wide as the 26-gauge flat wire which is to be used for the framework or outline.

The design

The design is drawn on a stiff piece of paper, and the framework constructed with pliers to match the design. The framework is placed on a rigid metal base such as cast iron, stainless steel, or mica sheet (see Fig. 324).

Frameworks may also be assembled after forming on a glass slab, and are held in place with gum tragacanth adhesive, or with casting wax melted at frequent points around the outer perimeter. These two methods of holding the framework containing the spirals, coils, etc., are usually employed when it is to be held rigidly in a block of plaster while being soldered.

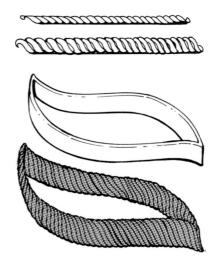

FIG. 323

Fig. 324

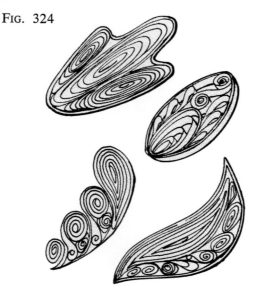

on the size of wire used (see Fig. 325). The jigs can be constructed of any material and with any winding variation as long as the desired end result is obtained. The jigs are made of brass, aluminum, or hardwood. The block may be held in a bench vise while the wires are being wound, or a base may be attached to it so that it can be clamped to the bench top. The pins, short lengths of piano wire, or any other steel wire are pressed or tapped lightly with a small hammer into predrilled holes set $\frac{1}{32}$ inch apart in a lengthwise line through the center of the block. The block need be only as large as 2 by 1 by $\frac{1}{8}$ inches.

A lifting plate can be drilled at the same time that the holes in the block are drilled (see Fig. 326). Jigs without the plate require lifting,

Pliers

Several different types of pliers, such as round-nose, snipe, flat, ring-bending, and end cutters, are used to form the wire framework. The metal is cut with end-cutting pliers, or with a small cold chisel to make a straight smooth and flat cut. In addition to the necessary pliers, a hand vise, ring clamp, and pin vise are also essential to aid in forming the wire with a minimum of scars and knicks.

Winding jigs

Winding jigs are necessary to wind the twisted wire networks. The networks can be constructed in various sizes and shapes depending

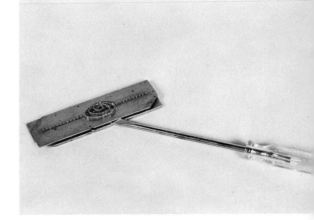

Fig. 326

tugging, and prying the wound wire pattern off of the pins and flattening it again.

The plate, the same size as the block and $\frac{1}{16}$- to $\frac{1}{8}$-inch thick, is clamped to the top of the block. Before removing the clamps and lifting the plate (after the drilling is complete), one end of the plate and the corresponding end of the block should be notched for easy positioning of the plate on the pins. The size of the holes for the pins in the block should be as close as possible to the wire diameter and, after drilling, the holes in the plate should be slightly enlarged so that the plate can be easily lifted off the pins. The purpose of the plate is to enable one to lift the wound wire filigree form as a flat unit. Because the windings are delicate, it is easier to construct a block with a lifting plate than to attempt to lift the wound wires with a knife or other tool.

Fig. 325

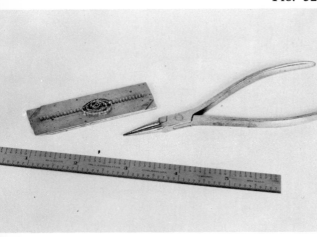

FIG. 327

smooth section of cast iron or mica sheet (see Fig. 329). A small cast-iron frying pan, even the smaller novelty ones used for ashtrays, can be used as a supporting base for the wire assemblage when soldering. Borax flux may be mixed with the gum tragacanth adhesive (used for enameling—see Chapter 27) to hold the solder in place when the torch is applied. Solder filings, borax, and the adhesive may be used as a flux-solder paste for soldering minute areas.

Solders

Filigree solder is made of filings of 14k gold solder, or of silver solder mixed with powdered borax. A good solder for silver consists of two parts fine silver to one part brass. Brass parts from alarm clocks, alloyed with the silver,

Some practice may be necessary to master the art of winding the small networks to fit into a specific area. Brass or copper wire of the same gauge used for the actual design, when rolled to the suggested thin gauge, can be used for practice windings.

Different pin arrangements on winding jigs will give different patterns. These can be used as fill-ins for areas in a pierced section of metal that is not strictly a filigree piece. Windings for leaf veinings and borders can be placed in open areas and held in place by tension alone during soldering.

The windings, after removal from the winding jig, can be carefully hand-formed to fit the shape of the frame, or placed in the framework and then arranged and adjusted gently with the pliers. There should always be tension on the coil to hold it in place in the frame. An orangewood stick sanded to a wedge shape on one end, and a round taper on the opposite is handy for nudging the windings into a corner or pocket loop of the framework (see Fig. 327).

Soldering the windings and framework

The contact areas are coated with a thin paste of gum tragacanth adhesive. The adhesive is used to hold the metal framework to a solid metal base. The framework is placed on a

FIG. 327A Pin, filigree, chasing, repoussé sterling silver with blue star quartz. By Sharr Choate.

FIG. 328

FIG. 329

cooled, and flattened can be filed into solder powder. Small amounts of zinc may be added a little at a time to lower the melting point of the solder to the desired degree.

Mexican filigree is soldered with an alloy of 50 parts brass to 50 parts fine silver. Another alloy is 1 ounce copper to 2 ounces fine silver reduced to filings. Any formula of solder filings is always mixed 3 parts solder to 1 part borax to form a paste together with gum tragacanth adhesive. All solder powders can be used dry by sifting or dusting them into the desired areas on the surfaces, which have been coated with plain gum tragacanth adhesive. The solder dust must be applied before the adhesive solution has a chance to dry.

Kilns and torches for soldering

Enameling or casting kilns and furnaces may be used for soldering a filigree piece. This will eliminate the possibility of melting wires which frequently occurs if the torch is held too close to the delicate wire assemblage. The filigree framework and windings are assembled on a section of cast iron or other support materials and held in place with the gum tragacanth adhesive. The flux-solder filing mix is dusted on the piece, and the entire assemblage, including the base, is eased into the warm furnace a few inches at a time to ensure that the adhesive is completely dry (see Fig. 329). The furnace is then brought up to soldering temperature.

If a torch is used for soldering, the article, still assembled on the cast iron, is placed on a grid on a soldering tripod, and the heat applied from underneath. The heat is applied slowly at first and increased as the metal heats. With this method it is easy to watch the soldering procedure so that additional solder dust may be added as needed without cooling and reheating the metal.

After soldering, the metal is removed from the cast-iron sheet, placed in a cold pickling solution, and brought up to near boiling point to remove the flux and any oxides. The metal will emerge clean and bright.

Indirect soldering

An indirect method that works well for all metal techniques where it is necessary to avoid melting small or delicate parts incorporates the use of dental plaster. The metal framework and windings are assembled and embedded in sheet wax on a glass slab. The assemblage may also be placed in a shallow container such as a plastic lid or box. All the metal parts are fluxed and solder-dusted. A small amount of dental plaster is mixed and poured in to cover the metal completely. After the plaster has set (7 to 15 minutes) the mass is placed for one hour in a kitchen oven or casting-enameling furnace at 350°F. to melt the wax and dry out the plaster for the soldering step.

The dried block, exposed metal side up, is supported by a web on a soldering tripod and heated from underneath (see Figs. 330 and 330A). The exposed metal, when heated, will indicate by its red color that the block is heated through. The torch is continually played

Fig. 330A

Fig. 330

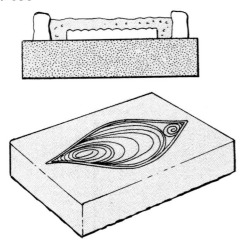

over the undersurface and around the sides of the plaster block to heat it. When the soldering is completed, the entire block is immersed in cold water to disintegrate the plaster. The thermal shock of the cold water on the very hot block will leave only small particles of plaster to be removed from the soldered piece. These are easily removed by scrubbing with a fine-bristle toothbrush. Stubborn particles will dislodge in the pickling solution.

Filigree frames and coils can also be held in place by looping U-shaped lengths of binding wire around them and embedding them slightly in the surface of a sheet of wax (see Fig. 331). The small short wire ends will stick straight up. The joints of the silver or gold wire, strips, or cloissonés are fluxed, and a creamy coat of dental plaster or dental casting investment is poured over the assemblage. When the plaster has set, the mass is turned over and the wax melted, either by placing the entire piece in a pan of boiling water, or by dissolving the wax with a wax solvent. Small particles of plaster are removed with a dental pick or a heavy darning needle inserted into a dowel wood handle. Solder filings or borax mixed in a paste are applied and heated at the juncture points along with the entire mass. When the soldering is completed, the plaster is broken away gently by immersing it immediately in cold water so that the small wire loops can be removed.

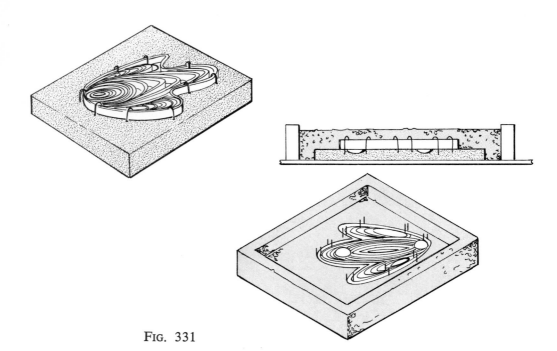

FIG. 331

Balls, beads, and grains

Balls and beads, used for the centers or junctures of filigree windings (see Fig. 332) are made by melting small bits of metal or filings in hollows of a charcoal block. The hollows can be made in the charcoal by gently pressing a dapping-die punch into the block, or by using a small carriage bolt for the same purpose. If a flat bottom is preferred on the grain, the metal can be melted on the flat surface of the block or on an asbestos sheet and, after cooling, pickling, and rinsing, filed flat on the bottom. Beads of one size can be made by cutting sheet scrap into identical squares, or by winding wire around a mandrel or dowel wood shaft. The wire coil is sawed in the same manner as when making rings for chains, etc. (see Chapter 12). Fine grains and shot are made by melting metal filings and screening them to obtain various sizes.

Large beads are made by melting the end of a section of heavy wire until it forms into a ball. As the metal melts, one can determine the size desired. Large leaves can be made in the same manner or by melting a sufficient amount

of silver, and while the metal is still molten, inserting a wire tip coated with flux into the ball. Small leaves, to be used with the filigree designs, are constructed similarly by melting the end of a section of wire to form a ball. While the ball is still hot, it can be pressed against a flat metal surface or tapped gently to flatten it. The ball and wire are allowed to cool slightly before dipping them in pickling solution, after which they are flattened to leaf thickness and filed to shape. The wire stem is not cut until it is attached to other parts of the article and the proper length for it determined.

Beads or grains are positioned on the filigree windings and soldered along with the coils and framework. If added after the initial soldering is completed, there is a risk of melting the filigree with subsequent soldering. The beads are added to the assemblage with soft solder after the findings have been attached to the underside.

Previously soldered sections will not become loosened easily if they remain free of flux during subsequent soldering steps of other portions of the article. They may be further

FIG. 332   Necklace, filigree, 14k gold.   Mexican (Oaxacan) design.

FIG. 333

FIG. 334

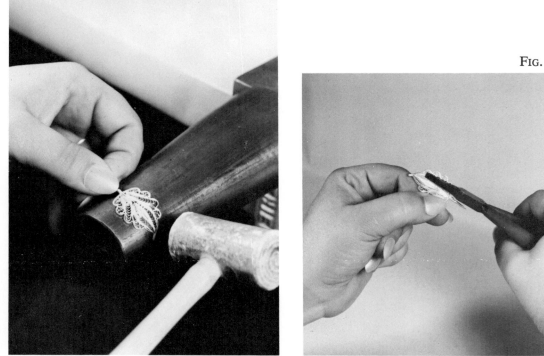

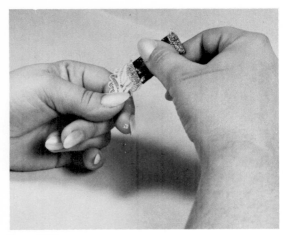

FIG. 335

FIG. 335A

protected from loosening and from fire scale by coating them with antiflux.

Forming after soldering

After soldering, the article must be shaped into graceful curves and swirls by placing the filigree sections on a curved stake and tapping them lightly with a rawhide mallet (see Figs. 333 and 334). Distortion may occur if this step is attempted with hand and finger pressure. The soldered forms are added to other fabricated sections of filigree or metalwork in a second soldering step. Findings are then added with easy-flow or soft solder.

Finishing

After all the soldering steps are completed, excess solder is removed from visible areas, and the entire piece is gently buffed with bobbing compound, followed by a good scrubbing with a fine nylon bristle brush and a household detergent (see Figs. 335 and 335A). When buffing the article, it should be held firmly, with due regard for the correct position, so that the buffing wheel does not grab the metal from the hands. A nylon bristle brush is used with a paste mixture of either whiting and alcohol or pumice and water to polish filigree articles.

CHAPTER 23

Fused Metals—Granulation—Drop Casting

FUSED METALS

METAL IN VARIOUS FORMS OF SHEET, WIRE, shot, filings, etc., can be combined without solder to form intriguing pieces. The entire object need not always be made up of scrap. Small fragments of new sheet, sections of wire, and coarse filings can be fused to a new sheet section to be used as a base (see Fig. 336). Metal scrap may be melted onto a base, preformed of sheet metal to match a planned design. Usually, 20-gauge metal is used for the base. Because of the buildup of fused metal, the base should be kept as thin as possible but still sturdy. Both the base metal and the fragments are pickled and fluxed to assure a good strong bond between the metal parts. Small fused sections may be formed before adding them to a preformed backing piece, and then bezels or other mountings can be added later for gemstones.

By experimenting with bits of metal, it will be found that the metal when heated will sag and fall into shapes that are impossible to form in any other way. The metal fragments can be piled up in various ways, and new material can be cut with shears into free-form, free-flowing shapes, including small coils of wire spread irregularly or bent slightly. Metals with higher melting points may be added to the fused mass; however, they must be confined to small fragments, shot, and filings. The rounded corners and edges, the general flowing form accented by the "orange-peel" texture that results from overheating the metal, gives the effect of a cast piece (see Fig. 336A).

FIG. 336

207

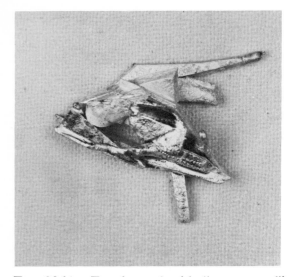

FIG. 336A Fused metal with "orange peel" finish, scrap sterling silver.
By Sharr Choate.

Gemstones in the mass

Gemstones may be added to the small swirled pockets of metal if desired in any one of many ways described in Chapter 11, but the attractiveness of the metal oxidized, buffed, and polished to bring out highlights, or covered with a patina-like coating will give all the accent actually needed for objects made in this technique.

Metal preparation

The metals to be used must be free of dirt, grease, and oxides before they are fused. They are then placed in a cold pickling solution of sulfuric acid and water (see Chapter 4). The solution is brought to a temperature just below the boiling point, and the metals are kept immersed until they are bright and shiny.

Small shot and filings can be poured into a cone of filter paper to prevent their loss in the clear water bath. The metal sheet base, if used, must be pickled also before the metals are fused.

Metals to be fused without a base section are arranged, stacked, overlapped, and intertwined with each other as desired after they have been coated with liquid soldering flux. If dry flux powder such as household borax is used, it can be sprinkled on the metals after they have been arranged. Often the original

amount of metal will melt too quickly, flow in the wrong direction, or simply reduce more than is expected. Additional scrap metal may be added to take care of this but it should be prepared in advance to save time when fusing the metals. The clean fluxed metal may be added to the mass with tweezers, or gently pushed toward it with the long soldering rod while the torch remains on the metal.

Fusing

The torch is applied to the metal in the beginning stages with a regular flame and, as the mass settles and begins to take some semblance of a fused piece, the flame is adjusted to a needlepoint. In this way the metal can be heat-molded with the torch as needed. By this it can be seen that the torch not only heats the metal, but is used to bring about interesting and unusual formations.

One must be careful not to overmelt the metal or the rounded edges will disappear into a big molten puddle.

Use of solder

Silver solder may be used to ensure a sturdy but delicate framework. The use of solder is of course dictated by the assemblage of the metal fragments. As the fusing progresses, it must be ascertained whether or not the object is sturdy enough to hold its shape when cool. Often additional pieces of metal or wire may be required to beef up a weak area.

After the fusing is completed, the mass is air-cooled (not quenched) before it is dipped in pickling solution and rinsed in running water.

Surface finishing

In some instances after the fusing is completed, protrusions, abutments, or sharp corners may need filing and sanding, but the effect is lost if excessive treatment with tools is evident. The beauty of the piece lies in the spontaneity apparent in articles made by the heat-molding technique.

The underside of the mass usually picks up the texture of the asbestos sheet or charcoal block, and this should be sanded smooth on sandpaper that is supported by a smooth hard surface. After sanding, the article is buffed and polished.

Usually the bright white color of fused silver pieces is sufficiently beautiful with the frosted "orange-peel" texture, and no other surface treatment is necessary. However, there are several finishing possibilities such as slight buffing to accent particular areas, oxidizing, and polishing the metal to bring out highlights, or covering with a patina coating.

GRANULATION

Granulation can be considered a branch of the metal overlay (appliqué) technique as well as the metal fusing process. Actually, this technique consists of attaching, without soldering, micromini-sized beads, spheroids, or other small shapes to a metal surface for decoration (see Fig. 303B). However, larger granules or shapes that require solder for attachment can be considered a variation of this technique. Granulation can be applied only after an article is completely formed and surface-finished.

Fig. 337

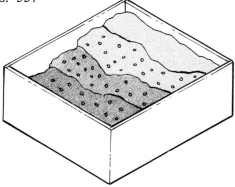

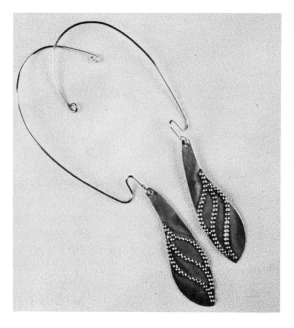

FIG. 337A   Earrings, granulation on sterling silver. Earrings hang over the ears and loop in front of the earlobes.
By Wayne Smith.

Making beads

Small beads (granules) are made from particles that are produced by filing clean oxide-free metal with coarse files (bastard or vixen cuts). These are placed on a charcoal block and separated so that each particle when heated with the torch melts into a single bead. The heat of the torch combined with the reducing properties of the flame (more gas than oxygen) produces a hot, oxide-free surface suitable for fusing. The particles must be separated enough from each other so that when heated they will not travel to each other and form a larger mass. The beads can be as small as ¼ mm ($\frac{1}{100}$-inch) or as large as 1 mm ($\frac{1}{25}$-inch) (larger sizes are called shot).

Another method of forming small beads is to place particles in powdered charcoal, cover them with more charcoal, and apply enough heat to transform them into spheroids (see Figs. 337 and 337A). When cool, the spheroids are separated from the charcoal by washing them in a fine screen container and afterwards sorting them through screens of various mesh sizes.

Making shot

Metal for each shot (pellet) is cut from wire or from a sheet. Naturally, the size of the pellet will be determined by the size of the slug or square.

The diameter of the bead or shot and the gauge of the metal sheet or base must be comparable in dimension for satisfactory results, because small beads will melt before thick metal has heated sufficiently.

Fusing the beads

An adhesive (gum tragacanth and water mixed to a paste) is applied on the clean pickled metal at all contact areas. The beads are placed on the metal either with tweezers or with a small soft camel-hair brush that has been dipped in the adhesive. The adhesive must be thoroughly dry before the metal is heated.

For adequate fusing of high-karat content golds and fine silver, the adhesive must be mixed with equal parts of copper carbonate or cupric hydroxide and made into a paste with distilled water. This mixture is necessary because of the higher degree of heat required to fuse these metals. Lower-karat golds and silver alloys can be fused by using heat and adhesive without any additives.

The heat applied to the metal must diffuse evenly as it is essential that both parts arrive at the fusing temperature at the same time. The temperature of pure gold should be 1750 to 1775°F., and of fine silver 1575 to 1600°F. Lower-karat gold and silver alloys will fuse at lower temperatures.

Joining shot

Shot is attached by applying a mixture of powdered flux, gum tragacanth, and water to the contact areas and placing a very small snippet of solder beside each pellet (see Fig. 338). The metal is heated to attach all the shot to the surface at the same time.

FIG. 338

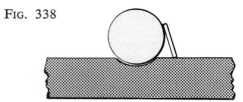

Cooling and pickling

When the fusing or soldering process is completed, the metal is air-cooled to make sure that all the grains are attached. Premature quenching will loosen the grains. When cool enough to handle with the bare fingers, the article is placed in a pickling solution, which is brought to near boiling, and left until the surface is bright and free of oxides.

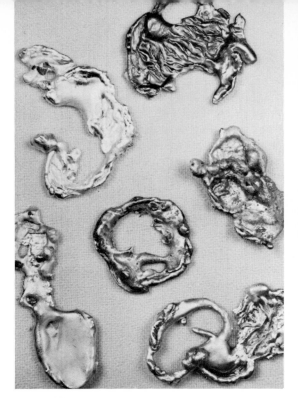

FIG. 339

Final assembly

All regular soldering with lower melting points that is necessary to assemble sections and findings is done after the granulation decorating procedure is complete.

DROP CASTING

An innovation for creating free-flow articles called "metal drop" or "ice-water casting" affords an excellent use of scrap metal pieces and filings for they can be remelted and dropped again and again until a pleasing shape results (see Fig. 339). This is done by heating metal scrap to the rolling stage, and then dropping the hot metal in a perpendicular pour into a stainless steel pan of ice water (see Fig. 340). Glass dishes, even pyrex, may break from the thermal shock of the molten metal and the ice water. The action of the molten metal as it drops into the water forms various nonrepresentational, one-of-a-kind shapes (see Fig. 341). The only way such pieces can be duplicated is by means of a mold-making and casting technique.

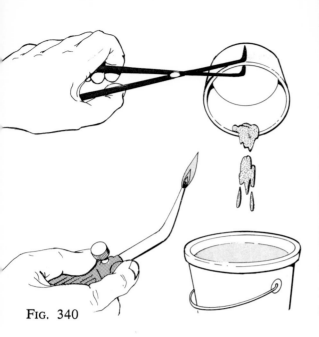

FIG. 340

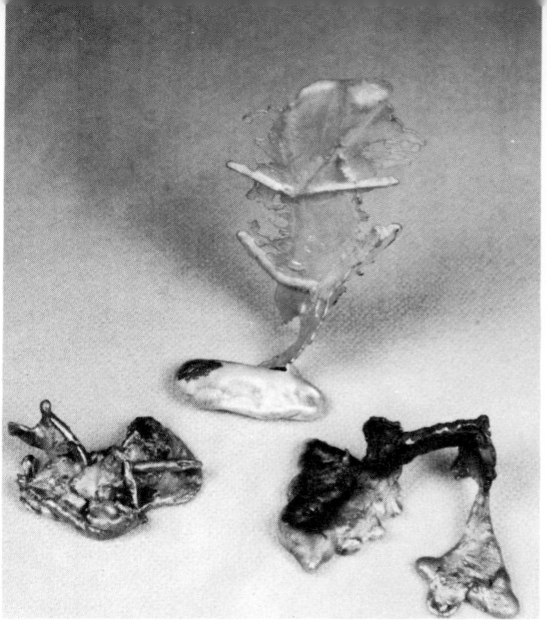

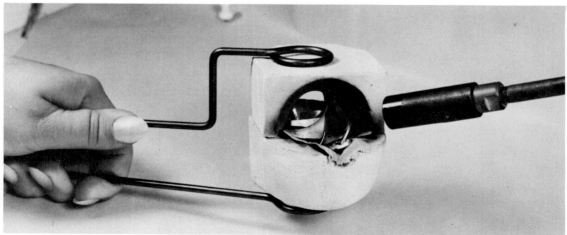

FIG. 341 "Sculptures," drop casting, sterling silver.
By Sharr Choate.

Metal preparation

The scrap to be melted is placed in an asbestos-lined crucible, such as is used for sand casting (see Figs. 342, 342A, and 342B), in a small fired clay dish lined with the same asbestos material, or in a hollowed-out area in a charcoal soldering block. If the charcoal block is used, the depression should be fairly deep with a small groove cut into one side from the outer edge of the block to act as a trough for the molten metal when it is poured into the water (see Fig. 343).

The pan should be deep enough to allow for at least 3 to 3½ inches of water, ice cubes, or slush. The scrap metal (if this is being used

rather than new metal) should be cleaned of as much debris as possible before melting. This includes saw blade fragments, buffing lint, strings, paper from designs, etc.

Heating the metal

As the metal is heated, it should be sprinkled with powdered borax (household type) which is a flux and will cleanse the metal of impurities and oxides. A scum or dross that forms on the surface of the metal as it melts must be skimmed off with a small stick. Additional flux is sprinkled on top while the metal is molten. The torch should remain on the metal until the crucible is tipped for the pour. The

FIG. 342

Fig. 342A

crucible is held with tongs over the water-filled container, and the contents dumped quickly, not dribbled, into the water.

Temperature and "drop" variations

Experimenting with different heights for the drop, different metals, and different water temperatures will show how fascinating this method can be. The hot metal can also be poured over slushy ice, ice cubes, or into a hollow in a small cake of ice. This gives more dimension to the free forms than does a simple drop into very cold water.

Pouring molten metal into water in a tall container produces long podlike shapes (see Fig. 344), and a straight perpendicular pour close to the water's surface produces a rounded lump shape (see Figs. 345 and 345A). Metal poured over ice cubes will solidify before the ice melts, taking the shape of the cube corners and emerging to resemble small sculptures (see

Fig. 342B

Figs. 346 and 341). Forms vary from small to large molded shapes depending on the amount of silver used. Often the metal "freezes" (solidifies) into interesting crystal shapes or clusters (see Fig. 347).

Preserving surface finish

Metal often emerges from the water without any surface oxides that would require pickling. Silver, because of its copper alloy constituent, cools into a gold-tinged silvery color, but addi-

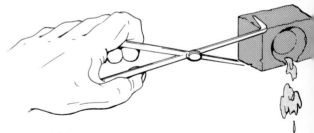

Fig. 343

tional heat applied for soldering requires pickling which destroys the attractive coloring. If this gold-tinged color is not desired, or if firescale is evident, the forms may be pickled to produce the usual frosty surface of silver.

Other metals used

Other metals such as gold, copper, brass, bronze—also foreign coins—can be melted down and used for "drop" castings. These can

FIG. 345   Necklace and earrings, drop casting, sterling silver.   By Hakon Jonnson.

be pickled, soldered, buffed, polished, and oxidized to give different effects.

Gold, when remelted, requires the addition of 50 percent new material or it will become quite brittle and hard to work. Scrap gold can be used without adding new material, but when it becomes unusable it must be sent to a refiner to be reworked.

Casting long seeds of metal

After dropping and cooling, the metal masses should be studied for various design possibili- ties. Pieces that seem incomplete by themselves can be soldered to other pieces to give interesting effects, and small bits can be used for appliqué and granulation techniques.

Small bubbles or "needles" that form on the metal as it is poured should also be saved. Metal dropped into a deep container will disintegrate on the bottom of the water container and form long slim pieces that make excellent necklace links. A larger mass dropped in the same manner will form into a pendant-sized piece.

FIG. 344

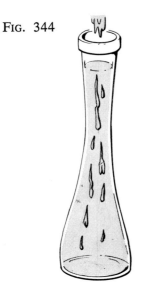

FIG. 345A   Earrings, drop casting, sterling silver with pearls.
By Pamela Healey.

FIG. 346

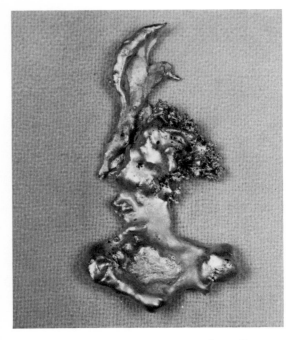

FIG. 347 Pin, drop casting, sterling silver. By Sharr Choate.

Steam bubbles in metal

Bubbly castings may have entrapped water which will explode as steam pressure builds up. This occurs when the metal is reheated for melting and casting, or when it is being soldered. The bubbles should be drilled to permit the escape of any water in an area that will not be visible when the article is completed (see Fig. 348). Holes that may show can be filled with solder or with small pieces of metal left in the container. Small spheres may be saved for decoration or joined with other dropped pieces, and then assembled by soldering or fusing into a single piece.

Metal finishing

Rough edges and tentacle-like extensions, if sharp, are trimmed and sanded if not amenable to the design concept. Often a gold or silver piece needs only a minimum of buffing to highlight the frosty silver surface. Other metals are usually completely buffed and polished. Any added gemstone attachments are soldered after the sanding and filing has been completed. Articles with a gold tinge (on silver) can be preserved by a thin coating of spray lacquer. The finished piece can be attached to a finding with soft solder, or to a regular prong mounting.

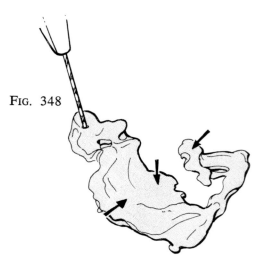

FIG. 348

CHAPTER 24

Forging

FORGING CONSISTS MAINLY OF FORMING METAL by hammering to alter the basic thickness and shape. The metal is first textured, after which it can be stretched—thinner, wider, longer; or condensed—thicker, shorter, narrower; and sunk or raised either convex or concave (see Figs. 349, 349A, 349B, and 349C).

Bending, twisting, wrapping, and folding are not referred to as forging steps, although they are part of handwrought metal techniques (see Chapter 5).

Forging on a massive scale is associated with blacksmithing and the forming of objects in ferrous metals such as iron and steel. Akin to this is the forging or handwrought metalwork done on a smaller and more detailed scale for jewelry and metalsmithing which employs a variety of small hammers on nonferrous metals. Working with nonferrous metals has its complexities because of the malleability and ductility of the metals, and the fact that after annealing, they are worked cold instead of red-hot as in the case of ferrous metals.

Precious metals can be worked hot but this is a technique reserved for the very experienced craftsman. The metal is struck when hot, but the temperature is extremely critical with very little leeway; therefore, striking the metal at an incorrect temperature causes the metal to crack or become grainy or sugary so that it crumbles. The shapes of forged metals are, like those produced in the casting techniques, difficult to produce by any other method.

Forging techniques—sinking and raising

Metal is forged to shape by raising it with a cross-peen raising hammer or planishing hammer over a stake (see Fig. 350). This indicates that the metal is worked and shaped from the outer surface. Sinking, another forging process, shapes the metal by working it from the inner surface. Generally this means that the metal is hammered down into a preformed hollow of hardwood or metal with a sinking or embossing hammer (see Fig. 351). Simple or basic forging consists of hammering flat metal with a cross-peen raising hammer on a stake or anvil to stretch the metal in different directions while at the same time thinning it (see Fig. 352).

Bouging

As the metal is worked it is bouged to remove humps and wrinkles from the working area.

FIG. 349   Plate, forged and pierced, feather and resin inlay, brass.   By Sharr Choate.

Bouging is done with a rawhide or wooden mallet with round ends on the inner surface of sunken objects and on the outer surface of raised objects with a wooden or rawhide mallet. The objects are supported on either a hard wooden or a metal surface when bouged from the inside, and supported by an appropriate stake when bouged on the outer surface (see Fig. 353). The metal is hammered only where it makes a flat contact with the supporting surface (see Fig. 354).

Planishing

Planishing, which is a finer smoothing step, is done on the outer surface of the metal with planishing hammers—flat or dome-faced, regardless of how it is formed. The metal surface to be treated in this way must always be parallel with the anvil when struck with the hammer.

Planishing metal on a stake requires that the surface contour of the stake and the inner con-

FIG. 349A   For-spo-kni (fork-spoon-knife-in-one), forged with stone nugget inlay, sterling silver with garnets and peridot.   By Sharr Choate.

FIG. 349B Plate and drawer pulls, forged and stone inlay. Plate: sterling silver, brass, bronze copper, nickel silver. Pulls: brass with malachite inlay.
By Sharr Choate.

tour of the raised metal object exactly match in the area where it is to be hammered on the outer surface (see Fig. 355). Only after annealing can bouging and planishing be done, and additional annealing is necessary before the sinking and raising procedure can be continued.

Metal hardness retention

If hardness is desired in the piece after the forging process is completed, the final annealing is omitted. Soldering and other work with the torch are completed without quenching the hot metal in water or pickling solution. It is air-cooled and when cool enough to handle with the bare fingers is placed in warm pickling solution which is brought to near boiling point. When the oxides are removed, the metal is taken from the solution and rinsed in water.

FIG. 349C Pin and earrings, forged shapes, sterling silver.
By Sharr Choate.

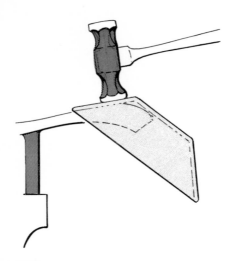

FIG. 350

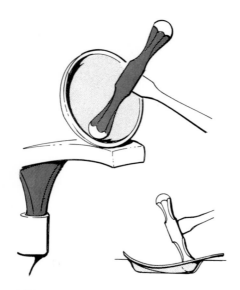

FIG. 351

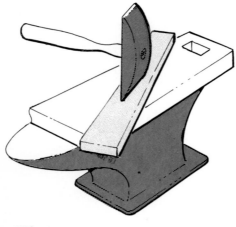

FIG. 352

Metal requirements

Metal requirements for sunken objects do not need to be increased in size to allow for the normal stretching of the metal; however, the thickness of the metal must be increased for deeper vessels. A vessel of 2-inch diameter (18-gauge) can be sunk 2 inches just as a 12-inch-diameter (14-gauge) vessel can be sunk 12 inches, but the metal must be thicker so that it can be shaped free from cracks and holes in thin areas (see Fig. 356).

Raised objects are made of thin metals, or in the thickness desired in the finished article, because the basic metal thickness does not change throughout the forging process (see Fig. 356). The outline size must be increased

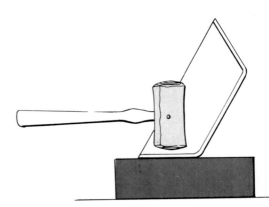

FIG. 353

as the metal is formed over a shape and therefore requires more metal to cover a curved area. A shallow dish 2 inches deep with a 2-inch diameter requires a metal disc of $5\frac{1}{16}$-inch diameter. A 2-inch diameter dish 1 inch deep requires a disc of $3\frac{1}{4}$-inch diameter. Other examples are as follows:

Dish Diameter (in.)	Dish Depth (in.)	Disc Diameter (in.)
2	$\frac{1}{2}$	$2\frac{1}{4}$
4	1	$4\frac{3}{4}$
4	2	$6\frac{1}{2}$
5	1	$5\frac{5}{8}$
5	2	$6\frac{1}{8}$
6	2	$7\frac{3}{4}$
6	3	$9\frac{5}{8}$

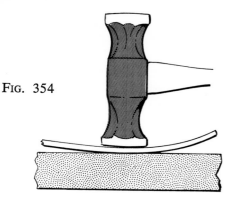

FIG. 354

These calculations are based on measurements made around a curved surface in cross section. Metal measurements can be determined by drawing a cross section of the object, and then measuring around the curve with string or soft wire (see Fig. 357). The string or straightened wire is measured to obtain the diameter of the disc. Asymmetrical, oval, or oblong shapes require additional cross-section diagrams for measurements, so that the length and width of the metal can be determined (see Fig. 357).

Metals for sinking and raising range in thickness from 10- to 24-gauge, and those for regular forging can be any thickness, even as much as several inches thick, depending upon the degree of forging and spread of the metal

FIG. 357

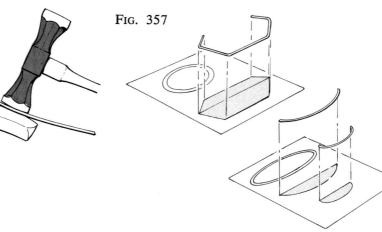

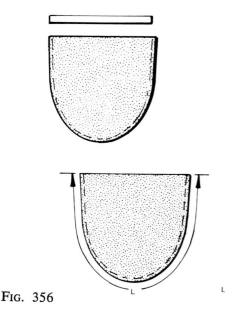

FIG. 355

FIG. 356

when completed. Objects that will require a thickened edge, usually of 6-inch diameter or larger, will need an additional ¾ inch of metal around the circumference. Larger pieces require a corresponding increase in metal requirements.

Stakes

Stakes are used to support metals when they are formed either by raising, or in later steps, when planishing sunken metal (see Fig. 358). The stake surfaces must be kept smooth and free of any nicks or scratches that would transfer to the metal being worked. The surfaces should be coated with a thin film of fine oil when not in use to prevent the formation of any rust. Rust particles hammered into the metal would make a surface difficult to buff and polish

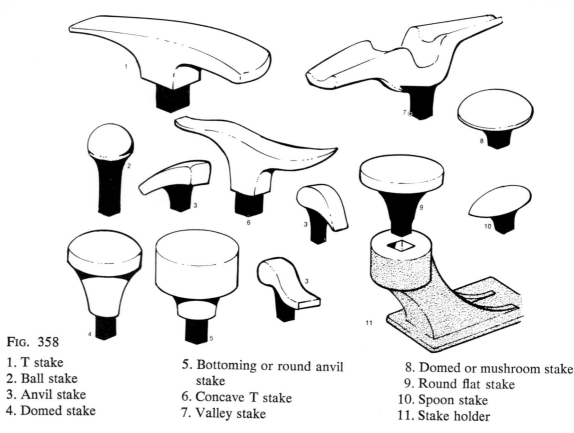

FIG. 358

1. T stake
2. Ball stake
3. Anvil stake
4. Domed stake

5. Bottoming or round anvil
   stake
6. Concave T stake
7. Valley stake

8. Domed or mushroom stake
9. Round flat stake
10. Spoon stake
11. Stake holder

properly. The stake must never be struck directly with a hammer as the surface could be damaged beyond repair.

Basic stakes are purchased as a start, and others added as required for a specific project or purpose (see Fig. 359). The stake holder is standard, and all stakes are interchangeable to fit the base. The stakes offered by different manufacturers are standard, even to the color-ful names used to identify each, so that one need not look to only one supplier for tools.

Standard stakes, in addition to the stake holder and anvil, are T stake, mushroom or round, and anvil. For larger projects, anvils with stake receptacles (a square hole in the flat surface) are often used in place of a standard stake holder. A sturdy bench vise with ¾-inch jaws can be used for the same purpose if

FIG. 359

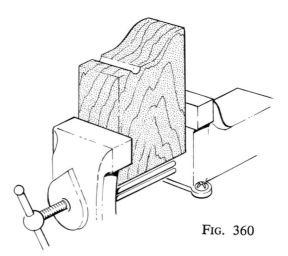

FIG. 360

attached to a strongly built workbench, securely attached to floor or wall. Wooden stakes
when used are usually held in a bench vise, and
a flat space is needed on a wooden workbench
top in addition to space to place a pitch box or
sandbag (see Fig. 360).

In addition to regular stakes, ring and bracelet mandrels are also used for forging processes.

Various forming supports

Machined depressions in hardwood blocks give
good support to the metal during the sinking
process, but they permit only stereotyped
shapes (see Fig. 361). A greater variety of
shapes can be improvised by adequately supporting the metal with stakes, sandbags, hardwood stump ends, and pitch bowls.

Hammers

Many different kinds of hammers are used for
the forging process, some for general use, and
others limited to specific techniques. These
hammers come in various sizes and lengths and
in different weights (see Figs. 362 and 362A).

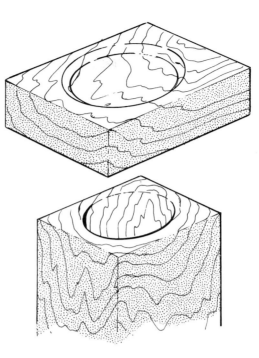

Fig. 361

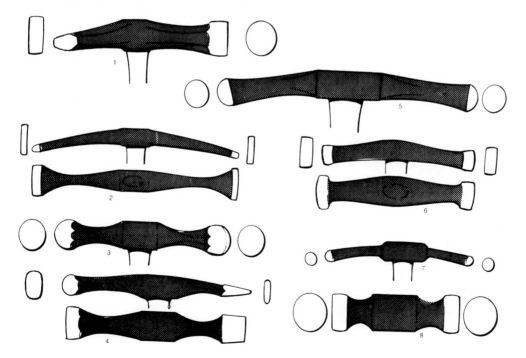

Fig. 362

1. Cross-peen raising hammer
2. Cross-peen raising hammer
3. Dome-faced embossing hammer

4. Collett hammer
5. Ball-faced sinking hammer
6. Cross-peen raising hammer

7. Ball-faced bottoming hammer
8. Planishing hammer

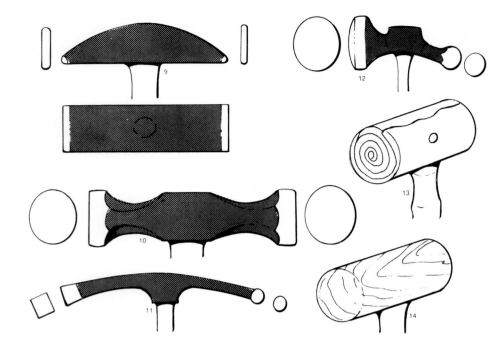

FIG. 362A
9. Forging (cross-peen raising) hammer

10. Dome-faced forging
    hammer
11. Box hammer

12. Chasing hammer
13. Rawhide mallet
14. Wooden mallet

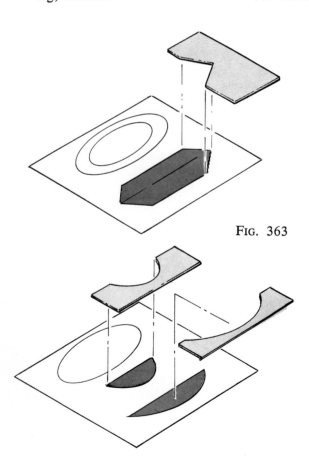

FIG. 363

Cross-peen raising hammers will flatten, spread, and flow the metal from point of impact at right angles to the main axis of the hammer face; flat-faced forging hammers will work the metal in all directions radially from point of impact (see Figs. 370 and 370A). These principles must be understood to determine which way the hammer must face when striking the metal.

Various types of cross-peen raising and planishing hammers other than standard forging hammers are used for raising the metal. Small bottoming and dome-faced planishing hammers are often used for leaves, flowers, petals, etc., in the manner described for the repoussé technique (see Chapter 18). Ball hammers are also used for sinking small areas. Box hammers are used for working in different areas, and to form a shoulder or base on the object. Collet hammers are also used for forming bases and for upsetting (thickening) the edges of vessels. Planishing hammers are used to smooth the outer metal surface when the bouging step of rough smoothing has been completed.

Hammers should be maintained free of any surface defects. The striking surfaces should be sanded to remove any nicks or scratches that will transfer (like a die stamping) to the metal surface. Rust, if permitted to accumulate on the surface, will be hammered down into the metal surface, making it difficult to clean and polish perfectly. The striking surfaces should be sanded on a carborundum wheel or on a piece of carborundum or emery paper cupped in the palm. This is followed by sanding with a rubber-bonded abrasive wheel, and then buffing on a hard felt wheel charged with Tripoli compound. The surface is mirror-polished on a medium felt buff charged with rouge.

The hammers, when not in use, should have a thin coating of fine oil on the striking surfaces to prevent the formation of any rust.

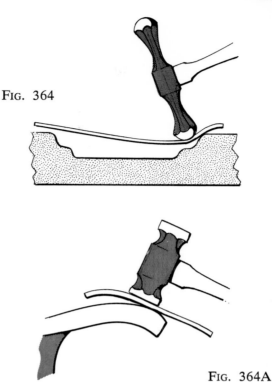

Fig. 364

Fig. 364A

Templates

Templates can be made of metal or heavy cardboard (see Fig. 363). The exact desired contour inside and out can be drawn on quadrille-lined paper and transferred to the cardboard. As the metal nears completion of the sinking or raising process, it is checked often with the contour gauge to determine areas that need additional work.

Multiple-piece forging

Complex or compound curves may present difficulties when forging a form from a single section of metal. Sections can be forged separately and then assembled by soldering or riveting.

Sinking

When sinking metal, the area with the greatest degree of depression is hammered first and the blows are directed successively out to the edge of the depression area but not to the metal edge itself. Metal travels on impact with the hammer in a definite direction, depending upon the angle of the face of the hammer when striking the surface. The metal must be held firmly against a surface plate or hardwood block when hammered. Before starting the hammering, the metal is tilted so that the point of impact (directly under the scribed line) will be at a 25 to 30° angle (see Fig. 364).

The first row or circle of hammer marks is made from a scribed line in the center of the article or from where the sinking is to begin. As the hammering continues, the metal is turned either clockwise or counterclockwise so that the previous blow can be seen.

When sinking or raising a deep vessel and the metal appears to lean or slant, the rotation of the rows of hammer blows should be reversed so that one row will be hammered clockwise and the next row counterclockwise. This is done as soon as the slant of the metal is obvious, not when the sinking or raising is almost completed. Small sections of metal can be rotated to the right continuously throughout the hammering steps. As each consecutive row of hammering is started, the blows must overlap not only the preceding blow, but also the finished row of hammering.

Hammer blows should be light, coming from a wrist action, not from the elbow. The metal is struck with the hammer in a rhythmic count of three consecutive strokes, each overlapping the other slightly. The hammer handle and the forearm are maintained in a straight line. The hand is moved so that the head of the hammer is raised only a few inches from the metal surface.

Annealing

When forming metals, annealing is usually necessary after each complete rotation of the circle or spiral. The metal will seem stubborn and a sudden hardness is evident when annealing is necessary. The metals are annealed to the regular suggested temperatures for annealing (see Chapter 4).

When sinking metal, the thickness of the stretched metal can be gauged in any area with calipers, according to the capacity of the caliper jaws. By frequently checking sections that have been sunk extensively, holes, sometimes inadvertently made by hammering metal to its absolute thinness, can be avoided. Holes are difficult to close and require a soldering operation which, being impossible to remove in the surface finishing, will be visible in the finished piece.

Raising

When raising metal to a shape, the same principles described for sinking are followed except that the metal is worked on the outer surface and the forming is begun close to the outer edge or perimeter of the metal disc. Wrinkles will form in the metal as it is raised. When the metal is completely rotated, any wrinkling tendencies should be removed (by bouging) before proceeding to the next complete circle of hammer blows. (see Fig. 353). By removing them progressively they will not develop into large wrinkles which could be difficult to correct later on when the hammering is completed.

When raising metal on a stake the hammer face and the stake surface should be parallel with each other and separated by the metal (see Fig. 354). If a bracelet stake or tapered mandrel is used, the metal is held at right angles to the striking surface, not to the stake or mandrel axis which would put an unwanted taper on the formed metal.

Deep vessels are raised on long anvil or horn stakes (see Fig. 358). The metal is raised from the outer edge until about one-third done, then raising is continued from the base. When another third of the forming is completed, the metal is moved on the stake, alternating the work area between the two sections until forming is completed.

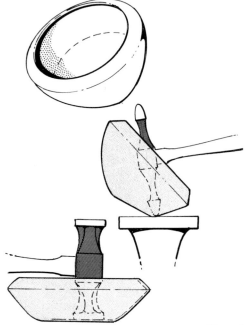

FIG. 365

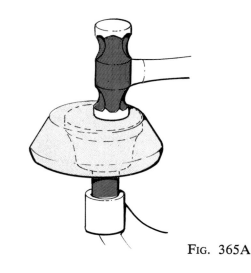

FIG. 365A

Bases are formed on sunken objects when the metal has been formed to the desired depth. A scribed line is made on the inner surface to indicate where the angle for the base is to be made. A collet hammer or flat-faced planishing hammer is used to form the angle with the metal tilted to 25 to 30° at the planned radius of the base (see Figs. 365 and 365A). The hammer blows must be even and overlapping. A flat-faced planishing hammer or raising hammer is then used to flatten the area inside the angle (see Fig. 366). This is done on a surface plate to ensure an absolutely flat base. Sunken bases can be formed after this primary base is completed by using the same type of hammers on a wooden stake and followed by leveling the base on the surface plate.

Bases are made on a raised object as it is formed so that the raising process can be stopped when the correct base diameter is reached. The angle needs only to be defined with a flat-faced planishing hammer on the inside surface.

After the base is completed a mark is scribed on the outside of the object with a pair of calipers (see Figs. 367 and 367A) to indicate the edge of the vessel, which is then trimmed with shears and filed smooth.

Upsetting the metal edge

Hammering directly to and off the edge of the metal will thin the edge. If hammering is done

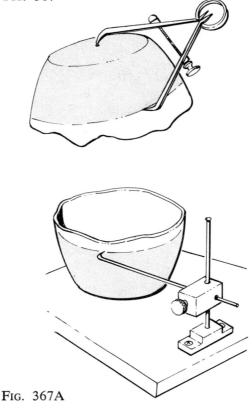

FIG. 367

FIG. 367A

and any flares, flutes, or crimped areas in the edge of the object are made on a valley stake with a planishing hammer (see Fig. 369). Small fluted sections are made in a crimping stake having the groove for this step in the upper surface. The sections are very gently marked off with a scribe to keep the size uniform and the areas symmetrical with the main body of the article.

Forging flat metals without stakes

When forging a strip of metal into a shape such as a spoon or fork, the bowl or tine sec-

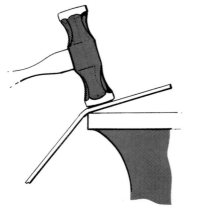

FIG. 366

close to but not on the edge, this will maintain some of the thickness. When working close to the outer edge of the metal, after each complete rotation of hammering the metal is placed on a flat surface or a sandbag. A collet hammer is used in a horizontal position to hammer the edge in order to thicken it (see Fig. 368).

Decorative forging

When all raising or sinking, bouging, and planishing is completed, the edge is trimmed evenly,

FIG. 368

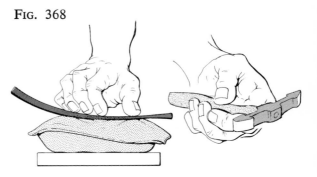

Fig. 369

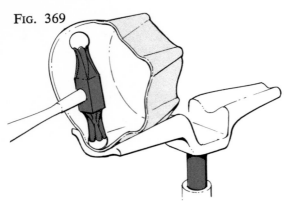

ished metal surface. If the metal tends to form a taper as it is hammered, it is because the hammer is not being kept parallel with the anvil when struck.

After the metal is flattened with the cross-peen hammer to the desired thickness, it is sunk into the hardwood bowl, formed over a spoon stake for a spoon, and over a round stake for the tines of a fork (see Figs. 371 and 349A). The narrower but slightly thicker shank (neck) section is then formed. The handle is forged and shaped from the shank (neck) portion out to the end to avoid over-extending the metal. In this way, any excess metal can be removed from the handle, which would not be possible if the bowl and shank were not completed first.

If the shank section is too short, it can be elongated by drawing. This is done by hammering opposite surfaces alternately. As the hammering continues, there will be a slight mushrooming effect on the edges. If the drawing is to produce a squared shape, the hammer-

tion is made first in one end of the metal. The metal is flattened by starting at the beginning of the bowl area opposite the end and working the cross-peen raising hammer in successive overlapping blows out to the end of the metal (see Figs. 370 and 370A). The metal is then turned over, and the blows are continued out to the end, starting in the same area, directly opposite the initial hammer blows. Smooth overlapping blows, and a minimum of hammer marks from the highly polished surface of the hammer face will produce a plan-

Fig. 370

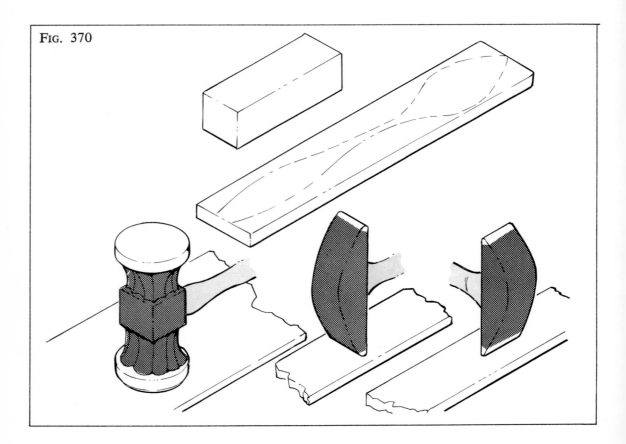

FIG. 370A

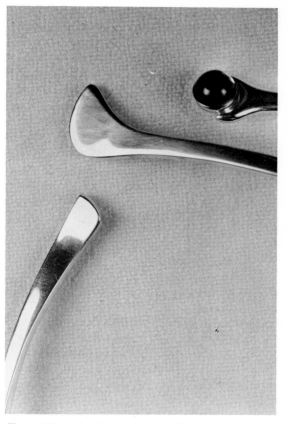

FIG. 372   Necklace tip detail, simulated forging (lamination).
By Sharr Choate.

FIG. 371

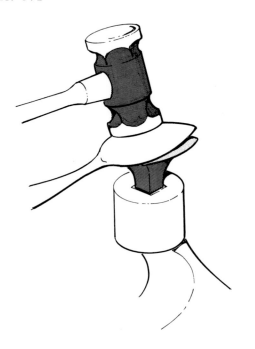

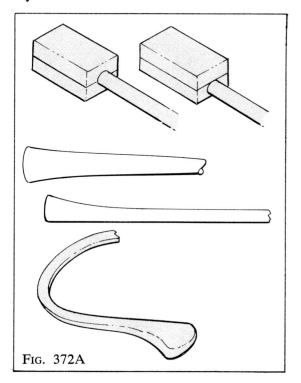

FIG. 372A

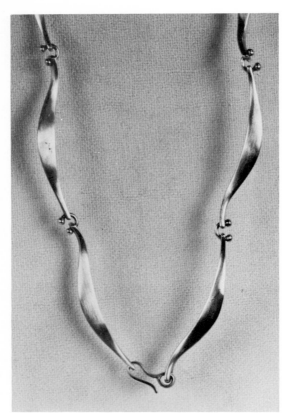

ing is done equally on all four sides. By tapping only on opposite sides, a rectangular shape (in cross section) is produced.

Simulated forging

Simulated forging done today often consists of soldering a double thickness of metal to the end of a small square wire and then flattening the ends, widening them to a flare (see Figs. 372, 372A, and 373). Ordinarily the ends, when flattened, would be extremely thin, therefore with this method a greater degree of thickness is maintained on the tip ends of a forged necklace or bracelet. Short sections to double the thickness can also be soldered in the strip center. After soldering and forging the ends, the entire piece is filed to shape with half-round files to produce a piece of jewelry apparently forged from one section of metal. This eliminates drawing out a heavier section of metal to form thin sections required by the design.

FIG. 373 Necklace detail, forging, sterling silver.
By Sharr Choate.

CHAPTER 25

Metal Spinning

Spinning metals is a method of forcing a rotating metal disc over a wooden or metal form with a tool held against a fulcrum for support. As the metal spins, it is gradually stretched over the wooden chuck to form a predetermined shape that can be reproduced on identically sized metal discs in any amount desired. The shapes are stereotyped and limited to the outline of the various chucks.

Basically, this is similar to the raising process done with hammer and stakes, but here the metal is bent in a mechanical operation on a lathe. The rotation of the metal will produce round shapes of varying depths, but no free-form or asymmetrical bowls or vessels.

It is best for the beginner to start with simple articles such as shallow dishes for enameling and small ashtrays with bases that can be removed with a jeweler's saw and made more elaborate with translucent gemstone or petrified wood sections. Other more difficult projects are spun plates for etching, tier trays with gemstone or exotic wood posts, silent butlers and lids with wooden or gemstone handles, candlesticks, lamp bases, covered candy dishes, tumblers, goblets, and chalices.

Spinning tools and equipment

Metal spinning requires the use of a metal, woodworking, or spinning lathe (see Fig. 374). The swing (distance between the spindle center and the lathe bed or track) will determine the maximum disc size for objects that can be spun on a specific lathe. The lathe is operated at 500 to 3000 rpms for spinning. The first requirement is a contoured maple,

FIG. 374

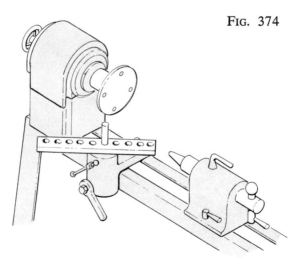

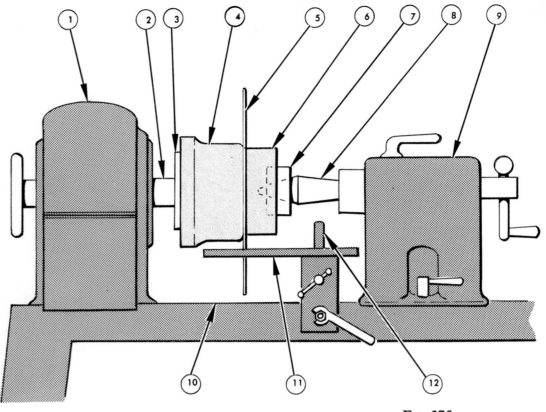

FIG. 375

1. Lathe arbor	7. Spinner
2. Spindle	(ball-bearing)
3. Faceplate	8. Tapered center
4. Chuck	9. Tailstock
5. Metal disc	10. Lathe bed
6. Follow block	11. Fulcrum bar
	12. Fulcrum pin

cherry, or birch hardwood block called a chuck, which is produced on a woodworking lathe to fit a particular design pattern (see Fig. 375). This is attached to a lathe faceplate from the back, either by a hob threaded to fit the spindle, or by a shaft fitted to the block and inserted into a large-sized collet. The block, which constitutes the pattern, must run absolutely true or the metal cannot be spun. It is best to have the block mounted on its attachment before shaping it. If this is not possible, it must be trued after attaching it to the lathe spindle, which will result in a reduction in size. This is done with the regular woodworking tools and sandpaper.

The chucks can be made with concave bottoms or bases if this is desired in the finished article; however, the follow block that holds the disc against the chuck must be shaped convexly to mate with the chuck (see Fig. 376). Often deep shapes require a progression of contoured forms (chucks) which should be formed and aligned for true centering before work is begun (see Fig. 377).

Hollow or flat chucks for shallow dishes and

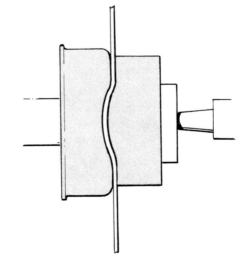

FIG. 376

ashtrays can be spun on a chuck with a concave surface. The depth of the concave area should not exceed one-fourth the diameter of the finished piece. The metal is placed over the hollow and tacked to the chuck on the face or on the edges. The form is made with the flat tool, and when completed is removed from the chuck, and the edges are sawed, filed, and finished. Split chucks can also be used.

If a sufficient number of faceplates are not available, and the chuck must be removed to make a change, an extra hole is drilled in the faceplate and in the chuck so that the chuck can be replaced and realigned. A short section of dowel wood acts as an aligning pin as the parts are attached to each other (see Fig. 378).

As blocks of hardwood for large-size chucks are not readily available, they can be made by clamping and gluing flat sections of hardwood together with a good woodworking glue or epoxy.

back center (see Figs. 379 and 375). The follow block is drilled on one side with a ¼-inch recess for the ball bearing spinner and is then placed between the bearing and another hardwood block and rounded off to size while rotating. The block should not be attached to the lathe faceplate during this sizing procedure.

The race is placed over the tapered center of the tail stock and the follow block (with its diameter never more than ½ inch smaller than the base of the chuck) is placed against the race so that the spun metal will turn a well-defined corner at the base (see Fig. 375). The complete assembly is moved to the chuck, the disc is placed between the chuck and the follow block, and the tail stock is tightened. The follow block must be pressed firmly against the disc so that it will not slip between but rotate with the two wooden sections. The outer diameter (periphery) of the block must be equidistant from its center. This can be determined only when it is rotating with its ball

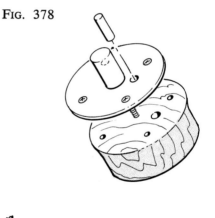

FIG. 378

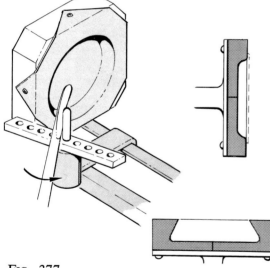

FIG. 377

Chucks, after forming and sanding, should be glazed with soap or wax to close the pores. The backing stick is used for this purpose while the chuck revolves.

Follow blocks

Because the follow block rotates with the metal disc, it is necessary to place a ball bearing race with a 1-inch arbor size between it and the

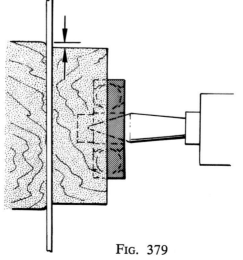

FIG. 379

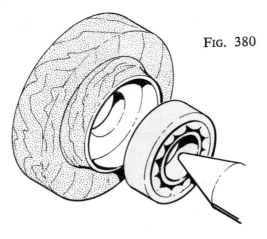

FIG. 380

ning tool is supported by the pin (fulcrum) as the tool is held against the metal surface, forcing it over the spinning hardwood chuck (see Figs. 381 and 375). The pin is moved to succeeding holes as the work progresses.

Spinning tools

The spinning tools are hardwood shafts (hickory or maple), round or rectangular, with ends formed and sanded to round or flat tapers (see Fig. 382). Metal spinning tools of carbon steel, usually purchased, come in a variety of shapes for different forming steps, such as getting into small areas to form a well-defined pedestal on the base of the article, to produce a bead or groove, and to roll an edge. All spinning tools must be maintained in tip-top condition. There must be no sharp edges or nicks and gouges that would prevent smooth travel over the spinning metal surface. Wooden tools wear quickly, but are more easily maintained than metal tools.

The spinning tools are held on the tool holder at an angle directly below the spindle axis. If held higher, they will chatter, chip, break, or hang up on the metal.

The basic spinning tools and their uses are as follows: a flat-back tool—flat on one side and domed on the other like the back of a

bearing race on the tail stock. An end support, as used for closet clothespoles can be glued to the block (instead of drilling) to act as a retaining ring for the bearing race (see Fig. 380).

Tool holder

A tool holder or rest consists of a flat oblong bar or block drilled with holes 1 inch apart to fit a $\frac{5}{16}$ to $\frac{1}{2}$-inch pin. The tool rest is positioned between the operator and the spinning metal slightly lower than, but parallel with, the lathe spindle axis. It is placed as closely as possible to the spinning metal edge. The spin-

FIG. 381

spoon—is used for the main forming steps; a rounding tool, a blunt taper, is used for forming small curves and radii; trimmers, either diamond-shaped or chisel-shaped, are used to true the edges. A ball tool, a shaft with a sphere of metal on the end, is used to remove marks made by other tools (similar to burnishing) (see Fig. 382). A back stick—an ordinary piece of wood—is used in combination with the flat-back tool to prevent wrinkles in the metal as it is spun.

Often when the metal is rotating at a slow speed, two spinning tools are needed to guide the metal as it is formed. One tool is held between the fulcrum pin and the metal, and the

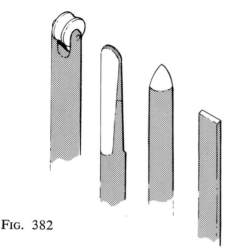

Fig. 382

remaining tool is held between the metal and the hardwood chuck. By working the tools in tandem the metal is gradually forced evenly toward the chuck (see Fig. 381).

Metals for spinning

Spinning metals, ranging in thickness from 12- to 28-gauge, include gold, silver, copper, brass, bronze, aluminum, pewter (britannia metal), stainless steel, and monel metal. Various other metals are also spun, but are primarily used for industrial and space projects. Aluminum is the easiest metal to spin and should be used for experimentation by the novice before advancing to the other metals. All the metals, except aluminum and pewter, will harden as they are spun and will require annealing before beginning the spinning operation, also several times during the completion of the process.

The various gauges of metal used are as follows: gold and silver 16- to 22-gauge; pewter 14- to 20-gauge; aluminum 18- to 20-gauge; stainless steel 24- to 26-gauge; copper, brass, bronze, monel metal 20- to 26-gauge; and nickel silver 24- to 26-gauge. The nickel silver will work-harden much quicker than the other metals and will require more frequent annealing than the others.

Spinning speeds

The metals are spun at speeds ranging from 500 to 3000 rpm. Metals to be spun should be calculated at 500 rpm for each 1 inch of diameter—a one-inch circle of metal = 500 rpm, two-inch diameter = 1000 rpm, a three-inch circle = 1500 rpm, etc. When the metal diameter exceeds 6 inches, the rpm should be figured at 250 rpm for each inch of diameter up to 10 inches. Circles larger than this are turned at 200 rpm for each inch of diameter.

Thicker metals are run at slower speeds and 500 rpm should be deducted for each lower gauge number below 20-gauge, such as is illustrated in the following example:

A 10-inch disc is spun at 2500 rpm if the metal thickness is 20-gauge or thinner. If the metal thickness is increased to 18-gauge, the metal disc is spun at 2000 rpm. Further increase in the thickness to 16-gauge will decrease the rpm to 1500 rpm.

Preparing the metal disc

The metal disc should be scribed to the desired outline, remembering that the metal requirement will be greater than the finished diameter. This is determined by measuring across the contoured surface of the chuck (a slight allowance can be trimmed from the upper edge before the spun shape is removed from the lathe). The disc is trimmed or sawed to shape and filed to the outline. It is placed between the contoured chuck and the follow block as close to dead center as possible.

A triangular-shaped wedge of wood is inserted in the lathe bed with the long point downward to align the metal disc so that it is in the exact center of the chuck and follow

FIG. 383

the tool tip moves outward on the revolving metal, the distance between it and the spindle increases. Wherever too much pressure is used, the metal thins out, causing wrinkling and an increasingly uneven surface as the forming progresses (see Fig. 384).

As the edge comes up toward the chuck during the final stages of the spinning, some wrinkles may appear, and the back stick is used in tandem to support the metal as it is formed against the chuck (see Figs. 384 and 381). If this does not alleviate the problem, the lathe will have to be stopped, the shell re-

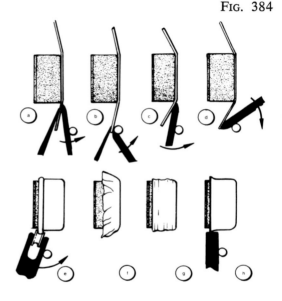

FIG. 384

block (see Fig. 383). When this is done, the lathe should be running at minimum speed. If the lathe is started at high speed, the misaligned disc may fly out centrifugally and injure the operator.

The aligning block is held with the left hand and pressed against the rotating edge of the metal disc. The right hand slightly loosens the tail stock and follow block to permit easy alignment, and as soon as the disc rides on center, the tail stock is tightened to hold the metal firmly for spinning.

The disc may be lubricated slightly on the follow block side to minimize any frictional contact with the spinning tools. A thin film of oil or detergent and water is sufficient. Another useful metal lubricant for the spinning tools is made of 1 part machine oil to 4 parts tallow, which is melted to mix with the oil. This must be applied sparingly to the metal surface.

If the metal disc has a tendency to slip while rotating or while forming the shell, and the tail stock has already been tightened adequately, a small amount of rosin placed on the face of the follow block next to the metal disc will eliminate the problem.

Forming the spun shape

Spinning tools are at least 24 inches long, a large portion of this being the handle which is held against the body, under the forearm and elbow. The tool is placed below the spindle center and with a light pressure is moved in an even sideways swinging motion of the body. As

moved, annealed, and hammered on a stake to remove the wrinkles before continuing with the spinning.

When the object is nearing completion, a smaller spinning tool is used to force the metal into undercuts or recessed areas to form a base platform or pedestal on a dish or bowl (see Fig. 385). Simple bases are made by starting the spinning at a line scribed on the metal surface facing the follow block. To prevent spinning the metal to a smaller circle, the follow block should be the same size as the scribed circle so that the contour will begin at this point (see Fig. 385).

When all forming is complete, the edge is

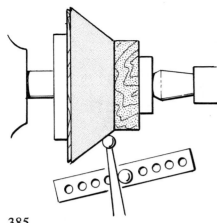

Fig. 385

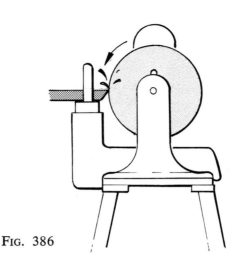

Fig. 386

trimmed before the metal is removed from the lathe. (If preferred, the edge could be trimmed when half formed.) A discarded file sharpened to a wedge shape is held, with the sharp edge up, firmly against the metal as it rotates (see Fig. 386). This trims the edge evenly, as long as the tool cutting edge is maintained at an absolute 90° to the spindle axis. The tool is held below the rotating center of the spindle and cuts into the metal as it turns against the knife edge. After trimming, the metal edge is filed smooth with a single-cut file held against the edge and slightly above the center.

If a rolled edge or curved lip is desired, the spinning is stopped ½ inch from the edge. The edge is then trimmed as detailed before in this chapter. The small bead, rolled edge, or lip is made on the metal with two spinning tools and two fulcrum pins placed close together and at

the left end of the tool holder, with only enough space between to insert the two tool tips so that they can be held on each side of the spinning metal edge (see Figs. 387 and 381). The left-hand tool will force the edge over into a bead, as the right-hand tool supports the metal on the inside curve and prevents spreading of the main portion of the bowl when pressure is exerted. A commercial beading tool can be used if desired.

Spinning speeds should not exceed 1800 rpm until some skill is developed with this particular technique.

To remove an object that has formed so tightly against the chuck that it cannot be moved, the ball tool is passed over the surface again to stretch the metal slightly so that air enters between the chuck and the metal (see Fig. 388). Solid chucks can be center-drilled

Fig. 387

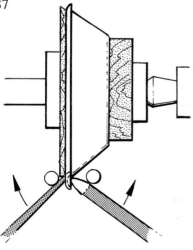

Fig. 388

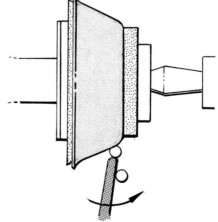

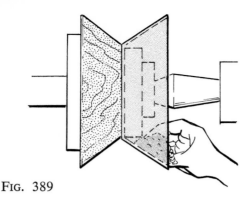

FIG. 389

through the chuck with a ⅛-inch hole to permit the air to enter.

Surface finishing

Defects such as scratches, tool marks, and other surface irregularities are removed with 400-grit emery paper and 000 steel wool before removing the metal from the lathe. The inside of the article should be finished to match the outer surface unless enameling is to be done on both or either surface.

The inner surface of any shallow spun object, visible when the spinning is completed, is sanded by removing the spun metal from its wooden chuck and placing it in the lathe between the wooden chuck and the follow block in a reverse position (see Fig. 389).

Collapsible chucks

Vessels with smaller openings than their largest part are spun on collapsible segmental chucks. When designing an object for spinning, the opening in the object must be large enough to permit removal of the chuck segments (see Fig. 390).

Breakdown chucks

If the object is quite deep, it is first spun on a breakdown chuck to form the metal partially (see Fig. 391). The breakdown chuck is formed into a stubby cone, instead of ending in a tapered tip. The smaller end is turned to the exact size of the finished article. The angular sides are equal in length to the height of the finished object. The breakdown chuck is made individually for each vessel as it is not inter-

changeable on differently contoured objects. When the forming is completed to this point, the metal is positioned on a collapsible core or chuck. It is then spun, as in the normal method, and when the object is completely formed, the rim or edge is trimmed, smoothed, rolled, and the surface sanded. The core and the metal shape, still intact, are then removed from the lathe.

Making a collapsible chuck

Collapsible chunks require four different-sized blocks of hardwood that are shaped as follows:

1. A hardwood block 2 inches thick and 2 inches larger than the largest diameter required by the design is attached to a lathe faceplate, and reduced to a diameter only 1½ inches larger. A 1¼-inch hole is drilled 1½ inches deep in the center of the block. Another hole ¾-inch deep, and equal to the diameter of the opening of the design object, is drilled in the same end of the block (see Fig. 392a).

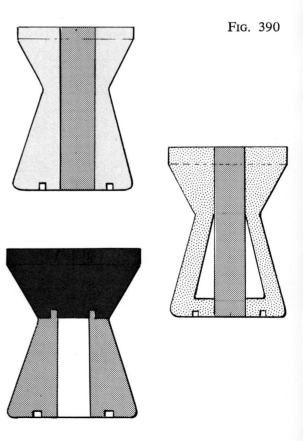

FIG. 390

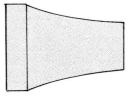

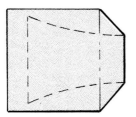

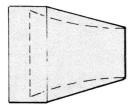

FIG. 391

2. A long block of wood 1½-inch square, and several inches longer than the overall length (or height) of the design object, is put on a lathe and turned down to 1¼-inch diameter to fit into the smallest hole drilled in the first block. After the long block is checked for fit in the drilled hole, it is returned to the lathe and turned down to a diameter equal to ¾ inch less than half the diameter of the widest part of the design object, except for 1½ inches at one end. At the point where the diameter changes there should be a ⅛-inch radius. The turned shaft or core is now ready to be glued into the smaller of the two openings in the first block (see Fig. 392b). Objects with wide main portions and narrow mouths will require removal of a part of the wide center portion of each segment.

3. A 2-inch-square wooden block is used to make a turning mandrel, which is necessary to hold the chuck block while it is turned to shape. The block is placed in the lathe and turned to 1½-inch diameter. A short shaft

FIG. 392
a. Chuck holding block   d. Contour template
b. Core   e. Chuck
c. Chuck mandael   f. Ring

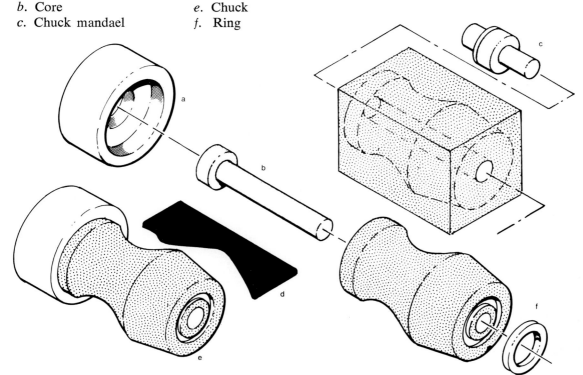

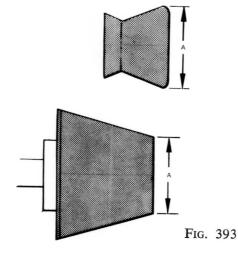

FIG. 393

section 1 inch long and equal to the shaft diameter of block no. 2 in diameter is made in one end of this block, and a ¼-inch radius is made on the shaft section, so that the large chuck block can be pressed tightly on the shaft to hold it in the lathe (see Fig. 392c).

4. A block of wood, slightly larger than the diameter of the design, and several inches longer than the height, is drilled lengthwise through the center to make a hole equal in diameter to match the diameter of the shaft of block no. 2. The chuck block is placed on the turning mandrel which is attached to the lathe faceplate, and the opposite end of the chuck block is held tightly in place with the follow block. The chuck block is turned to match the design outline in cross section. A contour gauge made of heavy cardboard or thin metal can be constructed to aid in checking the contour as it is turned on the lathe (see Fig. 392d). The end of the chuck block, which is shaped to match the top of the object, should be 1¼ inches longer than the design requires (see Fig. 392e). This leaves a section of the segmented chuck to insert into the core block.

The base of the chuck must be identical to the flat cone section of the breakdown chuck so that the partially formed metal will fit as closely as it fits the breakdown chuck used to form it (see Fig. 393). When the chuck is completely shaped and sanded, a groove is made in the base to fit a copper, brass, bronze, aluminum, or hardwood ring (see Fig. 392f). This

ring will hold the sections of the chuck together as the metal is spun. The width and depth of the groove are cut to match the ring used for this purpose. The groove should be cut after selecting the ring to be used. A follow block with a smaller diameter is used to hold the chuck while cutting a groove (see Fig. 394). The regular follow block covers the inserted ring when the chuck is turned to shape.

The chuck is removed from the mandrel and placed upright on a saw table and band-sawed into sections as indicated in the diagram. The sections should be marked off and identified with numbers or letters before sawing (see Fig. 395a). The block must remain vertical and be secure against the table during sawing to ensure straight cuts.

The key segment must be sawed with the correct angles so that it can be slid easily to the core area to be removed. The outer radius of the key segment must not be any wider than the diameter of the core (see Fig. 395k). Larger segmental chucks will require more segments for easy removal than the basic set of seven as illustrated.

When the sections have been sawed, the edges are sanded to remove any saw feathers or splinters. One edge of each section is then faced with shims of thin wood veneer or cardboard strips equal in thickness to the saw blade and glued in place (see Fig. 395e). This is necessary to bring the formed chuck back out to its original shape and contour. If these shims are left out, the metal as it is turned will show ridges at each sectional joint.

Spinning the metal

The chuck is placed on the core and inserted into the opening in the faceplate block, and

FIG. 394

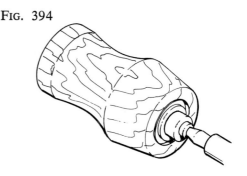

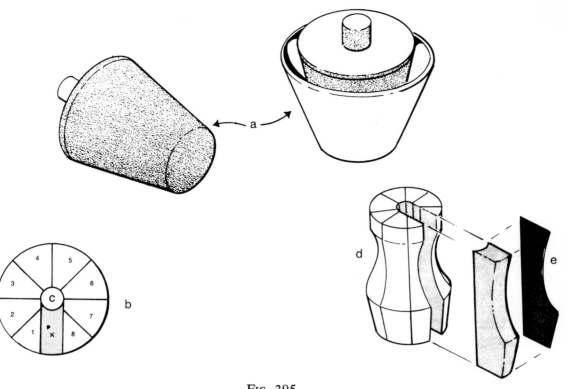

FIG. 395

a. Breakdown chucks
b. Band sawing diagram
c. Core

d. Collapsible chuck
e. Shim

the follow block is placed against the partially formed metal shape so that the spinning can be completed. The edge is trimmed, filed, rolled if desired, and the entire outer surface sanded smooth.

Removal of chuck segments

The spun metal object with its collapsible chuck intact and the retainer ring at the base are removed, followed by removal of the core (c) section (k). The smallest chuck section, "1" or "8," is then removed by pushing it into the center vacated by the core and the key segment (see Fig. 395). Each section is then removed in turn from the vessel. The breakdown chuck with its matching collapsible chuck and all attachments, including the contour guide and design sketch, should be identified as a set and stored as a unit for future use.

Shells can be formed on a breakdown chuck and then transferred to a straight-sided chuck for what is called air-spinning. This technique

can be done only after much practice. The tool is held against the outer surface, and with the backing tool supporting the edge, the flat back or rounding tool forms the curve in the surface without any chuck support underneath.

Soldering the attachments

Outer attachments, such as handles, knobs, bases, pedestals, feet or legs, pouring spouts and hinges that are to be soldered to the spun object, must be filed to fit the contour of the metal exactly. Areas of the spun object that are removed for any attachments must be sawed carefully, and filed to fit the opening perfectly.

The surfaces are cleaned as in the basic soldering steps, and the parts clamped or wired to hold them in place during soldering. Objects can be filled with sand to aid in holding them in position and to cool the metal so that it will not overheat. The joint is fluxed and positioned so that the solder will flow across or

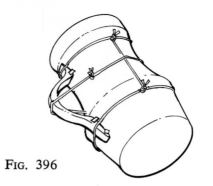

FIG. 396

along it (see Fig. 396). The solder is placed on the attachment, not on the spun surface. If excessive solder is evident, it is carefully removed with a scraper, files, or sanding paper across the spinning direction, but not with it (see Fig. 397).

Final finishing and coloring

Final buffing, polishing, and coloring on spun objects is described in Chapters 8 and 10.

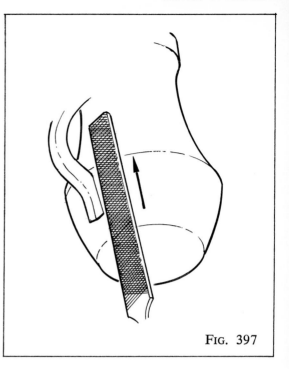

FIG. 397

CHAPTER 26

Blued Steel

EXPERIENCED METALSMITHS HAVE LONG BEEN aware that the heat necessary to anneal the metal during the forming process produces various surface colors that can be used for decorative finish. The colored metal combined with precious metals produces eye-catching contrasts of light and dark designs (see Figs. 398 and 398A).

The color or coating is an oxidation produced by heating the metal. The oxidation increases in thickness and varies in color as the temperature of the metal escalates. The colors ordinarily appear in this order: pale yellow, dark yellow, brown-yellow, brownish red,

FIG. 398   Pin, blued steel with pearl. By Sharr Choate.

purple, violet, dark blue, cornflower blue, bright blue, and a bluish green-gray (see Chapter 19 for steel colors when sharpening and hardening engraving tools).

During the application of heat, the metal is observed continuously until the desired color is obtained, at which time the torch is removed and the metal is allowed to cool. It is not dipped in pickling solution, as this would remove the oxides. The color is permanently preserved with clear lacquer applied by spray coating, rather than by brush coating.

Copper can also be used in place of steel, and the colors for this metal range from reddish orange, blue-purple, dark purple, iridescent shades of dark red, bronze, to a final color of brown or chestnut. The preferred colors are in the range of the iridescent shades of dark red. The copper is cooled in the same manner as steel, and spray-lacquered. Brushing the lacquer on the surface may disturb or brush off the lighter oxide colors.

The brighter colored precious metals used for contrast are produced by filling chased lines or grooves (see Chapter 18) in a flat or raised surface with hard solder before it is heat-colored (see Figs. 399 and 399A). As the metal is heat-colored, the solder remains bright rather than darkening as silver does. Only water

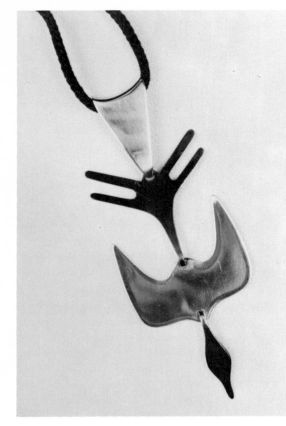

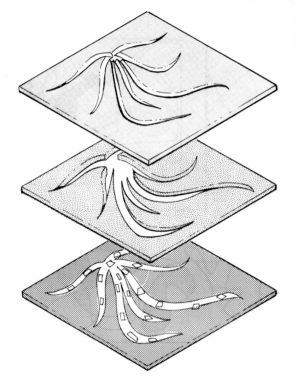

FIG. 399A   Three types of contrasting metal design.
a. Chased lines.
b. Pierced metal with backing sheet.
c. Painted or rubber stamped surface design.

FIG. 398A   Pendant, blued steel and sterling silver.
By Sharr Choate.

is used to cool the surface after applying the contrasting metal. Dipping in pickling solution would pit the surface and start an immediate corrosive action on the steel.

Designs can be applied on the surface of copper by etching rather than chasing or graving the surface (see Figs. 400 and 399A). This metal preparation follows the standard procedure for etching metals (see Chapter 20), except that the excavation is shallow, and should be confined to small areas. Large areas of etched surfaces requiring contrasting metals

may have a concave surface. Hard solder, when used in areas other than lines, strips, and small circles, should be pieces slightly thicker than the depth of the area in which it is placed. A good hard solder to use here is 100 parts silver and 48 parts brass by weight. The metals are melted in a crucible and poured into a hollow in a charcoal block to cool. The mass is hammered and rolled to the thickness needed. It can also be cut into small paillons and used for inlay along chased and engraved lines. The combination of brass and silver produces a

FIG. 399   Cuff links, blued steel with silver solder inlaid in chased design, set in sterling silver bases.
By Sharr Choate.

yellowish-white metal that resembles a very pale gold.

The grooves, filled with silver solder, are later sanded level with the surface of the base metal. The solder remains bright during the heat-coloring step and provides the design detail of the article. Only the copper pieces can be dipped in pickling solution to clean the surface of undesirable oxides prior to the heat-coloring step. They must not be dipped after the coloring has been completed.

Designs can also be applied to a metal surface by cutting a piece of rubber eraser into a stamp. It must be remembered that the imprint will be a mirror image of the stamp. The stamp is dipped in liquid flux and pressed down on the clean metal surface (see Fig. 401). Small paillons of solder are placed in the center of each flux-coated area, and the metal is heated from underneath. The solder will flow only on the fluxed surface within the outline of the stamped design.

A strip of aluminum, copper, or cast iron is placed across two firebricks and the solder-

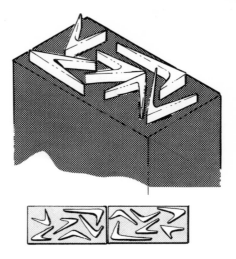

FIG. 401

FIG. 400   Plate, blue steel, with painted solder design.
By Sharr Choate.

coated steel piece is placed on it, design side up (see Fig. 402). (Aluminum transfers heat quickly and will not adhere to any metal.) The steel piece must be absolutely clean, free from all fingerprints, and highly polished before applying heat for color.

The flame of the torch is directed back and forth underneath the metal strip with the heat concentrated on the soldered steel piece above. Carbon steel colors blue at 570 to 600°F. The heat cannot be applied directly to the design surface or to the underside of the design, as it will not color evenly. The metal is heated until the desired color is obtained. When the steel becomes blue, it is cooled, and then sprayed with clear lacquer. It must be handled by the edges only until the lacquer is dry. If spots appear on the blued surfaces, the piece was not clean, completely polished, or the heat was not equally transferred. The remedy is to resand the piece with 400-grit paper and buff and

FIG. 402

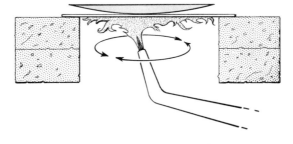

FIG. 403

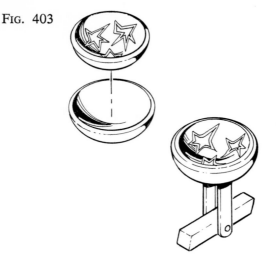

polish it again. Continued heating of the metal after the desired color appears will change the metal to the next color. If the final color possible has been reached, the prolonged heating will result in a peeling of the color, which is only a crust on the surface of the metal. This crust or oxidation is removed from steel by thoroughly cleaning the surface with steel wool so that the heat-coloring process can be redone. A copper article can be cleaned by heating and dipping in pickling solution.

Carbon steel and copper are available from all suppliers in small quantities in all gauges and shapes such as sheets, bars, and rods. Old lapidary diamond saw blades, copper or steel, far beyond recharging or reworking economically, are used for the main portions of the designs.

Metal sections decorated with contrasting metals and heat-colored can be inserted in silver mountings (see Fig. 403), such as bezels and prong settings, but care must be taken when burnishing the metal that the tool does not damage the heat-colored insert. Bezels or prongs should be made of fine silver whenever possible, because the softer metal will burnish much more easily without tool marking. Buffing and polishing must not be done on silver portions as this would damage the colored surface.

CHAPTER 27

Enameling

THOUGH ENAMELING IS A VERY ANCIENT ART, the fundamental process has not changed to this day except for improvements in equipment and materials. The use of various techniques that make possible the combination of many types of enamels with metal foils broadens the field considerably. Careful study of all the possibilities this decorative process affords will be very rewarding to the craftsman.

Enamels

Enameling is the fusion of a vitreous material that is basically glass or silica, but which includes other components of potassium nitrate, arsenic, sodium carbonate, and metal oxides. Hundreds of different color hues can be created by combining varying proportions of metal oxides with three types of enamels. The metal oxides that provide the coloring include selenium, antimony, iron, nickel, gold, silver, cobalt, copper, chromium, manganese, tin, and iridium.

The combined ingredients, after being melted in a furnace at 2000°F. for approximately fifteen hours, are poured like a batter onto cold iron slabs. When cool, the slabs are broken into chunks that can be purchased and ground to specified grit sizes as the craftsman desires, although it is more usual to purchase the chunks after they have been reduced to fine powder by the manufacturer.

Colors should always be sorted according to the manufacturer's number rather than by color alone. The correct number, together with the color designation, will make it possible to re-order whenever additional material is necessary. Also, a few grains or a bit of fired metal paillon (thin piece of metal) attached to the lid to show the color after firing will enable one to match colors and type exactly to the originals.

Enamels cannot be mixed like oil or water-color paints as each color retains its own distinct hue even after firing. Transparent and opalescent colors cannot be combined to produce an opal-like type of enamel.

Enamel types

Enamels are divided into three distinct types according to fusing times and temperatures. Soft-fusing enamels mature (become glossy) in 2 to 4 minutes at 1400°F. Such soft enamels are usually used for a second firing when a second color is added. If put through successive firings they would burn away. Medium-fusing, the most commonly used, matures in 2 to 4 minutes at 1450° to 1500°F. The hard-fusing enamels are fired 2 to 4 minutes at 1600°F. and are usually used for counterenameling and for pieces that require successive firings.

Enamels are opaque, translucent, opalescent, and transparent. Opaque materials, of course, show no light or signs of metal through them as translucent and opalescent materials do. Transparent enamels naturally permit all areas and surfaces to be clearly seen. They can be fired over opaques in successive firings to give a rich, pool-like effect.

Not all colors are available in the soft, medium, and hard types because of their indi-

Fig. 404

vidual chemical characteristics. For example, opaque black, orange, and red are usually soft while all transparent enamels are usually hard.

Enamel sizes

Enamels (or frit) in powdered form, lumps, and threads can be ground to suit in a steel, porcelain, or agate mortar with a porcelain pestle, but they must never be touched with bare fingers. Chunk enamel is ground to grains or fine powder from 80 to 250 mesh. (Eighty-mesh enamel would mean that the particles will pass through a screen having 80 openings to the square inch.) The grain size of 80-mesh enamel is equal in size to table salt and that of 250-mesh resembles flour.

Cleaning the frit

A solution of 1 or 2 drops of nitric or hydro-chloric acid added to a pint of water is poured over the enamels and set aside to decant. This first solution is then poured off, and replaced with a fresh solution which is poured off after decanting or when the liquid no longer appears cloudy when stirred with a glass rod. The enamel is then washed several times in running water. The container should be tilted at an angle to allow the running water to fill it and run over the side (see Fig. 404).

Storing enamel

Whenever enamels are not to be used at once, they are stored after washing in the same container and covered with distilled water so that they will be clean and ready for use at a later time. If the enamel is to be stored indefinitely, it should be dried by heating in an oven in order to eliminate all moisture and then stored in either sealed containers or tightly capped bottles.

Making rods or threads

Often one may require a certain color of enamel rods or threads that are not immedi-

Fig. 405

FIG. 405A

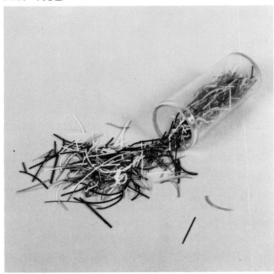

FIG. 405B

Using the rods and threads

The threads can be placed in the sifted enamel that is applied on the first coating, but they are usually placed on a prefired enamel surface that has been ground to remove any imperfections from the initial firing. Threads applied in the sifted enamel of the first coating emerge as an irregular veining, while, if thick enough, those placed on a previously underfired surface retain their original shape (see Fig. 406). Thinner threads will melt into a thicker line. Threads may be used to define a design outline to produce a cloisonné effect. The threads should be selected for uniform size. They are then broken into short lengths approximately ⅛ to ¼ inch long and placed with tweezers onto the adhesive coated surface.

Metals to be enameled

Metals used for enameling are gold, silver, and copper. Golds used for this technique should be alloys of 12 to 18k. Alloys above 18k, because of softness, are difficult and expensive to enamel. However, the lower the karat alloy the greater the tendency for the metal to oxidize. Solder must always match the metal in karat content. Whenever a solder is used on a metal, the range of enamel melting points is lowered to those that have a fusing point below the melting point (mp) of the metal and the matching solder.

FIG. 406   Enamel plaque, copper. By Sharr Choate.

ately available. These can be produced easily by melting lumps of enamel on a clean metal sheet. A scrolling tool, a steel rod filed to a point and bent at a right angle at one end, is used to dip into the hot enamel and lift out threads of the color. The threads cool immediately, and a slight tug or side pressure will release them from the molten base. These are stored in a tall glass jar or plastic bottle (see Figs. 405, 405A, and 405B).

The common gold karat alloys and their melting points are:

		Metal mp (°F.)	Solder mp (°F.)
10k	yellow	1615	1425
14k	yellow	1645	1450
14k	white	1825	1675
18k	yellow	1700	1550
18k	white	1730	1580
24k		1945	1895

The solders melt at approximately 150°F. lower than the metal mp.

Fine (pure) silver and sterling silver are both used; however, the pure silver is preferred. The copper content (.075 copper to .925 pure silver) of sterling silver will tend to oxidize and create gray streaks in the metal. These streaks can be removed in a pickling solution if they are not covered with transparent enamels. The melting point of fine silver is 1740°F., and of sterling silver is 1640°F. Solder mp is 150°F. less than metal mp. Because the silver alloy melting point is close to the high fusing point of most enamels, lower melting point enamels are required. The copper content that comes to the metal surface when heated is removed in a pickling solution. This procedure leaves a pure silver skin on the sterling article and eliminates the gray streaks without altering the melting point range.

Copper with a melting point of 1981°F. is the metal most frequently used for enameling because it can withstand successive firings without excessive warping or otherwise losing its shape. Also, increased prices for precious metal makes it best to experiment with copper.

Electroplating after enameling

Enameled articles made of silver or of copper can be gold-plated to change the color of exposed metal areas. When gold-plating is to be used, a full color sketch should be made to indicate contrasts in colors that might blend too closely.

The nonadhesive quality of brass, bronze, and aluminum makes them unsuited for enameling. However, the nonadhesive quality of

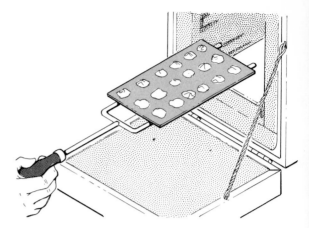

Fig. 407

brass is an advantage in the plique-à-jour technique (see page 261).

Enamel test-firing sampler

Enamels to be used on silver should be tested for their melting point on small scraps of the metal in order to ensure the maximum temperature necessary to fuse them properly.

The melting or fusing points of enamels to be used on all metals other than silver are checked by placing small dabs of different-colored enamels on a clean sheet of copper that, after firing, resembles an artist's palette (see Fig. 407). The higher melting point of the copper gives the craftsman a better opportunity to experiment with different colors and temperatures. Fine silver and sterling are too close to the firing temperatures to be used economically by the beginner.

The copper sheet is placed on a wire grid supported by a tripod soldering stand. The sheet is covered with a #1¼ tin can with a side opening cut out so that the enamels can be observed continuously to note how much time is required for each color to melt (see Fig. 408). The melting time is then recorded on each container. In this way colors that are to be used in combination can be selected from those that have similar or relatively close melting points.

Small, thoroughly clean squares of copper for use as samplers may be fired with single basic colors of each type enamel. As one grows more adept, other samplers can be produced.

Some transparent colors require firing on either gold or silver scrap to ascertain correctly color tones and other characteristics. To avoid costly mistakes, colors fired over clear or white flux, over gold and silver foil, or in various other combinations should be checked in this way before starting a project. Enamels, even single colors, take less time and produce better results with two or three applications and firings than one heavy thick firing.

Preparing the metals

Gold and fine silver are prepared for enameling by cleaning and pickling the metal. It is then rubbed with fine (00) steel wool to produce a satin finish which is preferred under transparent colors. Transparent colors are richer when the prepared surface has been reworked with fine steel wool. If all trace of the steel wool is not removed, however, it will show up glaringly in the fused colors. When a highly polished surface is desired, the metal is buffed and polished before annealing and

FIG. 408

pickling. If the metal is to be counterenameled, it is not necessary to anneal it.

Sterling silver used for enameling must be treated so that a layer of pure silver covers the surface to be enameled. The metal is buffed with Tripoli on a felt wheel and then with a wire brush. The buffing compound is removed with soap and water and the metal is polished with rouge on a muslin or cotton buff; the polishing compound is removed in the same manner. The clean metal is placed in a heated kiln (900°F.) until it becomes a light pink color. It is then immediately removed, air-cooled and placed in a hot solution of sulfuric acid and water (1 : 10) for several minutes. The solution removes the copper oxides that come to the surface. The metal is rinsed in running water and burnished gently with a wire wheel at medium speed. Heating, cooling, pickling, rinsing, and burnishing steps are repeated until all traces of the dark copper are removed, leaving a pure silver coating on the surface that will not be contaminated by the copper oxides found on untreated sterling silver surfaces. The metal is then recleaned with a detergent, rinsed, and dried.

Metal surfaces that have been pickled must be made alkaline for the best adherence of the enamel. To accomplish this, the surface, untouched by the fingers, is wiped with a paper towel or facial tissue which has been moistened with household ammonia or detergent, but not with regular soap or tap water, as they contain oils and other elements that prevent a perfectly fired glaze. The surface is dried before applying the adhesive and the enamel powder. Surfaces cleaned in this manner will have a smoother, shinier, more professional appearance. If the underside is to be enameled, it must be cleaned at the same time in the same manner.

Gold and silver should be fired first with a transparent flux which is a colorless enamel usually used as an undercoating (1500°F.; 1 to 2 minutes). The colors, which will appear more vivid than on copper, are added in subsequent firings.

A full-scale sketch of the design in color should be made before applying the powdered enamels to the prepared metal surface. Areas of gold or silver that will not be enameled can be protected from fire scale by covering the exposed areas in any one of three ways: with a coating of paste made of yellow ocher and water, with a commercial antiflux paste, or with a saturated solution consisting of powdered boric acid and a reagent alcohol (not isopropyl). The solution is painted onto the surface and ignited with a match so that the alcohol burns off, leaving a thin powdery film. To increase the effectiveness of the saturated solution, either of the pastes can be applied on top of the dried powdery film of boric acid. Before pickling the metal, the paste must be completely removed.

Soldering investment can be used to protect all soldered joints that would be inclined to loosen if fired at a temperature too close to soldering temperatures.

Enameled articles preferably should be of one piece, requiring findings only. Findings are soft-soldered into place in the final assembly. High-temperature soldering usually cannot be done after enameling. Jewelry findings can be attached to the metal before the enameling step if hard solder having a higher melting point than any of the enamels is used. As soldered joints are visible through transparent enamels, it is best to use opaque types of enamels. A small area must be left free of the adhesive coating and enamel so that findings for jewelry pieces can be securely attached to the base metal with soft solder.

Counterenameling

Warpage caused by the expansion and contraction stress of the metal during successive firing and cooling stages can be eliminated by counterenameling. This is always done on silver and, though not necessary, is best to do on other metals as well. The adhesive coating and enamel, usually transparent flux, are applied in the same manner as when preparing the design side of the metal. The design side of the piece is coated with antiflux to prevent fire scale.

The article is placed underside up on a grid, stilt, firing stand, or trivets and underfired (1500°F. for 2 minutes). The firing will be completed when the enamels on the design surface are fused. Whenever possible, the counter-

FIG. 409

enamels with the highest melting points should be used.

Simultaneous enameling consists of firing the two sides of the metal at the same time. The underside receives the counterenameling coating and the topside is fired with the initial color or a flux.

The viewing or finished side of the article is coated with the adhesive, and a transparent flux or enamel color is dusted on and dried. The metal is then turned over and the same operation repeated. When completely dry the metal is placed on the firing stand or trivets and underfired (1500°F. for 2 minutes) with the back or underside up. When the metal has cooled, the marks made by the firing stand and any small cracks or bubbles on the viewing side are ground away and the additional colors are added in a successive firing. The final firing should be at 1600°F.

Applying the enamel

The clean metal surface is coated with an adhesive called gum tragacanth, which can be purchased in powdered form from a druggist or enamel supplier. This adhesive is mixed into a paste made up of 1 teaspoon of adhesive dissolved in 1 teaspoon wood alcohol and added to 1 quart of distilled water and allowed to decant for 12 to 16 hours. The thin solution on top is used for spray (see Fig. 409) and the thicker substance at the bottom is used for the curved surfaces.

Commercial enameling gum can be used also. The gum is mixed to a paste of 3 parts water to 1 part liquid gum and used in the same manner as the tragacanth adhesive.

The colors are added dry and sifted onto the adhesive-coated surface through 80- to 250-mesh screen baskets (see Figs. 409 and 410). The enamel, previously washed, is taken from its storage container and dried on a sheet of stainless steel either over a low flame or on the open door of a heated kiln. When the enamel is dry it is transferred to a sheet of paper, rolled into a funnel, and a portion transferred to the sifting basket. The remainder is put into a clean dry container. Damp, freshly

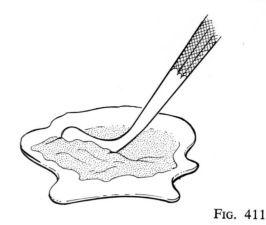

FIG. 411

FIG. 410

edge, or by placing the article under a heat lamp.

Enamel is also applied in a paste made by mixing the finely ground colors with pine or lavender oil that when too thick can be thinned with a few drops of turpentine. A small spatula is used to apply the substance to the metal surface.

Different effects are produced by first firing an enamel color that has been applied in damp or paste form with subsequent firings, using contrasting colors of sifted enamels (see Fig. 412). This technique requires a pretest for the enamels, with higher-melting-point enamels applied to the surface first.

washed enamel can be applied without drying. A small spatula is used to apply the enamel, and a scribelike pointer is used to push the enamel into small areas. The enamel is smoothed into an even layer (depth equal to the metal thickness) with a small-diameter rod bent at an angle. Old discarded dental tools work well for this step (see Fig. 411).

The enamel, either dry or damp, is applied to the metal surface which is continually sprayed with the adhesive. This does not affect the enamel, but controls it by holding it in place. Thicker coatings should be applied on curved, concave, or angular surfaces.

Enamel should not be thicker than the metal. When fired, enamel will reduce 50 percent of volume. Because enamels tend to recede during firing, they are placed at the extreme edge of the desired area. Excess moisture is removed from the metal by applying a blotter to the

FIG. 412

FIG. 413

FIG. 413A

Firing

Enamel-coated surfaces must be dry when fired. Room-temperature drying may take as long as 2 to 3 days. This time can be shortened by placing the enamel-coated metal in a kitchen oven at low heat (200°F.) for 20 to 25 minutes or under a heat lamp for 2 to 3 hours. The enamels may also be dried quickly by placing the coated metal in a hot kiln for 3 to 5 seconds. An alternative kiln-drying method is to place the coated metal article on the open

door of a heated kiln and allowing the metal to remain until there is no longer any steam arising from the surface.

Standard enameling or metal-casting ovens are used for fusing enamels. The furnace should have a pyrometer for immediate visual temperature observation and should be heated to 1600°–1700°F. before placing an enamel-coated article in the furnace. When the furnace door is opened, the pyrometer is observed until the indicator needle drops to the desired temperature, at which time the metal object is placed in the furnace. Furnaces or kilns with a solid floor are the only types that should be used. Exposed muffles or coils will be damaged by the excess enamel that may drip off of overloaded metal surfaces.

Ceramic trays, available from the enamel suppliers, are used to protect the furnace from excess enamel glaze. Small ceramic stilts or trivets and stainless steel stands are used to elevate and support the metal during the firing (see Fig. 413). The article is placed on the supports with a kitchen spatula, casting, or wire tongs.

Bunsen burners attached to domestic gas or butane torches can be used for fusing enamels which are placed on a wire grid tripod supported by a soldering stand (see Fig. 414).

FIG. 413B

However, this method is best used by experienced craftsmen because there is no way to determine temperatures, and the piece must be fired until the fusing of the glaze becomes obvious.

Because fusing times vary from a few seconds to 3 or 4 minutes, the enamel must be continuously observed. The enamel when fused ranges in color from a shiny dull red to a cherry red (1450–1500°F.), according to its melting point.

Another quick-check method to determine whether or not the enamel has matured (fused) is to hold the spatula over the metal. If the tool has been polished it will be reflected in the shiny surface of the enamel. Shiny enamel capable of reflecting is an indication that the fusing is complete.

When removing the enamel from the firing oven, all drafts must be avoided. A temperature change during the cooling will crack the surface. The permanent color of the fired enamel is evident when the piece is cool enough to touch with the bare hands.

As soon as the article is taken from the kiln, it is placed on the open door, and the fused enamel surface is checked for areas that are incomplete or that have receded too much. After the enamel has cooled slightly, such areas are scraped with a sharp tool or glass fiber brush until they appear bright (see Fig. 415). The surface is then coated with adhesive, and additional enamel is added.

The enameled metal article is replaced in the

FIG. 414

kiln for all subsequent firing only when the supports in the oven are red-hot. When the fusing is complete, the heat is turned off and the article is left to cool in either the furnace or in a protected area that is free from any draft. Enamels are never quenched in water or immersed in pickling solution while warm.

Firing times and temperatures are very important. An interval timer (the type used in a photo darkroom) should be used for timing the fusing periods. When the rim of a piece be-

FIG. 413C

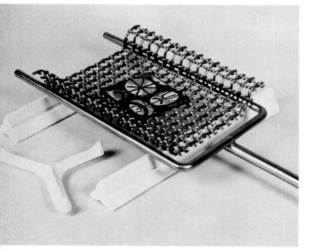

FIG. 415

comes blackened, overfiring is indicated. If a dark rim is not desired for an effect, the piece must be discarded; to restore the bright original color is impossible.

A dull, lumpy uneven surface indicates underfiring. This can be corrected with additional firing to smooth out the surface and put on a glossy finish.

Elimination of firing problems

Metal surfaces that, after firing, emerge darkened with oxides or fire scale are cleaned by dipping the cooled silver or copper into a cool solution consisting of 1 part nitric acid to 6 parts water. The solution should be stirred with a glass rod or feather as long as the enameled article remains therein to prevent etching of the metal, especially under the edges of the glaze and around the oxidized areas. The object is to remove the scale, not the metal around it.

Gold is immersed in a solution of 1 part sulphuric acid to 10 parts water, then rinsed in running water, buffed, and polished. After buffing, the enamel can be given a high polish on a separate hard felt wheel charged with tin oxide (a polishing powder used on fine gemstones).

After pickling, the article should be scrubbed with bicarbonate of soda and water. Care must be taken not to touch it with the bare hands. Enamel is removed from a damaged or improperly fired area by heating the metal to a dull dark red and immediately plunging it into cold water. This procedure will crack the enamel so that it can be lifted from the metal. The remaining enamel can be removed by submerging the metal in a hydrofluoric solution consisting of 1 part acid to 1 part water. As the acid is extremely toxic the fumes must not be breathed and the acid must never be allowed to touch the skin. Also, the acid/water solution must always be used out of doors rather than in a presumably well-ventilated room. Hydrofluoric acid is highly corrosive and should be poured from its original plastic container into a hard rubber container when used. Glass vessels could be used; however, because the acid attacks the glass, it

should be returned to its regular container as soon as possible.

When the metal is cool, the enamel can be removed by flaking it with a ball burnisher that is no longer being used for its original purpose. Bits of enamel that remain can be loosened with hydrofluoric acid which is washed off by rinsing several times in running water. The metal must then be recleaned, the coating and enamel added, and the fusing process as previously outlined repeated to completion.

On surfaces that will require two or more firings, some surface treatment may be necessary, especially on those using transparent

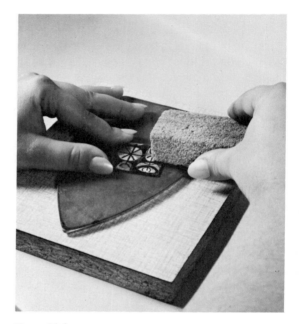

FIG. 416

colors. Opaque colors, when observed as the firing progresses, can be removed from the kiln at the shiny stage and cooled for surface work. If no pits or bubbles are visible, the firing can continue to the glossy stage and then the article is removed and cooled. Surfaces of opaque enamels and transparent colors need to be surface-ground after cooling to eliminate the pits and bubbles (see Fig. 416). These imperfections are the result of unclean metal, unclean enamels, damp enamels placed in the furnace for firing, or a combination of any of these. Small cracks are created by tension in the metal as it expands and contracts in the heated kiln or by enamels applied thicker than the metal. Uneven areas are produced either by underfiring or by irregular leveling of the enamels when applied. Unless a lumpy effect is desired, the colors should be smoothed out as level as possible.

Second firings

When the enamel in the first firing has reached the shiny (but not glossy) stage, it is removed from the furnace and cooled. If warpage is evident, the metal is handled as soon as possible with asbestos gloves to reshape it to its original form if possible. It should then be prepared for additional firings. If there are no surface blemishes requiring attention, the fire glaze is removed from the exposed metal portions (unless an antioxidant has been used) and the surface cleaned and dried preparatory to application of the second coat of enamel. Surfaces needing removal of pits, bubbles, or other flaws, are completely cooled and held in a container constantly refilled with running water. The surface is ground in a circular motion with a carborundum stone or 600 silicon carbide cloth (see Fig. 416). The running water immediately washes away the ground enamel plus any grit particles from the grinding stone. The stone particles, if not washed away, will scratch the surface and require additional work to remove heavier scratches. The article is cleaned and dried for application of a second layer of adhesive and enamel.

When considerable grinding is necessary to remove the enamel, small particles of the grinding stone are apt to become embedded in the enamels. To remove these particles, the surface is swabbed with a tap water and hydrofluoric acid solution (1 : 1 ratio) and then rinsed away with running water.

If incidental grinding is all that is needed and the newly ground surface is to be the final coating of color, the surface can be polished with a felt wheel charged with pumice and water paste, or the article can be returned to the furnace to bring the surface to a glossy finish. If polishing is used for the finish, it must be remembered that the enamel is harder than the metal, and the metals should not be polished any more than necessary to prevent the wearing away of the exposed metal areas.

Surface finishing

The fused surface of the enamel is ground smooth with a carborundum or Scotch stone under running water as soon as the metal is cool. The enamel is stoned down as closely as possible to the metal surface. The grit, which tends to become embedded in the enamel, must be scrubbed away with a glass brush. The stone used for grinding the surface level will scratch and pit the enamel; therefore, additional enamel must be added to these adhesive-coated areas and refired at 1300°F. for a few seconds until the added enamel is fused.

A smooth but unpolished surface can be repolished by returning it to a heated furnace or by buffing it on a machine. If the article is to be returned to the furnace, the surface should first be washed with the hydrofluoric acid solution. The acid attacks all the minute grains that remain from the grinding stone, even though the surface has been washed several times. If the machine buffing method is used, a hard felt wheel charged with pumice works best, but care must be taken because the metal is softer than the enamel, and persistent buffing will remove the metal faster.

Soldering findings on the metal

If the article was counterenameled, the small area left unfired for findings is cleaned with ammonia or the vinegar solution to remove any fire scale. Some fire scale can be removed only by pickling solution. If pickling solution is necessary, it should be applied on a cotton swab instead of by immersion. As usual, the pickling solution is rinsed away with running water and the metal dried. The finding is positioned and a small piece of solder is applied with a pair of tweezers (not fingers) next to the finding. (It should be remembered that soldering must always be done after all enameling is complete because the heat would loosen any soldered joints). The kiln is turned to low heat and the article placed in the kiln just long enough to melt the solder so that it will flow.

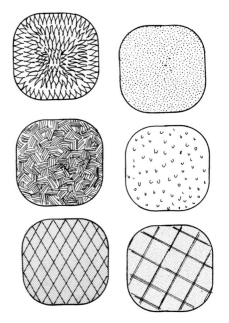

Fig. 417

Fig. 417A   Pin, enamel, champlevé, sterling silver.
By Sharr Choate.

Decorative surface treatment

Textured surfaces with fine detailing can be produced to show effectively through transparent enamels by texturing the surface in several different ways. A vibrotool is used to create numerous patterns such as circular, straight, wavy, crosshatch, vertical lines, stippling, etc. Flat gravers, used for florentine textures, can be used to "rock" and walk across the surface to produce a wriggly line pattern. Regular gravers may be used to produce a variety of different patterns, such as diamond or quilted effects (see Figs. 417, 417A, and 417B).

An additional method for decorating the metal is to use a rotating stick with a flat end that will button-polish the surface in small circles. The short section of wood doweling is placed in a flexible shaft handpiece and the end is dipped in oil and then in fine carborundum grit (see Figs. 418 and 418A).

Frosted translucent surfaces on enamel are produced with a hydrofluoric acid and water solution (1 : 1) which is applied to the surface and immediately washed away under running water. For contrast, selected areas can be left unfrosted by coating them with paraffin before applying the acid. After the acid has been washed away, the paraffin can be removed in very hot water.

Small bits of scrap metal can be melted on a charcoal block or asbestos sheet and made into half-domes or shot. These are used as is, or flattened with a hammer and placed on the previously enameled surface. Transparent

Fig. 417B   Pin and earrings, enameled champlevé, 14k gold.
By David Anderson, Oslo, Norway.

FIG. 418

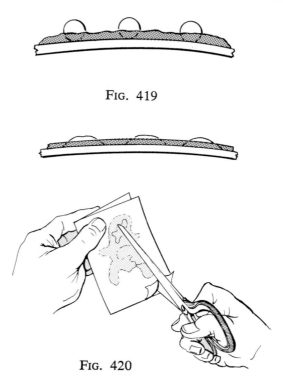

FIG. 419

FIG. 420

enamel is filled in around them and, after firing, the surface is ground level, revealing the odd shapes emerging through the enamel (see Fig. 419).

Liquid metallic lusters are used with transparent enamels for a pleasing crackle effect. The solution for the crackle finish consists of metallic salts dissolved in an oil. The metal is counterenameled, and the viewing surface is fired with a soft-firing enamel. After cooling, the viewing surface is wiped clean with a paper towel moistened with cleaning solvent, lighter fluid, or carbon tetrachloride. The metallic

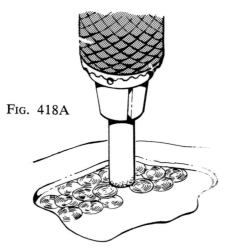

FIG. 418A

luster solution is painted onto the surface and dried. The metal is then fired at 1150 to 1250° F. for 2 to 3 minutes until the luster brightens. After cooling, a transparent enamel is dusted onto the surface and fired at 1450°F. 2 to 3 minutes to produce the crackle finish.

Gold and silver foil technique

Precious metal foil is used with transparent colors for different decorating effects. The foil is purchased in small booklets consisting of leaves or panels of the metal (numbered 4, 6, 8, 10, etc.). The number indicates the total grains in each sheet. The foil, never touched with the fingers, is handled entirely with tweezers or tongs. The metal article is cleaned and coated with adhesive, and then simultaneously fired with a hard fusing enamel on both sides. The enamel is fired at 1500°F. for 1 to 3 minutes, or until the surface is glossy.

The foil is prepared while the enamel metal is cooling. The foil design is drawn on one side of a piece of tracing paper and then folded at the edge of the design. The foil is transferred to the folded paper with the tweezers, and the design is cut with small surgical or manicure scissors (see Fig. 420). The cut design, still inside the double thickness of tracing paper,

FIG. 421

is placed on a piece of wood, and the section is pricked with tiny holes, usually equal to about 150 to 200 mesh. This is done with a small tool, made by inserting embroidery needles in a cork. Dressmaker's tracing wheels may also be used; however, this makes a larger hole. The cut design, still inside the paper, is transferred to the adhesive-coated prefired surface by lifting the foil from the paper with a small artist's camel-hair brush moistened with distilled water (see Fig. 421). The brush is used to move the foil into position. A soft paper towel or facial tissue is used to press the foil firmly but carefully to the surface and to remove any wrinkles in the foil. After the surface is dry, the article is fired at 1200°F. for one minute or until cherry red. The article is removed from the kiln while still hot and a blunt instrument (like the dull side of a knife) is used to tamp the foil down, thus removing any air bubbles which may have formed under the foil, and to ensure that the foil is adhering to the enamel. This is followed by an additional quick firing at the same temperature to ensure proper adherence of the foil in the enamel undercoat. The article is then cooled and a light coat of transparent enamel is sprinkled on the entire surface and fired at 1450 to 1500°F. for 2 to 4 minutes or until the flux is shiny.

Combinations of gold and silver foil can be made and used on one piece, if desired. In this way scrap foil can be used up, leaving little or no waste.

Making metal foils

Foils used for enameling are alloys of copper, silver, and gold which have been melted into a homogenous mass, hammered to flatten, and frequently annealed and rolled to the thinness of foil. When alloying the metals for foil, the copper portion should be melted first and the others added later. The molten mass is poured out into a hollow in the charcoal block, which in effect becomes an ingot mold (a shallow mold is preferred to a deep one). After cooling, the metal is hammered flat, a procedure that will require several annealings before it becomes fairly thin. When it reaches approximately 14- to 16-gauge it can, after annealing, be rolled in alternating rolling and annealing steps until it is finally reduced to a foil thickness—.0005 inch to .002 inch. The following table gives metal percentages required to produce the different colors of gold foils:

Yellow gold foil	9 carats (weight)* 18 72	24-karat (fineness) gold fine silver pure copper
Red gold foil	20 carats 16 18	24-karat gold fine silver pure copper
Blue foil	4 carats 2 16	24-karat gold fine silver pure copper
Green foil	1 carat 6 10	24-karat gold fine silver pure copper

* 1 carat = 3.1 grains

TYPES OF ENAMELING

Cloisonné

Cloisonné consists of forming small cells or cloisons of flat wire to form a design which is stood on edge on a new or previously fired surface. The cells are filled with enamel and fired. The fine wire separation acts as an outline or border between the colors and prevents them from running together when fired (see Figs. 281, 281A, 422 and 423).

The steps for cloisonné enameling with either gold or silver are the same except that the choice of colors differs. Colors must be chosen which are in contrast to the metal color.

Rectangular wire is used for the cloisons. The wire ranges in size from 20 to 34 gauge in thickness and 16 to 22 gauge in width. The optimum size is 30 gauge by 18 gauge wide (.010 × .040 inch). Wire selection depends upon whether or not the cloisons are to be ground down flush with the level of the fired enamel, or left slightly elevated and exposed. The wire is annealed before using and bent to shape with round-nosed, needle-nosed, flat-jawed, and ring-bending pliers. The ends of the wires should be bent so that the cloisons or cells hold their shape without any tension whatsoever. Tension would permit the wires to spread when heated, thus leaving gaps in the cloison walls.

The wire ends are pulled back past their contact points and then gently returned to position, similar to bezel forming (see Chapter 11). Because fine silver wire and #660 gold wire have a minimum of oxidation, they are preferred for enameling. Sterling wire oxidizes because of the alloy. The base metal should

Fig. 422

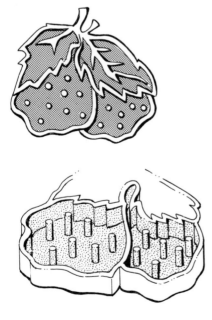

be at least 18-gauge.

Wire that can be ground down after the cells are filled and fired is preferred because the grinding operation hardens it and makes it stronger, whereas wire that remains elevated is soft and becomes dented if handled frequently. Wires are not ground when depth for color and effect is desired. Round wire can also be used for the cloisons, but is not ground down because the different levels of grinding would produce an irregular width of exposed wire. The wire is left as is and gold-plated after enameling is completed.

A thin coating of powdered yellow or clear transparent flux is usually applied as the first coating or counterenameling step when using the cloisonné method. When this is dry, the metal is turned over and the surface is coated with adhesive and dusted with the transparent flux. Fluxes are available for each different metal. When the adhesive and enamel have dried, the piece is placed in the preheated kiln on the supports, underside up, and fired at 1500°F. for approximately three minutes or until the flux is clear and the surface smooth. When the enameled surface has cooled after firing, it is coated with the adhesive solution, and the cloisons are placed in position and set aside to dry.

The cloisons, placed on a prefired surface, may be put into the heated furnace and fired at 1500°F. for 1 to 2 minutes. This permits the cloisons to sink slightly into the surface, thus positioning them securely. A flat-bladed tool may be used to press the cloisons gently down into the hot enamel. This can be done while the article is still sitting on the trivets in the kiln. Cloisons can also be placed on a clean unfired adhesive-coated metal surface, filled with enamel before firing, and set aside to dry.

When the enamel surface has cooled, it is coated again with adhesive solution painted on with a small artist's camel-hair brush or sprayed on with an atomizer. While the solution is moist, the powdered enamel colors are sifted or dusted into their particular areas. The cells are filled to the brim with enamel powder which has been moistened to a thin paste and then placed in the walled-in areas with a small spatula or small camel-hair brush. The filled cells must be completely dry before firing. If additional enamel is needed to fill the cell, it is

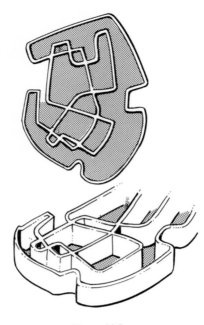

FIG. 423

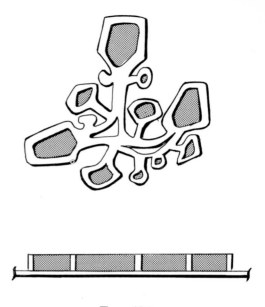

FIG. 424

filled, dried, and given a second firing. When this step is necessary, the cell is filled as full and as high as possible.

The enamels are fired at 1400 to 1450°F. for 2 to 4 minutes. The temperature should never exceed 1450°F. when firing the filled cells. After the firing and cooling are completed, the surface is finished by stoning with a carborundum stone, followed by a Scotch stone. Both are used on the enamels while under water.

Areas of enamel may be returned to a glossy state by adding additional enamel to the stoned areas and refiring at 1300°F. for a few seconds until the gloss is restored.

Cells in cloisonné enamel or in etched metal pieces can be filled with liquid plastics for an enameled effect. Metal scraps, wire bits, and fabric sections with a well-defined weave, such as burlap, linen, and buckram when embedded in plastic are attractive in their simplicity.

Cloisonné pieces can be gold-plated (copper or silver base metal); however, the cloisons must all make contact with each other. Preferably, they should be soldered to the base metal so that direct contact is produced in the plating solution. If the wires are placed in a transparent flux and do not sink deep enough into the flux coating to make contact, it will be impossible for them to be plated. The cells should be posi-

tioned on the clean metal with only a coating of the adhesive to hold them in place.

Enameling electroformed surfaces

Surfaces that have areas left clear to be built up with additional metal by means of the electroforming process can be enameled (see Chapter 28). These areas can be electroformed before enameling, if desired, but the surfaces to be enameled must be masked off. Electroformed surfaces can also be enameled.

Small wire (28 gauge) is bent to form a design and is attached to the metal surface with the gum solution. When dry, the article is attached by appropriate wires to the electroplating apparatus to form an encrustation on the exposed metal outlines.

Thin foil strips can be used for a base if height and body are desired on a wide flat area, or the surface can be electroformed without using any wire.

Champlevé

Champlevé enameling is similar in some respects to cloisonné, but it requires depressed areas in the metal surface which are filled with enamels instead of having enamels built up on the surface and held in place by tiny cells or enclosures. The depressions are made by etching the metal in an acid solution to the desired depth (see Figs. 417A and 417B). This is the same step used for regular acid etching of metals (see Chapter 20).

As described in Chapter 20, all metal areas that will not be subjected to the acid solution must be masked off with black asphaltum paint. Metal etching mordant consists of nitric acid and water in a 50-50 combination. In approximately ten hours the submerged metal should be etched in the exposed areas to a depth of $\frac{1}{16}$ inch. The surfaces should be brushed lightly with a feather, especially if bubbles form, to prevent a scalloped or irregular edge.

When the etching step is completed, the depressions, called excavations, are filled with wet enamel and set aside to dry. When completely dry, the object is fired at 1450°F. for 2 to 4 minutes.

Champlevé pieces may be plated if the metal in the excavations is ground level with the metal after firing. The stoning process is done underwater in a circular motion only. The enamels are harder than the metals, and the stoning steps must be halted frequently and the surface inspected to be sure that the enamel is being ground down to the metal and that the metal alone is not being removed. This usually happens when a back and forth grinding motion is used. Buffing and polishing follow the stoning to remove any scratches. Refire at 1400°F. to restore gloss to the enamel.

Plique-à-jour

Plique-à-jour enameling is similar to the effect of a stained-glass window. It employs trans-

parent enamel areas with no visible metal base or backing (see Fig. 424). The design is drawn on metal and drilled, sawed, or pierced, and the edges filed smooth. Plique-à-jour enameling also resembles cloisonné in that a webbing of cells has been produced from a single piece of sheet metal, but there the similarity ends, for the metal is not attached to a base metal section. Metal used for this technique should be at least 18-gauge (.040) and annealed before using.

The pierced metal is placed on a sheet of mica or aluminum bronze which is coated with the regular gum adhesive. The openings (80-mesh) in the metal are filled with wet enamel which is applied with a small spatula to ensure that all areas are filled. After drying, the article is fired at 1450 to 1500°F. for 2 to 4 minutes. If the piece is fairly large, it and the mica undersheet should be supported on a thin piece of iron. When firing, low areas must be checked and more enamel added, if necessary.

A variation of the plique-à-jour technique is to construct the design by means of grouping cells formed with the same size and type of wire used for cloisonné. The cells are held in place on a mica sheet with gum tragacanth adhesive during enameling. Formed shapes such as bowls may be produced by this technique.

A bowl or shape is formed of thin copper sheet, and a framework of metal wire is made as used for cloisonné (see Fig. 425). The wire is attached with the adhesive to the copper form using either the convex or concave surface. The cells are filled with enamel, fired, and after cooling, the entire article is immersed in an acid solution (5 parts nitric acid to 5 parts

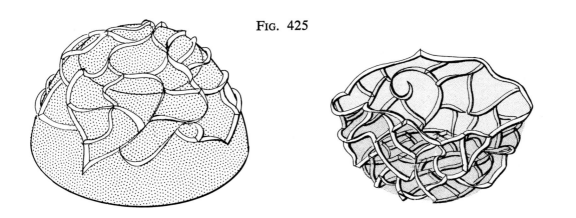

Fig. 425

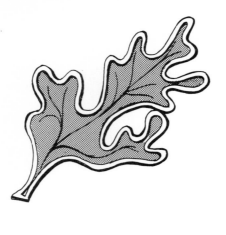

FIG. 426

Basse-taille

The basse-taille process is used on thinner (24-gauge) metals which are formed and detailed in repoussé technique and textured as desired. The transparent enamel coating, after firing at 1450°F., is ground level so that some portions of the metal may be elevated more than others in order to give depth (see Fig. 426).

Encrusté

Encrusté enameling is similar to basse-taille in that the metal surface is usually worked in the repoussé technique, but the enamel coating is applied evenly over the entire surface following the contours of the metal, and the surface is not ground away for a leveling-off after firing at 1450°F. (see Fig. 427).

Limoges

Limoges enameling is commonly referred to as wet enamel. The colors are ground 200 to 400 mesh, and using a small spatula, are mixed with alpine oil on a glass slab. The enamels are mixed to an oil painting consistency. When too thick, they can be thinned with turpentine. Colors mixed with the oil may be stored if more enamel was prepared than was needed. The prepared colors are painted (on a prefired surface) just as is done when painting with oils (see Fig. 428). The metal is held at the open door of the kiln before placing it inside so that the oil and turpentine may be burned away be-

water). The thin copper is soon dissolved in the acid, leaving only the delicate tracery of metal surrounded by enamel.

A bowl may be fashioned from 18-gauge metal using the plique-à-jour technique. The pierced work is completed in the flat sheet and then it is gently formed to a shallow shape. A similar bowl of thin copper is shaped to fit inside or out to hold the enamel for firing. The supporting bowl is removed by immersing it in the acid solution. Forms may also be enameled in this technique by using a nonfusing metal such as brass or aluminum bronze. Flat pieces and those with form may be completed without the supporting metal becoming attached to the cloisons, the pierced grill, or the network. Small shallow brass bowls are ideal for beginners in this technique. The supporting surface must be highly polished and smooth. The cloisons of silver wire are attached to the bowl with heavy adhesive solution. When they are all in place, the cells are filled with the enamel.

A heavier wire is placed around the rim, and a wide band is placed on the curve for a base. The bowl is fired upside down at 1450 to 1500°F. 2 to 4 minutes or until the enamel is glossy. When cooled, the highly polished brass bowl should separate from the enameled article with a slight tap or two.

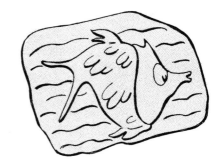

FIG. 427

FIG. 428   Pin, enamel, Limoges, 14k gold.
Antique.

FIG. 430

fore firing the enamels. The enamel should be fired at 1350 to 1450°F. for 2 to 3 minutes.

The standard 80-mesh enamel powders may be mixed with the gum tragacanth solution, or mixed with distilled water and painted onto a prefired surface, but the result will be a defined color separation instead of the delicate blending evident in the Limoges technique.

En résille

En résille technique involves the treatment of the surface of rock crystal. The crystal is scored

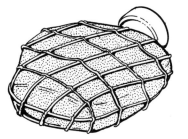

FIG. 429

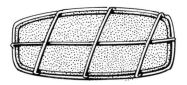

in a crisscross netlike pattern with engraving tools, and fine gold wires are laid in the grooves (see Fig. 429). The compartments formed by the wires are filled with enamels, and the entire article is then fired at 1350°F. for 1 to 2 minutes.

Grisaille

Grisaille refers to a gray or neutral-toned enameled surface which is built up in multiple layers of white, gray, and yellow enamels on a black enameled surface in successive firings. This gives a Wedgwood, or bas-relief effect (see Fig. 430).

Stencil

In the stencil technique, the metal surface is prepared and fired with an opaque coating of enamel. When cool, the stencil is placed on the surface which has been slightly dampened with water to hold the stencil in place. The open areas in the stencil are sprayed with the adhesive solution in a small atomizer. Enamel powder, preferably 100 mesh, is dusted into the open portions of the stencil (see Fig. 431). The dampened stencil is removed with tweezers, and the metal is medium-fired at 1450°F. for 2 to 3 minutes and then cooled.

Stencils can be made by cutting them from thin cardboard similar to that used on the

FIG. 431

back of scratch-paper tablets. The stencil is placed over a paper towel or tracing paper and the design drawn, thus protecting the original stencil design for later use. Dressmaking fabric used for stiffening in lapels, etc., can also be used for the expendable stencils.

For a pseudostencil technique, the fired enamel surface is coated with the adhesive solution in the areas to be fired with the contrasting color. This means that the design must be painted on the surface with the adhesive solution which should be thick enough to hold where painted. The wet adhesive-coated area is dusted with the chosen color and then tipped up and tapped slightly to remove rebel grains from the surface. The article is medium-fired at 1500°F. for 2 to 3 minutes, or until the surface appears glossy.

For a dry-brush effect, the prefired surface is cleaned with ammonia or the vinegar solution (see p. 269) and dried. Dry enamel powder is sprinkled on the enameled surface (no adhesive is used here) and then the dry enamel is brushed away to reveal the enameled surface beneath. The article is then fired at 1450°F. for 1 to 2 minutes, or until glossy.

Sgraffito

The sgraffito technique entails the use of 100-mesh enamel powders dusted on a prefired surface that has been freshly coated with adhesive. A metal scribe is used to scratch the design in the unfired enamel powder, thereby exposing the previously fired coating underneath (see Fig. 432). After drying, the piece is fired at 1450°F. for 2 or 3 minutes or until smooth and glossy. If the lines are too faint or thin after firing, adhesive is applied and more enamel is added to the surface. The design areas are scratched with a thicker tool followed by another firing at the same temperature.

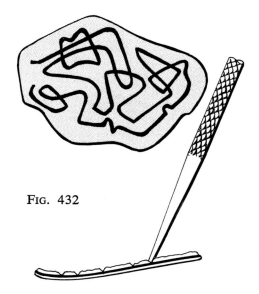

FIG. 432

Sculptures

Simple, uncomplicated sculpture objects can be enameled also. The design, executed in flat metal, is shaped by hand pressure or with any of the metalworking tools, using little or no annealing to strengthen the form.

Metal pieces may sag when fired, but areas can be held in place with iron binding-wire. The metal form should be enameled on all surfaces in the first firing.

Electroformed surfaces

See Chapter 28 for electroforming masked-off areas of enameled articles.

Electroplating and Electroforming

ELECTROPLATING

ELECTROPLATING IS A METHOD OF DEPOSITING various coatings of metal on other metals to produce different colors, to improve the appearance of dull metals, and to provide tarnish-resistant surfaces.

The thickness of the metal deposited electrically as a coating on another metal can be as thin as one-millionth of an inch (0.000001 inch), or as thick as two-thousandths of an inch (0.002 inch).

The plating is done by electrolysis—the passing of low-voltage direct current through a metal object (cathode) suspended in a chemical solution called an electrolyte which contains an anode (see Fig. 433). An anode is a strip of metal which dissolves and forms a thin transparent layer of metal (plating) on the object. As the anode wears away gradually in proportion to the thickness of the metal deposited, it can be used many times.

Plating equipment

Plating equipment consists of a plating machine, pyrex beakers or containers for solutions, steam cleaner, hot plate, instant-reading ther-mometer, and copper wires (see Fig. 433). Materials include masking lacquers, anodes, and solutions for stripping (removal of previous plating deposits), cleaning, plating, and rinsing.

The kind of metal in the object, and the kind and thickness of the metal for the plating dictate the type of solution, temperature, voltage, and immersion time for the plating process. Some solutions are used in varying degrees of heat for different metals, while others are used at a constant temperature. The solutions should never be heated beyond their recommended temperatures.

Anodes

Anodes are pure copper, pure or high-karat gold, fine silver, brass, stainless steel, pure nickel, platinum, and titanium (used instead of platinum for rhodium plating). Sterling silver is not usable as an anode material.

When suspended in the plating solution, the anodes will discharge and deposit a thin transparent plating on the metal surface when the electric current is activated.

To reduce plating time, anodes can be bent around an article, keeping all platable areas

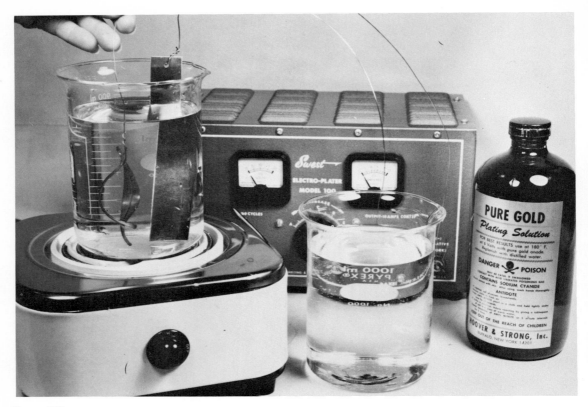

FIG. 433

equidistant from it (see Fig. 434). This method can also be used to reduce the time for electrostripping.

The surface area of the anode must always be greater than the surface area to be plated, but it does not have to be reduced for small articles. An additional anode will be required for large objects with a platable surface no more than four inches from the anode.

Anodes should not be left in the solution overnight or longer as the metal content of the solution increases unnecessarily. They should be rinsed after each use and stored in a dust-proof wrapping. Copper anodes exposed to the air become corroded and must be thoroughly cleaned and sanded before reuse.

Plating solutions

Plating solutions are concentrated liquids mixed with *distilled* water before being used. To avoid contamination, solutions are stored in glass containers and tightly capped. As some solutions tend to erode, it is advisable to store the containers in plastic tubs. These can be made by cutting off the lower portion of bottles used for distilled water (see Fig. 435). Each solution has specific instructions for dilution and use which must be strictly adhered to if perfect plating is to result. Water levels must be maintained and everything that has to do with the plating kept meticulously clean. Solutions must be stored in tightly capped glass bottles to prevent evaporation. Plastic or rubber gloves should be worn when working with plating substances because of their extreme toxicity.

Different metals can be plated with anode and solution combinations made up of the primary plating solutions of gold, silver, copper, rhodium, and nickel as follows:

Gold on copper, nickel, or brass produces different shades of gold; gold on silver (gold on other white metals is possible, but any exposed soft solder must be plated first with copper); silver on copper, nickel and brass (the nickel and brass should be plated with copper first); platinum on gold; platinum and rhodium on silver and also on nickel, copper, and brass (the copper and brass must be nickel-coated first).

If a white metal surface is desired on copper or brass, a nickel finish on copper can be used as a final coating instead of silver or rhodium.

Gold-plating solutions

Gold-plating solutions consist of gold cyanides, sodium cyanide, or potassium cyanide and other metallic salts. *Plating solution fumes must not be inhaled.* Copper salts added to the solution produce a pinkish metal color, nickel salts a white color, and silver salts a greenish hue. The salts are deposited on the metal along with the gold from the gold anode (see Appendix).

Gold-plating colors are slightly enhanced by the kind of metal underneath the plating. Gold plating on silver produces a rich yellow, on copper a pinkish tinge, and on nickel a slightly greenish hue.

Gold-plating solutions, properly formulated, are available in bright yellow 24k and 14k, rich deep yellow 24k and 18k, light rose, dark rose, flesh, pink, lavender, green, antique green, and white gold.

Silver can be used as a base metal for gold-plating. Nickel or brass requires a base plating of copper to prevent peeling or spottiness in the final plating. Rhodium requires nickel as the undercoat. The regular procedure is followed for the base coat plating after which the article is thoroughly rinsed in running water.

The gold in the solution can be used for plating without an anode but the gold content

Fig. 434

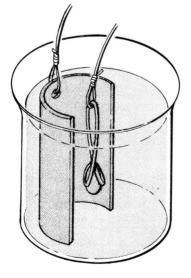

Fig. 435

must be replenished oftener than when one is used. Electrical conductivity is effected by means of a stainless steel anode.

The small amounts of gold remaining in a weak solution can be removed by a process called "plating out." The wires from the negative and positive poles are both attached to stainless steel anodes and inserted in the gold solution. The gold will collect on one of the anodes and can be reused for subsequent platings. The stainless steel anode does not discharge any metal except the gold, as it acts simply as a conductor of the electrical current. Individual stainless steel anodes must be used for each gold color.

Silver-, copper-, and nickel-plating solutions

Silver solutions contain silver cyanides and sodium cyanide as the main constituents; copper solutions contain copper carbonates and sodium cyanide; nickel solutions contain nickel sulfates and nickel chlorides.

The salts in the solutions are deposited on the metal along with the pure metal from the anodes that are mated to each solution—silver anode with silver solution, etc. (see Appendix). Rhodium-plating solutions contain rhodium sulfates and sulfuric or phosphoric acids. Rhodium plating, unlike the others, comes from the metal deposits in the solution. A platinum or titanium anode is used, but the metal is not deposited on the metal surface from the anode as it simply acts as an electrical conductor.

The solution must be recharged with a rhodium syrup to maintain a strong plating solution. Because the deposit comes from the solution, the action is stronger on surfaces of the article that are closest to the anode. To equalize the thickness of the deposit, the article must be rotated continually while plating.

Articles to be rhodium-plated are dipped after the electrocleaning step in an acid solution of 3 parts water and 1 part sulfuric acid, and then rinsed in running water.

Rhodium is best plated over a silver base metal. Other base metals must be precoated with nickel. The wires from the machine must always be platinum.

Before using, all solutions must be filtered through a paper filter contained in a glass funnel, as dust particles or sediment left in the containers will contaminate the plated surface.

Unbalanced plating solutions and home-made anodes with incorrect grain structure will produce unsatisfactory plating. When the anodes and solutions are maintained at a proper metal content balance, the anode will dissolve in direct proportion to the deposit without any waste or heavy buildup.

Plating machines

A plating machine (rectifier) with a voltage control capable of 12 to 16 volts operates on a normal household electrical current (see Fig. 433). Dry cells and storage batteries can be rigged to provide low-voltage direct current; however, the machine plater is preferable because the voltage can be better controlled (see Fig. 436).

Copper wire (or platinum wire for rhodium plating) capable of a 25- to 50-amp load is used from terminal to anode and from terminal to cathode (see Figs. 433 and 436). The wires must not touch each other and should be used in wide-mouthed beakers of at least quart capacity.

Before plating, the article is finished in exactly the same procedure used for articles that are not to be plated. Plating does not cover surface imperfections, scratches, and discoloration. The surface must be kept aseptically clean—continually free from all grease and fingerprints.

FIG. 436

Steam cleaning and boil-out

Articles for plating are steam-cleaned with a small jet cleaner consisting of a coil of copper tubing ($\frac{5}{16}$ inch, inside diameter) covered by a stainless steel cover, open at the bottom with vent holes around the top or solid end (see Fig. 437). One end of the coil is attached to the water supply and the opposite end has a tapered tip for the jet spray. The coil is heated on a small *gas plate*. While the jet cleaner is heating to build up steam, the buffed and polished article is suspended on a copper wire dipstick in a pyrex beaker or saucepan of boil-out solution (see Fig. 438).

The solution consists of one part detergent (ordinary soap must not be used because of fats and oils in it), 3 parts water and 2 tablespoons of household ammonia. The article is left in the solution as it is brought to a boil and should remain therein for 5 to 10 minutes. During the boil-out period the jet cleaner is heated to produce a moist steam.

The article is removed from the boil-out solution still suspended on the wire because it cannot be touched with the fingers again until the plating has been accomplished. In order to hold the article securely under the jet spray. it is transfered to self-locking tweezers or wire *without touching the fingers*. It is held in the tweezers and under the jet spray to remove any remaining traces of dirt or grease. The article is transferred back to the copper dipping wire and immersed again in the boil-out solution. These steps are repeated until no oil, dirt, or grease remains on the metal. The article held under running water will have bubbles forming on the surface if there is any trace of grease or dirt. If the surface is absolutely clean, water will flow freely across the surface in a smooth film without any bubbles.

Electrocleaning

All metals are electrocleaned after boiling out to remove any tarnish or fire scale. The article is attached to a copper wire (20-gauge) and immersed in a commercially prepared electrocleaning solution or one prepared by combining 1 ounce of household cleaner such as Oakite, Spic and Span, etc., with 1 quart of water. The solution is heated to 180° (the

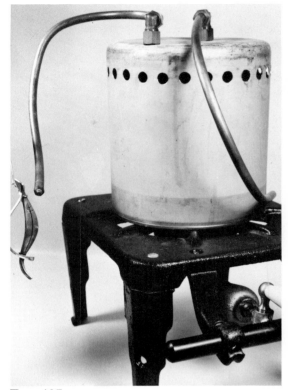

FIG. 437

FIG. 438

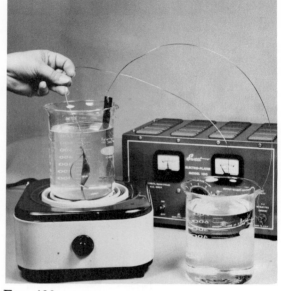

FIG. 439

FIG. 440

temperature is determined with an instant reading thermometer available at photo supply stores). The wire from the article is attached to the negative terminal and a stainless steel or brass anode is connected by a copper wire to the positive pole of the plating machine (see Fig. 439). *Wires holding anodes must never make contact with solutions during any kind of process.* The machine is set at 6 volts and the article agitated in the solution until clean. Neither the article and its wire nor the anode and its wire must touch the other at any time. The machine is turned off, and the article rinsed under running water either while still attached to the wire or after it has been transferred to locking tweezers. *It must not be touched with the fingers.*

The article is checked for cleanliness in the same manner as described for the "boiling-out" process. It is then immersed in a container of clean water while the plating setup is implemented.

Electrostripping

Articles with unsatisfactory or worn plating must be stripped before attempting additional plating. Commercial stripping solutions are preferred, but a solution can be made by combining $\frac{1}{3}$ teaspoon of sodium carbonate, and 1 ounce of sodium cyanide with 1 quart of distilled water. The solution is stirred with a glass

rod until clear and then heated to 200°F. The article is attached to a copper wire that is connected to the positive pole, a stainless steel or brass anode is wired and connected to the negative pole (see Fig. 440). This reverses the wires on the two machine terminals and creates a "reverse plating." The anode, instead of discharging metal to the article and the solution, is itself plated with the accumulation being removed from the surface of the article. The anode and the article with their respective wires, which must never be allowed to make contact, are suspended in the heated solution. The machine is set to 10 volts, turned on, and the article is agitated in the solution for approximately three minutes, or until the surface is clean and free from any evidence of previous platings or accumulation. The machine is then turned off and the article disconnected from the machine and rinsed under running water. The surface must always be carefully checked for cleanliness when this process is completed. The article may remain in a rinsing beaker while preparation is being made for the plating process.

Nickel stripping

Nickel is stripped in a cold solution consisting of 2 parts nitric acid, 1 part water, 4 parts sulfuric acid, and $\frac{1}{16}$ part hydrochloric acid. These constituents are combined by adding the nitric

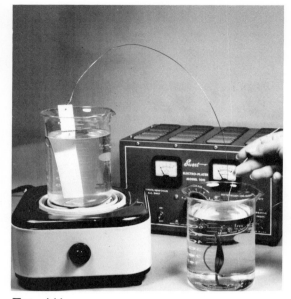

FIG. 441

FIG. 442

acid to the water (never the water to the acid), then adding the sulfuric acid, and when the solution is cool, adding the hydrochloric acid.

The article is immersed in the solution only long enough to remove the old plate, after which it is rinsed in running water. Acid solutions such as this should not be used in close proximity to open containers of cyanide (plating) solutions.

Electroplating the metal

When the cleaning, boil-out, and stripping operations have been completed, the machine is set up with two beakers in front of it, one of which is placed on a hot plate. The left-hand beaker is filled with distilled water and the right-hand beaker (on the hot plate) with the proper plating solution. The article is attached to a wire and then connected to the negative terminal on the plating machine. The other wire, attached to the proper anode, is connected to the positive pole, and the anode is then suspended in the plating solution (see Fig. 433).

The plating solution is heated, and the machine is set to the voltage requirement recommended for the particular metal and solution. The machine is turned on, and the article is agitated for the specified time span, after which the machine is turned off and the article rinsed in a separate container of distilled water (see Fig. 441). The container used for rinsing after electrocleaning is never used for rinsing the

plated article. If the new plating color is satisfactory, the article is transferred to self-locking tweezers, rinsed under running water, and then released from the tweezers without being touched into a box of hardwood sawdust to dry without spotting.

Postplating treatment

Gold-plated articles after plating and rinsing are rubbed with ordinary baking soda (sodium bicarbonate) and rinsed in running water. This adds luster to the metal finish and neutralizes any acids remaining on the metal. Copperplated articles require thorough rinsing to prevent any peeling of the plating. Rhodium-plated

FIG. 443

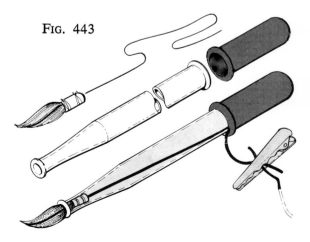

articles are thoroughly rinsed and then dipped in household alcohol (rubbing or isopropyl type) for neutralizing and luster.

Overplating or excessive metal deposit

Overplated articles will build up a frosty coating of plating material. There are three possible causes for this, namely, incorrect temperature, and/or voltage setting, and extended immersion in the plating solution. Thin encrustations can usually be removed by rubbing with baking soda and water mixed to a paste. A thick encrustation will require stripping and replating.

Partial plating for contrast

Portions of a clean article can be plated to provide a color contrast with the original metal. The parts of the article that will not be seen when worn need not be plated. Any areas to be left unaffected by the plating solution are painted with a mask-off lacquer (see Fig. 442). After plating, the lacquer can easily be removed, without rubbing, with thinner or acetone.

When a cold plating solution is used, the mask-off can be made with a wax pencil or paraffin. After plating, the wax is easily removed by immersing the article in warm water approximately 135°F. or by dipping it in a wax solvent.

Brush-plating

Articles can be brush-plated by combining a brush with a medicine dropper to form an applicator (see Fig. 443). A small quill brush (the bristles must be bound with nylon thread or stainless steel wire) is inserted in a medicine dropper with the squeeze bulb removed. An anode small enough to fit inside the glass or plastic barrel of the dropper is connected with two wires of the same material as the anode. One of the wires, approximately 20-gauge, is attached to the positive pole on the machine. The other wire of 28- to 30-gauge extends down through the bristles to make contact with the article. The article itself is simply attached to its regular wire and the negative pole. The barrel of the dropper is filled with plating solution and the squeeze bulb replaced. When the bulb is squeezed, one drop of solution at a time

FIG. 444   Pin, electroformed copper over natural leaf.
By Sharr Choate.

flows to the bristles to be spread over the surface as desired.

Plating soft solder

Solf solder can be plated if copper is used first as a base coating. Areas that do not need to be copper-plated are masked off. The article is immersed in the copper solution with the copper anode for one minute, then rinsed and the mask-off removed. After the metal is electrocleaned and rinsed, the gold or silver plating process is done.

Metal finishes under plating

Because the plating is a transparent color coating, different finishes must be effected on the metal surfaces before plating. High luster requires a high polish. Satin finishes are made by brushing the surface with a scratch brush, and a softer satin finish is accomplished by coating the scratch brush with pumice, and then buffing.

Plating articles containing gemstones

Articles can be electroplated with stones intact if the stone can withstand the temperature of the cleaning and plating solutions. Some stones such as opal, pearls, turquoise, and coral cannot be immersed in any solution at any temperature.

Plating inner surfaces of bowls

Bowls or other vessels to be plated on the inner surface are cleaned thoroughly, and the plating solution is placed inside the vessel. The wire to the negative pole is clipped to the vessel, and the anode, attached to the positive pole wire, is immersed in the solution-filled vessel, and the switch turned on for necessary plating time. The plating procedure is as described and only the article is handled differently.

ELECTROFORMING

Electroforming requires the same plating machine and other equipment used for electroplating. The process is also the same, except that the buildup of metal is considerably thicker and, instead of a base metal, a matrix (form) of disposable material can either remain as a core or be eliminated after the deposit of metal is complete. This technique produces basically the original object in exact detail and also the encrustation or buildup of metal (see Fig. 444).

Matrix materials

The matrix or basic form is made of wax, styrofoam, fabric, plastic, wood, thin metal sheet such as foil or opened and flattened toothpaste tubes and the like, or any similar material that will hold a shape as well as a coating of electrically conductive material.

Commercially produced low-melting-point metals such as Millots metal, Cerro-base, and Cerrobin can also be used for the matrix. The same voltage settings, temperatures, solutions, and anodes used for electroplating are employed; however, buildup time is longer, sometimes taking as much as several hours.

The matrix should be lightweight, structurally sound, but not bulky. A bulky matrix, when removed, will leave a flimsy collapsible form.

Fabrics are coated with fabric spray, thin resin coatings, clear lacquer, or any substance

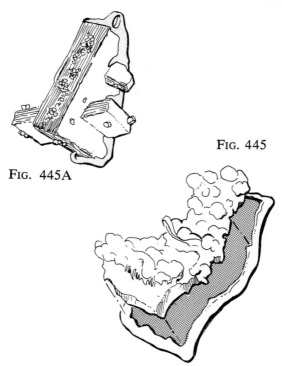

FIG. 445

FIG. 445A

impervious to water that will make the material substantial enough to hold its shape.

Plastic, wax, wood, and metals are worked with ordinary tools such as wax carving, metal and woodworking tools, soldering irons, small torches, etc.

Commercial metals are usually cast into a form (mold) which becomes the matrix. They can also be poured out into a sheet and, when set, worked with various tools to produce the desired shape.

Electroforming around gemstone materials

Soft materials such as crystal specimens, shells, gemstones, etc., which cannot stand the heat of casting or the pressure required to burnish down prongs, can be mounted on or in a wax matrix. If the buildup around the gem material is not sufficient to hold it in place, prongs are constructed of any material and, like the matrix, covered with a conductive coating (see Figs. 445 and 445A). *The conductive coating must not be allowed to touch the gemmy material,* because an unwanted metal buildup on it will occur.

No soldering can be done to electroformed objects containing gem material of any kind. Metal findings can be attached to the matrix and coated with a plating "stop" or clear lac-

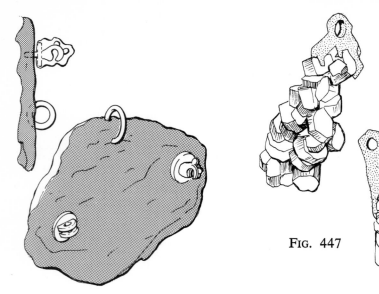

FIG. 447

FIG. 448

FIG. 446

quer to prevent a metal buildup on them when electroforming the entire piece. The stop is not to be applied to the portion of the finding that is to be attached (see Fig. 446).

Pendant bails used to suspend single crystal or other gem material can be constructed around the article with matrix material and covered with a conductive coating (see Fig. 447).

Before electroforming around gem materials, a sample piece of scrap gem material should be encased in a matrix and immersed, then checked to see if it is in any way adversely affected by the plating solution.

Conductive coatings

Commercial coatings are preferred as they contain the best constituents for metal attraction and electrical conductivity; however, there are several other substances that can be used. White graphite powder or silver dust mixed with resin to form a paste, or metal powders (copper, silver, or bronze) mixed with wax, shellac, clear lacquer, or synthetic resins also give good results. All coatings must be impervious to water. Coatings are brushed onto the surface with a small brush or a dental spatula and smoothed out as the electroforming will follow the contour of the coating. All surfaces must be completely free of all grease, dust, and dirt.

Anodes and solutions

The anodes and solutions for electroforming are used up much faster than for electroplating; therefore, the anodes must be thicker and the solutions replenished more often. All solutions must be filtered before each use in order to maintain their effectiveness. Filtering the solutions through fiberglass fabrics is preferred as it eliminates the greatest amount of contamination.

First coating

Matrices should have a base copper coating, as other metals have a greater affinity for it, and in addition, the copper color aids in determining whether or not the plating (or forming) metal is completely covering the matrix.

The electric current is directed to the object by inserting a wire that has been heated with a torch into any area that will not be visible on the completed article. One end of the wire must be inserted far enough to make contact with the coated surface, and embedded firmly enough to hold the article suspended in the solution (see Fig. 448). The opposite wire end is attached to the negative pole on the plating machine.

Form buildup

As the immersion time is lengthy, making it inconvenient to hand-hold the object, the anode and the object are suspended on a brass rod positioned over the beakers. The wires from the two poles on the machine are attached with alligator clips to these wires (see Fig. 449). After the machine is turned on, the object is left immersed in the solution for at least 10 minutes. In this time the metal will have begun to deposit around the wires making contact with the coated surface of the matrix. Gradually, the metal will build up and spread to the rest of the object. Agitation of the object in the solution accelerates the plating action and gives better results. When the buildup has reached the desired thickness (usually about as thick as an index card), the current is turned off and the article removed from the electrolyte and rinsed in running water.

Elimination of matrix

After the electroforming is completed, small holes are drilled in the underside where they will not be visible so that the base material can evacuate as carbon or fumes when it is turned from a solid to a liquid or ash (see Fig. 450). For the burning-out process the article is placed on a grid or small support stand in a 170–500°F. furnace. Nonmetallic matrices eliminated in a furnace or kiln will often produce oxides on the deposited metal surfaces. These are removed from the surface by immersing in regular pickling solutions.

Of course, articles containing gemmy material are never placed in a furnace. The matrix is not removed, but remains as a part of the piece unless it is of wax which can be removed by immersion in a wax solvent.

Electroforming bas-relief forms

Matrices for bas-relief articles are constructed of wax, wood, plastic, or clay (see Fig. 451) and a dam of the same material is made to surround the model. Wax or wet casting plaster is then poured into the enclosure and over the mold. When the material has set up, the sections are separated, producing a negative mold. Talc or graphite is dusted onto the surfaces of the model to act as a mold release before it is covered with wax or plaster.

A positive mold is made by filling the impression with wax or plaster. When wax is used for molds, a small amount of white vaseline melted in with the wax produces a pliable material, thus preventing brittleness that may cause breakage when cool. The duplicate positive mold is separated from the negative mold, coated with a conductive substance, and preparation for the electroforming process is made.

An alternative method to produce bas-relief matrices for electroforming requires coating the original model with a conductive substance without making a duplicate. After electroplating, the metal article is used as a mold. The disadvantage of this method, however, is that if unsatisfactory electroforming occurs, the matrix must be completely reconstructed.

FIG. 449

FIG. 450

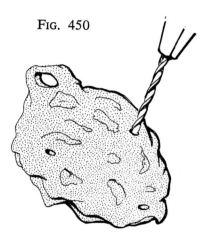

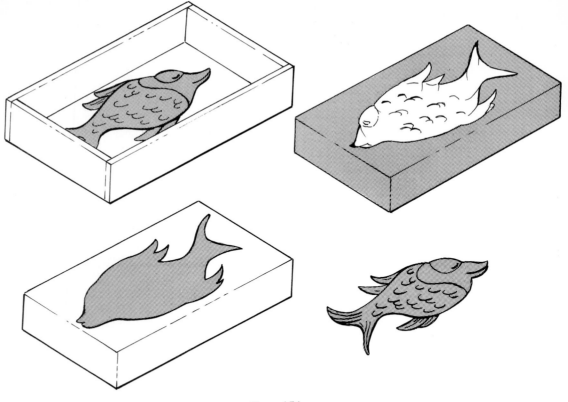

Fig. 451

If the coating for bas-relief articles is applied with a circular motion of the brush, even the smallest crevices and convolutions of the mold will be coated. The models should be checked for any traces of conductive coating on the underside because if it is allowed to remain, it will attract the deposit material, making it difficult to remove from the mold later on.

Electroformed surfaces can be enameled. The encrustation can also act as a divider (as in cloisonné) for different enamel colors (see Chapter 27).

Electroetching

Electroetching is a quick method for etching a metal surface using electroplating equipment. The areas that are to remain unetched are masked off, as in regular etching procedures. When the mask-off is dry, the metal is suspended in the plating solution on a wax-coated copper wire that is attached to the positive pole on the plating machine. The regular anode is also suspended on a wax-coated copper wire

and attached to the negative pole. This reverses the plating process, for here the anode is plated with the metal from the article. Naturally, the plating solution and the anode must match the metal to be etched. *Etching mordants are never used here.*

The plating solution is heated to 70°F. and maintained at this temperature during the electroetching process. The metal and the anode must be removed frequently from the solution and rinsed in distilled water to check the etching depth and to remove any accumulation of gasses which may have formed on the metal surfaces. This process must be continued until the etching is complete.

If some areas are to be electroformed after etching, surrounding areas, including newly etched excavations, are masked off, and the wires are switched on the poles on the electroplating machine. The metal deposited on the anode during the electroetching step is used to build up the unmasked areas on the design metal, and the normal electroforming procedures are followed.

Appendix

COMPARATIVE WEIGHTS AND MEASURES

Avoirdupois weight

Drams	Ounces	Metric Grams	Pounds	Troy Grains	Troy Ounces
1	.0625(1/16)	1.7719	.0039	437.5	.91146
16	1.	28.35	.0625	7,000.	14.58
256	16.	453.60	1.		
	34.20	1,000.00 (1 kilogram)	2.20		

Troy weight (used for precious metal weights)

1 dram = 1/18 troy ounce

Grams (Gm.)		Grains (Gr.)		Pennyweights (dwt.)		Ounces (Oz.)		Pounds (lb.)		Metric Grams
0.065	=	1	=	.0416	=	.0020	=	.00017	=	.0648
(15.43 grains		24	=	1	=	.05	=	.00416	=	1.5551
= 1 gram)		480	=	20	=	1	=	.08333	=	31.10
		5,760	=	240	=	12	=	1(13.17 oz. avoir)	=	373.24

1.0 troy oz. = 1.10 oz. avoirdupois
14.58 troy oz. = 1 lb. (16 oz.) avoirdupois
Only the troy oz., divided decimally, is used for a standard

Apothecary weight

Grains	Scruples	Drachmas	Ounces	Metric
1	.05	.01666	.00208	.0648
20	1	.3333	.04166	1.296
60	3	1	.125	3.888
480	24	8 (1 fl. oz.)	1	31.1035
20 fl. oz. (1 pint)				

The apothecary pound is obsolete

Linear measure

1 meter = 1.0936 yards
     = 3.2808 feet
     = 39.37 inches
     = 10 decimeters
     = 100 centimeters
     = 1,000 millimeters
     = 1,000,000 microns

1 decimeter = 3.937"
1 centimeter = .3937"
1 millimeter = .0393"   1/25"
1 micron = .000039" = 1/25,400"

1 inch = 2.54 centimeters
     = 25.4 millimeters
1 foot = 304.8 millimeters
     = 30.48 centimeters
     = 3.0408 decimeters
     = 0.3048 meter
1 yard = 0.9144 meter

Fluid measure

1 cubic centimeter = 16.23 minims
1 ounce = 29.57 cubic centimeters
1 dram = 1/16 ounce = 1.85 cubic centimeters
16 ounces = 1 pint
32 ounces = 2 pints = 1 quart = ¼ gallon
128 ounces = 4 quarts = 1 gallon

1 cubic centimeter of water weighs 1 gram

Carat weight

1 carat = 200 milligrams = 1/5 gram = 3.086 grains
     .007 ounce   100 points

½ carat = .50 point
¼ carat = .25 point
5 carats = 1 gram
1 Troy ounce = 155.54 carats
1 pennyweight = 7.777 carats
1 avoirdupois ounce = 141.76 carats

Carat weight for stones is based on the metric carat of 200 milligrams

METAL SHEET AND WIRE GAUGE EQUIVALENTS

Gauge	Inches (Decimal)	Drill
0	.325	21/64
1	.289	L
2	.257	F
3	.229	1
4	.204	6
5	.182	14
6	.162	20
7	.144	27
8	.128	30
9	.114	32
10	.102	38
11	.091	42
12	.081	46
13	.072	49
14	.064	52
15	.057	53
16	.051	55
17	.045	56
18	.040	60
19	.036	64
20	.032	67
21	.028	70
22	.025	72
23	.022	74
24	.020	76
25	.018	77
26	.016	78
27	.014	79
28	.012	80
29	.011	
30	.010	
31	.009	
32	.008	
33	.007	
34	.0063	
35	.0056	
36	.005	

DETERMINING LENGTH OF BEZELS

Bezel wire lengths are calculated by multiplying the diameter of the planned bezel by π (3.1416) and adding 2 mm for filing and fitting ends.

For oval bezels, add diameters of narrow and long axes of bezel and divide. Multiply the dividend by π to get length and add 2 mm for filing and fitting.

If a stone is measure for bezel, multiply diameter by $3\frac{1}{7}$ to get circumference or bezel length.

GEMSTONE SIZES

Gemstones purchased commercially are cut to specific sizes calculated in millimeters. 1 mm = 0.0394". (1" = 25.3998 mm). Oval stones are cut to fit commercial mountings in the following popular sizes:

mm	mm	mm
2 × 3	10 × 14	15 × 25
3 × 4	10 × 18	15 × 30
4 × 5	10 × 20	15 × 32
5 × 7	10 × 22	18 × 25
5 × 20	10 × 24	18 × 35
6 × 8	10 × 28	18 × 40
6 × 10	12 × 14	19 × 25
7 × 9	12 × 16	20 × 30
8 × 10	12 × 18	22 × 34
8 × 14	12 × 20	24 × 30
8 × 16	12 × 26	25 × 38
8 × 22	13 × 18	25 × 50
8 × 28	13 × 24	27 × 38
9 × 11	13 × 35	30 × 40
9 × 14	14 × 16	30 × 45
9 × 16	14 × 20	32 × 60
9 × 18	14 × 24	35 × 50
10 × 12	15 × 20	50 × 80

Rectangular or cushion-shaped gemstones are available commercially in the following common mm sizes:

6 × 8	10 × 12	12 × 16
8 × 12	10 × 14	13 × 18
8 × 13	11 × 15	14 × 16
8 × 16	12 × 14	

When lapidary equipment is available, the stones can be cut to any dimension called for in the design.

To determine the approximate fractional dimensions of gemstones, convert the millimeters to decimal equivalents and then to fractions. There are no mm dimensions (in round figures) that match simple fractional or decimal dimensions.

To convert millimeters to inches:
    millimeters × .0394   inches
To convert inches to millimeters:
    inches × 25.4   millimeters

COMPARATIVE SCALE OF METAL MALLEABILITY AND DUCTILITY

Range	Malleability	Ductility
1 (best)	Gold	Gold
2	Silver	Silver
3	Copper	Platinum
4	Platinum	Iron
5	Palladium	Nickel
6	Iron	Copper
7	Aluminum	Palladium
8	Tin	Aluminum
9	Zinc	Zinc
10	Lead	Tin
11	Nickel	Lead

COMPARATIVE WIRE AND DRILL COMBINATIONS

Wire Gauge	Diameter	Nearest Fraction	Drill Number	Diameter
26	.016″	1/64″	77	.018″
20	.032	1/32	64	.036
16	.051	3/64	54	.054
14	.064	1/16	51	.067
12	.081	5/64	44	.086
11	.091	3/32	3/32	.0937
8	.128	1/8	30	.1285
5	.182	3/16	13	.185
2	.257	1/4	"G"	.261

WEIGHT AND TEMPERATURE CONVERSIONS

Ounces troy to avoirdupois ounces:
 Multiply the troy oz. by 1.0971
Ounces avoirdupois to troy ounces:
 Multiply avoir. oz. by .09115
°Centigrade (Celsius) to °Fahrenheit:
 Multiply centigrade figure by 9, divide product by 5, add 32 = 0°F. Example:
 50°C. × 9 = 450 ÷ 5 = 90 + 32 = 122°F.
°Fahrenheit to °Centigrade (Celsius):
 Subtract 32 from Fahrenheit number, multiply the remainder by 5 and divide the product by 9. Example:
 122°F − 32 = 90 × 5 = 450 ÷ 9 = 50°C.
Troy Weights to Decimal Conversions:
 Grams to grains—
  multiply grams by 15.43
 Grams to oz. troy—
  multiply grams by 0.3215
 Grams to oz. avoir.—
  multiply grams by 0.03527
 Oz. troy to grams—
  Multiply oz. troy by 31.1035
 Oz. avoir. to grams—
  multiply oz. avoir. by 28.3495

METALS—MELTING POINTS (0°F.)

Aluminum	860–1240
Brass	930–2075
Bronze	1290–1890
Copper	1981
Gold	
24k	1945
18k	1700–1810
14k	1625–1765
10k	1580–1665
Iron, Cast	2060–2200
Wrought Iron	2700–2900
Lead	621
Lead, Alloys	140–640
Mercury	—38
Nickel Alloys	2160–2950
Nickel Silver	1832
Pewter	392–440
Palladium	2820
Platinum	3223
Rhodium	4442
Silver	
(1.000 Fine)	1761
.925 Sterling	1640
.900 Coin	1615
Tin	450
Tin Alloys	370–1155
Tungsten	6098
Zinc	787

COMPARATIVE SAW BLADE AND METAL SHEET COMBINATIONS

Saw Blade Number	Thickness	Nearest Fraction	Metal Sheet Gauge	Thickness
8/0	.0063″			Use for
6/0	.007	Less than 1/32″.		file or
4/0	.0086			rasp.
2/0	.0103	1/32″	28	.012″
1/0	.011	1/32	28	.012
3	.014	1/32	26	.016
7	.0173	1/32	24	.018
14	.0236	1/32	22	.025

HEAT COLORS (0°F.)

Faint red (barely visible	650– 700
Dull red (faint glow)	700– 900
Medium dark red	900–1280
Bright red	1280–1590
Cherry red	1600–1750
Salmon—orange	1800–1850
Bright yellow	1875–1925
Light yellow	1950–2125
White	2210–2300
Blinding white	2732 and up

TAPS, TAP DRILLS, AND WIRE SIZES

Tap Size	OD (0.00″)	Tap Drill	No. & Size (0.00″)	Nearest Wire Gauge & Size (0.00″)
1–64	0.0730	53	0.0595	12—.0808
2–56	0.0860	50	0.0700	11—.0907
3–48	0.0990	47	0.0785	10—.1019
4–40	0.1120	43	0.0890	9—.1144
5–40	0.1250	38	0.1015	8—.1285
6–32	0.1380	36	0.1065	7—.1443
8–32	0.1640	29	0.1360	5—.1819
10–24	0.1900	25	0.1495	4—.2043
12–24	0.2160	16	0.1770	3—.2294

Taps (.022–.076″) with mating dies can be purchased if smaller thread holes are needed. Taps are generally 25 percent larger than the tap drill and wire or shaft to be threaded is approximately 10 to 15 percent larger than the tap before threading.

ANNEALING TEMPERATURES (0°F.)

Aluminum	650
Britannia metal	None
Pewter	None
Brass	800–1300
Bronze	800–1200
Copper	700–1200
Gold	
Red	1100–1200
White and yellow	1400
Nickel silver	1000–1400
Silver	900–1200
Stainless steel	1200

TEMPERED STEEL HEAT COLORS (0°F.)

No color	200	Scrapers
Pale yellow	390	
Bright yellow	430	
Straw yellow	450	Punches, chasing tools
Dark yellow	470	
Brownish yellow	480	Engraving tools
Brownish red	500	Hammers, drills
Purple	520	
Violet	540	
Dark blue	550	Cold chisels
Cornflower blue	570	Screwdrivers, knives, saws
Bright Blue	600	Springs
Bluish green/gray	630	

PICKLING SOLUTIONS

Metal	Solution
Gold-Silver-Copper-Rhodium	1 part sulphuric acid *added to* 8 parts water (most commonly used solution)
Silver-Copper	*1 part nitric acid added to 8 parts water
Gold, with stubborn oxides	1 part sulphuric acid added to 8 parts water with ¼ oz. potassium dichromate added to solution
Silver-Copper-stubborn oxides	¼ oz. potassium dichromate 1 part sulfuric acid and 1 part nitric acid added to 7 parts water
Platinum	†Aqua regia (3 parts hydrochloric acid to 1 part nitric acid. Can be diluted 1 : 1 with water if desired (for weaker solution)
Gold-Silver-Copper-Brass-Bronze	Sparex #2. A commercial preparation consisting of a powder which is combined with water to make a saturated solution
Gold-Silver-Platinum-Copper	Prevox. A commercial ant-flux preparation. Metals, after dipped in solution, will not oxidize through 3–4 reheat steps

* Silver, copper, brass, bronze are soluble in nitric acid.
† Gold, platinum are soluble in aqua regia.

CONSTITUENTS OF SILVER SOLDERS

Solder Hardness	Pure Silver	Brass
Hard #1	7 parts	1 part
Hard	5	1
Medium	3	1
Easy grade	2	1
Easy flow	2	½

SOLDER MELTING POINT (0°F.)

Gold			
	14k	Hard	1450
		Medium	1410
		Easy	1360
	18k	Hard	1520
		Medium	1485
		Easy	1390
	22k		1610
Silver			
		Hard	1460
		Hard #1	1425
		Medium	1390
		Easy	1325
Soft			358-484
Aluminum			650

ESSENTIAL INFORMATION OF ELECTROPLATING
AND ELECTROFORMING PROCESSES

Electroplating

Step	Anode	Solution	Temp. (0°F.)	Voltage	Immersion Time
Steam-clean	—	Tap water through steam cleaner	200–212	—	Optional
Rinse	—	Distilled water	68–72	—	Optional
Boilout	—		212	—	Optional
Electro-clean	Stainless steel	Commercially prepared	180	10	30 secs.– 1 min.
Electro-strip	Brass or stainless steel	Commercially prepared	200	10–12	2–3 mins.
Copper plate	Copper on stainless steel wire	Commercially prepared	100–160	6	30 secs.– 1 min.
Nickel plate	Nickel	Commercially prepared	70	12	3–4 mins.
Gold plate	Gold	Commercially prepared	140	1–2	30 secs.– 1 min.
Silver plate	Fine silver	Commercially prepared	70	2	30 secs.– 1 min.
Rhodium plate	Platinum on platinum or gold wire	Commercially prepared	100	1–2	30 secs.– 1 min. (max.)

Electroforming

Step	Anode	Solution	Temp. (0°F.)	Voltage
Copper on copper or nickel	Copper	Commercial plating solution for copper or sulfuric acid 10 oz. per gal. of distilled water and copper sulfate 32 oz. per gallon water	80–100	6V max.
Gold on gold, copper, silver, nickel silver	Gold, any karat desired or stainless steel which uses only metal salts from solution	Commercial plating solution for gold or potassium gold cyanide 2 oz. (troy) per gal. of distilled water	140–160	1½–3V
Silver on silver, copper or nickel silver	Fine silver	Commercial plating solution for silver or 5 oz. sodium cyanide 3 oz. silver cyanide 3 oz. sodium carbonate ½ oz. sodium hydroxide added to 1 gal. distilled water	75 min. to 110 max.	2–4V
Silver strike used under electroforming as a base coat	Stainless steel or fine silver	1½ oz. silver cyanide 9 oz. sodium cyanide 1 gram copper cyanide to 1 gal. distilled water	75	2–4V 15 sec. to 1 mm. immersion time

RING SIZES AND DECIMAL EQUIVALENTS

0	0.458″ inside diameter
½	.474
1	.490
1½	.506
2	.522
2½	.538
3	.554
3½	.570
4	.586
4½	.602
5	.618
5½	.634
6	.650
6½	.666
7	.682
7½	.698
8	.714
8½	.730
9	.746
9½	.762
10	.778
10½	.794
11	.810
11½	.826
12	.842
12½	.858
13	.874
13½	.890
14	.906
14½	.922
15	.938
15½	.954
16	.970
16½	.986
17	1.002

Each full ring size is .032″ (32/1000ths) larger than the previous size.

Shanks are measured by determining ring size, inner diameter, and circumference based on the inner diameter. The shank length is equal to the circumference plus 1½ times gauge thickness.

Example:
Size 6 (16-gauge) ring shank =
.650″ diameter = 2.04 (2 3/64″)
plus .050
$\times$ 1.5
.075 (5/64″) or 1½ × thickness
at 16 gauge
2.04
+ .075
Ring shank is 2.115″ (or approx. 2⅛″ long).

COMPARISON OF MILLIMETERS, B&S WIRE GAUGE SIZES, AND DECIMAL EQUIVALENTS

B&S Wire Gauge (most generally used sizes)	Millimeters	Decimal Equivalents 0.000″
8	3	.128
10	–	.101
12	2	.080
14	1½	.064
16	1¼	.050
18	1	.040
20	¾	.032
22	–	.025
24	½	.020
26	–	.016
28	⅓	.012
30	¼	.010

TO FIND THE CIRCUMFERENCE OF A CIRCLE

Multiply the diameter by 3.1416 (π) or $3\frac{1}{7}$

3.1416 (π)
$\times$ 2″ diameter
6.2832″, or 6¼″ circumference

CIRCLES

Dia. (Inches)	Circumference (Inches)
1/16	13/64
1/8	25/64
3/16	19/32
1/4	25/32
5/16	63/64
3/8	1-11/64
7/16	1- 3/8
1/2	1-37/64
9/16	1-49/64
5/8	1-31/32
11/16	2- 5/32
3/4	2- 23/64
13/16	2- 35/64
7/8	2- 3/4
15/16	2-15/16

1	3- 9/64
1- 1/8	3-17/32
1- 1/4	3-15/16
1- 3/8	4- 5/16
1- 1/2	4-21/32
1- 5/8	5- 7/64
1- 3/4	5- 1/2
1- 7/8	5-57/64
2	6- 9/32
2- 1/8	6-11/16
2- 1/4	7- 1/16
2- 3/8	7-15/32
2- 1/2	7-55/64
2- 5/8	8- 1/4
2- 3/4	8-41/64
2- 7/8	9- 1/32
3	9-27/64

TO DRAW AN ELLIPSE (OVAL) IN ANY SIZE RECTANGLE #1

1. Determine the length and width of the desired ellipse. Use these dimensions to draw the major and minor axes. Mark the major axis AB and the minor axis CD. Mark the point of intersection X.
2. Measure AX and use as a radius pivoting from point C. Draw an arc to intersect with major axis at E and F.
3. Place pins at C, E, and F and tie a string tightly around the three pins. Remove the pin at point C and insert a pencil inside the loop (mechanical pencil works best).
4. Hold the string taut and draw the ellipse by moving the pencil inside the string loop.

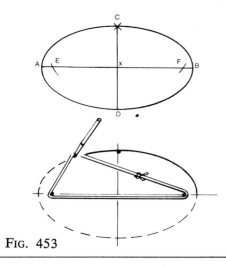

FIG. 453

TO DRAW AN ELLIPSE (OVAL) IN ANY SIZE RECTANGLE #2

1. Draw on the edge of a square or a piece of square cut paper the major and minor axes of the desired ellipse. Mark the major axis AC and the minor axis AB.
2. Divide two pins on a straight line with distance between pins equal to AC.
3. Measure the length of AC and BC and divide in half. Tie a string tightly equal to this length and place over the pins.
4. Place a pencil inside the loop (mechanical pencil works best) and with the string held taut, draw the ellipse inside loop.

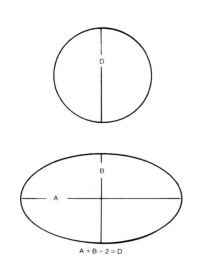

FIG. 452

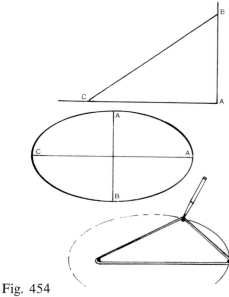

Fig. 454

TO MAKE A SMALL COMPASS FOR DRAWING CIRCLES

1. Drill small holes (just large enough to insert a pencil lead) in a short scale at ⅛″ increments in the first inch and thereafter at each inch on the scale.
2. Place the left-hand hole over a pin and insert pencil point in any other hole to equal the radius of the circle. For even-sized holes use drilled hole opposite 1″ as a pivot point and if fractions are desired then the pin will be inserted over one of the fractional divisions in the first inch on the scale. Remember that the radius will be less than the numbers indicated on the scale because the first inch is used for fractional pivot holes (see Fig. 455).

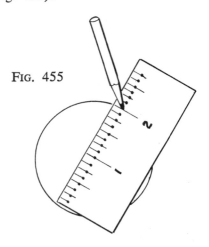

FIG. 455

TO DIVIDE A STRAIGHT LINE INTO EQUAL PORTIONS

1. Draw two parallel lines approximately 3″ apart. (Distance is optional.)
2. Divide the lower line (length optional) into desired number of portions using ¼″, ½″, or 1″ spacing. Mark outer limits as a and b.

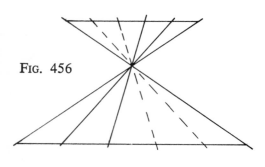

FIG. 456

3. Mark exact length of line to be divided on top line and mark outer limits A and B.
4. Draw straight line from A on top line to b on lower line. Draw another line from B on top line to a on lower line.
5. Place straight edge on any segment on lower line and draw a line through intersecting point of lines A-b and B-a up to the top line. Repeat until all segments on the bottom line have been transferred to the top line.

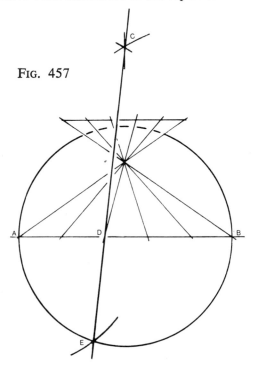

FIG. 457

TO DIVIDE THE CIRCUMFERENCE OF A CIRCLE INTO EQUAL PORTIONS

1. Divide the diameter of the circle into equal portions as desired around the circumference. Use the rule for dividing a straight line into equal portions. Mark the outer limits of the diameter A and B.
2. Draw an arc with a compass using AB as the radius and A as a pivot point. Draw another arc (same radius) using B as a pivot point. Mark the intersection of the two arcs C.
3. Place a straight edge on C and draw a line from this point through the second segment on the diameter line AB now marked D and extending out to the circle marked E.
4. Place a compass on points A and E to obtain distance of each portion and mark them off around the circle.

ALLOYING GOLD SOLDERS TO MATCH VARIOUS KARAT CONTENTS

Gold solder is alloyed to closely match the gold content of the article. Take four parts of the karat gold being used and one part fine silver. Measure the metals with the gold scale. The same alloy percentage is applicable regardless of the specific karat content.

12k gold solder	4 parts 12k gold	1 part fine silver
14k " "	4 " 14k "	1 " " "
18k " "	4 " 18k "	1 " " "

Place the metals in a crucible or in a hollow in a charcoal block. When the metal mass is molten and rolling, sprinkle borax flux over the metal and remove any slag with an orangewood stick. When the metal has cooled, flatten it with a forging hammer or rolling mill to standard sheet-solder thickness (28 gauge or .012").

(speed of driving pulley)
2¾"—diameter of driving pulley

$$3,450 \quad \frac{10,000}{6,900} \quad \frac{}{3,100} \quad \frac{}{3,450}$$

GOLD   ALLOYING

The metals for alloying are weighed in troy ounces, and it is necessary to understand the weights used.

12 oz. troy = 1 pound troy
1 oz. gold (troy wt.) = 20 pennyweight (dwt.)
1 dwt. = 24 grains (gr.)
= 480 grains = 31.10 grams
1 grain = 0.065 gram (gm)
1 gram = 15.43 grains
31.10 grams = 1 oz.

Weights are reduced to decimals for correct calculations. To convert:

1 troy ounce to grams: multiply the ounce by 31.10
grams to 1 ounce: divide grams by 31.10
grains to grams: multiply grains by .0648
grams to grains: multiply grams by 15.43

Fine gold is 1.000 in fineness and must be 99.9 percent pure gold. Other karat golds are listed according to their percentages of pure gold:

(24k)	(1.000)
22k	.9167
20k	.8333
19k	.7917
18k	.7500
16k	.6667
14k	.5833
12k	.5000
10k	.4167
9k	.3750
8k	.3333

Some of the gold/alloy metal percentages for different colors and karat contents are as follows:

22k Yellow
Gold	92%
Silver	5%
Copper	2%
Zinc	1%

18k White
Gold	75%
Nickel	10%
Palladium	10%
Zinc	5%

18k	Red	Pink	Yellow	Green
Gold	75%	75%	75%	75%
Copper	20%	17%	12½%	5%
Silver	5%	8%	12½%	20%

14k	White %	Red %	Dk Yel %	Lt Yel %	Green %
Gold	58½	58½	58½	58½	58½
Silver	15	7	15	21½	24½
Copper	—	34½	26½	20	17
Nickel	20	—	—	—	—
Zinc	6½	—	—	—	—

To increase 1 ounce troy of 14k gold to 18k, the following method of calibration is used to determine the additional pure gold necessary to raise the fineness of the gold:

20 dwt. × 18k = 360
20 dwt. × 14k = 280
360 − 280 = 80
80 ÷ 6 = 13.33 dwt., 7 gr. of 24k gold required.

The divisor (6) is determined by subtracting the karat gold desired from 24k. The dwt. requirement—13.33 (or 13⅓ dwt.)—is reduced to grains by determining what percentage the .33 dwt. is of 20 dwt.

To increase 12k gold (1 oz.) to 14k gold, the following example is used:

20 dwt. × 24 = 480
20 dwt. × 18 = 360

280 − 240 = 40
24k − 14k = 10
40 ÷ 10 = 4 dwt. pure gold to raise the 12k
      gold to 14k quality.

When lowering the karat content of gold, the divisor is the karat number of the end product.

To lower 1 oz. troy 24k to 18k quality, the following example is used:

20 dwt. × 24 = 480
20 dwt. × 18 = 360
divided into
480 − 360 = 120
120 ÷ 18 = 6 dwt. 16 grains of alloyed metal
                  required to reduce to 18k
Fractional grains are divided into 24 grains

(1 dwt.)

$$\begin{array}{r} 6 \\ 18\overline{)120} \\ 108 \\ \hline 12 \end{array} \qquad \frac{12}{18}=\frac{2}{3}$$

$$\begin{array}{r} 8 \\ 3\overline{)24} \end{array} \qquad 8 \times 2 = 16 \text{ gr.}$$

To lower 24k to 14k:

20 × 24 = 480
20 × 14 = 280
480 − 280 = 200
200 ÷ 14 = 14 dwt. 7 grains of alloy metals
                    required to make 14k

Determining the cost of gold in an article

To determine the cost of gold in an article, the item is weighed and the total is converted to decimal equivalents of a troy ounce and then multiplied by the cost of the metal per troy ounce. Decimal weights are always in troy ounces of fractions thereof, and it is very important to keep the decimal point straight.

If a piece of 24k gold of a given size weighs	.09 oz. troy
22k in the same dimensions will weigh	.082
18k	.0725
14k	.0627
9k	.0535
Fine silver	.0495
Sterling	.0490
Copper	.0415
Nickel	.0414
Brass	.0375
Aluminum	.012

TEST FOR GOLD CONTENT AND KARAT

If there is uncertainty as to whether or not a metal is gold, or to determine the karat content of unmarked gold, the following tests can be made to verify such characteristics. Tools required are a touchstone (slate), small file, small bottle of nitric acid, small bottle of hydrochloric acid, one set each of yellow, white, green, and gold needles (see Fig. 18).

To make the gold test, a small mark is filed in the edge of the metal on an area unseen when viewed in normal position or anywhere on an edge of plain stock metal. On assembled items it is absolutely necessary to file a mark to get down to base metal beneath any layer of precious metal deposited on the surface. A drop of nitric acid is applied to the scratch with a glass rod. Brass or copper will cause the acid to boil and turn green. Yellow gold (6k and below) will boil and sizzle, 10k yellow will darken, and 12k yellow or more will show little or no reaction. Platinum and stainless steel resist nitric acid; therefore, there is no reaction.

To determine the karat quantity of gold with gold needles, a streak is made on the touchstone by rubbing the gold against it. A needle is chosen from the correct gold needle set. The needle closest in color to the gold streak is chosen and a mark with this needle is made on the plate alongside the original streak. Draw a glass rod previously dipped in nitric acid across the streaks. The first streak to dissolve is of lower karat quantity. If the solution does not dissolve the metal, then aqua regia is used. Aqua regia consists of 10 parts hydrochloric acid and 3 parts nitric acid diluted with 10 parts distilled water to slow the dissolving action. The solution deteriorates and should not be saved. A new batch should be mixed each time the test is made.

Aqua regia attacks all gold, but attacks lower karat golds the fastest. If the reaction or color change is the same as the color-streak test, then the exact karat is already determined. In this solution 24k gold dissolves to a yellow liquid. Copper in yellow gold turns the streak greenish. Nickel content in white gold also makes the streak greenish, and silver turns it to a cheese-like white.

To test for white gold, palladium, and platinum (used with white gold and/or platinum needles), a solution consisting of the following substances (troy weights) is used, one drop to the scratch area:

> 1¼ oz. hydrochloric acid
> ¾ oz. nitric acid
> 1/20 oz. potassium nitrate

The drop of solution is left on the metal for one minute. There will be:

> no action on platinum
> pale bright yellow color if 18k
> deep yellow if 14k
> light brown color on 12k with platinum
> dark brown on 10k with palladium

White metals can be tested with a blowpipe to determine type of metal; however, one should practice this test on known alloys. Pure and precious metals, such as gold or platinum, melt smoothly and the resultant bead will cool without any trace of darkening or oxides. Stainless steel will darken before it melts. Palladium, like silver, will melt smooth but both will spit as they cool and silver will turn black. Because of the presence of nickel, copper or chrome will darken the metal as it cools. Base metal or pot metal in large amounts will reduce to a blackened clinker.

TESTING METAL FOR SILVER CONTENT

The metal is scraped in a small underside area and a drop of solution consisting of the following ingredients is used:

> 6 parts nitric acid
> 1 part chromic acid (2 parts bichromate of potash may be substituted for this acid)
> 2 parts water

If the metal contains silver, the scratch area will turn to a blood-red spot and the higher the silver content the more intense the red color will be.

To determine the amount of silver in an article, it is weighed and reduced to troy ounces (including pennyweights and grains). The constituents of silver solder are as follows (by weight):

DISTINGUISHING BETWEEN WHITE GOLD, PALLADIUM, PLATINUM, NICKEL, STAINLESS STEEL, AND DENTAL ALLOY

A drop of solution is applied to a scratch area as follows:

The metal is cleaned and a scratch area prepared. A drop of nitric acid is applied to the area. If the area is slow to etch or discolors, it indicates that the metal is 10–14k white gold, palladium, dental alloy, or nickel. If there is no action, a drop of aqua regia is applied (3 parts hydrochloric acid, 1 part nitric acid). Both acids should be heated when used and applied to the metal with a small glass rod. The solution is allowed to remain on the metal for thirty seconds. The acid-coated scratch area is blotted with blotting paper and the metal is washed and dried. The metal is then compared with the blotting paper and the metal is determined according to the following tests.

Metal	Effect with Nitric Acid		Effect with Aqua Regia	
	On Metal	Paper Stain	On Metal	Paper Stain
18k white	Ø	Ø	quick to etch dark stain	Ø
14k white	slow to etch	brown stain	slow to etch	green
10k white	slow to etch	brown stain	slow to etch	green/yellow
Platinum ⎰ Palladium ⎱	slow to etch no color	Ø	slow to etch	dark brown
Nickel	quick to etch	blue green	quick attack no color	no color to faint green
Stainless steel	Ø	Ø	quick attack no color	yellow/brown
Dental alloy	Ø	black stain	quick action no color	Ø

Ø—none

COATED ABRASIVE AND GRIT SIZES

	Garnet, Aluminum Oxide, or Silicon Carbide (Carborundum)		Emery
Very Fine	600, 500	—	
	400	10/0	
	360	—	
	320	9/0	
	280	8/0	
	240	7/0	
	220	6/0	
Fine	180	5/0	3/0
	150	4/0	2/0
	120	3/0	—
Medium	—	—	0
	100	2/0	—
	—	—	1/2
	80	0	1
	—	—	1-1/2
	60	1/2	—
Coarse	—	—	2
	50	1	—
	—	—	2-1/2
	40	1-1/2	—
	36	2	—
Very Coarse	—	—	3
	30	2-1/2	—
	24	3	—
	20	3-1/2	
	16	4	
	12	4-1/2	

COMPARATIVE SIZES OF SAW BLADES AND DRILLS

Blade No.	Thickness	Width	Drill
8/0	.0063	.0130	80
7/0	.0065	.0135	80
6/0	.0070	.0140	79
5/0	.0080	.0150	78
4/0	.0085	.0170	77
3/0	.0095	.0190	76
2/0	.0103	.0204	75
0	.0110	.0230	73
1	.0115	.0250	71
1½	.0125	.0255	71
2	.0135	.0270	70
3	.0140	.0290	68
4	.0150	.0310	67
5	.0160	.0340	65
6	.0173	.0370	58
7	.0189	.0400	
8	.0200	.0480	55
10	.0215	.0510	51
12	.0236	.0655	51
14	.0240	.0689	50

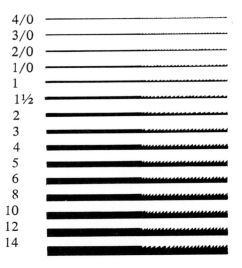

4/0
3/0
2/0
1/0
1
1½
2
3
4
5
6
8
10
12
14

FIG. 458

AVOIRDUPOIS OUNCES AND POUNDS TO OUNCES TROY

Avoir. Oz.	Troy Oz.	Avoir. Lbs.	Troy Oz.
1	.9115	1	14.583
2	1.823	2	29.167
3	2.734	3	43.750
4	3.646	4	58.333
5	4.557	5	72.917
6	5.469	6	87.500
7	6.380	7	102.083
8	7.292	8	116.667
9	8.203	9	131.250
10	9.115	10	145.833
11	10.026	11	160.417
12	10.937	12	175.000
13	11.849	13	189.583
14	12.760	14	204.167
15	13.672	15	218.750
		16	233.333
		17	247.917
		18	262.500
		19	277.083
		20	291.667

COMPARISON OF TROY WEIGHTS OF VARIOUS METALS
IN SQUARE INCH SECTIONS

B & S Gauge	Thickness in Inches	Fine Gold Dwts.	18k Yellow Gold Dwts.	14k Yellow Gold Dwts.	10k Yellow Gold Dwts.	Fine Silver Ozs.	Sterling Silver Ozs.	Coin Silver Ozs.	Platinum Ozs.	Palladium Ozs.
1	.28930	59.0	47.5	39.8	35.3	1.61	1.58	1.58	3.27	1.83
2	.25763	52.6	42.3	35.5	31.4	1.43	1.41	1.40	2.91	1.63
3	.22942	46.8	37.7	31.6	28.0	1.27	1.26	1.25	2.59	1.45
4	.20431	41.7	33.6	28.1	24.9	1.13	1.12	1.11	2.31	1.29
5	.18194	37.1	29.9	25.1	22.2	1.01	.996	.992	2.06	1.15
6	.16202	33.1	26.6	22.3	19.8	.899	.887	.883	1.83	1.02
7	.14428	29.4	23.7	19.9	17.6	.800	.790	.786	1.63	.912
8	.12849	26.2	21.1	17.7	15.7	.713	.704	.700	1.45	.812
9	.11443	23.3	18.8	15.8	14.0	.635	.627	.624	1.29	.723
10	.10189	20.8	16.7	14.0	12.4	.565	.558	.555	1.15	.644
11	.09074	18.5	14.9	12.5	11.1	.503	.497	.495	1.03	.574
12	.08080	16.5	13.3	11.1	9.85	.448	.443	.440	.913	.511
13	.07196	14.7	11.8	9.91	8.77	.399	.394	.392	.813	.455
14	.06408	13.1	10.5	8.82	7.81	.356	.351	.349	.724	.405
15	.05706	11.6	9.37	7.86	6.96	.317	.313	.311	.645	.361
16	.05082	10.4	8.35	7.00	6.21	.282	.278	.277	.574	.321
17	.04525	9.23	7.43	6.23	5.52	.251	.248	.247	.511	.286
18	.04030	8.22	6.62	5.55	4.91	.224	.221	.220	.455	.255
19	.03589	7.32	5.89	4.94	4.38	.199	.197	.196	.406	.227
20	.03196	6.52	5.25	4.40	3.90	.177	.175	.174	.361	.202
21	.02846	5.81	4.67	3.92	3.47	.158	.156	.155	.322	.180
22	.02534	5.17	4.16	3.49	3.09	.141	.139	.138	.286	.160
23	.02257	4.60	3.71	3.11	2.75	.125	.124	.123	.255	.143
24	.02010	4.10	3.30	2.77	2.45	.112	.110	.110	.227	.127
25	.01790	3.65	2.94	2.46	2.18	.0993	.0980	.0976	.202	.113
26	.01594	3.25	2.62	2.19	1.94	.0884	.0873	.0869	.180	.101
27	.01419	2.89	2.33	1.95	1.73	.0787	.0777	.0773	.160	.0897
28	.01264	2.58	2.08	1.74	1.54	.0701	.0692	.0689	.143	.0799
29	.01125	2.29	1.85	1.55	1.37	.0624	.0616	.0613	.127	.0711
30	.01002	2.04	1.65	1.38	1.22	.0556	.0549	.0546	.113	.0633
31	.00892	1.82	1.46	1.23	1.09	.0495	.0489	.0486	.101	.0564
32	.00795	1.62	1.31	1.09	.969	.0441	.0435	.0433	.0898	.0503
33	.00708	1.44	1.16	.975	.863	.0393	.0388	.0386	.0800	.0448
34	.00630	1.29	1.03	.868	.768	.0350	.0345	.0343	.0712	.0398
35	.00561	1.14	.921	.772	.684	.0311	.0307	.0306	.0634	.0355
36	.00500	1.02	.821	.689	.610	.0277	.0274	.0273	.0565	.0316
37	.00445	.908	.731	.613	.543	.0247	.0244	.0243	.0503	.0281
38	.00396	.808	.650	.545	.483	.0220	.0217	.0216	.0448	.0250
39	.00353	.720	.580	.486	.430	.0196	.0193	.0192	.0399	.0223
40	.00314	.641	.516	.432	.383	.0174	.0172	.0171	.0355	.0199

OUNCES TROY TO POUNDS AND OUNCES AVOIRDUPOIS

Oz. Troy	Lbs. & Oz. Avoir.	Oz. Troy	Lbs. & Oz. Avoir.	Oz. Troy	Lbs. & Oz. Avoir.
1	1.1	36	2- 7.5	71	4-13.9
2	2.2	37	2- 8.6	72	4-15.0
3	3.3	38	2- 9.7	73	4- 0.1
4	4.4	39	2-10.8	74	5- 1.2
5	5.5	40	2-11.9	75	5- 2.3
6	6.6	41	2-13.0	76	5- 3.4
7	7.7	42	2-14.1	77	5- 4.5
8	8.8	43	2-15.2	78	5- 5.6
9	9.9	44	3- 0.3	79	5- 6.7
10	11.0	45	3- 1.4	80	5- 7.8
11	12.1	46	3- 2.5	81	5- 8.9
12	13.2	47	3- 3.6	82	5-10.0
13	14.3	48	3- 4.7	83	5-11.1
14	15.4	49	3- 5.8	84	5-12.2
15	1- 0.5	50	3- 6.9	85	5-13.3
16	1- 1.6	51	3- 8.0	86	5-14.4
17	1- 2.7	52	3- 9.1	87	5-15.5
18	1- 3.8	53	3-10.2	88	6- 0.6
19	1- 4.9	54	3-11.3	89	6- 1.7
20	1- 6.0	55	3-12.4	90	6- 2.8
21	1- 7.1	56	3-13.5	91	6- 3.9
22	1- 8.2	57	3-14.6	92	6- 5.0
23	1- 9.3	58	3-15.7	93	6- 6.1
24	1-10.4	59	4- 0.8	94	6- 7.2
25	1-11.5	60	4- 1.9	95	6- 8.3
26	1-12.6	61	4- 3.0	96	6- 9.4
27	1-13.7	62	4- 4.1	97	6-10.5
28	1-14.8	63	4- 5.2	98	6-11.6
29	1-15.9	64	4- 6.3	99	6-12.7
30	2- 1.0	65	4- 7.4	100	6-13.8
31	2- 2.1	66	4- 8.5		
32	2- 3.2	67	4- 9.6		
33	2- 4.3	68	4-10.7		
34	2- 5.4	69	4-11.8		
35	2- 6.4	70	4-12.8		

Millimeters to Inches (Basis: 1 inch = 25.4 millimeters)

Millimeters	Inches	Millimeters	Inches	Millimeters	Inches	Millimeters	Inches
1	0.039370	26	1.023622	51	2.007874	76	2.992126
2	.078740	27	1.062992	52	2.047244	77	3.031496
3	.118110	28	1.102362	53	2.086614	78	3.070866
4	.157480	29	1.141732	54	2.125984	79	3.110236
5	.196850	30	1.181102	55	2.165354	80	3.149606
6	.236220	31	1.220472	56	2.204724	81	3.188976
7	.275591	32	1.259843	57	2.244094	82	3.228346
8	.314961	33	1.299213	58	2.283465	83	3.267717
9	.354331	34	1.338583	59	2.322835	84	3.307087
10	.393701	35	1.377953	60	2.362205	85	3.346457
11	.433071	36	1.417323	61	2.401575	86	3.385827
12	.472441	37	1.456693	62	2.440945	87	3.425197
13	.511811	38	1.496063	63	2.480315	88	3.464567
14	.551181	39	1.535433	64	2.519685	89	3.503937
15	.590551	40	1.574803	65	2.559055	90	3.543307
16	.629921	41	1.614173	66	2.598425	91	3.582677
17	.669291	42	1.653543	67	2.637795	92	3.622047
18	.708661	43	1.692913	68	2.677165	93	3.661417
19	.748031	44	1.732283	69	2.716535	94	3.700787
20	.787402	45	1.771654	70	2.755906	95	3.740157
21	.826772	46	1.811024	71	2.795276	96	3.779528
22	.866142	47	1.850394	72	2.834646	97	3.818898
23	.905512	48	1.889764	73	2.874016	98	3.858268
24	.944882	49	1.929134	74	2.913386	99	3.897638
25	.984252	50	1.968504	75	2.952756	100	3.937008

MILLIMETERS TO INCHES AND COMMON FRACTIONS OF AN INCH TO MILLIMETERS

Common Fractions of an Inch to Millimeters (Basis: 1 inch = 25.4 millimeters)

4ths	8ths	16ths	32nds	64ths	Decimal inch	Millimeters
				1	0.015625	0.396875
			1		.031250	0.793750
				3	.046875	1.190625
		1			.062500	1.587500
				5	.078125	1.984375
			3		0.093750	2.381250
				7	.109375	2.778125
	1				.125000	3.175000
				9	.140625	3.571875
			5		.156250	3.968750
				11	0.171875	4.365625
		3			.187500	4.762500
				13	.203125	5.159375
			7		.218750	5.556250
				15	.234375	5.953125
1					0.250000	6.350000
				17	.265625	6.746875
			9		.281250	7.143750
				19	.296875	7.540625
		5			.312500	7.937500
				21	0.328125	8.334375
			11		.343750	8.731250
				23	.359375	9.128125
	3				.375000	9.525000
				25	.390625	9.921875
			13		0.406250	10.318750
				27	.421875	10.715625
		7			.437500	11.112500
				29	.453125	11.509375
			15		.468750	11.906250
				31	0.484375	12.303125
2					.500000	12.700000
				33	.515625	13.096875
			17		.531250	13.493750
				35	.546875	13.890625
		9			0.562500	14.287500
				37	.578125	14.684375
			19		.593750	15.081250
				39	.609375	15.478125
	5				.625000	15.875000
				41	0.640625	16.271875
			21		.656250	16.668750
				43	.671875	17.065625
		11			.687500	17.462500
				45	.703125	17.859375
			23		0.718750	18.256250
				47	.734375	18.653125
3					.750000	19.050000
				49	.765625	19.446875
			25		.781250	19.843750
				51	0.796875	20.240625
		13			.812500	20.637500
				53	.828125	21.034375
			27		.843750	21.431250
				55	.859375	21.828125
	7				0.875000	22.225000
				57	.890625	22.621875
			29		.906250	23.018750
				59	.921875	23.415625
		15			.937500	23.812500
				61	0.953125	24.209375
			31		.968750	24.606250
				63	.984375	25.003125
4	8	16	32	64	1.000000	25.400000

NOTE: Table is exact; all figures beyond the six places given are zeros.

TO FIND THE SPEED OF A DRIVEN SHAFT

Multiply the diameter of the driving pulley by its speed and divide the product by the diameter of the driven pulley.

```
   3,450 rpm drive pulley speed
 ×    4″ (drive pulley)
 ─────
  13,800

  (driven pulley)
          6,900 rpm—speed of driven shaft
     2″  13,800
```

TO FIND THE DIAMETER OF A DRIVING PULLEY

Multiply the diameter of the driven pulley by its desired speed and divide the product by the speed of the driving pulley.

```
   5,000 rpm (desired speed)
 ×    2″ driven pulley
 ─────
  10,000

  (speed of driving pulley)
             2¾″—diameter of driving pulley
   3,450  10,000
           6,900
           ─────
           3,100
           3,450
```

Bibliography

ABBEY, STATON. *The Goldsmith's and Siversmith's Manual,* 1952.

AMERICAN DENTAL ASSOCIATION. *Guide to Dental Materials,* 1962–1963.

AMERICAN SOCIETY OF TESTS AND MATERIALS. Special Technical Bulletin 318, *Applications, Uses and Prospectus of Electroforming Metal.*

ASHBEE, C. R., Trans. *The Treatises of Benvenuto Cellini on Goldsmithing and Sculpture,* 1967.

BATES, KENNETH F. *The Enamelist,* 1967.

BAXTER, WILLIAM T. *Jewelry, Gem Cutting and Metalcraft,* 1950.

BOWMAN, JOHN J. *The Jewelry Engraver's Manual,* 1954.

———, and HARDY, R. ALLEN. *Jewelry Repair Manual,* 1956.

CIRINO, ANTONIO, and ROSE, AUGUSTUS F. *Jewelry Making and Design,* 1967.

DELTA POWER TOOL DIVISION, ROCKWELL MANUFACTURING CO. *Getting the Most Out of Your Lathe,* 1954.

DIXON, INC. *Sal-Hyde Plating Manual* (Mimeographed bulletin, n.d.).

EMERSON, A. R. *Handmade Jewelry,* 1953.

HUGHES, GRAHAM. *Modern Jewelry,* 1963.

JOACHIM, E. E. *Jewelry Making Step by Step,* 1967.

LEWES, KLARES. *Jewelry Making for the Amateur,* 1965.

LINICK, LESLIE. *Jeweler's Workshop Practices,* 1948.

MEILACH, DONA and SEIDEN, DONALD. *Direct Metal Sculpture,* 1966.

MILLER, JOHN G. *Metal Art Crafts,* 1948.

MEYEROWITZ, PATRICIA. *Jewelry and Sculpture Through Unit Construction,* 1967.

NEUMANN, ROBERT VON, *The Design and Creation of Jewelry,* 1961.

OSBRUN, BURL N., and WILBER, GORDON O. *Pewter, Spun, Wrought, Cast,* 1938.

REAGAN, JAMES E., and SMITH, EARL E., *50 Metal-Spinning Projects,* 1941.

ROTHENBURG, POLLY. *Metal Enameling,* 1969.

SMITH, ROBERT E. *Etching, Spinning, Raising, Tooling,* 1951.

———. *Forging and Welding,* 1956.

SOUTHWEST SMELTING AND REFINING. *Plating for Profit and Ease,* 1964.

THOMAS, RICHARD. *Metalsmithing,* 1960.

WEINER, LOUIS. *Handmade Jewelry* (2d ed.), 1960.

WINEBRENNER, KENNETH. *Jewelry Making,* 1955.

WINTER, EDWARD. *Enamel Art on Metal,* 1958.

UNTRACHT, OPPI. *Metal Technique for Craftsmen,* 1968.

Index

Illustrations and photographs are indicated by **boldface** type.

293

Forging, 16, 215; annealing metals, 19, 216, 224; anvils, 215–16; bases on objects, raised, 225, **366**; bases, sunken, 224, **365, 365A**; basic, 225–26, **370, 370A**; bench stakes, 24, **31**; blocks, 24, **32**; bouging, 24, 29, 215, 224, **353**; decorative, 225, **369**; edge-thickening, 29, 225, **368**; edge-trimming, 225, **367, 367A**; edge-upsetting, 229; hammers, 16, **20, 22**, 215, 216, 221, 222, **362, 362A, 400**; hammers, ball-faced sinking, 222, **362, 362A**; hammers, bottoming, 222, **362, 362A**; hammers, box, 222, **362, 362A**; hammers, care of, 223, **362, 362A**; hammers, collet, 222, **362**; hammers, cross-peen raising, 222, 225, **362, 370**; hammers, dome-faced planishing, 222, **362, 362A**; hammers, flat-faced forging, 222, **362, 362A**; hammers, planishing, 222, **362, 362A**; hammers, raising, 224, **362, 362A**; hardness, metal, retention, of, 217; lamination (simulated forging), 228, **372, 372A**; lead blocks, 25, **34**; metal requirements, 218–19, **356–57**; multiple piece forging, 223; planishing, 29, 216, 219; raising, 16, 24, 215, 218, 219, 224; raising deep objects, 224; sandbags, 24–25, **221**; sinking, 16, 24, 215, 218–19, 223, **354, 355, 364**; sinking, large areas, 29; spoon, forging, 226, **370, 370A**; supports for metal, 216, 221, **350–51, 361**; templates, 223, **363**; warping, 29; wrinkles, removal of, 224

Fractional dimensions of circles, 283

Fractional to decimals chart, 291

Fractional to millimeters chart, 291

Fused metals, 207, **336A**; cleaning metal, 208; fluxing, 208; fusing, 208; metal requirements, 207; orange peel, 209; soldering, 208; surface finish, 208

Fusibility. See Metals

G

Gallery wire, 77, 82

Gas-air torches, 20

Gauges, comparison of metal, 228; gauges, wire, 8, **15**

Gemstones, design nucleus, 4; electroplating with, 272; size standards, 278. **See also** Mountings

German scrollwork, 161

German silver. **See** Nickel silver

Gilding, 72

Glass beads, 6, **14**

Glycerine, 74

Goblet buffs, **89**

Gold, 7, 9; alloying, 9–10; 15–17, 285–86; annealing, 19; annealing temperatures, 280; characteristics, 9–10; chloride of gold, 9, 72; electrum,

9; flux, 61; foils, 9, 257–58; gauging, 11, 12; gold-filled items, 11; "gold" jewelry, 9–10; heat colors, 279; karat content, 10, 287; karat, testing for quality, 287; karat, testing for quantity, 286; measuring, 11, 12; melting point, 248, 279; pickling, 19, 280; plating chart, 281, **see also** Electroplating; removing solder from gold, 68; skin discoloration, 10; solders, 11, 58; solders, melting point, 280; stamping karat content, 11; tests, cost of metal in article, 286; tests, content of gold, 286; tests for white gold, 287; weighing, 12; weight, comparison to other metals, 289

Granulation, 209–10, **337, 337A, 338**

Graphite rods, 10

Gravers. **See** Engraving

Grisaille, 263, **430**

Gypsy setting, 92, **155**

Gum, tragacanth: enameling aid, 250; holding flux, 61; soldering with, 170, 199, 201–2, 250, **282**

H

Half-domes, 28

Hallmarks, 11

Hammers: care of, 16–17; types, 16, **20, 22**, 24, **30, 333, 400. See also** Forging; Texturing; Chasing

Hard solder. **See** solders

Healey, Pamela, **345A**

Heat colors of metals, 279; blued steel, 180, 241; soldering, 64; tempering, 173, 180

Hydrochloric acid, 68, 70, 186, 270, 280, 286, 287

Hydrofluoric acid, 73, 254, 255, 256

I

Indian stamping tools, 18, **23**

Indirect soldering: filigree, 203, **303, 303A**

Inlay, amalgams, 149–50; enamel, 258–66; etched, 188; metals, 139; niello, 149–50; solder, 143; stone, 165; Toledo, 144

Iodine, 70

Iron oxide, 70

Iron perchloride, 186

J

Japanese engraving, **302D**

Jeweler's saw, 31, **43**

Jonnson, Hakon, 158, 162–64, **173, 302, 303A, 322A, 345**, and color plates

Jump rings, 114–15, **203, 203A**

K

Karat, 7; content in alloys, 285; content of gold, 10; percentage, determining, 285; quantity, test for, 286. **See also** Gold

Kerosene, 75

L

Lathes, buffing, polishing, 48–50, **82**; spinning, 229, **374–75**

Lead, 15; blocks, 18, 25, **33**

Lead acetate (sugar of lead), 71

Leather buffs, 52, **86**

Limoges, 262, **428**

Linde A powder, 57

Linear measure, 277

Lines, dividing equally, 284

Liquid solder flux for coloring, 71

Liver of sulfur (potassium sulfide), 69, 70

M

Mallets, 24, **30**, 206, **333. See also** Hammers

Mandrels, carbon soldering, 132, 241; bracelet, 24, **30**; buffing, 43, 45, **69, 75, 76**; polishing, 43, 45, **69, 75, 76**; ring, 81, **123, 124, 240**; sanding, 43, **69, 70, 75, 76**

Manganese bronze. **See** Brass

Matte dip, 75

Matte finishing, 75

Matting tools, 18, **23**

Measuring equipment: calipers, 8, **15**; drill, 8; gauges, 8, **15**; gem scale, 8, ·**17**; gold scale, 8, **17**; scale, triple beam, 8, **16**; sliding, 8, **15**; wire, 8, **15**

Measuring gold, 11–12

Measuring metals, 11–13

Melting points of metals, 12–14, 279

Mercury, in gold amalgam, 72, 148, **269–73**

Mercury, in silver amalgam, 12, 149, **269–73**

Metal coloring and finishing, 69–71; coloring, gilding contrasting metal, 72; coloring, gold bright dip, 74; coloring, nitric acid as color agent, 72; coloring, patina S-72, bright dip, 75; coloring, silver bright dip, 74; coloring, silvering contrasting metal, 72; coloring, sulfuric acid, matte dip, 75. Finishing, bright dip, 74; finishing, brush wheels, 51, 73, 75; finishing, burnishing, 47, 73–74, **80, 112**; finishing, emery paper, 74, **110**; finishing, florentining, 73; finishing, matte dip, 75; finishing, polishing wheels, 74; finishing, satin finish, 73; finishing, steel wool, 74. **See also** Electroplating

Metal inlay, 139; amalgam, 148–49, **269–73**; backing sheet, 140, **253, 255, 280A**; cleaning, 144; finishing, 144; fitting sections, 138–41, **254–56**; metal requirements, rolling metal, 147, **267A**; mokume, 146–47, **265–67**; niello, 149–50, **274**; saw blade and metal gauge comparisons, 279, 288; sawing sections, 139–42, **251A, 252**; solder, 143, **399, 399A**; soldering, 139, **253**; strip, 142, **257–59**; surface "inlay," 144, **399A**; Toledo, 144, **260–**